THE TIME OF
Yeats

ENGLISH POETRY OF TO-DAY
AGAINST AN AMERICAN BACKGROUND

BY

Cornelius Weygandt

NEW YORK / RUSSELL & RUSSELL

COPYRIGHT, 1937, BY
D. APPLETON-CENTURY COMPANY, INC.
COPYRIGHT, 1964, BY CORNELIUS N. WEYGANDT
REISSUED, 1969, BY RUSSELL & RUSSELL
A DIVISION OF ATHENEUM PUBLISHERS, INC.
BY SPECIAL ARRANGEMENT WITH
APPLETON-CENTURY-CROFTS
DIVISION OF MEREDITH CORPORATION
L. C. CATALOG CARD NO: 68-25053
PRINTED IN THE UNITED STATES OF AMERICA

To

A. M. W.

Poetry Comes into Its Own

THE poets considered in this volume have all written for America as well as for England. Many of them have published their verses in American magazines. A good few have visited us and read their verses to us. This "barding" has had something to do with the more general acceptance of poetry during the past thirty years. The accent of the spoken word so noticeable in recent verse is partly the result of the poet's belief that verse is a something to be heard as well as to be read quietly under the lamp. There is growing up the feeling that a poem is no more a poem until it has been heard than a play is a play until it has been seen.

The seeing and hearing in America of the English poets of our day has added to our willingness to accept them as belonging to us as well as to England and her colonies. They are, for the most part, fellowly men, and they have been brought up as we have been brought up, on the institutions of democracy and on the masters of our English tongue. Shakespeare and the Bible, Milton and Herrick, Bunyan and Swift, English-speaking folk on both sides of the Atlantic have as a common heritage. The outstanding English writers of the eighteenth century are well represented in libraries that have come down to us from Colonial times. Burns had as great a currency here as in his native Scotland, and a greater currency than he had or has in England. The Georgians were quickly taken to heart in the States, and the Victorians were appreciated here as generally as were the New England poets and Poe. Stevenson and Yeats and Hodgson were welcomed here as peers of Walt Whitman and Emily Dickinson and Robert Frost.

All the English poets considered in this book are seen against our American background. I have tried to record what each one means to us. One and all are judged, though, I hope, by the standards of what is best in all poetry in English.

I began buying contemporary poets in 1892. Shelving that fills the wall space of a room is necessary to hold them now. There are first editions, among these books, of *The Countess Kathleen* of Yeats, of *A Shropshire Lad* of Housman, and of *Salt Water Ballads* of Masefield. All the poets have been read and reread and quarreled about with men to whom poetry is one of the first things of life. During nearly forty years the elders among them have been talked about to college classes. The younger men found place in those talks as they came along. Writing about them, begun in 1896, led to correspondence with some of them, Henley and Yeats, Davidson and Symons, Russell and Hodgson. I have talked about poetry with Yeats and Noyes, Binyon and Masefield, Stephens and Dunsany, Riley and Frost.

Poetry is the first art of the English-speaking peoples, the very foundation of their literature, the final touchstone by which we determine the greatness not only of verse, but of prose, too, whether of novel or play or essay. It has come into its own with the waning of the novel and with the eclipse of the drama by the talkies. What Yeats fought for in *The King's Threshold* has come to pass. The poet has his place again at the high table of the king.

* * *

The scope of *The Time of Yeats* does not admit of the consideration of poets from the British dominions. Men like Lindsay Gordon and Kendall in Australia and Lampman and Bliss Carman in Canada have done interesting work. The most considerable Colonials, however, like Kipling of India and Roy Campbell of South Africa, have found their way eventually to England, and hence are considered here. The loss by the non-inclusion of the Colonials is a loss of much picturesque and exotic writing, but of no poetry of the first rank. Ezra Pound, T. S. Eliot, and other Americans associated with England or resident in England are not considered.

ACKNOWLEDGMENTS

The author wishes to acknowledge his indebtedness to the following publishers and individuals for permission to use material from these publications:

Jonathan Cape, Ltd., for quotations from Oliver Gogarty (*Wild Apples*) and the *Poems of W. H. Davies* (1934), copyright 1916 by W. H. Davies.
The Dial Press for quotations from Sylvia Townsend Warner. (*The Espalier*) and Roy Campbell (*Adamastor* and *The Flaming Terrapin*).
Dodd, Mead and Company for quotations from Lascelles Abercrombie, Arthur Christopher Benson, Rupert Brooke, Olive Custance, John Davidson, Ernest Dowson, Monk Gibbon, "Laurence Hope," Henry Newbolt, Stephen Phillips, Owen Seaman, Arthur Symons, Herbert Trench, and Margaret L. Woods.
Doubleday, Doran and Company, Inc., for quotations from Walt Whitman (*Leaves of Grass*); Virginia Sackville-West (*Collected Poems*); and Humbert Wolfe (*Requiem*).
Mrs. Kipling and Doubleday, Doran & Company, Inc., for quotations from "A Song of the English" and "The Flowers," from *The Seven Seas*, copyright 1893, 1921; "The Ballad of East and West," "In the Neolithic Age," and "The Ballad of Fisher's Boarding-House" from *Departmental Ditties and Barrack Room Ballads*, copyright 1892, 1920; "To the True Romance," from *Many Inventions*, copyright 1893, 1921; "My New-Cut Ashlar," from *Life's Handicap*, copyright 1891, 1918; "Lichtenberg," "The Return," and "Sussex," from *The Five Nations*, copyright 1903, 1931; "A Charm" from *Rewards and Fairies*; and

ACKNOWLEDGMENTS

"A Song of Travel" from *Songs from Books*, copyright 1912.

Gerald Duckworth and Co., Ltd., for quotations from Hilaire Belloc (*More Beasts for Worse Children*).

E. P. Dutton & Co., Inc., for quotations from Siegfried Sassoon (*Picture-Show*); Mary Webb (*Poems and the Spring of Joy*); John Davidson (*Holiday and Other Poems*); Winifred M. Letts (*The Spires of Oxford* and *Songs from Leinster*); and Arthur Symons (*The Romantic Movement in English Poetry*).

Funk & Wagnalls Company, for quotations from Ethna Carberry (*The Four Winds of Erin*).

Harcourt, Brace and Company, Inc., for quotations from Anna Wickham (*The Contemplative Quarry* and *The Man with a Hammer*); John Freeman (*Poems New and Old*); and T. Sturge Moore (*The Little School*).

Henry Holt and Company, for quotations from A. E. Housman (*A Shropshire Lad* and *Last Poems*) and Walter De La Mare (*Collected Poems, 1901-1918*).

Houghton Mifflin Company, for quotations from Katharine Tynan (*The Years of the Shadow*); Laurence Binyon (*The Cause*); John Drinkwater (*Poems, 1908-19*); T. Sturge Moore (*The Sea Is Kind*); and Edith Sitwell (*The Sleeping Beauty*).

Mitchell Kennerley, for quotations from Richard Middleton (*Poems and Songs*, First and Second Series) and John Davidson (*Fleet Street and Other Poems*).

Liveright Publishing Corporation, for quotations from L. A. G. Strong (*Dublin Days*).

Longmans, Green and Company, for quotations from Eva Gore-Booth (*Unseen Kings* and *The One and the Many*).

The Macmillan Company, for quotations from Thomas Hardy *Winter Words, Human Shows, Far Fantasies, Songs and Trifles*, and *Collected Poems*); Stephen Phillips (*Nero*); Richard Rowley (*Selected Poems*); George W. Russell

ACKNOWLEDGMENTS

(*Vale and Other Poems, Voices of the Stones,* and *Collected Poems*); James Stephens (*Insurrections, The Hill of Vision, The Crock of Gold, A Poetry Recital, The Rocky Road to Dublin,* and *Songs from the Clay*); William Butler Yeats (*Autobiographies, The King of the Great Clock Tower,* etc., *Essays, The Collected Poems of William B. Yeats,* and *The Collected Plays of William B. Yeats*); Moira O'Neill (*Songs of the Glens of Antrim* and *More Songs of the Glens of Antrim*); Padraic Colum (*Poems*); Ralph Hodgson (*Poems*); Ruth Pitter (*A Mad Lady's Garland*); Laurence Whistler (*Four Walls*); John Masefield (*Selected Poems, King Cole, The Taking of Helen and Other Prose Selections, Reynard the Fox, The Poems and Plays of John Masefield,* Vol. I, and *With the Living Voice*); Charlotte Mew (*Saturday Market*); Sidney Royse Lysaght (*Horizons and Landmarks* and *Poems of the Unknown Way*); Wilfred Wilson Gibson (*Collected Poems, 1902-1925,* Poems (*1904-1917*), *Fires,* and *Womenkind*); Laurence Binyon (*Selected Poems* and *Collected Poems of Laurence Binyon,* Vols. I and II); Katharine Tynan (*Collected Poems*); T. Sturge Moore (*The Poems of T. Sturge Moore,* Vols. II and III); and Harold Monro (*Real Property,* Parts I and II).

Coward McCann, Inc., for quotations from *The Complete Poems of Francis Ledwidge.*

Methuen and Company, Ltd., for quotations from Humbert Wolfe (*The Unknown Goddess*).

The Oxford University Press, for quotations from *Poetical Works of Robert Bridges;* Lascelles Abercrombie (*The Poems of Lascelles Abercrombie*); and Gerard Manley Hopkins (*Poems of Gerard Manley Hopkins*).

A. D. Peters, for quotations from Edmund Blunden (*Poems, 1914-30*) and A. E. Coppard (*Collected Poems*).

G. P. Putnam's Sons, for quotations from Lord Dunsany (*Fifty Poems*); Charles Hamilton Sorley (*Marlborough and*

Other Poems); and Maurice Hewlett (*The Village Wife's Lament*).

Random House, Inc., for quotations from W. H. Auden (*Poems*); Stephen Spender (*Poems*); Cecil Day Lewis (*Collected Poems* and *A Hope for Poetry* and *A Time to Dance, Noah and the Waters and Revolution in Writing*); and Andrew Young (*Winter Harvest*).

Charles Scribner's Sons, for quotations from Robert Louis Stevenson (*The Weir of Hermiston* and *Complete Poems*) and William Ernest Henley (*Poems* and *Views and Reviews, Literature*).

Martin Secker & Warburg, Ltd., for quotations from James Elroy Flecker (*The Collected Poems*).

Peter Smith, for quotations from W. H. Davies (*Collected Poems*).

Frederick A. Stokes Company, for quotations from Alfred Noyes (*Collected Poems*, Vols. I and III).

The Viking Press, Inc., for quotations from Sylvia Townsend Warner (*Time Importuned*); Wilfred Owen (*Poems*); and D. H. Lawrence (*The Collected Poems of D. H. Lawrence*, Vol. I).

Yale University Press, for quotations from W. H. Davies (*The Captive Lion*).

CONTENTS

CHAPTER		PAGE
I	Forces in Poetry, 1882-1936: The American Invasion, Science, and Internationalism	3
II	The Beginnings of the New Order: Henley, Stevenson, and Davidson	30
III	The Old Main Line	67
IV	The Victorian Aftermath	121
V	The Song of Empire: Kipling and Newbolt	134
VI	The Catholic Rhapsodists	144
VII	The Decadents: Arthur Symons and Ernest Dowson	154
VIII	William Butler Yeats and the Irish Literary Renaissance	167
IX	A. E. Housman	252
X	The Penetration of Thomas Hardy	261
XI	Charles M. Doughty, Sturge Moore and Gordon Bottomley	284
XII	Alfred Noyes	306
XIII	John Masefield: Apostle of Beauty	315
XIV	Realists of the Countryside	336
XV	The Last Romantics	363
XVI	The Latest Phases of English Poetry	386
XVII	Of Poetry and Propaganda	429
XVIII	The Hope for the Future	444
	Index	447

THE TIME OF YEATS

CHAPTER I

Forces in Poetry, 1882-1936: The American Invasion, Science, and Internationalism

THE FORCES that were to break up Victorianism in England were actively at work by 1882. They were, in considerable part, of American origin. Some of these forces were carried across the Atlantic in the books of poets and prophets, others were machinery and ways of business invented here, democratic institutions first tested here, art forms developed here more quickly than in the Old World. A good many of these forces were resented before they came into general acceptance in England: harvesting machines that changed rural customs; manhood suffrage and public schools that challenged the old order; the short story and the out-of-door essay that seemed needless innovations. Of more recent years invasions of American ways in theaters and newspapers have troubled England still more.

It was Whitman who had most to do with breaking the mold of Victorian poetry, though Emerson had been a liberating force for a generation before Whitman's example and precepts were taken to heart by any large number of writers or by any large part of the audience for writers. We have the testimony of Matthew Arnold himself that when he was an undergraduate at Oxford (1841-1844), Emerson's was one of the voices in the air, "a clear and pure voice which, for my ear, at any rate, brought a strain as new, and moving, and unforgettable, as the strain of Newman, or Carlyle, or Goethe." This means that to Arnold Emerson was one of the prophets, "the friend and aider of those who would live in the spirit."

Leaves of Grass (1855) was made known to all England in the truncated Rossetti reprinting of 1868. Robert Buchanan, James Thomson, John Addington Symonds, and T. W. Rolleston were staunch advocates of the American. Stevenson discussed him in *Familiar Studies of Men and Books* (1882). Edward Carpenter (1844-1928) made pilgrimage to America in 1884 to visit Whitman, and imitated his rhythms and chanted of similar subjects in *Towards Democracy* (1886).

It is a matter of real difficulty to determine just how much of the new freedom of form in English verse of the past half-century is due to the influence of Whitman. Whitman's form itself owed something to *Ossian* and to the prophetic books of Blake and to the cadences of the King James Bible. These books were, of course, all of them better known to English writers than was *Leaves of Grass*, despite the enduring and loud controversy over *Leaves of Grass*. There had been no length of time that unrhymed verse other than blank verse had not had its adherents during the hundred years prior to 1882. Longfellow and Matthew Arnold are but two of the poets in our earlier half-century that practised unrhymed measures successfully. Henley owed as much of the impulse that set him to work in his free rhythms to Arnold as to Whitman, and Stevenson, too, and William Sharp, and all the many who before the day of what is now known specifically as "free verse" tried their hand at unrhymed forms of irregular rhythm.

It was Whitman, however, who was the chief challenger of the old orders of rhymed verse, who made the loudest noise in the world with his "barbaric yawp." His unconventionality of theme, his determination to sing the whole of life, his setting of his face so resolutely to the future, his insistence on common forms of speech, his wilful assumption of jargon as part of his vocabulary—these were just as influential on the English poetry of late Victorian times as were the rhythms he felt his way to so uncertainly. His greatest service was to prove that there was another poetry of the mid-nineteenth century than the poetry of "music and moonlight," that there was poetry in things that had heretofore been held common and mean. Even if more recent generations than that he shocked reject nine tenths of what he wrote as impossible of being, lifted to poetry, his catalogues and the like, there is enough of poetry of high order in the remaining tenth to prove his theories sound. It has been said again and again, and truly, that he did not turn to his free rhythms until he found he could not be at ease in the old verse forms, that he could not, in fact, master them. Such a failure does not invalidate, in the least degree, however, his claims for the free forms, or minimize his success in them. If there is exultation and exaltation in these forms, if there is glamour, if there are natural falterings and victorious bursts, if there is about them "the light that never was on sea or land," he is certainly of the poets. All these attributes his verses have, and he himself is sure of his place.

Certain of the repellent phases of current poetry are as directly traceable to Whitman as certain of its excellences. A stridency; a false accent; an inability to maintain a sustained tone; an insistence on uglinesses that cannot be made lyric by the feeling underlying their appreciation or that cannot be lifted even to a grotesque beauty; a swagger; a braggadocio; and poses not easily pardoned can be attributed to his influence. What he did for poetry, however, was of inestimable advantage to it. Above everything else he humanized it, as Burns had humanized it two generations before him, and, although he did not make his sort of poetry quickly accepted of the crowd, he made many see the poetry of familiar things. Those who did see what he pointed out, the sense of space he gave to everything he presented, the light in him and the heat, the warm-bloodedness, the tonic earthiness of his best, were often able in their recordings of material like to his to come closer to the hearts of the people. Whitman made audiences for what used to be considered "rough stuff" in poetry, he broke the way for Henley and Kipling and Masefield. He joined effort with the so totally different Meredith in establishing the right of the poet to sing of all things, no matter whether they had previously been considered fit material for poetry or not.

Let it be always remembered that, formally, Whitman blazed the trail for the writers of free verse, Americans most of them, Amy Lowell, Ezra Pound, T. S. Eliot, Richard Aldington. Whitman, so far from serene in his writing, was adjudged a Greek by Havelock Ellis, and by many another, too. Even if he were not, he won the imagists a hearing, the chance to present the cold, clear images that have given to contemporary poetry a solidity and hardness it sorely needed.

Thoreau is the most quoted of all American writers by the later Victorians and Edwardians and Neo-Georgians. One might almost say that Thoreau is the most quoted of all modern writers in English. It is, of course, his propagandist writing that has won a part of this wide acclaim. His voice has traveled around the world to India. His "civil disobedience," adopted by Gandhi, nearly brought the rulers of the British Empire to their knees in 1931. Thoreau's return to the simple life in the cabin by Walden Pond underlies all the widespread rebellion against the complexities of modern civilization and the enslaving city life that there is in so much writing of the past half-century. It was only the rarer souls that went the whole way with him in his preaching of the necessity of the wild. It took the absence of jobs in town from 1929 on to stem the flow of the young folks from country to city.

Emerson had preached the greatness of country things before Thoreau, holding that "man in the bush with God may meet." Thoreau, however, had an intimacy of knowledge of country things that Emerson lacked, and a country tang to his writing that lured his readers afield. There are parallels between Emerson and Whitman, too. Whitman, however, is in no sense the follower of Emerson, as Thoreau was. Emerson was the inspirer of Thoreau, the teacher of Thoreau, the master of Thoreau, though he never passed on to his disciple his own instinctive sympathy with the old order of things. For all his revolutionary doctrine Emerson was deep down in him at one with the strong souls that ruled the world. Thoreau was not. Thoreau never had much to lose. Emerson had a good deal of this world's goods. And even when Thoreau does follow some thought laid down by Emerson, he gives to its expression the quality of his own voice.

Emerson's voice, too, has gone far around the world. You cannot read any essay of Maeterlinck without coming on Emersonian doctrine. Poe, too, influenced Maeterlinck. That sense of something terrible about to happen, so insistent in Poe, is present, too, in nearly every play of Maeterlinck. It is especially insistent in *The Intruder*. Emerson's preachments and his hierophantic manner have both been thoroughly assimilated by George W. Russell, the Irish mystic better known, perhaps, as "A.E." Irish literature of the past fifty years owes a great deal to Emerson. It owes something, too, to Poe, several of whose characteristics are shared by Mangan. Mangan has a trick of refrain, a sense of loneliness, and a sense of inescapable sorrow about to fall such as has Poe. Emerson and Poe are influences, too, at second hand, through Maeterlinck, on Yeats. In some of the early plays, such as *The Countess Kathleen* (1892), and in certain later plays, *Deirdre* (1908) for one, you are aware of Maeterlinck's influence. Yeats, too, has taken to heart Whitman's injunction that Lady Gregory quotes at the outset of her *Poets and Dreamers* (1903):

Will you seek afar off? You surely come back at last,
In things best known to you finding the best, or as good as the best,
In folks nearest to you finding the sweetest, strongest, lovingest,
Happiness, knowledge, not in another place but this place, not for another hour but this hour.

In *Ideals in Ireland* (1901), which Lady Gregory edited, you again find a passage of Whitman, this time as prelude:

Dear Camerado! I confess I have urged you onward with me, and
    still urge you, without the least idea what is our destination,
Or whether we shall be victorious, or utterly quelled and defeated.

A lost cause, as here suggested, has always appealed to the Celt, and the insistence on his own order, no matter what the world thinks or does, that the earlier quotation suggests. It is still further significant that of the seven signers of the first memorial out of Britain approving Whitman two were Irish, Edward Dowden of Trinity College, Dublin, and J. B. Yeats, the portrait painter and father of the poet.

The preface of Synge to his *Poems* (1908) is so wholly in the spirit of Whitman I must quote much of it. As Synge wrote here so he must have talked in those "Bloomsbury nights" Masefield tells us of in "Biography," and handed on his theory of poetry to the younger man. At any rate this credo applauds just the art of poetry Masefield practised. Synge writes:

> The poetry of exaltation will be always the highest; but when men lose their poetic feeling for ordinary life, and cannot write poetry of ordinary things, their exalted poetry is likely to lose its strength of exaltation, in the way men cease to build beautiful churches when they have lost happiness in building shops.
>
> Many of the older poets, such as Villon and Herrick and Burns, used the whole of their personal life as their material, and the verse written in this way was read by strong men, and thieves, and deacons, not by little cliques only. . . .
>
> . . . it is the timber of poetry that wears most surely, and there is no timber that has not strong roots among the clay and worms. . . .
>
> . . . It may almost be said that before verse can be human again it must learn to be brutal.

As I have said, it is Thoreau, though, that is more often mentioned by the British writers who have come to the fore since 1882 than any other American. Stevenson expatiates upon him, and men as different as Swinburne and Watts-Dunton, Edward Thomas and De La Mare, Joseph Campbell and Brett-Young use thoughts of his as starting points for their own thinking. In the time of my boyhood, the seventies and early eighties, Thoreau was to most Americans a writer of out-of-door essays. My own greatest joy in reading him was to find bits of spring and summer and winter caught in brief passages that are as surely poems as any lyric of Emerson or Emily Dickinson. As I grew older his values of things in life and literature came to mean more and more to me, but they have never displaced in my interest his picture of old pastures growing up to apple-trees, or his appreciation of the return of the flicker in March. You will find them poohpoohing Thoreau as a naturalist nowadays, but the latest specialist on turtles has to fall back on him for a description of the way *Chrysemys picta* lays her eggs. Neither Jefferies nor Hudson, prose poets both, had been as they are had not Thoreau preceded them.

Of Poe's influence on the Pre-Raphaelites I have already spoken. Through Baudelaire and Mallarmé, as well as through Maeterlinck, there comes back on English literature another influence of Poe, a decided influence if at second hand. There are those who believe Poe affected Turgenieff, and that the sense of the imminence of tragedy in the Russian, like its so kindred quality in the Belgian, originates in Poe. Francis Thompson owes much to Poe, too, as he does to so many poets his predecessors, and De La Mare and Dunsany have borne frank testimony to their inspiration by Poe.

I have often thought that the influence of Hawthorne on English novelists would be an interesting study. Eustacia Vye has always seemed to me to owe something to Zenobia, though there are few points of contact between *The Return of the Native* and *The Blithedale Romance*. Watts-Dunton's *Aylwin* shows a study of Hawthorne, and there are many other romances that show their authors are familiar with *The Scarlet Letter* or *The Marble Faun*. Matthew Arnold considered Hawthorne a great writer, "the finest, I think, which America has yet produced." When Lionel Johnson was only twelve, or so he says, he was haunted by that "voice borne over the waste sea," and "the golden gloom" of Hawthorne's style has been an element in the formation of styles as different as those of Pater and Dunsany. Hawthorne, of course, had made himself beloved and disliked in England by *Our Old Home* (1863). Emerson spent a good deal of time in England, too, and found there and in his reading the material of his *English Traits* (1856).

The American invasion has never ceased. Harte took his practice of local color with him when he went as consul to Glasgow. He practically expatriated himself as Henry James did actually at a later date. Harte was the dominant influence on the art of the short story of Kipling, and James has left an indelible impression on the English novel, even so great a man as Conrad going to school to him. "The Return," that early short story, is decidedly in the manner of James. Stephen Spender testifies to his influence on the youngest of the English poets to-day.

"John Oliver Hobbes" shook the dust of Boston from her feet and settled in England. She added little of American quality to English writing, carrying on the Meredith tradition in her novels and collaborating with George Moore in *Journeys End in Lovers Meeting,* one of the favorite curtain-raisers of the Irving-Terry trips to America.

Between the century's end and the war in 1914 quite a few Americans migrated to England for longer or shorter stays. Ezra Pound went there, by way of Italy, in 1908, and spent twelve years in England before moving on to Paris and the Italian Riviera. Through his verse, as well as by active propaganda, Pound did much to forward, if not to initiate, new movements in writing. It is claimed for him that he created the term *imagist,* though imagism had been in poetry from the beginning. He gathered together his anthology *Des Imagistes* in 1914. Amy Lowell, in a way Pound's disciple, though older than he, carried on the work he had begun. For a while resident in England, she, too, proved an influence on English as well as on American poetry.

Robert Frost went to England in 1912, returning early in 1915. His important contacts there were with Ezra Pound, Abercrombie, and Edward Thomas. Set in his own way, Frost was uninfluenced by any of these men. He lent, indeed, some of his theories of art to Abercrombie, and he directly inspired the verse of Edward Thomas. *North of Boston* (1914) and *New Hamp-*

shire (1923) have left their mark on English verse no less surely than on American verse.

T. S. Eliot has been the American, however, who, since the day of Henry James, has most definitely set himself to the task of influencing English literature. Settling down in London in 1914, he has published all his verses in England, and through his domination of *The New Criterion* he made himself something of a literary dictator. There is disillusion and satire and anger with life in his verse, and moments of lonely beauty, as in "Marriana." He keeps to himself, even more than does Yeats, the key to the meanings of his verse, and it is a question if the world will take the trouble to ferret out his meanings. It has taken that trouble with Yeats, as it has with Browning and with Donne, but, though a writer who has created a little world of his own, Eliot is not of the stature of the Titans and he may not inspire similar efforts. His criticism is so clear and scholarly and cogent that the obscurity of his verse seems a wilful assumption. Whether you agree with his criticism or not, you come quickly to know his standards of value and his purposes. In *For Lancelot Andrewes* (1929) he owns "a general point of view which may be described as classicist in literature, royalist in politics, and Anglo-Catholic in religion." Eliot owes as much to Pound almost as he does, self-confessedly, to Arthur Symons, who revealed the French Symbolists to him. The practice of Eliot's verse harks back to Browning, in its jumbling together of various arts and conditions of life. It would seem that the theory that scholarship should underlie creative writing comes also from Browning, by way of Pound. Eliot, however, is able to "consolidate" his scholarship, to organize it into a code in support of his theories, and he realizes that there are other ways to arrest attention than the provocative.

POETRY AND SCIENCE

It chances that 1882 was the year in which Charles Darwin died. Twenty-three years before his death, in 1859, he had published *The Origin of Species*, a book that aroused as much controversy and brought about as much readjustment of belief as any English book ever did. By the time of his death the world had pretty well adapted itself to his revelations. The vexed controversies with theologians were over. In 1882 orthodox parents even in far America did not object to evolutionary talks to their children in lectures on chemistry and geology and paleontology. To that I can personally testify. It was in that year I moved on from dame-school to academy and met the popularization of the new revelations. Edward Drinker Cope and Joseph Leidy were not assailed for the scientific views they pronounced when I sat under them in college in the late eighties. There was an echo here and there in the community round about Philadelphia from the heated controversies of the sixties and early seventies, in which Huxley had borne the brunt of the battle, but there was as often a questioning of Darwin by the scientists who differed with him as by the old-fashioned theologians. Darwin lost ground somewhat after his death, many middlemen of science coming to make more and more of Alfred Russel Wallace.

There were no discoveries of science in the whole nineteenth century, however, so quickening to the imagination as those of the Copernican astronomy and the finding of new lands and new peoples to Renaissance times. Applied science has brought comforts into life since 1882 that would be unbelievable to Mid-Victorians could they come back and see them. The movies and the talkies and the radio have made the entertainments of the center accessible to the farthest back-country places, but none of the discoveries and the changes have destroyed the old values in life, or influenced materially any of the characteristics of human nature. The automobile and good roads, the extension of the telephone and rural free delivery of mail have made many places easy to live in that were out of the world a half-century ago. Prophylactic medicine, the advances in surgery and in sanitation have made life sounder and longer for many of us.

Science has not, however, revolutionized poetry as it was expected to do. Science has made the world even more interesting than it was before, or interesting in other ways than it was before. Science has revealed a great deal that was not noticed or understood before. We can see things more as they are and we can therefore communicate impressions of them more accurately through all the arts. Science has made poetry more faithful to the world in which we live, to its landscapes, its birds and beasts, its trees and flowers, its rainbows and northern lights, its clouds and stars, its human moods and emotions and phases of character. T. S. Eliot knows the difference between the songs of woodthrush and hermit-thrush as Whitman did not. Edward Thomas is a better botanist than Richard Jefferies. Such accuracy of knowledge does not make necessarily for better poetry, but it helps to keep out of poetry certain falsities that cheapen it and lessen its effectiveness. A John Burroughs of to-day would find few contemporary poets, American or English, who would err in details of out-of-door things as those he finds at fault in that chapter of *Pepacton* (1881) called "Nature and the Poets."

THE LITTLE EFFECT OF INTERNATIONALISM

Internationalism was from the beginning a burden of the preaching of socialism. All through the half-century that has followed on the foundation of the Fabian Society, in 1883, resolute socialists like Shaw and Wells have set their faces sternly against patriotism in the old sense of the word. Earlier than their internationalism was the cosmopolitanism that his early years at Neuwied, his service as war correspondent in Italy, and his travels in France and the Alps had forced upon George Meredith. Not a socialist himself, he paved the way for the coming of the socialists' internationalism by his insistence on cosmopolitanism.

Some of his friends thought William Morris might have been a great poet were it not for his socialism. It seems to me, though, that if there had not been his socialistic activity to sap his vitality some one or other of his various artistic or social or business activities would have been magnified into as severe a tax on his wonderful physique and energy. There is comparatively little reflex of his beliefs in his writing intended as art, and almost none of it in his best poetry.

Rupert Brooke, a convinced Fabian, never allowed his political or economic theories to intrude into his verse. Nor could a Labor government find in the verse of Masefield any allegiance to the doctrines of socialism. In the famous colloquy of the parson and Saul Kane, Masefield seems to declare that the present system of things is doing a pretty good job in getting the world up in the morning, through the day's work, and to bed again at night. Masefield was probably chosen for the laureateship by MacDonald as the chief rival in popularity to Kipling, whose Toryism the socialists could not brook. Then Masefield had celebrated the common man, and in his very first volume, *Salt Water Ballads*, long before he wrote those epics in little of the common man, *The Everlasting Mercy*, *The Widow in the Bye Street*, *Dauber*, and *The Daffodil Fields*.

It has been said of this poet and that, in the newspapers, that he is an internationalist, but if that is the truth about a Sassoon or a Sitwell, he has not put internationalist propaganda into his poetry. It remained for Auden, Spender, and Day Lewis to do that. It is only in satiric or in philosophical poetry that any large amount of propaganda can intrude without precipitating the poetry. Somehow we are more ready to accept propaganda in the play and the novel, though it has weighted the plays of Shaw and the stories of Wells with so much quickly outmoded matter that old works of theirs read like last year's newspapers. Young intellectuals are likely, like other youths, to go through a radical stage, and then, if they succeed in making a place for themselves in the world, to accept at least tacitly the system under which they made their place.

It was, of course, the spectacle of Tolstoi that began the conversion of the artists to socialism. The spectacle of the man who had the ear of the world abjuring art, and holding the betterment of man, economically, socially, and morally, a something far more important than art, was too startling not to stun artists everywhere

FORCES IN POETRY, 1882-1936 15

to acquiescence with his views. Underlying the spectacle of Tolstoi was that old quarrel of the lover of beauty with the ugliness of civilization, and the fact that the artist of whatever sort is none too quickly recognized by the system that runs the world, and even when recognized none too highly valued. The young poet has the hardest row to hoe of them all. Yeats, as W. H. Davies points out, never got such a return at the height of his power for a poem as Augustus John for a drawing. John, after he arrived, could make fifty pounds by an hour's work, while Yeats, for a lyric, would get only a few guineas.

THE IMPERIAL NOTE

Queen Victoria was proclaimed Empress of India on January 1, 1877. The famous "Durbar" from which that event was heralded throughout the world marked the heights of Oriental splendor. The proclamation itself was a symbol to all the English of the might and power and far-flung dominion of the Empire. Those ceremonies doubtless stirred the small boy who was to be the leading apostle of imperialism in the years through which it flourished. There had been declarations of the love of England, the countryside and the nation, from the beginnings of English poetry, but patriotic poetry as we understand it to-day is comparatively modern. If you look up patriotic poems in the anthologies devoted to such verse, such as *Poems of the Love and Pride of England* (1897), collected by Frederick Wedmore and his daughter, you will find, before Wordsworth, only twenty-five excerpts or sets of verses of a patriotic nature. Copyright privileges kept Tennyson out of this volume, and Kipling, for reasons not stated, is not represented. Kipling's omission serves a good purpose, however, in emphasizing that there was the spirit of Empire in English poetry before him, even if there was no other writing man who knew so much of the Empire as he, and who had so resolute a desire to sing the glories of Empire. Kipling in his most excited state has never been so truculently John Bullish as Sidney Dobell in "England's Day," written at the time of the *Alabama* claims. Dobell includes us of America with Russian and Prussian as shaking our fists at England. England, he avers:

> carries a flag unfurled
> That shall flog you off the waves
> Of the world.

The imperialistic spirit breaks out with a vengeance in:

> The North waves roll from pole to pole,
> Ha, ha, ha, ha, ha!
> From pole to pole the south winds troll,
> Ha, ha, ha, ha, ha!
> From air to sea, from sea to air,
> The cross-clang clamors everywhere,
> Ha, ha, ha, ha, ha!
> From Baffin Bay, by Matapan,
> Round Hindostan, and far Japan,
> Back, back, to where it first began,
> Ha, ha, ha, ha, ha!

All this circumnavigation of the globe in spirit piles up a realization that all the seas wash English shores, that the sun never sets on the British Empire. It is precious poor stuff, this "England's Day," of Sidney Dobell, such stuff as even his worst enemy could not wish cheaper or weaker; but for that matter all but all patriotic poetry is poor poetry. It seems to be the fate of poets to sink into rhetoric when they wax patriotic or take to writing hymns.

Sir Lewis Morris wrote "A Song of Empire" in 1887 for the fiftieth anniversary of the coming to the throne of Queen Victoria. He cried:

> Oh England! Empire wide and great
> As ever from the shaping hand of fate
> Did issue on the earth, august, large grown!
> What were the Empires of the past to thine,
> The old old Empires ruled by kings divine—
> Egypt, Assyria, Rome?

Again I have to write a passage down as poor poetry and stout patriotism. Swinburne, Watts-Dunton, Henley, Sir William Watson, too, all tried their hand at celebrating the might of greater England. Their results were rather better than those of Dobell and Morris, but nothing to brag about at that. It remained for Kipling to give the world a volume worth while almost wholly in praise of the people and institutions about the seas dominated by England. The keynote of *The Seven Seas* (1896) is struck in "A Song of the English," in which Kipling declares that "the Lord our God most High . . . hath smote for us a pathway to the ends of all the Earth." After Kipling come Sir Henry Newbolt and a score of lesser men, Colonials and men of the home counties alike, who luxuriated in patriotic and imperial verse in and out of season until the World War.

The World War developed new sorts of patriotic verse. Kipling himself changed his tone after his first few poems inspired by it. He lost his boy Jack in the war. He half apologized to America, after we came into the war, for "An American" and other knocks. Yet something of the old spirit of patronage still remains. It is difficult to be imperialistic without being patronizing.

The celebration of the might of empire seemed pretentious and cruel to a country losing the flower of its youth by thousands on thousands. There were publicists not a few who held that it was Germany's ambition of empire that provoked the war. A number of the younger poets who saw service in the trenches bitterly attacked war. Sassoon and Graves and Nichols found war something very other than "the lordliest life on earth." The World War put a quietus, for a time at any rate, on imperialistic verse. It had won to itself, in its heyday, many poets of the generation of Kipling, and it will long be remembered as a characteristic of the age of Cecil Rhodes. There were signs that it was failing even before the war began. The war, of course, cost all poetry dear. Edward Thomas was killed, and Rupert Brooke and Wilfrid Owen and Charles Sorley, to name only four from whom we would have had good verse had they lived. So much, too, was taken out of life by the war and its aftermath. Men were so burnt out by it and so disillusioned, things held priceless before were so cheapened by it, that the desire to make things of beauty went out of the hearts of many young artists, poets, painters, composers of music. Blunden almost alone of the poets who knew the war's horrors retained his dream in the days immediately following its close. Things are now righting themselves somewhat, but another generation of poets who did not know the war will have to grow up before the old joy in life will return fully to poetry.

HARDY'S PRACTICE OF THE HIGHER PROVINCIALISM

English poetry from its beginnings has considered the countryman, but it was not until Burns that he had his due. Chaucer cheapened him, Shakespeare made him a clown, Walton idealized him, Gay made a half-effort to paint him as he was. It required, perhaps, the return to nature of the eighteenth century to enable Wordsworth to present him as he does in a score of different guises. The little nine days' wonders that Bloomfield and Clare aroused did not really dignify the countryman. The attitude of the public was that it was a marvel that even second- or third-rate poetry should come from the farm.

Country things had had from early times a far more sympathetic treatment. Birds and flowers and gardens had been praised in verse and prose, hunting and fishing and country gentlemen's contentments of all kinds had had books devoted to them, but the yeoman and the peasant had received scant consideration. There was a stout carl sympathetically portrayed, a Piers Plowman or a Little John or a Clym o' the Clough, but it was not until the doctrine of liberty, fraternity, and equality was loud in the land that the farmer, the yeoman, and the farm laborer could come into their own.

Tennyson gave us some inimitable pictures of the countryside, and in "The Northern Farmer" and other poems painted pictures of men and women definitely of the soil. Scott and George Eliot had made country types familiar to all readers by Mid-Victorian times. Richard Jefferies had done two services to the country by the time our period was well under way. In his earlier work, such as *The Gamekeeper at Home* (1878), he described details of country life, birds' ways and beasts', with loving particularity, and later, in *The Story of My Heart* (1883), he caught effects of beauty from the changing seasons and times of day that had not been caught before. He rhapsodized about his discoveries with so lyric a fervor that all out-of-doors took on aspects that few had seen before.

It remained for Hardy, though, to give us more about the country folk and the countryside in which they live than any writer of them all, and to give both a dignity they had not had before. Wide as was Wordsworth's appeal, Hardy's was wider. In a succession of novels that everybody read, beginning with *Under the Greenwood Tree,* in 1872, and ending with *Jude the Obscure* in 1895, he revealed rural England as none of his forerunners had revealed it. He brought his art of the center to the material of the province. What was most interesting to him was what he had known all his life, his family first, then his neighbors, then the other folks of his Dorsetshire. Everything about family and neighbors and Dorsetmen generally was important to him. Their houses and dooryards and orchards come down to them from old time were studied faithfully; and that old time in all its aspects as faithfully as to-day. Nothing escaped him, prehistoric conditions in the countryside, Roman ruins, churches and their graveyards, the Elizabethan timbered cottages and the eighteenth-century manor houses, the picturesque customs that lingered on into the days of his youth, dancing about the Maypole, witch-doctoring, the old-time singing to serpent and violin and bass viol in the church services.

There is condensed in the verse of Hardy even more of the past and present of Wessex than in his novels. Story on story that might have expanded into a novel is outlined or intimated in a few stanzas of verse. From his prose stories descend the country verses of A. E. Housman. From his prose stories and his verses the narrative verse of Masefield and Abercrombie and Blunden, the other important poets to accept his doctrine of the higher provincialism.

It is a mistake to regard Hardy's irony as his principal characteristic. Deep sympathy, which, because it is quiet and unobtrusive, is not noticed by the half of his readers, informs all his writing. It is a sympathy extended to every sort of man and woman, to all indeed which has life, to wounded pheasant and hunted fox and overdriven horse. As a matter of fact Hardy is almost too sensitive, too keenly aware of all sorrow and suffering. He is hurt by the ways of the world almost as sharply as his own Jude.

There is less humor in his verses than in his prose, but humor you will find in the verses, in "The Fire at Tranter Sweatley's" and in "The Milkmaid" and in "The Dark-Eyed Gentleman." Poetry needs humor to keep it sweet as all sorts of literature need it, but humor ceased to be put into poetry after the coming into dominance of the Miltonic school. It came back in Burns, if without the broad laughter of Chaucer and Shakespeare, but there was little of it again in the higher kinds of poetry until Hardy. Byron has humor, but the most of it is perilously close to satire. It is strange there is so little humor in the lyricists who write verse close to *vers de société*, for Herrick has shown how it might be imprisoned in such verse. There is a cackling jocosity in Browning in his less inspired moments, as well as a more constant loud heartiness that clears the air. There is not often in him, however, the heart-easing humor you find in Chaucer and Shakespeare and Hardy.

Meredith has, like Hardy, less humor in his verse than in his prose. Humor there is, however, in "Juggling Jerry," "The Old Chartist," and "The Sage Enamored and the Honest Lady." There is a sort of "acrid Asiatic mirth," a satiric laughter, a grotesquerie, in the verse of Kipling as well as the farcical laughter of many of his stories and the youthful high spirits of *Soldiers Three*.

There are moments of humor in Masefield, too, in *Reynard the Fox* more often than elsewhere, but in general he is as prodigiously serious as are most modern poets. There is laughter in Noyes, but it is but an echo of Elizabethan mirth, not a something in the fiber of the man. The laughter of Pound and of T. S. Eliot is no more than chuckling. You must turn to *The Flaming Terrapin* (1924) of Roy Campbell to find in contemporary youngsters what in any large sense may be called humor. The spectacle that poem affords of the great turtle pulling Noah's Ark half way round the world would have delighted the men of the Mermaid as it to-day delights the men who once met at the Cheshire Cheese.

Hardy published his *Wessex Poems* in 1898 and his *Poems of the Past and the Present* in 1901. His verses did not exert a great influence from their first appearance. It was not, indeed, until the third volume, *Time's Laughingstocks*, came out in 1909, that he broke in his audience to the kind of poetry he fashioned. From 1909 until to-day his influence has widened and widened. The poets of to-day, nine out of ten of them, hold Hardy a great poet. He has proven that with insight and knowledge, with sympathy and understanding, with faithfulness and singleness of aim, the poet can make a whole countryside, men and women and the places they live in, of immediate concern and of endless appeal to all the world. It was Hardy who reaffirmed, for the twentieth century, what Burns and Wordsworth had discovered to earlier eras, the dignity and the inexhaustible humanity of the common man. No country place, no matter how out of the world and primitive and backward, can ever again be without interest and wonder to the thinking man.

Many elements have joined to bring about the return to the country that has developed in all English-speaking lands during the past thirty years. It has been only of most recent years, however, that it has come to balance the drift to town of the young people from the farms. While these young folks were still seeking the bright lights and allurements and easier jobs of the city, men and women of an older generation were making homes as far out in the country as their city employments would allow. They were moving out so that they could bring up their children in the better conditions of country life, in good air and elbow room and freedom from the slum. The parents themselves, many of them, were feeling the necessity of relief from the noise and vitiated air and sense of exhaustion always present in the city. They were feeling the urge to raise things, shrubs, flowers, vegetables, livestock. They were hungry for prospects of field and wood and hill that bring peace in the seeing. They had had enough of the city. They preferred the "dullness" of the country to the drive of the city. They began taking up the farms that the country folk had deserted because of the heavy labor or the increased capital necessary to make a living there.

Such back-to-the-landers had found out they wanted the country, not the wilds. The vogue passed of the books of the lure of this or that wild place. Camps on lakes and bungalows by the sea accessible or comfortable only in summer began to seem less desirable than farms to which they could escape of week-ends all the year. Country people began to see there must be a great deal to value and cherish and love in the country places in which city people were so anxious to find homes for at least a part of the year.

It remained, however, as I have said, for hard times to send more people to the country than came from the country to town. Thousands were driven back to the farms they had deserted. Nature study in the schools and the spreading of the Old Home Week habit had a share in the good work. But the writers who drove home a realization of the dignity of country life, who made the country-born feel that they were not bumpkins, yokels, hayseeds, heckers, rubes, played their part in turning the tide.

The size of the audience for an accurate portrayal of country life in verse and essay and novel suddenly increased, and even the play of country life, witness Eden Phillpotts' *Farmer's Wife* with its four-years' run in London (1924-1928), took on comparative popularity. The verse of Hardy, Masefield, Gibson, Abercrombie,

FORCES IN POETRY, 1882–1936 23

Davies, and Blunden was widely read, and not for a generation had prose outside of that of the novel and short story and play won such a response from the English public. Hudson, neglected for years, became a classic in his old age. Edward Thomas made a living out of the prose of criticism and the essay. Maurice Hewlett turned in his last days to description of loved places in the Wiltshire Downs. The critics no longer had to review Cunninghame Graham as a story-teller but could own him as essayist. E. L. Grant Watson abandoned Australasian novels for the nonce and did a book of out-of-door essays, *English Country* (1924). In a form nearly allied to the essay, the travel sketch, Doughty was acknowledged a great artist, and the fame of *Arabia Deserta* (1888) spread wherever English was spoken. Norman Douglas woke suddenly to find his books collectors' items.

THE POETIC SUGGESTION OF IBSEN

The reiteration by Ibsen of the poetry and hidden romance close about us and deep in us had its effect on the English verse that grew up after his plays were translated into English and revealed on the English stage. It was in 1880 that the first performance and the first translation were made. By 1890 Ibsen was known to all in England with any curiosity at all about foreign masters of letters. Taken by many people as a propagandist, Ibsen always insisted that he was first and last the poet. And that, of course, is what he is. All his greatest plays are instinct with poetry. Even *Ghosts* has in it a sense of the indifference of nature to the little lives of men that comes home to us with all the thrill of poetry. The aurora you see through Mrs. Alving's French windows, and the wind you hear without the walls of her house still you as poetry stills you. Their effect on you is the effect of lyric feeling. They give you an intense sense of Northernness, and at the same time bring you a sense of their power to heal all the illness in the world. In *Little Eyolf* the Northern forests, full to the tree-tops with quivering light and fresh scents of fir and spruce, are symbolized by Rita. In *John Gabriel Borkman* the primitive ways of the gnome that are inherent still in civilized man and civilized man's kinship with the most elemental things are revealed in the broken miner. In *Rosmersholm* all the high tragedy there is in the ending of an old and noble house speaks as clearly as it does in *The Bride of Lammermoor*. *The Master Builder* is a revelation, in poetical wise, of that dread of height that Francis Thompson hymns and of that intoxication of freedom that has so often gone to the heads of leaders of men.

Through Maeterlinck, too, comes to English poetry, to Yeats, to Sharp, to De La Mare, an influence at second hand from Ibsen. Without Ibsen, as without Emerson and Poe, Maeterlinck could not be Maeterlinck. The romance of that many-willowed lowland we discern behind the action of *Pelleas and Melisande* comes, perhaps, out of Broceliande, but the symbolism of the ring lost in the fountain, the hidden depths of the hearts of the lovers, and the quiet clash of will on will are out of the Northern master. Davidson owes almost as much to Ibsen as he does to Nietzsche in those testaments and strange plays that brought his activities to their close. Through the drama, of course, that Ibsen inspired in England, he was an indirect influence on all English thought on life. Ibsen was, in a sense, always looking over the shoulder of every other English writer from 1880 to the World War.

THE EFFECT OF MUSIC-HALL RHYTHMS

However popular the verse of Masefield and Gibson and Kipling may be, it can hardly be claimed for it that it is popular in the sense that the songs of the music-hall are popular. It can hardly be claimed that these poets are popular as Weatherly is popular or Oxenham is popular. At any rate, the publishers of the accredited poets do not claim that their collections "sell beyond the million mark" as do the war verses and songs of the men who can swing the crowd. *The Angel in the House* did sell over a million, but it took more than a generation for it to reach that figure. Martin Farquhar Tupper's *Proverbial Philosophy* must have had even better sales, but it is to be doubted if any collections of verse in English, Scott, Byron, Macaulay, and Longfellow not excepted, have sold as well as certain music-hall "hits."

The directness of such verses, their rough vigor, and their address to appetites and emotions shared by all cannot be denied, and when their low-aimed content is allied to a catchy tune they "go over big" as no other form of verse can possibly be expected to "go over." It is natural enough that poets should be curious to try to do something with such forms, to try their luck in casting a poem now and then in a music-hall rhythm. John Davidson has verses to "Tararaboomdeay" and to "After the Ball," but you can hardly include either set among his successes. Kipling was an even earlier experimenter with such forms. You find music-hall rhythms in *Departmental Ditties*, and he has never abjured them from that day to this. Noyes, too, likes their thump and go, witness "The Barrel Organ" and "Forty Singing Seamen" and "The Lord of Misrule." Masefield made his bow with something very like them in *Salt Water Ballads*. In America Vachel Lindsay has found music-hall rhythms grist to his mill. No one has gotten better affects out of the negroid and jazzed elements in them than he.

That the vogue of music-hall rhythms has resulted in many verses that are at once poetry and singable is perhaps the least of their excellences. That they make the man in the street feel that poetry may be a companionable and everyday sort of thing is certainly not the least. Yet it can hardly be claimed that many kinds of poetry can be written in such rhythms with hope of a large popular appeal. It is only that kind of poetry that can be understood and felt and fully fathomed on first hearing or reading that is wholly congenial in music-hall dress. From Shakespeare's *Sonnets* to *The Tower* of Yeats there have been many poems of the first power that had to be read and lived with and reread before they revealed their full meaning and their furthest implications. It is virtually only the song and the ballad that can be completely successful in music-hall rhythms.

In the times of the Elizabethan song-books poems carrying

meanings other than those to be quickly taken in were popular. A possible explanation of the wide appeal of songs deeply burdened with thought may be in the fact that such songs were pretty generally learned by heart, and, recurring again and again to the memory of those who knew them, had the chance to reveal their full meaning by such repeated and unlabored repetition.

THE OBLIGATION TO THE EAST

Japan was opened to foreign commerce by the negotiations of Commodore M. C. Perry in 1854. That was only one of the proofs of Japanese responsiveness to American suggestions. Twenty-two years after that opening there were exhibitions of Japanese and Chinese art at the Philadelphia Centennial of 1876 that changed standards of taste in America, that brought a new interior decoration into our homes and, momentarily at least, a new landscape gardening in our parks and large estates. Our clipper-ships had bound us to the Far East with many ties, even in the eighteenth century. Old houses from Salem in Massachusetts to Charleston in South Carolina had in them objects of art from China and Japan. They had, too, many of them, Chinese and Japanese shrubs in their windows and cool greenhouses. As it was in America so it was in England. So fascinated were all sorts and conditions of men there with eastern decoration that English Lowestoft china was copied in China and shipped in quantity to England. To a lesser degree it was made in China for the American market, too. I know sets of Lowestoft with monograms on them intact after a hundred and fifty years of use. Canton china was made in Staffordshire a hundred years ago, as it is made to-day in Trenton.

It was Judith Gautier who began the popularization of Chinese poetry in the Occident with her *Book of Jade* in 1867. It was Gilbert who first popularized Japanese decoration and Japanese motives in England with *The Mikado* (1885). It was the Japanese art at the Philadelphia Centennial that ensured the so quick taking to heart of this operetta in America. From Gilbert's day to to-day there has been no cessation of borrowing of Japanese and

Chinese effects. The Noh plays of Japan are responsible for Masefield's *The Faithful* (1915) and for some of the effects of the later plays of Yeats; Pound's versions from the Chinese, after Fenollosa, appeared in *Cathay* (1915). Arthur Waley put out his *A Hundred and Seventy Chinese Poems* in 1919. Certain plays and tales of Dunsany show how he took to heart suggestions from the art of the East. Imagism certainly owes a large debt to China, and several contemporary English poets, Blunden not least among them, have struck new lodes to follow through residence in Japan. One cannot help wondering whether such years there will give us, sooner or later, a new book of verse from Ralph Hodgson to put on our shelves alongside that nuggety little volume of 1917.

THE EFFECTS OF THE NEW PSYCHOLOGY

"Not proven" is still written across the Freudian psychology, as across other large areas of this new science. It has had its influence, unquestionably, during the past thirty years, but it has by now fairly run its course, and it is no longer dominating any artistic intelligence of the first power. Whether it ruined a fine writer in D. H. Lawrence, or whether the hysteria in the very innermost being of the man developed with his decay of health it is impossible to say. Sex was an obsession with him. There was no appeasement of desire possible to him. The signs that point to his obsession were apparent in him from the first, although they were not so clear in his early verse as in his early novels. *Love Poems* (1913) is freer of them than *Sons and Lovers* (1913). It is in his novels rather than in his verse that his poetry is at its best.

His tragedy is the greatest in all the tragic annals of the poetry of our hundred years. With incomparable gifts for both poetry and the novel he squandered them all, and his work, much of it and of diverse forms as there is, remains variations on frustrations. That a man who could write the poem "Violets" with its deep human sympathy and beauty of feeling should come to his later novels is a phenomenon for the alienists to explain.

THE OLD MAIN LINE

Two fresh treatments of Greek myth by Stephen Phillips and Sturge Moore brought most of what was new to the old main line of English poetry after 1882. The rest of the group went on in the safe way that had come down to them from Spenser and Milton and Gray, Wordsworth and Tennyson and Arnold. The attempts of Bridges in his new prosody and his labored code in *The Testament of Beauty* are interesting, but they have led to no poetry of power. Sir William Watson held resolutely to the end the standards he assumed in his youth. Francis Coutts and A. C. Benson and Binyon, the other principals of the group, have done good work in verse, but no one of them has achieved a poem sure of a place in the anthologies of the future.

THE LAST PHASE OF THE ESTHETIC MOVEMENT

Of the leaders of the Pre-Raphaelite movement Morris and Swinburne were writing after 1882, the year in which Rossetti died, but all their best work had been done. Morris lived on to 1896 and Swinburne to 1909. Pater, apostle of the later development of the movement they brought to full fruition, came into his own as a master of prose in the eighteen-eighties. He founded a school of prose writing of which Arthur Symons and George Moore were shining lights. The new estheticism handed on certain of its credos to Yeats, the most strongly individual poet that ever came from the movement from the days of *The Germ* (1848) until to-day. Wilde was, however, the last writer wholly of the movement.

THE CELTIC RENAISSANCE

George W. Russell thought the Paterian values a blight on literature, and few of the younger Irishmen hold to the artistic theories of Yeats. Wilde, who was not affiliated in any way with the Celtic Renaissance, owed a good deal to Pater, and you come on an echo of his standards now and then in Dunsany and Gogarty.

Russell, Synge, and Stephens held to far other doctrines and values, and the younger men like Strong and Higgins and Austin Clarke are entirely out of the esthetic tradition.

There is no movement of these last fifty years that has brought forward so important a group of writers as the Celtic Renaissance. Yeats, from many points of view, is the outstanding poet of the half-century. Like other men who have won to a position of individuality, he did 'prentice-work in the styles of other men, but he soon freed himself and attained a mastery all his own. He has struck new notes in poetry, he has made a new music of English words, and he has gotten new colors into English verse. There was nothing like "Tread softly because you tread on my dreams" and like "The dews drop slowly and dreams gather" until Yeats wrote such lines. And since Milton there has been no such august dignity in English poetry as that of Yeats, save that of Wordsworth in his highest mood. Nor has there ever been, since Shakespeare, phrasing more pregnant and perfect, and life stories of men and women told more wholly in brief passages of from one line to three.

There has been in our time no such discoverer and provoker of writers as Yeats. It may be that he cost Dunsany five years of productivity by putting him upon the wrong track, but I doubt if we should have had Dunsany without Yeats. Synge Yeats discovered in Paris and sent to the Aran Isles. Moore's third phase, that from *Evelyn Innes* to *Hail and Farewell*, is due to Yeats. And Yeats stood sponsor to the early work of Masefield. Yeats countenanced Pound, and he asked a hearing for all the imagists down to T. S. Eliot.

CHAPTER II

The Beginnings of the New Order:
Henley, Stevenson, and Davidson

WILLIAM ERNEST HENLEY (1849-1903) was a man of prose who had his heart set on being a poet. And so good a craftsman was he, so interested in the rhythms and images of verse, so full of life, so overflowing with feeling, that when he forced his prose into the forms of verse, he made it lift now and then to poetry. So, too, had Landor, another man of prose, made his writing in verse kindle rarely into poetry. So, too, had not Dr. Johnson and Dean Swift, prosemen both and nothing more, though they tried their hardest to be lyrical. Sheer creative force in literature must have an innate lyrical quality to it to break out in poetry. A passage charged to the highest intensity with feeling will not, for that reason, turn lyric. It is Henley who has pointed out this, in the preface to *English Lyrics* (1897), illustrating his contention by the cases of Johnson and Swift cited above.

There was a lyric vein in Henley, but it was thin, and quickly exhausted after the first lines of a poem. Time and again, when I have come to the reading of him, with glowing memories of some poem, I have found that poem less than my memory of it. I have remembered certain images he used, maybe a line or two of the poem, its lilt and go, but before I have gone far with the rereading, the glow has gone out of it all. I have had this experience with "The nightingale has a lyre of gold," and with "The April sky sags low and drear." With "the downs, like uplands in Eden" the glow does not begin to fade until I come to the third stanza. One mood is sustained in stanzas one and two, and then another succeeds to it in stanza three. The intrusion of death in the third stanza, even though thoughts of it create "a rapture of boding," is like a feast's last course served in cups made from skulls. Again the light of a poem will go out suddenly like the light of a candle quickly snuffed. So it is in "Moon of half-candied meres." What has happened is, I think, that his inspiration has failed him, that he feels the need of an additional stanza, but he has not the material for it, and falls back on a contrast or a conceit to help him out.

Curiously, it was in two opposite poles of verse that Henley was most successful. In that strait-jacketed form, the ballade, he did his best poem, "Of Dead Actors." He liked the theater; he wrote, with R. L. S., plays for it, he had a brother, Edward John Henley, an actor and a good actor, as I who saw him with Margaret Mather in *Cymbeline* can testify. In those old days of the end of the century, when movies and phonographs were not, the art of the actor passed with the actor. Even to-day, with all our modern equipment, a talkie is still no more than a ghost of a play. Henley felt deeply the temporary quality of the actor's art. All that life and brilliancy, all that savor and tang of changing personality, as it was now in one part and now another, gone with the last curtain fall!

> The curtain falls, the play is played:
> The Beggar packs beside the Beau;
> The Monarch troops, and troops the Maid;
> The Thunder huddles with the Snow.
> Where are the revellers high and low?
> The clashing swords? The lover's call?
> The dancers gleaming row on row?
> Into the night go one and all.

It is all so true, and so universal an experience. We have all thought of it and deplored it often and often. It is all so easy to understand and to feel and to visualize. There is nothing baffling about it, as there is about so much verse, in the estimation at least of those not bred to verse.

And yet there are only four lines of poetry in it all, and they reduce to one line four times repeated, the inimitable refrain, "Into the night go one and all." There is a toll to that, slow and ominous and weighted with the inevitable. One other line, "The Thunder huddles with the Snow," is close to poetry, but only "Into the night go one and all" is impassioned and musical and burdened with intimations of things beyond consciousness.

In the freest of free rhythms Henley did his other finest poetry. The "Praeludium" to *Hawthorn and Lavender* (1901), for all its wanton close, is, I think, about the best of this sort. It is, indeed, *largo expressivo*.

> In sumptuous chords, and strange,
> Through rich yet poignant harmonies:
> Subtle and strong browns, reds
> Magnificent with death and the pride of death,
> Thin, clamant greens
> And delicate yellows that exhaust
> The exquisite chromatics of decay.

The poet who wrote this is the man Henley with all his interests quickened to their utmost. We find here the student of music, the critic of painting, the lover of the countryside, as well as the lifelong reader of poetry, his memory stored with all the great odes from Spenser to Patmore. And yet, fine as it all is, it is hardly impassioned writing, hardly more than the admirably nervous prose the man can write.

There are times, indeed, when I wonder if his prose is not the best of him, his early prose, recovered from "the shot rubbish of some fourteen years of journalism" that he reprinted, rewritten, in *Views and Reviews* (1890). My copy, which I did not procure until 1898, is marked up from first page to last. "Read him on Walton, Herrick, and Homer and Theocritus," I have written on the fly-leaf at the end, and to-day, on a rereading, I say what I said more than thirty years ago, and add to that "Read him on Longfellow, too." How I rejoiced in "Master Piscator," precious-

BEGINNINGS OF THE NEW ORDER 33

ness and all: "It was rather the pretext . . . of a day in the fields: where the skylark soared, and the earth smelled sweet, and the water flashed and tinkled as it ran, while hard by some milkmaid, courteous yet innocent, sang as she plied her nimble fingers, and not very far away the casement of the inn-parlour gleamed comfortable promises of talk and food and rest. . . . He had the purest and the most innocent of minds, he was the master of a style as bright, as sweet, as refreshing and delightful, as fine clean home-spun some time in lavender."

There is plenty to quarrel with always in Henley. A few lines below those I have quoted, he declares: "After all it is only your town-bred poet who knows anything of the country," citing Milton and Herrick in support of his paradox, and conveniently forgetting Wordsworth and Tennyson.

Turn over the page from Walton and you have Herrick:

In Herrick the air is fragrant with new-mown hay; there is a morning light upon all things; long shadows streak the grass, and on the eglantine swinging in the hedge the dew lies white and brilliant.

Of Longfellow Henley has this to say:

In his verse the rigging creaks, the white sail fills and crackles, there are blown smells of pine and hemp and tar; you catch the home wind on your cheeks; and old shipmen, their eyeballs white in their bronzed faces, with silver rings and gaudy handkerchiefs, come in and tell you moving stories of the immemorial, incommunicable deep.

I have no space left to quote you Henley on Homer and Theocritus. There are finer passages on these poets than those I have quoted, but as they have been picked out by certain commentators on Henley, I chose the less familiar ones on Walton and Herrick and Longfellow. As I said, I am not sure that such are not the best of Henley, better than any of the verses even, and much better than the prose of *Views and Reviews: Art* (1902), or of *Burns: Life, Genius, Achievement* (1897), or of any of the essays on Fielding, Smollett, Hazlitt, Byron, and T. E. Brown collected after his death.

What the world values most in Henley is other than any of these poems or passages in prose I have mentioned. What the world values most is the poem "Out of the night that covers me," largely because it was Theodore Roosevelt's favorite poem. Almost from the time it was printed in *A Book of Verses* (1888) its phrases were on the lips of men, and all its sixteen lines in the memory of every other school-boy. "The master of my fate" and "The captain of my soul" soon became distressingly familiar, and "My head is bloody, but unbowed" overemphatic.

In this same *Book of Verses* appeared:

> Or ever the knightly years were gone
> With the old world to the grave,
> I was a King in Babylon
> And you were a Christian Slave.

Those lines, you will recall, became the favorite reading of the resourceful butler hero of *The Admirable Crichton* (1903), after the yachting party were wrecked on a far Pacific island. Whether the quotation by Crichton of this stanza helped the circulation of Henley when the play was first published in 1918 I do not know, but I do know that the "picturization" of the play into *Male and Female* sold out all the copies of Henley's poems containing it that were in America. You couldn't buy *A Book of Verses* (1888) or *Poems* (1898) in Philadelphia or New York or San Francisco for love or money. I know because my edition of *Poems* was "borrowed," and I had to send to England to get another copy. I made the round of bookstores in Philadelphia, but there was a copy of Henley's verses nowhere, not even an old copy at Leary's. Friends tried for me in the other cities, with like results. The publishers, too, were out of them. It is helpful to an author to have Sir James M. Barrie quote him, and for that quotation to be flashed on the screen. The stanza on the screen before them, the populace naturally were curious to see what the rest of the poem was like.

BEGINNINGS OF THE NEW ORDER

There was a time when *The Song of the Sword* (1892) and *London Voluntaries* (1893) went to my head as quickly as cognac. I still value them for many bracing declarations on life, for certain passages striking rhetorically, and for certain lines that have become part of our speech. *The Song of the Sword* puts the theory of the survival of the fittest into verse that is bright and glittering, but of a metallic ring. Metallic he is apt to be nearly always. There are few strings and little woodwind in Henley's orchestra, and no French horns. It is nearly all trumpets, with a trombone or two, brasses that have here the suggestion of steel. There is a drum, too, that he borrowed in his last years from Kipling. And there are bells.

There is still magic for me in the opening of *London Voluntaries*. The poem sinks, however, to the clang of prose, when it changes from *Grave* to *Andante con moto*. Most of what is memorable in the rest of *London Voluntaries* is memorable in the way of prose. "Death with his well-worn, lean, professional smile" is good prose. So, too, are "matrons heavy bosomed and aglow With the mild and placid pride of increase," and "desirable and frankly fair," and the designation of the world as "Wanton and wondrous and forever well."

In his first book of verse, the privately published *Voluntaries* (1888), Henley had proved he was a master at limning things seen. The series "In Hospital" gave his impressions while he was a patient in the Old Edinburgh Infirmary from 1873 to 1875. He went there for treatment of a "beastly form of tubercle." It was here he met Stevenson, whom Leslie Stephen brought to see him, and whom he described so accurately in "Apparition." Stevenson did the like for him in "Talk and Talkers," where Henley appears as "Burly," and in *Treasure Island* (1883), for which he was pranked out as John Silver.

Henley had just as firm a hand a quarter of a century later, when in 1898 he did Bus-Driver and Beef-Eater and Bar-Maid in *London Types* to cuts by William Nicholson, as he had used on nurses and visitors and doctors in "In Hospital."

To his own time Henley was most important of all as editor.

He had charge of *London* in 1877 and 1878; of *The Magazine of Art* from 1882 to 1886; of *The Scots Observer*, afterwards *The National Observer*, from 1889 to 1894; and of *The New Review* from 1894 to 1898. His idea of an editor's duties was not to make his magazine pay its owners, but to publish good literature and, if possible, of a new sort. It is to be wondered he held any of the jobs as long as he did. You cannot get the temper of the man better than by what he wrote me of *The National Observer*, in November, 1897, just as he was about to give up the editorship of *The New Review:*

It bulked large and luminous while it lived. But it was far too aristocratic—in art, life, politics, morals—to live long. Still, it served its turn; and the English Press is not exactly what it was before we came. I had the young men with me—Kipling, Whibley, Barrie, G. W. Steevens, Street, Marriott-Watson, Arthur Morrison, Gilbert Parker. Decidedly it served its turn, and was as well hated (by the right people) as any journal that has been.

This is not the place to speak of the other writers, many of them later distinguished in letters, from Stevenson on, to whom Henley gave a chance. I must, however, mention that Yeats owns his first good work was done for *The National Observer;* and that the story with which Conrad reached his mastery of style, *The Nigger of the Narcissus*, was first printed in *The New Review*.

George Moore, so far as I can recall, makes nothing of Henley's labors as an interpreter of French impressionism. Henley, perhaps, had ignored Moore. Henley was, however, as deeply interested in impressionism as Moore, and interested as early as the author of *Modern Painting* (1893). Henley was proud of his *Catalogue* (1888) of the French and Dutch pictures in the Edinburgh Exhibition. One citation must suffice to show his methods in establishing standards. Of the art criticism of R. A. M. Stevenson, Robert Louis Stevenson's cousin, and the "Spring-heeled Jack" of "Talk and Talkers," Henley writes: "A good Corot, a good Wordsworth sonnet, the *Andante* of the G minor symphony, a passage in *Paradise Lost* or the *Agonistes*, the *Lances*, the 'Troubled Soul' in Gluck's Orphée—with these he was at home." And with these best things of the arts Henley, too, was at home. And the personality of the man Henley! It was a thousand pities he could not more often transmute that into poetry. Perhaps one reason was that clear intelligence of his was always in the saddle and drove him on remorselessly to the daily task, a task that was only other than hackwork because he made it so. Perhaps it was he was too busy to listen for the inner voice. Perhaps it was that he went to school too early to Pope and the eighteenth century.

Good craftsmanship was instinctive to Henley, and a realization of things as they are, and romance. He demonstrated once and for all that there is no inherent contradiction between realism and romance. In that most realistic sequence of phases of hospital life, Henley calls a twenty-line poem of his that is bare and unadorned and stark, "Romance," and rightly. It is a sailor's talk of seeing old men and boys, late in the Civil War, training for arms on a wharf at Charleston. They are "Poor old Dixie's bottom dollar."

> It looked like fighting,
> And they meant it too, by thunder!

Clear, kindly, human, Henley always was. Intolerant generally, too, he was, violent often, luxuriating in John Bullishness of a simon-pure Tory brand. No man has, indeed, written a poem with rounder praise of England than his "England, my England," one of several militantly patriotic poems gathered into *For England's Sake* (1900) during the Boer War. Always Henley retained the towering optimism of the Englishman who believes he is appointed of God to rule and to overcome whoever challenges his right to rule.

> That race is damned which misesteems its fate,
> And this, in God's good time, they all shall know,
> And know you too, you good green England, then—
> Mother of mothering girls and governing men!

Henley in "Shoreham River" saw himself as an old wreck "stranded in midstream," as he later saw himself as "A tool on His workshop floor, Worn to the butt." It was this feeling, I think, that explains the violence of his expression of patriotism, and of his desire for life at the full bent of being.

At the very end Henley turned his hand to the motor-car as material for poetry. *A Song of Speed* came in 1903. I have sat up all night, when it was fresh from the press, discussing with young men the question as to whether it is poetry or not. In one memorable bout we decided about daylight that it was not. The Mercedes he celebrates is shapeless, unhandsome, and unpaintable, but still a good thing because of its speed. The song about the Mercedes is like in kind, hardly poetry but a thrilling experience for any reader. What you remember from it on a first reading is what you remember from a ride with some youngster who will not take his foot off the gas, no matter what is ahead; a sense of power let loose; and a sense of speed. You remember power and speed and some pictures of the countryside at a second reading. At each reading thereafter the pictures of the countryside bite in on you more clearly:

>   the horse on the tow-path,
>   Tugging in dreams
>   At the long barge that hangs
>   Like a dream on his collar;

and the

>   Beechwoods that burn out
>   The life in their leafage.

It was not for nothing that he was Anthony Warton Henley's brother. William Ernest Henley, too, was a landscape painter. Maybe after all is said and done these bits of the England which he so loved will last longest in memory:

>   Low-low
>   Over a perishing afterglow,
>   A thin, red shred of moon

> Trailed. In the windless air
> The poplars all ranked lean and chill.
> The smell of winter loitered there,
> And the Year's heart felt still.

There is a landscape, with its feeling, its connotation, its values, all in thirty-six words. And I have to say of it, as I have had to say of so much of Henley, that its power is the power of prose, of unimpassioned prose.

There was no dream in Henley's eyes; there was no such music in his ears as compelled his lines to fall into magical cadences; there was no such tumult in his brain as drove him to ecstasies. Eyes and ears and brain functioned at high power, but almost always they were the servants of the man writing. They seldom took hold of him and forced him to build better than he knew. The man was master of what he wrote in all but a few poems. The writing only two or three times in his life possessed him to the exclusion of himself, and made him merely the mouthpiece for intimations and emotions, melodies and harmonies, that were roving about just below consciousness, and to be caught by the poet only in such moments of possession. So it is that, admirable craftsman in verse as he is always, Henley is the lyrical poet only now and then.

ROBERT LOUIS STEVENSON

When an author is as well known and as well loved as Robert Louis Stevenson (1850-1894), everything that he writes becomes interesting because of him, even if it is not interesting of itself. We look to this poem or that essay to see how much of the man who wrote *Treasure Island* or *David Balfour* or *Weir of Hermiston* there is in it. It is because of this attitude we have toward Stevenson that we pay heed to certain verses of his in which he expresses more pithily than elsewhere his cheerful philosophy of life. He would not falter in his "great task of happiness." He would be "up and doing"; he asks it be given him:

> Unfearing and unshamed to go
> In all the uproar and the press
> About my human business!

If it were not for this philosophy, I doubt if "The Celestial Surgeon" and "Our Lady of the Snows," from which I quote, or "The Vagabond" or "If This Were Faith," would long detain us. They are not good poems, any of them. They are verses which give us in a few of their lines his philosophy of life, high-hearted and well phrased. Such lines as:

> All I ask the heaven above
> And the road below me

strike that note of vagabondage that was so deep-seated in the man. Back of all the douce Balfours and the pawky Stevensons there must have been some old reiver or cattle-lifter of the Border whose blood reasserted itself in R.L.S. There are those who will tell you that lines such as:

> My mistress still the open road
> And the bright eyes of danger

are but part of the pose of the play-actor he undoubtedly was; that he was no adventurer at all, but as sedentary a literary man as ever stuck night after night to lamp-lit desk. So it is well enough to say, but no one can deny his gallant air in illness, or the fact that he braved the sharp Pacific gales in a seventy-four ton schooner. That he would have been as happy as a man of action as he thought he would be, I doubt. There was, as Henley said, a good deal of Hamlet in him, and out of brooding and self-analysis comes writing. There is no doubt, however, that he wrote in all sincerity those lines in "If This Were Faith":

> If still in my veins the glee
> Of the black night and the sun
> And the lost battle, run.

BEGINNINGS OF THE NEW ORDER

At the same time we may admit that there was in Stevenson something of the invalid's envy of hardihood, which made him put a higher value on all that is the outcome of hardihood than would the well man. He would have liked to be a man strong enough and adroit enough and resourceful enough to risk his neck with an even chance of coming out safely. Stevenson believes wholeheartedly what he says when he declares:

> For still the Lord is Lord of Might;
> In deeds, in deeds, He takes delight.

But all this which I have quoted is merely bracing philosophy, not poetry. Stevenson himself made light of all his verse, child's verse, epistles, poems of places; and his family and most of his critics have followed him in this profession of his. It should not be taken too seriously, however, this profession of a lack of seriousness of intention in his verses. He belittled the art that made him famous, speaking of literature as an "art of prostitution," in one place, and, in another, in verse, as a "childish task Around the fire," a playing "at home with paper like a child." That he wrote so much verse as the omnium-gatherum of it in the *Complete Poems* (1922) shows he did, is proof positive that he aspired to be a poet. Once in a while, too, his secret longing betrays itself in his letters or in some passage in his criticism.

In "To the Muse" Stevenson writes:

> Resign the rhapsody, the dream,
>   To men of larger reach;
> Be ours the quest of a plain theme,
>   The piety of speech.

Good craftsman and good critic that he was, Stevenson knew well that he was little of a poet in either prose or verse. What he says about the success of *Underwoods* (1887), in a letter to Sidney Colvin, shows that he put about the right value upon his verses. "You see, the verses are sane; that is their strong point, and it seems it is strong enough to carry them." Yes, the verses of *Underwoods* were sane, and that was enough to carry them to a passing success, but not further. There is little left of them to-day. Pick up your copy of them, reader, you who are a lover of poetry, and note how many passages you have marked. Shut the book, and try to summon to your lips lines of it. You know it would be idle to try to recall a whole poem. There is not one set of verses, not even "Requiem," you so cared about that it made you remember it, or made you get it by heart. "Envoy" is verse of a pleasant eighteenth-century flavor. "A Song of the Road" is a summing-up of its maker, an allegory in little of his life and what it amounted to, a realization of the futility often the end of all, that is not in keeping with his customary optimism:

> There's nothing under heav'n so blue
> That's fairly worth the traveling to.

"The Canoe Speaks" is pleasant, too, not more. "It is the season now to go" is an unimpassioned little lyric of calf love, better in its kind than most of his verses. "The House Beautiful" has its memorable line, as has perhaps every fifth set of verses of his, a good eighteenth-century line, "The incomparable pomp of eve." And so it goes through all the thirty-nine titles, epistles, occasional verses, epigrams. There are many different kinds of pleasantness, but of ecstasy very little, and of music almost none at all. Yet Stevenson does strike a note now and then that is his own, the note of a prose Cotton, I should say, rather than of a prose Herrick, as Stevenson says, though that note is not so distinct as the note of either of the elder poets.

"A Lowden Sabbath Morn" is a pastoral of a sort distinctly better than the poems in English of *Underwoods*. It is in a Scotch which looks forbidding, a Scotch which is not that of Burns, so familiar to the America of yesterday. Burns, indeed, Stevenson owns, "has always sounded in my ear like something partly foreign." It is the speech of the Lothians that he uses, Stevenson tells

BEGINNINGS OF THE NEW ORDER 43

us. In the Skerryvore edition, in which I now read it, the hard words are mercifully translated on the margin, and so I can understand all of the poem without difficulty. "A Lowden Sabbath Morn" is all on one note, a note of kindly and smiling tolerance for all things of yesterday, Sabbaths, blue-stocking Presbyterians, precentors and long sermons. The tolerance quickens to a love of what he laughs at before the poem comes to an end. It is, indeed, to Stevenson, a poem of "mine own people."

It is not, however, a poem that could not have been written by anybody else. Of the verses of *A Child's Garden of Verses* (1885), alone of all his verses, can it be honestly said, only Stevenson could have written these. "A Lowden Sabbath Morn" is observant, true to life, sonsie, well-proportioned, memorable. It may be my own Presbyterian past makes me have a weakness for it, but I think my liking for the poem is more than a weakness. It appeals, I think, to all of us who have been brought up as Puritans in country places. It is a part of life in which a large part of the world has shared. From the Pentlands to the Selkirks, from the Alleghenies to the New Zealand Alps, men of British stock, Scotch, English, Welsh, and Irish, have been called to church, for many generations, by Sabbath bells. The place in Stevenson's poem is as Scotch as the language in which it is written, but all the ways of pastor and flock here chronicled are the same the world over among all Evangelical Protestants.

Ballads (1890) collects four narratives in verse, two of the Pacific islands and two of the Highland Scotch life, with hardly a suspicion of poetry about them. *Songs of Travel* (1896) contains the best that Stevenson has done in verse. The verses were written, most of them, after Stevenson went, in 1888, to the South Seas. During the last six years of his life in "these ultimate islands," so different in aspect and associations from the Scotland of his youth, his thoughts turned night after night to his home country about Edinburgh. There were found among his notes for the incompleted *Weir of Hermiston* these lines with the tang and color of the Lothians:

> I saw rain falling and the rainbow drawn
> On Lammermuir. Hearkening I heard again
> In my precipitous city beaten bells
> Winnow the keen sea wind. And here afar,
> Intent on my own race and place, I wrote.

They are a dedication of the novel to his wife, whom he had taught to see his home country through his eyes.

Places had always been a great deal to Stevenson. He fitted games to them as a child; he made stories and verses for them as a man. He found images in them for his poetry. It is a memory of the Castle Rock in Edinburgh that gave him these two lines in "The Unforgotten":

> Her starry silence smote my ear
> Like sudden drums at night.

A place in Scotland inspires his best poem but one, "In the highlands, in the country places"; and still another place, in his beloved Lammermuir, his best poem of all, "To S. R. Crockett." The celebrator of the Covenanters had dedicated a novel to Stevenson, and Stevenson wrote twelve lines in acknowledgment that gave us in a nutshell the moor country south of Edinburgh and just back from the North Sea. I know this country. I saw it last on a blowing day of late summer such as Stevenson recalls. An old woman in a shawl in the third-class compartment in which we were traveling pointed out to us "the graves of the martyrs" for Kirk and Covenant. We saw the megalithic monuments of the Picts rising gray above the red heather that clothed every fold of the rolling moor. We saw curlews and lapwings, his "whaups" and "peewees," and sheep on an hundred hills. Here, in this poem on Lammermuir, almost alone in the verse of Stevenson, is heart's cry and music.

> Blows the wind today, and the sun and the rain are flying,
>   Blows the wind on the moors today and now,
> Where about the graves of the martyrs the whaups are crying,
>   My heart remembers how!

That ends what there is to say about the poetry of Stevenson, and hardly a word said of *A Child's Garden of Verses*. Does that mean I hold there is no poetry of consequence in the verses that meant so much to the generations of children that were in the nursery from 1885 to 1914? The World War marked the end of the unquestioned reign of Stevenson in the nursery. "Lewis Carroll" held his more modest sway on through the war and beyond it with *Alice's Adventures in Wonderland* (1865) and *Through the Looking Glass* (1872); and A. A. Milne has now won first place in all childish hearts with *When We Were Very Young* (1925) and *The House at Pook Corner* (1928). Yes, it means that I hold there is very little poetry in the child verses of Stevenson. There is very little poetry, too, in Carroll and Milne. There are, however, things that are very fetching, engaging, captivating, making for the joy of life, in all three. There is a great deal of human nature, and of fun, and of a make-believe that is heart-easing, in them all.

A Child's Garden of Verses is a real dramatization, a dramatization of childhood, a recapturing of childhood through memory, and a presentation of that dramatization and recapture that has delighted many, many children, and nearly all grown-ups who have read the verses. No one has been juster to them than Stevenson himself. In a letter to Edmund Gosse, under date of March 12, 1885, he wrote: "They look ghastly in the cold light of print; but there is something nice in the little ragged regiment for all; the blackguards seem to me to smile, to have a kind of childish treble note that sounds in my ears freshly; not song, if you will, but a child's voice."

That these verses took men wholly captive I have more than one concrete example to prove. Yet one must do. A friend of mine, a man of my generation but city-born and bred, had never realized what he had missed in life through not knowing hayloft and barn and farm until he read *A Child's Garden* to his children. He was bowled out cleanly by "The Hayloft" and "Farewell to the Farm." His children must have, he determined, what he had not had. So off he went and bought a farm, without even consulting his wife. As might be expected, things being as they always are in this world, the children did not much care for the hayloft in the barn on that farm in Gwynedd. They, or his wife, saw to it that they did not have the farm for long. Its purchase proves, however, the power of literature in general, and of Stevenson in particular. *A Child's Garden of Verses* is literature, there is no doubt of it. It has a place in verse just as surely as society verse, or satire, or any other of the several sorts of verse that are unquestionably literature, but hardly poetry. Unfortunately, I was out of the nursery before these verses came along, contenting myself as well as I could with Whittier's *Household Book of Poetry*. I saw, however, a child of mine watch for Leerie the lamplighter and talk to an unseen playmate in the cellar window.

OSCAR WILDE

Every criticism of Oscar Wilde (1856-1900) that would come to the point at once must begin with a reference to his "Hélas." That sonnet, prefixed to his poems, questions:

> To drift with every passion till my soul
> Is a stringed lute on which all winds can play,
> Is it for this that I have given away
> Mine ancient wisdom and austere control?

Those lines explain, perhaps, not only his weakness in life, but his weakness in verse as well. That there was a definite Epicureanism in Wilde is true, of course, and an equally definite love of beauty, but he was so much of a poseur, so much of a chameleon, so much of a weathercock, that it is difficult to define just what of his powers was his own. He responded to so many influences of his time you are hard put to find any originality in him. His wit was largely from Whistler, his art of the stage widely eclectic, but owing much to dramatists as different as Congreve and Maeterlinck, Sardou and Ibsen. His early verse is overburdened with Pre-Raphaelitism.

BEGINNINGS OF THE NEW ORDER

His "Ballad of Reading Gaol" (1898) owes its form to "The Rime of the Ancient Mariner" (1798), and its clarities to *A Shropshire Lad* (1896). Wilde aped the Greeks, the French decadents, the Old Testament, and the Elizabethans. He aped Tennyson, he aped Morris, he aped Rossetti, he aped Swinburne, he aped whatever dominated him at the moment of writing, but he always aped with an air. He is an out-and-out Parnassian in:

> The almond groves of Samarkand,
>   Bokhara, where red lilies blow,
> And Oxus, by whose yellow sand
>   The grave white-turbaned merchants go.

Second-hand though most of what he wrote was, it was good enough to serve as model for Symons, a poet of about his own stature, and for Flecker, a better poet.

There was that in Wilde that prevented him from transcending the dilettante in letters. He thought himself, of course, a master of the art of life, and a full-fledged man of letters. He was prodigal of theories of life and of art, of esthetic code, of propaganda of art for art's sake, but despite the many kinds of writing at which he tried his hand he perfected himself in none. There are those who hold that his curiously contrived fairy stories are the best of him, but the flaw there was in his very nature clouds even them. There are others who think that his essays are profound as well as witty. There are many who think his plays true high comedy, but though he had an appreciation of the comic spirit it could not save him from letting his plays run in this place into farce and in that place into melodrama. There are no great characters in any of his plays. Ernest and Viscount Goring, his heroes most nearly himself, are nearest to being figures against the sky. They are not that, though. You have only to project them, in your mind's eye, on the horizon's edge, to see them thin away into caricatures.

Short story or novel, criticism or essay, play or poem—whatever Wilde set himself to do he juggled with successfully, but he never reached finality of accomplishment in any form. He suffered from the curse of cleverness, he trusted to cleverness to see him through whatever he tried. He never knew, until he was in Reading Gaol, what it was to be possessed by a subject. He had no strong personality to express, no new beauty of imagination or of form. The root of originality was not in him.

So it is that almost all the verses of Wilde read like variations on themes from his elders. There is no poem wholly his own save "The Ballad of Reading Gaol." In that poem only had he a subject, something of his own to sing, and discovery about life. Suffering had leached out of him when he came to write it the abnormality that had been so deep-seated in him. That abnormality was apparent, here and there, in the verses of his youth collected into the *Poems* of 1881. Previous to his imprisonment Wilde had only played that he was possessed by the deeper emotions. Now sympathy for the trooper who was condemned to death for killing the girl he loved took hold of Wilde as no emotion had ever taken hold of him before. It was a very agony of sympathy, and that agony was caught in the verses Wilde wrote to show the effect of the trooper's last days and death on his fellow-prisoners at Reading. Now for the first time Wilde felt and imagined himself into the place of another man. Previously he had played many parts, but only as an actor who superficially presents them. Now for the first time he was a man among his fellow-men. A poet, like every other artist, must be that before he can be a great artist. He must be, of course, what it is much more unusual to be than a man among men—he must be the master of his art. If he is not wholly human, however, his art will have but cold and colorless material with which to work, and it will be difficult for him to win to more than minor accomplishment.

Wilde was temperamentally aloof from many of the concerns of life, but he furthered that aloofness by his preoccupation with the theories that finally led to his complete absorption into the theory of art for art's sake. It is in the preface to Rennell Rodd's *Rose Leaf and Apple Leaf* that he announces the theory:

Now, this increased sense of the absolutely satisfying value of beautiful workmanship, this recognition of the primary importance of the sensuous element in art, this love of art for art's sake, is the point in which we of the younger school have made a departure from the teaching of Mr. Ruskin,—a departure definite and different and decisive.

His criticism on the whole is valuable only for its insistence on this point of view. It resolves itself in the end to a glorification of manner and to an indifference to matter. It did not help him in his own verse, and it narrowed his sympathies when he came to judging the work of others. What is most interesting in his critical writing, indeed, is his awareness, in the lives of others, of what he was later to experience in his own life. It is strange, almost uncanny, to find him writing of the effect of prison on Wilfred Blunt in terms that might be applied to the effect of prison on himself. "Prison," he said, "Prison has had an admirable effect on Mr. Wilfred Blunt as a poet." Stranger still is it that the words he quotes from Blunt's preface to *In Vinculis* should be exactly applicable to his own case. "Imprisonment," he quotes Blunt as saying, "is a reality of discipline most useful to the modern soul, lapped as it is in physical sloth and self-indulgence. Like a sickness or a spiritual retreat it purifies and ennobles; and the soul emerges from it stronger and more self-contained."

The most memorable saying of Wilde in "The Ballad of Reading Gaol" is not agreed with by many men. It is a generalization from his statement about the trooper condemned to death. That trooper had killed the woman he loved. Wilde declares that a like crime is committed by every man. "Yet each man kills the thing he loves," is this memorable saying. The declaration is almost a leading motive in the ballad. It was, perhaps, symbolically true of Wilde himself. There are those who hold it even more than symbolically true. There are those who say, cynically, that it was Wilde's crime caused his own death and that he himself was what he most cared for. It is unquestionably forcing matters, though, to declare that men kill what they love as a result of their own actions. Wilde, though, seldom comes closer to insight than here. As close perhaps are two two-line declarations from this same ballad. The one is:

> For he who lives more lives than one
> More deaths than one must die.

Lest any one misunderstand these, let me run the risk of explaining the obvious and say that Wilde means that he who can put himself in another man's place, and live another man's life, knows all the terrors of death, through imaginative sympathy, when that man comes to die. The other declaration, curiously close to one of Wordsworth, is:

> For flowers have been known to heal
> A common man's despair.

There is another Wordsworthian echo in this other generalization:

> But this I know, that every Law
> That men have made for Man,
> Since first Man took his brother's life,
> And the sad world began,
> But strews the wheat and saves the chaff
> With a most evil fan.

There is better poetry in that other leading motive of "The Ballad of Reading Gaol," frequently recurrent in the poem:

> I never saw a man who looked
> With such a wistful eye
> Upon that little tent of blue
> Which prisoners call the sky.

The situation, of course, gives the lines no little part of their significance. The prisoner, with only a short time to live, is shut out from all the beauty of the world, save this bit of blue sky above the prison yard. That must serve him as the only solace he can have from nature, that is all there is to enable him to recall places that for a moment might shut out the picture of the gallows that is always before him. He is a torment not only to himself but to his fellow-prisoners. The end is sharply presented, from the standpoint of those fellow-prisoners though, and not from the trooper's. The effect of the hanging on his fellows was:

> Something was dead in each of us,
> And what was dead was Hope.

In the earlier verse of Wilde there is no end of literary allusions. Æschylos, Sophokles, and Euripides have place there; and Homer and Dante; and Chaucer, Shakespeare, and Milton; Mazzini and Byron; Wordsworth, Shelley, and Keats; and Swinburne, Rossetti, and William Morris. Such frequency of concern with the poets is almost always a sign of little originality in a poet. It is certainly that with Wilde. There is nothing that Wilde has written in verse that is stamped with individuality, of which you could say that Wilde surely wrote it, that only Wilde could have written it. Without the form of verse to help him, Wilde could come nowhere near poetry. If you do not believe that statement turn to his "Poems in Prose," and be convinced. And as he takes color from this poet or that, most often from Rossetti or Swinburne or Morris, he takes, too, color from place. In Rome Wilde is of Rome and the Romans. In Oxford he writes: "The English Thames is holier far than Rome." The upshot of every consideration of Wilde is that he is not an individuality, but only a talent, a surprising and a striking talent.

LORD ALFRED DOUGLAS

Lord Alfred Douglas (b. 1870) is better known for his friendship for Oscar Wilde and for his gifts of controversy than for his poetry. What concerns us in that poetry is a few sonnets and still fewer ballads. You will find what little matters in him in *The Collected Poems of Lord Alfred Douglas* (1919). There is the ballad "Perkin Warbeck" and a half-dozen most carefully wrought sonnets. Not one of these sets of verses is as interesting as his prose note at the end of the slight volume outlining his beliefs on poetry. He insists on sincerity and on artistry, two requisites for poetry, but not the only requisites. There must be, too, deeply felt emotion and discoveries about life. Lacking these latter, he writes verse that never crystallizes into lines that stick in memory. What you do remember of him is his bitterness, a bitterness that gives the verse imprisoning it a quality close to satire. His "Sonnet on the Sonnet" fails of a place beside Rossetti's, but you recall for a while after reading them "Canker Blooms" and "The Unspeakable Englishman" and "Lighten Our Darkness." There is wholesale damnation of his countrymen in the sestet of the last-named poem:

> Judges and prelates, chancellors and kings,
> . . . . . .
> I looked behind their masks and posturings
> And saw their souls too rotten to be cured,
> And knew them all for liars, rogues and knaves.

His wife, who was Olive Custance, is a writer of verse of a tender and fragile charm. "Alas! I do not know" haunts me as does no verse of her husband. You will find it in *The Inn of Dreams* (1911). It records the passing of childhood and fear at the threatened passing of youth.

> Alas! I do not know on what sad day
> My childhood went away . . .
> . . . . . .
> And so I cannot tell when youth will go
> Although I love it so.

NORMAN GALE

Norman Gale (b. 1862) persuades himself that Arcady is still to be found in the English shires. It is in Warwickshire, his own home country, he comes upon it, and not very far, I expect, from

BEGINNINGS OF THE NEW ORDER 53

Rugby. There you may see Cupid sleeping on a bank, and nymphs, in the guise of country girls, bathing in a stream. There is a farmer who sets his hands to dancing after the day's work is done, and to romps "by starlight in the dew." There they still play cricket on the commons in the long twilights of summer. There are still parsons as gay as Herrick. It is all artificial enough, what happens, though the girls who have part in it are right enough English girls, clean-limbed and lithe, and the landscape their background the England we know. The rose is his flower, but his favorite bird is rarer, the white-throat, which he praises in season and out, and loves as did Gilbert White.

It is a fresh small voice, this of Gale's and it was grateful in the nineties, when so much of the music of the poets was of the town. Le Gallienne and Symons and Dowson were hopelessly cockneys, feeling there was no such friendliness anywhere as under the street lamps and no such blooms as those the flower-girls sold.

Orchard Songs (1893) was a book of its year. Title-page and cover design were by Will Rothenstein, and there was a special edition on Whatman paper and bound in vellum. Its verses were freshly phrased and undisturbing, full of little prettinesses and sure of the goodness of God. *Orchard Songs* had been preceded the year before by two series of *A Country Muse,* both dated 1892, but I did not come upon them until later and I never cared for either so much as for *Orchard Songs.* They had not the freshness for me of the first-found volume. That is the way it often is with the artificially charming. You find the bloom is off it on a second meeting.

Cricket Songs (1894) had more appeal, perhaps, in and about Philadelphia than anywhere in America, for in late Victorian times we still learned to play cricket in the backyards in Germantown and Merion and Haddonfield before we learned to play baseball on the corner lots. The verses of this volume are pleasant and slangy, but they are few of them even remotely poetry.

Gale issued his *Collected Poems* in 1914, but they did not gain in effect by so many verses of so little diversity of subject and feeling and treatment gathered together. He wrote very much in his old vein in *A Merry-Go-Round of Song* (1919). It has all the sound workmanship of aforetime, but it was certainly not to the tune of the time. What was prettily artificial in the eighteen-nineties seemed all compound of artifice at the end of the nineteen-tens.

JOHN DAVIDSON

John Davidson (1857-1909) has still his old magic for youth. I never put him on a reading list in my course in contemporary poetry but I get enthusiastic reviews of his ballads and eclogues, and even, sometimes, of his testaments. He is not to me now what he was when I was young. Yet I remember as if it were yesterday the time when he was wine to me. I was so weak from typhoid fever when Bert Brown brought me *Ballads and Songs* (1894) in the late April or early May of 1895 that it took all my strength to sit up in bed. It was a Sunday afternoon that he came with the book, in those old days when Sunday afternoon was still a part of the Sabbath. He read bits of it to me, among others, bits of "A Ballad of a Nun," which I recalled I had read in *The Yellowbook*, and some verses set to "Ta-ra-ra-boom-de-ay," which we all knew from the violent declamation of Lottie Collins. Davidson brought the music hall to me, and the *fin de siècle* magazine, but he brought, too, a glory of sun-swept countryside still drenched with rain:

>The adventurous sun took Heaven by storm;
> Clouds scattered largesses of rain;
>The sounding cities, rich and warm,
> Smouldered and glittered in the plain.

That seemed like a Turner to me, but I liked better than the poet's picture of so wide a landscape his pictures of smaller bits of landscape, a copse in spring, or an orchard in fall:

>Showers of sunlight splash and dapple
> The orchard park;
>And there the plum hangs and the apple
> Like smouldering gems and lanterns dark.

It all seemed rich in imagination; it was all prodigal of light and color; everything was dispensed with the free hand of youth. There was such a thrill of passion in it all, or so it seemed then, almost a sob of passion. There was such joy in the escape from the city to the country. In a word, it was all attuned to the eager boy who listened that day to it, and read and reread it all time and again. It helped to bring home to him the wonder of the world.

Yet the man who was so much to men who were young a generation ago, who is so much to young men even to-day, when attention is directed to him, has fallen almost wholly out of discussion. He is almost never mentioned when the talk turns to late Victorian poetry. Davidson is no more to most of those who read poetry than is Sir William Watson. No one poem of Davidson, indeed, is as much alive as *Wordsworth's Grave* (1890) of Watson. Even the circumstances of Davidson's hard struggle in London and of his strange suicide in Cornwall are forgotten. He has passed, as James Thomson and Robert Buchanan, of that same dour stock of the Scottish Lowlands, have passed.

It is doubly tragic, this passing, in that Davidson strove so to do great things. He would have been prophet as well as poet. In the obsession that grew on him toward the end he thought that he had discovered the secret of the ages. Listen to the assurance of the man as he writes in the "Dedication" to *The Testament of John Davidson* (1908):

> Thus I break the world out of the imaginary chrysalis or cocoon of Other World in which it has slumbered so long; and man beholds himself, not now as that fabulous monster, half-god, half-devil, of the Christian era, but as Man, the very form and substance of the universe, the material of eternity, eternity itself become conscious and self-conscious. This is the greatest thing told since the world began.

Was the man deaf to all the talk of science of his time, or was he just infatuate? If he means what the words he uses ordinarily mean, his discovery is no discovery at all, but only what a considerable part of the world had long guessed to be the truth, and what another part had come to hold to as gospel as a result of the development of natural science.

It sounds Nietzschean, this quotation, and so does much else in Davidson, too. This trend of his thought had developed early, and he indignantly protests that the idea it grew to, like all the other ideas he particularly cherishes, originated with him. "The only educational influences I acknowledge," he wrote me in 1896, "are my own passions, thought and experience." He owns, however, more than once in his writing, that he was a reader of Carlyle, so it may well be that his idea of the superman comes from *Heroes and Hero-Worship.* Davidson's creed is announced clearly for the first time in "A Woman and Her Son," in *New Ballads* (1896), though there are hints of it in *Fleet Street Eclogues* (1893-1895) and even as far back as *Smith: A Tragic Farce* (1888). There the right of individual liberty is deified into overmanship. Torturing his dying mother with his unbelief, the son of "A Woman and Her Son" declares:

> Oh, surely now your creed will set you free
> For one great moment, and the universe
> Flash on your intellect as power, power, power,
> Knowing not good or evil, God or sin,
> But only everlasting yea and nay.

Davidson is here working his way to the belief that he came in the end to hold, that might is right. Born a Puritan, with an inherited anger at a world gone wrong, he came to confess that matter, what is, the nature of things, is not only triumphant, but rightly triumphant, in human affairs. *Godfrida* (1898), a play in four acts, is said by Davidson in his prologue to have its "poles" in two of its passages. The one is:
>   no felicity
> Can spring in men, except from barbèd roots
> Of discontent and envy, deeply struck
> In some sore heart that hoped to have the flower.

And the other is:
> I have had a vision of the soul of life,
> And love alone is worthy.

BEGINNINGS OF THE NEW ORDER 57

Clearer than any contrast involved in these two quotations is that between the brainsick and healthy characters in the play. The healthy triumph, of course, those who have the will to live. In *Self's the Man* (1901), whether he arrived at the condition himself or under the influence of Nietzsche, Davidson is Nietzschean through and through. Davidson owns, of course, to a reading of Nietzsche.

"There are signs of a Nietzsche panic," wrote Davidson to the London Academy, "and the word 'overman' is supposed to be an index of evolution in humanity. This seems to me very foolish. Nietzsche has nothing to tell the Englishman of the 'overman', the Englishman is the 'overman', in Europe, in Asia, in Africa, in America, he holds the world in the hollow of his hand. Moreover, he has been stated in our literature again and again, the outstanding instances being these:—Marlowe's *Tamburlaine*, Shakespeare's Richard III, Milton's Satan, Carlyle's *Cromwell*."

Davidson had read Ibsen carefully before he read Nietzsche. And before he had read Ibsen, he had read Burns and Shakespeare. Influences of all four men can be traced in him. There is no close following of any one of them, but they undoubtedly helped him to find himself. He could free himself of masters, but he could not win freedom for himself in which he could "loaf and invite his soul." There was no chance of it at all unless his plays should please the public. There was no chance that his early plays, printed in Scotland from 1886 to 1889, could do that, but he was hopeful a successful adaptation of Coppée's *Pour la Couronne* (1894), for Mrs. Patrick Campbell and Forbes Robertson, might pave the way for plays of his own. He seems to have felt his only chance was, through adaptations, to gain a reputation that would lead to the production of his own plays, but at the same time he resented being judged as a playwright by his adaptations.

In his introduction to *The Theatrocrat: A Tragic Play of Church and Stage* (1905) Davidson says: "My own plays, *Godfrida, Self's the Man, The Knight of the Maypole*, and an unpublished Arthurian play remain unproduced. The dismay of it is this:—That my Testaments and Tragedies—the matter wherewith I propose to change the mood of the world—remain, those that are issued, unknown; and those that should be written, unwritten: whereas the successful production of my four plays, the likeliest poetical plays written for the English stage in these times, would have placed me in an independent and dominant position from which all my writings could have come with that adventitious authority the world is powerless to disregard."

No one of these three published plays that he mentions is a thing of sustained power. *The Knight of the Maypole* (1903) is just the usual thing, with the Charles II we all know, and the dispossessed heir we were brought up on in *Guy Mannering*. It is comedy, *Self's the Man* (1901) tragedy, and *Godfrida* (1898) melodrama. There is the excitement of arms and love in old Provence in *Godfrida*. The romantic hero cuts his way through a hundred swords to his lady and carries her away, on horseback, to safety in the North. There is still more war and sounding arms and still more love and more intrigue in *Self's the Man*. Urban, the hero, fails because he had not the courage of his desires. He put aside his mistress Saturnia, whom he really loved, and wedded Osmunda, whose father was the most powerful among the Lombard nobles. Urban would have stunned his world to absolute subjection had he married Saturnia. His choice of policy rather than a following of his instinct overthrow him, or shall I say, his choice of policy rather than ruthlessness overthrew him. Perhaps a third reason for his failure that I might advance is nearer still the real reason. Perhaps it was wabbling that overthrew him, his choice now of Osmunda, who came to love him, and his choice now of Saturnia, who never ceased to love him. Ruthless selfishness making itself one with a high aim seems to be what Davidson asks of his overman.

The characterization is not sharp in any of the plays. Indeed his best work in characterization will be found in his earliest book of verse, *In a Music Hall* (1891), in his men and women of the stage; and in the volume of verse he mailed to his publisher on the

BEGINNINGS OF THE NEW ORDER 59

night he threw himself into the sea, *Fleet Street* (1909). In "Rail and Road" there is a lusty Juventus-like youth done brown, though, like the music hall people, he is more a type than an individual.

Self's the Man was commissioned by Sir Herbert Beerbohm Tree, who, however, failed to produce it. One feels it might have gone well on the stage. It has plenty of action, and action it is easy to follow. It may be that Tree never put it on because he feared an audience would not sympathize with its hero.

In his later plays Davidson is so obviously the enemy of society that it is easy to account for their failure to reach the stage. *The Theatrocrat* (1905), *The Triumph of Mammon* (1907), and *Mammon and His Message* (1908) are all anti-social, and it is hardly likely, in his heart, Davidson had hopes of any of the three but *The Theatrocrat* being produced by any actor-manager. Nor had Davidson those personal contacts that would make it possible for him to arrange for productions by the independent theater associations. He had always been too downright in the expression of his opinions to have many interested acquaintances, and even his friends had found it harder and harder, as the years advanced, to remain his friends.

There is little poetry in any of these later plays. As Davidson said to Yeats, in the mid-nineties: "The fires are out, and I must hammer the cold iron." Yeats records the saying in *The Trembling of the Veil* (1922), but I heard it from him much earlier, on his first American trip in 1903-1904. It had evidently made a deep impression upon him. It is the opinion of Yeats, as he expresses it in this autobiography, that Davidson had burnt himself out. "Violent energy," writes Yeats, "which is like a fire of straw, consumes in a few minutes the nervous vitality, and is useless in the arts."

The work of Davidson that is in the anthologies is of the early eighteen-nineties. The early plays he published in Scotland, where he was a national schoolmaster, have more poetry in them than have his last plays, but they are weak in structure, and only now and then more than eloquent. There are good lines in them, in *Smith* (1888) particularly. Here we find:

>   one must become
>   Fanatic—be a wedge—a thunderbolt
>   To smite a passage through the close-grained world,

and

>   Business—the world's work—is the sale of lies.

In all Davidson you will find no lines more memorable. Of like arresting force are "And one against the world will always win," and "Only a splendid hell keeps Heaven fair." Not so pregnant, but at least interesting for their ideas are:

>   For every Mob exhales a poisonous breath,
>   And Socialism is decadence, is death.

And

>   great, indeed,
>   The world was and will always be, but good
>   It never can become.

Neither of these quotations is comforting to the socialists, whom, of course, Davidson held only part "of the litter and broken bits of a shattered society, the debris and wreckage of Christendom."

Of the testaments that Davidson intended to write he finished five, or six, if you wish to include the slighter "Testament of Sir Simon Simplex Concerning Automobilism." The five that contain his confession of faith are *The Testament of a Vivisector* (1901), *The Testament of a Man Forbid* (1901), *The Testament of an Empire Builder* (1902), *The Testament of a Prime Minister* (1904), and *The Testament of John Davidson* (1908). The first three are, on the whole, sane, though they have passages in them, particularly that on the vivisector, which indicate that "This way madness lies." The last two show unmistakable signs of having been written under an obsession.

From the beginning there was in the man an impatience of authority, an unwillingness to accept the ordinary regulations of

BEGINNINGS OF THE NEW ORDER

society, an insistence on self, hardly normal. There grew up in him afterwards a curiosity about suffering and cruelty that was even more ominous. What was a sensitiveness to pain and cruelty became a shuddering acceptance of cruelty and pain, and in the end a sort of delight in them. In one stage Davidson is struck with the incongruity of a thrush singing his tenderest notes as he devours a snail whose shell he has just pounded to pieces. A further stage is his objective presentation of the vivisector's study of pain in the broken-down horse. In the end Davidson rejoices, and makes God rejoice, too, in Abel's sacrifice of a white bull to God, a sacrifice in which the joy of killing and the welter of blood are insisted on *ad nauseam*.

Davidson believed that the world was against him, a condition of mind that is not, in some of its phases, very different from the persecution mania. He was curious, too, about madness, and eager to find signs of it in great men. In *A Rosary* (1903) he makes Ibsen say: "One word before I go. My Mystery. From *Emperor and Galilean* onwards, I have dealt with madness. That is my secret. I found out, as Shakespeare also found out, that madness is the thing. You cannot have the essence till the shell is broken and the kernel bruised."

So it is that the heroes in the Testament are "all to madness near allied." Their genius, such as it is, does not kindle their presenter to much poetry. There is satire, a good deal of it, in some of the testaments, very amusing satire of England, which is mingled with worship of England, in *The Testament of an Empire Builder*. "The English Hell," he holds, "Forever crowds the English Heaven." The materials of Hell are "all kinds of cowards who eluded fact," and "all deniers of the will to live." "It was good to see," he cries, "Dives in Heaven and Lazarus in Hell."

The Testament of an Empire Builder is prefaced by a parable that tells the whole story of its maker's development as a poet; what his accomplishment has been; what his unfulfilled aims are. Read it and "A Ballad in Blank Verse on the Making of a Poet," and you have Davidson's autobiography. He left it in his will that no one was to write his biography. There is no need. It is all in his writing, too much of the pain and unhappiness of it out of which no beauty has been made.

As I read them, the testaments reach their highest level in *The Testament of a Man Forbid*. The heat is again, I think, in the iron that he is hammering:

> The rainbow reaches Asgard now no more;
> Olympus stands untenanted; the dead
> Have their serene abode in earth itself,
> Our womb, our nurture, and our sepulchre.

That opens finely, even if it slips into rhetoric toward the close. In material it is, of course, his old attack on the illusions with which we content ourselves, but in this instance the attack is couched in gentler terms than usual.

There is a burden of preachment in the eclogues, too. His journalists discuss the topics of the hour, but fortunately they are a city-hating lot, and they escape to the country when they can. Bread and butter drives them back to town, of course, but as they bolt into tavern or office, or wherever it is they meet, they bring the country with them. It is sometimes there by sample, as when one of them brings a spray of hawthorn with him, but it is more often present, at second hand, in their words. So it is, that, though we have his Ninian giving us a story somewhat like that of Ibsen's *Ghosts*, we remember rather than that, and "the rotting match girls" and the slums about to rise, "The sheepbells and the cuckoo's mellow chime."

There are little pictures of real worth in the eclogues, now of hop-pickers, say, and now of basket-weavers. The beauty of the world is almost all there is in the world that does not rub Davidson the wrong way. Because he is driven, and tired, and compelled to do writing "for which people will pay," he is easily touched on the raw. He can then be as sore-headed as Smollett. Bird-song or a hedge in bloom eases him always. It was Epping Forest, northeast of London, to which he escaped oftenest, and which colors most of

BEGINNINGS OF THE NEW ORDER

his poetry of out-of-doors. He writes, too, of the Chilterns and Sussex and Kent. He likes water in a scene, and the Medway appeals to him more than most rivers. There are reminiscences of Scottish landscape, too, in the eclogues, and these both of his native Glasgow awa', and the Edinburgh he knew in his short university career. He grows intoxicated with the beauty of nature, and he can intoxicate you in turn with his rendering of his own possession:

> The lark from the top of heaven raved
> Of the sunshine sweet and old;
> And the whispering branches dipped and laved
> In the light; and waste and wold
> Took heart and shone; and the buttercups paved
> The emerald meads with gold.

If that is over-luscious to your taste, perhaps you will like better these two lines that follow. They are accurate description and impeccable verse:

> The blackbirds with their oboe voices make
> The sweetest broken music.

Do we all not now understand this unhappy man, a man whose whole outlook on life might have been changed had he had the money to buy him a little leisure? We can feel to the full, I think, how sincere he was when he said: "Heaven is to tread unpaven ground." There were many years of his life when he knew little walking save on the stone pavements of London.

The ballads of Davidson have, I think, been overpraised. Once I thought they could hardly be overpraised. There were special reasons, of course, why I should care very greatly for them and their maker. He wrote for newspapers, and so did I. He tried to fight in the newspapers for what was best in art and drama and letters, and so did I. He escaped, whenever he could, from the city to which the newspaper man is condemned for most of his time, and so did I. He knew his English out-of-doors, in all its details of bird and tree and flower, as I knew my American countryside. The greatest reason for my liking was, however, his youthfulness, the impetuosity of him, the power of feeling he had, the desire in him to make the old world over into something new and better. I liked, too, the ease of his writing, its swing and reach, the vigor of his onset in ballads and songs, the intensity that carried through with a rush whatever he put his hand to.

Now I can see that true as are all these qualities of his verse, it is lacking in depth; that he discovers the obvious; that he mouths the issue of the hour. "A New Ballad of Tannhäuser" seemed to me once as rapturous as the Venusberg music of Wagner. It seems doctrinaire to me now, too insistent on its thesis, and crude.

There are certain poets who are for youth almost only, poets who give free rein to their passions, who are defiers of convention, who have a deep vein of satire in them, and that cleverness which is so beguiling to awakening wits. Byron is one such, I think, before the time of Davidson, and Rupert Brooke another since the time of Davidson. Though no other of the three ever made the appeal of Byron, it is just as well that the youth of to-day who glory in Brooke should know how quickly another apostle of youth has passed. The passion of all three men leaves middle years cold, as the passion of Marlowe does not, or of Keats, or of Yeats.

The best of all the ballads of Davidson is "A Ballad in Blank Verse on the Making of a Poet." It is obviously his own story that he tells here, though he has sensationalized it. "Sensationalize" is an ugly word, but it is needed to convey the meaning of what Davidson has in this instance, and in others, done with life. Overstatement, overemphasis, an overdecorative style mar much of his work. He relaxes, and he clarifies his writing, when he turns to blank verse. Rhyme, though he calls it "a property of decadence," he likes and writes. "The re-echoing rhyme" of Poe leads Davidson to call him "the most original genius in words the world has known."

Blank verse Davidson likes best of all forms of verse. He

writes it best, too, witness the sea-piece in "Lammas" in *Fleet Street Eclogues*. "I know nothing," he writes in the note "On Poetry" in *Holiday*, "I know nothing so entertaining, so absorbing, so full of contentment, as the making of blank verse." He had, then, hours of happiness in his art, as well as in out-of-doors and with family and friends. He has written a good deal about his art, and somewhat contradictorily. Eventually, however, he had come to the opinion we find him expressing in "On Poetry":

> Poetry is matter become vocal, a blind force without judgment. Much there is a poet can control; he acquires a vocabulary, sifts and sorts; he can select the theme of his poem, and the weight and convolutions of his brain determine the power and variety of his rhythm, but the purport of his poetry is not within his own control.

Such a belief was not acceptable to all his fellow-poets or to all the critics. It was, like almost everything else in his life, a something that had to be fought for, argued over, put into print, and sent out as propaganda. There was almost nothing in his life that led to real relaxation. That happiness he thought of as coming to him and his fellows in *Fleet Street Eclogues*, when he wrote:

> and now we'll think
> Of Eden silently a while,

was a rare happiness indeed. Even his escapes to the country were haunted by a realization that they must be turned into copy, "things for which people will pay."

Certain passages that I have quoted are good in themselves and intimations of the finer things he could have done had he been "divinely blessed by leisure hours." As it is there are only one or two lyrics in all of Davidson's twenty-odd books of verse that are perfectly done, "In Romney Marsh" in *Ballads and Songs* and "Spring Song" in *New Ballads*.

Those who admire Davidson most always fall back on his poetry descriptive of out-of-doors as his greatest asset. Poetry descriptive of out-of-doors, though, must be something more than poetry descriptive of out-of-doors to be cherished in the memory. It must be background to a human figure or figures, or have some association with the common experiences of life, with hunting, say, or nutting, or daisying, or sapping, or ploughing, or logging. It must be a part of what has been experienced before by man. If it is not, then it must be as surprising in its difference from all experienced before as a new planet swum into our ken.

Davidson realized these truths, I think, and believed that he had humanized his descriptions in his eclogues by the topical discussions of their protagonists. He did humanize them, partly, but not altogether. Often the descriptions seem dragged in. In a sense his failure was a failure in knowledge of life. He knew, neither at first hand nor in imagination, much life other than that which school-mastering in Scotland—he called it "mental bootblacking" —or journalism in England—he called it "sixpenny reviewing"— had brought his way.

Not only had Davidson too little time to write, but too little time to live, to get to know life. Nor had he had much time to think. He believed that he had had time to think, but he had thought few things out. He had not had enough experience, either, to test the truth of the thoughts which came to him, or enough reading to know the relation of his thinking to that of other men. The necessity of making a living for his wife and two boys was always present to his mind. His nose was always to the grindstone. His health, too, had been long undermined with asthma, and he believed, toward the end, that he had cancer. It was the fear of cancer that drove him to suicide. He had written all, I am sure, that he could have had any happiness in writing, and all that the world could have had any happines in reading. Nor was the truth in him in his last years. The world had had of him, when he died, all he had to give, or all, perhaps I should say, that it had allowed him to give, or would ever have allowed him to give.

CHAPTER III

The Old Main Line

THERE has never been any general acceptance of Robert Bridges (1844-1930) by the reading public. That is a lot which has fallen to few poets. There has not been even any large acceptance of him by that smaller reading public which cares for poetry. That is a lot which has fallen to fellows of his no better poets, but of less severe and bare a style. Bridges was made laureate at the wish of the poets of England, a large number of whom felt that he was the man for the place. Those of the public who were at all interested, whether in England or America or the Colonies, were willing to agree that the poets should know, that since such men as Yeats and Newbolt, Stephen Phillips and Binyon, had said that Bridges was the proper choice, that he was the proper choice.

Certainly Bridges looked the part. Certainly he had the dignity and position and traditions that made him a worthy representative of the English poets of his time. Certainly he had been an influence, technically, on many of the younger generation of poets. Certainly he had written in all the accredited forms of English poetry, and always worthily. And, certainly, he had to his credit an accomplishment in lyric poetry, narrow in range, but of impeccable artistry, and of a new beauty. No one else had caught just those aspects of English countryside and English life that are to be found in "There is a hill beside the silver Thames," "Spring goeth all in white," "The Winnowers," "Nightingales," "The South Wind," and the two odes to spring, "Invitation to the Country" and "Reply."

These best poems of Bridges do not yield all that is in them on first acquaintance. There is, indeed, little of his writing that does. Nor is he to be appreciated on a second reading, or on a third. It requires rereading after rereading, in different moods, and at intervals, before his full significance makes itself apparent. He had no way with him, no irresistible felicities, no sudden bursts of music. He, himself, knew well his limitations, and he was candid in owning them. He confessed to "sluggish blood," that to him was denied "the best," that his "sense" was "hard," his style "so worn and bare." And yet he knew, as every true poet knows, that there was worth in what he had written.

Bridges was born on the Isle of Thanet, close by the meeting place of the great estuary of the Thames and the Channel. It was, he says, on

> a stony, breaking beach
> My childhood chanced and chose to be.

He knew sea and shore, inheriting with this knowledge that interest in ships that has been part of the Englishman from Anglo-Saxon times. He went the usual way of boys of his class, to Eton, further up the Thames, and then to Oxford, where the Thames is a little river indeed. The Thames was more to him, I think, than the sea, though the sea was much to him. It is the sight of the sea over the downs that lends spaciousness to "The Downs." It is the roar of the sea, reproduced in its sonorous rhythms, that gives such distinction to "The Voice of Nature." The sea is in "The Cliff-Top," "A Poppy," "A Passer-By," and in a score poems else, but it can hardly, in the nature of things, be made an intimate in the close and familiar way a river can.

"Elegy," that takes place as the first poem of his *Shorter Poems* (1890), is inspired by the Thames. The river is named and described in loving detail in "There is a hill beside the silver Thames." This poem is a very symbol of southern England, a cross-section of the Thames valley. It catches the look and feel and atmosphere of this old, old countryside. So much of Bridges is, indeed, the picturing of the countryside of southern England that you would say to an outlander overseas who wished to know what rural England was like: "Read Robert Bridges and you will know. Read 'There is a hill beside the silver Thames.' Read 'The Windmill.' Read 'The Winnowers.' Read 'The Garden in September.' Read 'North Wind in October.'"

And if you would know what the English code is, read "Founders' Day. A Secular Ode on the Ninth Jubilee of Eton College":

> Now learn, love, have, do, be the best;
> Each in one thing excel the rest;
> Strive; and hold fast this truth of heaven—
> To him that hath shall more be given.

It is not often that Bridges is so forthright as this. Not that he would deceive anybody as to what he felt and believed about things, but that he was by nature reticent and restrained, and that he held it bad form for a gentleman to give himself away. Say a third of what you feel and believe about things, and leave it to the understanding of that other fellow, your reader, to multiply your statement into what its underlying feeling and thought would have it be. This is a dangerous practice for a poet. So many people expect poetry to be emotional, sentimental, romantic, extreme, that the poet who soft-pedals all he has to say is often hardly heard.

The best things in Bridges, too, are often hidden away. "Eclogue I," for instance, that stands first in *New Poems* (1899), does not open very interestingly. Two old friends meet, literary fellows both, in Somerset, and reminisce. They exchange rhymes. You read along with a rather languid interest. You are off guard, and you may easily pass over the rare beauty of a passage like this:

> But if you have seen a village all red and old
> In cherry-orchards a-sprinkle with white and gold,
> By a hawthorn seated, or witchelm flowering high,
> A gay breeze making riot in the waving rye!

The picture you can hardly miss, but all is so quietly presented that you are not sufficiently quickened emotionally to realize to the full what color and movement there is in the passage. "A gay breeze making riot in the waving rye" is one of the most exactly descriptive lines in all English poetry. The irregularity of the accent pulls the line this way and that as the wind pulls a field of rye.

As you read "There is a hill beside the silver Thames," you expect it to continue to be what it starts out to be, a poem descriptive of landscape. You like its onset, stately for all its apparent simplicity. You like, more mildly, its second and third and fourth and fifth stanzas. Then, in the sixth stanza, you meet a human figure, a fisherman, who quickens your interest as the human figure always does. In the seventh stanza you meet a more memorable human:

> a slow figure 'neath the trees,
> In ancient-fashioned smock, with tottering care
> Upon a staff propping his weary knees.

If ever there was what George Moore calls "pure poetry" it is to be found in "Spring goeth all in white." Here is no moralizing, no comment of any kind by the poet, hardly any sense even of the personality of the poet. It is an almost completely objective poem, about hawthorne-time, which has never been better done:

> Spring goeth all in white,
> Crowned with milk-white may:
> In fleecy flocks of light
> O'er heaven the white clouds stray.

What a contrast this poem presents to the famous "Loveliest of trees the cherry now" of A. E. Housman! There is not so much of the spring, objectively, in the twelve lines of that poem as in the eight lines of Bridges, but how much more of the sharpness and sweetness of spring, how much more of youth and time and change. It is, perhaps, unjust to criticize a poem for not possessing what is outside of its intention, and there are poems of Bridges that have their own burden of the brevity of all good things. Yet it is fair to point out that Bridges lacks poignancy, that his poetry has been, most of it, by intention, a poetry without passion. By this I mean, not only without the passion of love, but without passionate feeling of any sort. What he lacks because of his "sluggish blood" is a real shortcoming to his poetry. That poetry has been, from the beginning, an old man's poetry. It is no less true poetry for this, but it is of a more restricted appeal because of this.

Years ago when I was reading Bridges I wondered if it might not be with my attitude toward him somewhat as it had been with my attitude in early life toward Milton. Milton had been a household book in the home of my youth. When my mother thought I was not being taught to "parse" properly in school she taught me to "parse," in her way, in *Paradise Lost*. To this day I know its opening lines as I know the opening lines of Cæsar's *Gallic Wars*. I had to study *Comus* as part of the required reading for admission to college, and it did not in those days become more to me than a thing I had to study. In college my teacher of literature was unsympathetic to Milton. At thirty, as a teacher of English literature, it became my duty to write college entrance examinations in English. I had to reread "Lycidas," "L'Allegro," and "Il Penseroso" to write questions on them. Even under such forbidding conditions the beauty of Milton could not escape me. The scales fell from my eyes. It was the bells at evening:

> Swinging slow with sullen roar
> Over some wide-watered shore

that began the loosening of the scales. From that day on I have been able to see for myself that Milton is the great poet all the English-speaking peoples declare him to be.

I thought, those years ago when I was reading Bridges and could not see him for more than a minor poet: "Perhaps the scales will suddenly fall from my eyes as they did when I was reading Milton, and I shall see Bridges as Binyon sees him, or Newbolt, or Yeats." I have to confess that the scales have not fallen. I can still see Bridges only as a minor poet.

You cannot say that Bridges, for all his predilection for the little things of the countryside, has wholly avoided great themes.

He has retold the story of Psyche and Eros in narrative verse; he has written after the manner of Milton on Prometheus and Demeter; and he has attempted plays on Achilles, and Ulysses, and Nero. There is no bad work in *Eros and Psyche* (1885), *Prometheus the Firegiver* (1883), *Demeter* (1904), *Nero Part I* (1885), *Achilles in Scyros* (1890), *The Return of Ulysses* (1890), and *Nero Part II* (1894). Nor, save in *Nero Part I,* is there any writing which stands out against the sky. There are touches of tragic power here, too, closet drama though it is. "This play," he tells us, "was not intended for the stage, as the rest of my plays are." It is hard to believe that the rest of his plays were intended for the stage, for they are all just as untheatrical as the plays of Stephen Phillips, say, are theatrical. Phillips built up the third part of his *Ulysses* (1902) on his kinsman's *Return of Ulysses,* and one wonders if it was not the elder poet's handling of Nero that suggested him to the younger as material out of which he could make "good theater."

There are passages to mark in narrative, masques, and plays, but there are not passages that impress themselves, willy-nilly, on your memory, so that you can no more forget them than you can the names of your children. Yet that is the way of truly great passages, they will not out of mind, and even of passages of rhetorical effectiveness less than great.

Eros and Psyche has a suavity and ease of progression rather unusual in Bridges. The verse of most of his poems, good as much of it is, is apt to be a little stiff, as if it fell none too easily from his pen. One wonders why he did not try narrative oftener. There is "Screaming Tarn," of course, good in a way, but conventional in make-up and tone. There is an approach to narrative, too, now and then, in the eclogues, but Bridges is, on the whole, a purely lyrical poet. You can dismiss all else than the lyrics, and you have left that by which he stands or falls.

The sonnet sequence, *The Growth of Love* (1889), is not a sequence in the sense that *Astrophel and Stella* or *Modern Love* is a sequence. It does not tell the story of a love, but records moments in the progress of a love, many of which have nothing to do with the feeling of the lover toward the lady of his choice. *The Growth of Love* is the first book of Bridges I owned. I bought it, in the Mosher reprint (1893), back in the nineties. That I have lived with it longest of my books of Bridges is why, perhaps, there are more marked passages in it than in any other of his books on my shelves. And yet that is not, I think, the only reason. There is more concern with his art in *The Growth of Love* than elsewhere in his writing, a subject on which he feels more strongly, perhaps, than on any other, and there is more speculation in it on the whys and wherefores of things than in any other of his poems.

In the very first sonnet there is an arresting four lines and a half:

> They that in play can do the thing they would
> Having an instinct throned in reason's place,
> And every perfect action hath the grace
> Of indolence or thoughtless hardihood—
> These are the best. . . .

There speaks the English amateur clearly and distinctly. Poet or sportsman, either one, would like us to believe that such is the way he attains, such is the origin of his "perfect actions." Bridges hardly puts himself among such "best." Indeed, he owns how hard he had to strive before he cast his chains, and became "Master of the art which for thy sake I serve." And yet one feels that he half-claims to attain both ways, by instinct, and by a hard-won and perfected art.

Bridges has said nothing more memorable than a half-dozen things he says here.

> The very names of things belov'd are dear,
> And sounds will gather beauty from their sense

we recognize as true from our own experience before we read on to his third line and find the concrete illustration that justifies his statement. In Sonnet 8 he lays down his credo about "beauty being the best of all we know." Again and again, in this sequence, and elsewhere, he repeats this belief, as again and again he returns to the expression of an aristocratic code of life. He likes:

> an ancient house where state
> From noble ancestry is handed on,

or any other like "relic of old splendour." He hates the "down-levelling of Socialism," and he frankly confesses his joy in the privilege that gives him:

My Japanese paintings, my fair blue Cheney, Hellenic Statues and Caroline silver, my beautiful Aldines.

But I am running on beyond *The Growth of Love*. Here Bridges tells us that "This world is unto God a work of art." Here he puts his feeling "So poor's the best that longest life can do." Here he laments "The perpetuity which all things lack." Here he writes down his realization of how lonely Adam was in Paradise "Before God of His pity fashion'd Eve." That is, I think, his greatest line, a line it is not an exaggeration to call Miltonic. If there were a hundred such in Bridges one might build up for him a claim to be a major poet.

There are not many "readings of life" in Bridges. There is, though, a definite philosophy that remained fairly constant through all the long years that he wrote. Like all men, he had in youth a quarrel with things as they are, "that old feud," he calls it, " 'Twixt things and me," but it passed quickly. At fifty-five he could write, in *New Poems* (1899):

> All my joys my hope excel,
> All my work hath prosper'd well,
> All my songs have happy been.

All three of these statements are given to few men to make, but of Bridges all three are true, the first and second completely true, and the third only a very little too sweeping. There are moments of unhappiness now and then in the poems, but even these are all but all passed before the poem comes to a close. It is rare in life for realization of joy to exceed man's hope of joy, and rarer, perhaps, that all a man's work has "prospered well," and rarest, perhaps, that a poet is able to say, "all my songs have happy been," which, indeed, Bridges can say with less qualification than any other English poet of his time.

It is not because Bridges has shut his eyes to ugliness and pain and wrong that he sees beauty and joy triumphant in life. In *Prometheus the Firegiver* he acknowledges:

> For many things there be upon this earth
> Unblest and fallen from beauty, to mislead
> Man's mind, and in a shadow justify
> The evil thoughts and deeds that work his ill.

He was a physician, with experience in London hospitals, and he had been brought face to face with things as they are. It was, I think, because what is beautiful or happy moved him so deeply that ugly and painful and unhappy things had little chance to register in his heart. The joy and delight in beauty filled his heart to the exclusion of all else. A fortunate lot in life and a temperament that responded intuitively to all that was happy and beautiful undoubtedly contributed to his optimism and to his discovery of so much beauty everywhere.

Happiness and beauty were very closely affiliated in his mind. It was the happy things in life and art that he found beautiful. "For howso'er man hug his care," he declared, "The best of his art is gay." And yet, with such an experience of the rich happiness of human things, Bridges can claim:

> Divinity hath surely touched my heart;
> I have possessed more joy than earth can lend.

The mood in which he so felt was, however, a rare one. Commoner was that he expressed in "Dejection," in which he worked himself from a state of care to a height at which he could write:

> I praise my days for all they bring,
> Yet are they only not enough.

For many years Bridges lived the life of a country gentleman in the hills near Oxford. He made journeys to the Continent, Italy leaving more impress on his art than any other country, but only a slight impress at that. He came to America in 1925 on the foundation for visiting artists of the University of Michigan. He did not find much happiness or beauty in America. He was at home only in that sheltered life of England he celebrated in those two odes, "Invitation to the Country" and "Reply," in Book II of *The Shorter Poems*. "Reply" evidently tells us how Bridges found delight in his London days, before he knew well-being at Yattendon or Boar's Hill. Terence, Plato, and Socrates, he reads, who crown:

> the mind supreme,
> And her delights divine.

In "Invitation to the Country," Bridges tells us:

> And country life I praise,
> And lead, because I find
> The philosophic mind
> Can take no middle ways;
> She will not leave her love
> To mix with men, her art
> Is all to strive above
> The crowd, or stand apart.

You can easily put your finger on the objects that stir him to such ecstasies. He has a long poem, "A song of my heart," in which he enumerates what things of the country most delight him. In other poems he tells us of his love for the little out-of-the-way hamlets in the downs. It was his greatest art to picture bits of the countryside; a village; a stretch of mountainside; a tree; a bird; a team, ploughing, against the sky. It is trees that stirred him most. Of a score of such descriptions I quote two, one of a willow, and the other of a larch:

> The woodland willow stands a lonely bush
> Of nebulous gold.

That is much in little, and so is this:

> The larch thinneth her spire
> To lay the ways of the wood with cloth of gold.

It must be in the Lake County that Bridges found Dunstone Hill, on

> The purple mountain-side, where all
> The dewy night the meteors fall.

It was in his own hill country about Oxford, though, that he saw the team, ploughing, against the sky. These pictures, in which Bridges most often attained, are larger than miniatures, but they suggest the work of the miniaturist. They are exquisitely done. Though in the approved tradition, they are wholly his own. They art not, however, great poetry. Nor are they, relatively to great poetry, as important as the miniature-like novels of Jane Austen to the epical novels of Hardy. They are of the best of minor poetry, the rigidly artistic work of a man who would have life—I use his own words—

> all as this day,
> Simple, enjoyment calm in its excess,
> With not a grief to cloud, and not a ray
> Of passion overhot my peace to oppress;
> With no ambition to reproach delay,
> Nor rapture to disturb its happiness.

SIR WILLIAM WATSON

Sir William Watson (1858-1935) always insisted that the poet should be an integral part of the social and intellectual life of his time. He combated the latter-day idea that the "poet is a being who dwells apart from life as to all its larger manifestations, a person uninterested in politics, in science, in sociology, in the progress of the human species; a dreamy, ineffectual, and generally neurotic creature, concerned chiefly with the manufacture of strange epitaphs and the analysis of his own equally strange and not very important emotions." He would have the poet a man of affairs. He would have the poet concerned with public questions; and he lived up to this belief of his by his own comment on all the trying situations for English policy from the time of the Irish troubles of the eighties to the time of the disturbing problems that arose after the World War.

Watson would have the poet do his share in determining public policy, and he would have him take part in public life. If France can send a Claudel to Washington why not England an English poet to Paris? Though Watson had himself lived much in places remote from the center, in the Lake Country, and, after his marriage in 1909 to an Irish wife, in Ireland, he was always deeply interested in all the affairs of the center. He was interested not only in literature, but in travel and science and politics. A letter received in his youth from Darwin was among his most cherished possessions and he boasted proudly that Herbert Spencer read his writing because it was "in touch with the modern spirit." You will find a good deal about Liberal leaders in his prose. Campbell-Bannerman was his friend; Rosebery discussed the abolition of the laureateship with him; Asquith and his family were nice to him, and then "gave their guest away," involving him in all the to-do over "The Woman with the Serpent's Tongue." Lloyd-George was "The Man Who Saw," the savior of England in the World War.

It may be that all this gave Watson the right to say what he wrote down in the preface to *The Superhuman Antagonists* (1919) as to his having lived "a far from bookish life, in which I have seen something of many countries, have counted among my friends many famous persons, have known very varied fortunes, have had memorable and great experiences, and have lived intensely through much peace and war." A like experience is recorded in his verse.

Watson tells us there that he has "lived deep life," that he has "drunk of tragic springs"; but "deep life" and "tragic springs" are not the sources of his poetry. Its sources are such thoughts as are habitual to cultivated people of English race when they seriously discuss State, Church, Literature, Science, Travel, or the everyday problems of life. Sometimes, in brooding over the common themes, individual thoughts came to Watson; but usually it was the better conversation of the day that formed his material. This conversation, condensed to its essentials, and wonderfully clarified, he refashioned into verse that was at its average stately rhetoric and at its best sonorous poetry. Only in those rare moments when he was out of hearing of the talk of the time and some large mood of nature dominated him, or when his spirit lifted as he realized some greatness of his country, or when he was drawn out of himself by the call of old romance, could he attain the magic of high poetry; and even when so dominated or so uplifted or so enchanted he could not write without echoes of the great poets lingering among his own words. Even in his "Ode in May," where he is most himself, there are suggestions of likeness between lines of his and lines in older poets; and in "The Ode on the Day of the Coronation of King Edward VII," a structure of noble rhetoric raised on stern thought, the reader cannot admire without wondering which modern poet inspired this love of "old forgotten far-off things," who taught him to recapture this "old romance," so familiar is the cry and clang of singing line and sounding line. In these two poems, the best of those not confessedly derivative by choice of subject, Watson reëchoes others.

Indeed, nothing that he has written is so individual that were it published unsigned it could be surely attributed to him, unless it be his "Apologia," in which he defends himself against the criticism that he writes too much of older poets and that he brings "naught new." To the former charge he replies that he holds "singers' selves . . . to be very part Of Nature's greatness."

To the latter he replies that he indeed brings "nought new," "save as each noontide or each Spring is new." So he passes on to a third charge that has been made against his poetry, that it lacks the passion that Milton demands of poetry. He declares that he is a man such as other men are, that he, too, has blood in his veins, that he is not unresponsive to "human touch," but that there are higher raptures than those of the flesh, deeper transports and mightier thrills than those that come of "commerce with mortality." He ends by declaring that what he hopes for is that on his pages shall fall "The shadow of the summits," and that, at the same time they shall not lack "the human touch" to which he has already referred.

It is seldom that a poet has written of his own purpose and achievement so frankly and so justly. All that he claims with proud humility for his poetry may be granted him, except that his verse is new as "each spring is new." It is a fine retort, that he brings nothing new, "save as each noontide or each Spring is new," but it boasts of two widely differing qualities. One noontide recalls another, but each spring refreshes with a joy unknown before. There is one newness of the noontide, a newness that is the rebirth of known and remembered things, and this is Watson's; there is another newness of the spring, a newness that is the rapture of virgin things, and this is not Watson's.

All else that Watson boasts is his, even to the "high lineage" from "the mighty voices of old days." Subjects that have engaged Spenser's attention and Milton's and Wordsworth's and Tennyson's engage his. All these poets were seekers of "order beyond this coil and errancy"; so is he. Like them, he is largely concerned with political and social questions, from an outlook basically Puritan. But it is not only of this line of our poets, of natures strenuous yet rigidly controlled, that Watson may trace descent, but from that line that, beginning in Ben Jonson and continued in Dryden and Pope, has tended toward epigrammatic expression and delighted in rhetoric and satire. The problems that concern the individual as an individual furnish Watson the material for almost as many poems as do public affairs. He writes of man's relation to God, his place in nature, the why and whither of life; of love of woman; of the great poets; of nature; and most of all, of public affairs.

Public affairs seem to have interested him early. His first published volume, *The Prince's Quest and Other Poems* (1880) written in great part during his teens, naturally contains no reference to them; but the Soudanese campaign of 1885 and the Russian menace of that year provoked him to a series of fifteen sonnets on public affairs, which he entitles "Ver Tenebrosum." From that time on public affairs never ceased to inspire him, and in his "Ode on the Day of the Coronation" of 1902 they inspired him to his highest poetry of such kind.

As is to be expected of a poet who writes not so often out of possessed mood as on happenings or topics of the day, much of Watson's poetry is occasional. His poetry on public affairs must of necessity be largely occasional. Of such kind are the sonnets of "Ver Tenebrosum," "England to Ireland," verses praying for reconcilement during the Irish agitation of February, 1888; the sonnets of *The Year of Shame* (1897), wrung from him in bitterest despair at England's apathetic acquiescence in the Armenian massacres; the various poems of the Boer war; and the "Ode on the Day of the Coronation of King Edward VII." The latter poem is not only critical of the events of state of the hour in England but commemorative of England's "old greatnesses" and celebrant of England's imperial sway. In its warning to England it was frankly of the hour that realized the backwardness of the English army system and of English manufacturing methods. In its reference to old battles and its portrayal of strong rulers, it is commemorative of "old greatnesses"; and in its symbolizing of the vastness of the realm about the seven seas it is celebrant of England's imperial sway. It is in recalling the remote past of England and in following the sunset beyond "Druid mountains" and over the Irish Sea that the ode gathers to itself bewildering glamour.

No homely Saxon subject can attract magic as Dyvnaint and "Cumbria sunset-gazing," Morven, "wild Lorn," and Lochiel.

In all there are some hundred of these poems on public affairs. Most of them are critical of English governmental policy, and some of these very personal in their satire. Michael Hicks-Beach and Alfred Austin are told very plainly of their shortcomings. Gladstone is appealed to; Chamberlain and his orchid held up to scorn. Every man can understand, and almost every man outside the influence of party feeling can sympathize, at least theoretically, with Watson in his indignation at the Armenian massacres, the crushing of Greece by Turkey, and the South African war; but even he himself came to realize that most of his poems so inspired, and written at white heat, are not high poetry. It is not that they suffer any taint of political prejudice, but that they are rhetorical rather than poetical. They are effective, but their effectiveness is the effectiveness of rhetoric, not the effectiveness of poetry. The sonnets of *The Year of Shame* served to carry his name around the world, and one of them, written during the Venezuelan crisis, was deemed important enough as a public document to be cabled to America. Watson excluded almost all of these sonnets from his *Collected Poems* (1898).

Yet though Watson himself judged almost all of the poems of *The Year of Shame* ephemeral, and though most of them are ephemeral, that very quality makes them of historical importance. Of course his protests had no effect, and of course Salisbury's government felicitated itself that neither Gladstone nor Rosebery had left them so independent a laureate, and of course Alfred Austin answered the protests. It was altogether, maybe, only a pretty pother, but it showed that cultivated people of the English race would still listen to a poet who protested in the name of Christian morality against the despotism of commercial fact. G. F. Watts testified to his sympathy with the protests by allowing his picture, "The Recording Angel," to be reproduced as frontispiece to *The Year of Shame*, and the Right Reverend John Percival, Anglican Bishop of Hereford, prefaced it with a statement.

It was a serious effort, at any rate, to use poetry as a means, and it was taken seriously by people the world holds to be in high places; but, as is the case when poetry is anything but its own end, it was not high poetry. Nor, as I have said, did it accomplish anything.

The greatest compliment to Watson as a poet of public affairs was paid him by the American censorship during the World War. Five of the sonnets included in the English edition of *The Man Who Saw* (1917) were cut out of the American edition of that same year. These were "To America, Concerning England," "To Roosevelt," "To a Would-Be Umpire," "The Voice from the Sunset" and "America Once More." They must have come before the censors just about the time that we were entering the war in the spring of 1917, but *The Man Who Saw* was not published until June of that year. Even then, I suppose, some of the sonnets might have been distasteful to the powers that were, for they praise Theodore Roosevelt, and they have this to say of our entrance into the war:

> This, this is the America that we knew!
> Not she whose armor against Hell was reams
> Of ratiocination; who in streams
> Of most invincible ink was lost to view.

There is a certain power of satire in that, but it is not desolating satire. There are like satiric touches in other of the sonnets, and what is no more than good leader writing. There is no poetry in them anywhere, and they are hardly "golden rhetoric." Between "golden rhetoric" and "tinsel rhetoric" Watson has distinguished in *Pencraft; A Plea for the Older Ways* (1916). *Pencraft* is a not uneloquent argument for "book English." Watson would have literature written in a diction and a style derived from the writing of the past. He does not believe that literature can be leavened by speech from actual life. That means that he has not had contacts that would show him there is a highly selective use of words in traditional speech still used largely as it was used a century ago. It means that he does not know there is good speech still in country-houses, where old men and women of cultivation talk what is fit to print; in clubs, where wits meet and break lances; in country stores "in the States" where yarns are swapped in choice and rhythmical language. It means that William Watson ignored all the theory of William Wordsworth about the best diction for poetry being that of everyday life.

No man who holds to tradition can fail to have a certain sympathy with Watson in his plea for writing that is grounded on the good writing of yesterday. Yet he is an extremist. He leans all the way there is to lean toward the side of bookishness. He fails to understand that writing will inevitably be devitalized, and become stilted, without constant borrowings from speech. If you have not the sound of living speech in your mind as you write, it is difficult to have your writing take on those differences of tone which are analogous to the tones of the voice. It is Milton, I think, who has led Watson astray. Milton, he tells us, again and again, is his master, and a poet can hardly have a better master for technique. Yet Watson follows his master too far. He makes the mistake the eighteenth century made in imposing a too Miltonic diction upon poetry.

The most imposing poem of the class commemorative of England's "old greatnesses" is "The Father of the Forest." Musing by a yew so old that the "stars look youthful," it "being by," the poet broods over the past that the tree must have seen, until there unrolls before him a pageant of that past, beginning with Elizabethan days and extending back to the time when on the down beyond camped "the hosts of Rome." In the pageant pass Cranmer, Mary Queen of Scots, Sir Philip Sidney, Henry V, Edward I, Richard I, the Conqueror, the Viking hordes. When all are gone the poet falls again to brooding, and dreams that the tree whispers to him of a time when the "indomitable world" will have attained that which has for eternities been its goal, "its golden end— Beauty." "A New Year's Prayer" and "Jubilee Night in Westmoreland" are other poems inspired by "the high imperial past."

This "high imperial past" he now mourns as dead, the knell of chivalry he has heard rung, but even in that past England was not always righteous.

His poems celebrant of the British empire's vastness and power are not markedly successful; but here and there in poems of other inspiration he has written "imperial verse" up to his high standards. As far back as 1885, in the last sonnet of "Ver Tenebrosum," he celebrated England's trust in her colonies. A little later he wrote "England and Her Colonies" in the same strain. In those days, as to-day, he trusted his "Kin before the Muscovite," and declared he was not a cosmopolite, but "chiefly mere Englishman" of "island fostering." He is a lover of his country, but a lover not blind to her failings, who believes that some day she may be "appalled by her own crimson hands."

Born of typically English stock in Wharfedale, Yorkshire, Watson lived much in his younger years on the Lancashire coast of the Irish Sea, in the Lake Country, and in London. In such inheritance and surroundings he grew to manhood with an ever-increasing love of the beautiful in life and nature, and an ever-increasing admiration for the greatness of old times. At maturity he owned a love of order and law in all things, a reliance on precedent and authority, a veneration for those institutions that had survived out of England's past. He once declared he loved:

> So well man's noble memories
> He needs must love man's nobler hopes yet more.

As he grew older his temperamental conservatism grew on him, though even his concurrently growing pessimism did not dissuade him from Liberal tendencies. Closely grafted on this Liberal Conservatism is an aristocratic creed. This creed well accords with the manner of his poetry, which has always a high-bred air and pace. An idealist such a man must be; life for him must be a life chosen from many possible ways of living,—life sublimed,—and life must have style. With these things in conjunction realism has not to do. He does once declare, "Life as I see it lived is great enough for me"; but the life that he wills to see, though it inspire him to pessimism, is such life as I have indicated, above all a life concerned with great issues. Tragedy to him is not merely the triumph of the universal over the individual; it is "the overthrow of something great." He makes one or two perfunctory references to the plight of Demos, but he quotes with something of their author's scorn the Miltonic phrases "the nameless aggregated millions" who "grow up and perish as the summer fly." Not that Watson is unsympathetic—no one could accuse the writer of *The Year of Shame* and *For England* (1903) of lack of sympathy, but he feels keenly distinctions between men, between things. "The sense of oneness with our kind" he puts on record as one of "the things that are more excellent." Others are "the thirst to know and understand," "a large and liberal discontent." Friendship, too, he makes one of such good things. His tributes to friendship are writ large everywhere in his verses. Perhaps it is because he lived so much alone in remote parts of the country that such friendship as involves intellectual companionship came to mean so much to him.

How much friendship is to him he reveals in the number of his poems that are addressed to people. Of these some are occasional poems of compliment, in which the compliment terminates a lyric that has led to it gracefully. In this form he is particularly happy—witness the poems "To Richard Holt Hutton" and "To the Lady Katherine Manners." Others are epistles in the eighteenth-century manner, combining personal references with disquisition upon some contemporary problem, such as the ode "To Arthur Christopher Benson." Others still are almost solely critical of poetry, such as that "To Edward Dowden"; and yet others almost solely personal to the man addressed, as that "To Edward Clodd." "A Familiar Epistle" to Dr. Oliver Gogarty reaffirms his devotion to poetry amid all the turmoil and terrors of war. This insistence on the social side of letters is of a part with Watson's interest in recording social discussion of all kinds, and is one of several proclivities of his that ally him to the eighteenth-century writers. Watson makes Dr. Johnson say that "your modern poet would appear to be a taciturn and unsocial person who never opens his mouth until he comes where there are none but ravens and seamews to listen"; and in the same essay, "Dr. Johnson on Modern Poetry: an Interview in the Elysian Fields," Watson, as interviewer, admits to the Doctor "that in the failure to give classical literary form to the presentation of social life is the vulnerable side of modern poetry." Watson has given "classical literary form to the presentation" of the better conversational topics of social life, and in so far strengthens the defenses on this side of modern poetry; further he has not gone, and wisely, for it is indeed a hard and high endeavor.

Although in the eighteenth-century sense of the word a "philosophic" poet, being more concerned with the constitution of things than with the appearance of things, Watson has nowhere laid down definitely his philosophy of life, as he has in the "Apologia" definitely laid down the purpose of his art. His attitude must be learned from a declaration here and a declaration there; in "The Hope of the World," more fully than elsewhere, he states such philosophy as he has formulated. Law and love he would see the rulers of the world, he would have man live by them; man, who as far as he can judge, did not rise to his kingship through some purpose of nature's, but climbed there by chance. If so it be, what assurance is there that he will ever rise to more than mortal state, that he will put on immortality? There is no such assurance, he admits. "Equal, my source of hope, my reason for despair."

The past he knows had in it some good, therefore his eyes turn always lovingly on the past; there he sees the "burly oak," in the present only "the lissom willow swaying to the wind." Altogether it is not too cheerful a philosophy he professes, but one that holds to high ideals. If he does not always hold to Church and State, he does hold to the foundations of morality and religion, of law and order, on which Church and State are based; he holds to the institutions of his race.

Of the problems of life outside the domain of politics Watson has written some two hundred poems, of which about fifty may be classified as love poetry. The constitution of things, the laws of nature, the question of immortality, the incidents of social life, occupy him as often as does love; yet of love songs he is a skilful maker, and his verse has never so much lilt as here. His first poem is naturally enough a poem of love. *The Prince's Quest* is a quest for love, a development of a theme not unlike that of William Morris's *Love Is Enough*.

Watson has spoken rather derogatively of the "ardor of Eros' lips," and he has kept it from his own. His love verse is written out of the reverie of love, a reverie undisturbed by the tumult of passion. "Lux Perdita" and "Too Late" are gravely introspective in thought and marmoreally beautiful in style. "The Heights and the Deeps," with its Cumbrian setting and its simplicity and freshness and deep-heartedness, carries one back to Wordsworth. "Sonnets to Miranda" record his love for one "out of reach," first in "lace and braids," and then "in simple speech."

Admirer of Wordsworth that he is, Watson has written comparatively little verse descriptive of nature, and that little is not Wordsworthian. In "The Heights and the Deeps" he comes nearest to Wordsworth's way and tone. Even in "Wordsworth's Grave," where he might well have pictured the graveyard in Grasmere vale with the mountains brooding above, he mentions, until the very close of the poem, scarcely a detail save "the old rude church, with bare, bald tower," and the "cool murmur" of Rotha lulling the poet's rest. The note of the poem is the peace that is Grasmere's; and in his wish to give this peace, Watson does in some part describe twilight in the vale, "the sheen of the retreating day" behind Helm Crag and Silver Howe, the half-heard bleat of sheep coming from the hill pastures. In many other poems, as in this, there are references to nature; but neither here nor in the other poems that may be called nature poems are there any revelations of an intimate delight such as was Wordsworth's.

"April" is one of his most spontaneous lyrics, musical as with rain among the leaves. "Hymn to the Sea," a gallant attempt to do the impossible, is, despite its sounding elegiacs, hardly as rapturous as the spring and the sea whose pæan it raises. The "Ode to May" is the most exultant of Watson's poems, where for once he awakes to an appreciation of the "glorious energy of things," and captures and imprisons that energy in his verse, as he failed to capture and imprison in his hymn "the thunderous throes of life divine" in which "leaped the glad sea."

There came into Watson's life after he was fifty, and most of what he had that counted already done, two new inspirations. His Irish wife brought him the one inspiration, Ireland, and two visits to America in 1909 and 1912, the other, the United States. He had written about both countries from his earlier years, but with no such quickening of the blood as came to him after he knew the two countries through long stays in them.

There is descriptive verse of both countries in what he writes of them, but it is the hearts of the countries he is striving to explain in most of his Irish and American poems. It was to Florida, and then Cuba, he had fled, after the rebuffs he received in the Northern cities because of "The Woman with the Serpent's Tongue." This poem, he was baited into admitting, was in a way suggested by Mrs. Asquith (Margot Tennant) and Violet Asquith. His admission cost him dear. Lectures arranged for were canceled, invitations withdrawn, and the dream of a pleasant progress throughout the country completely dissipated. The open-minded stood by him, and he was grateful. He took it all very well, writing when he got to Havana:

Yet travel hath taught us lessons we scarce had learned in repose;
Our friends have been proven our friends, and our foes have been proven our foes.

The story of how Watson came to write "The Woman with the Serpent's Tongue" is too long and too involved to repeat in detail here, but it may be said that it grew out of what Watson considered a disparagement by the Asquiths of Sir Henry Campbell-Bannerman, Asquith's predecessor in the premiership. The pother over it all was ridiculous. Watson, of course, was foolish to have written the poem, more foolish to have published it, most foolish of all to admit the identity of the originals. Neither of the ladies concerned was in any way hurt by the satire. They had lived in public, and were used to all the ways of publicity. It was just a case of a guileless man, unused to the ways of the world, giving himself away, first in his social relations with the Asquiths, and then in the writing of the satire, and then in the admissions to the reporters.

Three years later, on his return to read a poem on the Dickens Centenary, he had been forgiven for what the press had loudly condemned as a great discourtesy. The satire, of course, is not poetry, and only fair satire. In "To the Invincible Republic," published along with "The Woman with the Serpent's Tongue" in *New Poems* (1909), and written before he had visited America, is a tribute to Washington and Lincoln that would certainly have made a warm welcome before him in America if it had not been for the unlucky satire. He is thoroughly sincere, and not currying favor, when he writes that no other country has memories of "nobler children." He pays whole-hearted tribute to Washington, to his final triumph at Yorktown and to his as great triumph of another sort in bringing his army through that memorable winter at Valley Forge. Lincoln, too, appeals greatly to him, not only as a leader of men, and as a freer of the slaves, but for his power over words. Sir William must warn us, as all men of older countries think it their privilege to warn men of younger countries, against falling short of traditional ideals, of losing "those large habitudes of soul" that were theirs in their beginnings. He does not deal with us so vigorously as did Kipling in "The White Man's Burden," but he never doubts his right to admonish us.

Even more forthright, and, of course, more informal, is his praise of the spirit of our country in "A Full Confession," written after he had been here the second time. Then he found us, not "the land of the dollar," not enthroning Mammon. There is no impassioned writing in all this about America, though, nor in that about Ireland, of which there is almost as much in quantity. The poet was too set in his ways when these late inspirations came to him to be really kindled by them. Watson knew this, of course, in his heart. He knew what poetry is. In "The Poet's Place in the Scheme of Life," prefixed to *The Muse in Exile* (1913) he says poetry is "an art whose function is to see the world through a kind of ecstasy." There is little ecstasy in all Watson, and but intimations of it in these later poems.

Watson mistook a lack of appreciation for his own poetry as a lack of appreciation of all poetry. His kind of poetry, the stateliest sort of rhetorical poetry, is out of fashion. And even if it were in fashion the world's approbation would not make it any better than it is. That the readers of our day like Masefield better, and Housman, and Kipling, should not be taken by Watson to mean that good taste in literature is lessening throughout the English-speaking world. Student of English poetry that he is, he must know one sort of verse is the vogue in this generation and another sort of verse is the vogue in another generation. He must realize that the old battle between the words of the street and the words of "pencraft" results now in the victory of the one and now in the victory of the other. In "Retrogression" he deprecates "the loose-lipped lingo of the street" for poetry, a phrase that might be applied to much of either Kipling or Masefield. In the prose of "The Poet's Place," he pays his respects again to what in *Wordsworth's Grave* he had called "the scholar's not the child's simplicity." Then I had thought he referred to Norman Gale. In the later reference I wonder if he is not referring to A. E. Housman.

Again and again Watson returns to the theme of the world's neglect of poetry, but the world does not neglect poetry. It does neglect the rhetorical poetry of Sir William Watson, because it is not greatly moved by it. It does not neglect at least a score of poets of our time; and it reads more and more the great poets of the past. What troubled Watson was that after the ten years of appreciation that fell to him as it falls to most poets, the world turned to some other sort of poetry. It is only the great who can hold the attention of the world for more than a decade.

Watson made his first decided appeal to the world with a critical elegy, *Wordsworth's Grave* (1890); but in his *Epigrams of Art, Life, and Nature* (1884) he had already written metrical critiques. *Lachrymæ Musarum* and *Lyric Love* were published in 1892, and the next year the prose *Excursions in Criticism*. Many notable critical-elegiac poems are included in his later volumes. All the poets he criticizes are of well-established fame, and the criticisms in little he makes are not flashes of insight that for the first time reveal a poet to the world, but accurate condensations in most pregnant and felicitous verse of the opinion of "those with special knowledge" in regard to that poet. Thus when he writes of Shelley as "the cloud-begot," as a man of "vain vision," who rides in "thin ether," "lost in a storm of light," no one who knows Arnold's essay but will recall "the beautiful and ineffectual angel beating in the void his luminous wings in vain."

In his essay, "Some Literary Idolatries," in arguing that Webster and Poe are not poets of the first rank, Watson says very plainly what he considers the qualities of greatness in poetry: "But the authentic masters, are they not masters in virtue of their power of nobly elucidating the difficult world, not of exhibiting it in a fantastic lime-light? And after all, the highest beauty in art is, perhaps, a transcendent propriety. The touches which allure us by strangeness, or which 'surprise by a fine excess' belong at best to the second order of greatness. The highest, rarest, and most marvelous of all are those which simply compel us to feel they are supremely fit and right." "A transcendent propriety" in art seems to Watson to exclude strangeness and excess, and yet strangeness and excess are the very being of romantic art. Watson is obviously a classicist, but there are few classicists that would lay down such a dictum.

Wordsworth's Grave, the first of Watson's important critical elegies, remains his most important. Written nearly forty years after Wordsworth's death, it is not in any sense a lament for the poet personally; it is rather a lament for our own age that lacks so great a voice. It is composed of seven parts that might each, with slight alterations, be printed as a separate poem. There are in all forty-seven stanzas of four lines each. Part I celebrates Wordsworth's grave itself, beside Rotha, in the shadow of the "old rude church" at Grasmere, and the power in his poetry that calls our age back to Wordsworth. Part II postulates that Wordsworth's great gift was the gift of peace, "peace, whose names are also rapture, power, clear sight, and love," and compares this gift with Milton's "keen, translunar music," with "Shakespeare's cloudless, boundless human view," with Shelley's "flush of rose on peaks divine," with Coleridge's "wizard twilight," with Byron's "tempest-anger, tempest-mirth." Part III analyzes Wordsworth more minutely, insisting that his song was impassioned and ecstatic. Part IV outlines in fourteen stanzas the history of poetry in the eighteenth century up to the publication of the *Lyrical Ballads* in 1798. Pope and his school, Collin's "lonely vesper-chime," Gray's "frugal note," Blair, Goldsmith, Burns with his "plowman's conquering share," are criticized in succession until "Those morning stars that sang together rose," the dreamer and the seer, Coleridge and Wordsworth. Part V sketches the progress of poetry down through the Victorians—from Swinburne, whose "empty music floods the ear," and Browning, who "the heart refreshing, tires the brain," to the "loquacious throng" that "flutter and twitter," for so Watson sees the minor poets of the eighties. Part VI contrasts Byron with "hot heart world-defiled," and Wordsworth, who was home, who was all but nature's voice. Part VII returns to the grave at Grasmere. The poem ends on the note on which it began, the note of rest and peace.

Lachrymæ Musarum, a threnody for Tennyson, was published immediately upon his death in October, 1892. It is only incidentally critical, as when Watson remarks of Tennyson's "honeyed words," that they are "rich with sweets from every muse's hive." Of Matthew Arnold, a follower of ideals not unlike those Watson followed so long, and like him an admirable critical poet, he writes with much sympathy, but with keenness. He puts the accomplishment of Burns succinctly. He sees more clearly than most Englishmen can just what a great poet Burns was. He makes no claim for him as prophet or seer, but he realizes to the full how avid he was of life, how fully he lived, how deep was his sympathy with the average man. What such a man sees he saw, just that and no more. He cannot, however, attain to the directness and simplicity of the poet he praises. He must cry him up rhetorically.

These that I have mentioned are the critical elegies. The critiques in fly-leaf poems, epistles, and other occasional poems are many. In a poem addressed "To Edward Dowden, on Receiving from Him a Copy of the Life of Shelley," Watson tells us of his own poetical development from a captive to Shelley's power to a captive to Keats's, to a freeman of Wordsworth's. Here again is true and well-put criticism of Shelley. Landor, Watson hits off in a line: "The bland Attic skies True-mirrored by an English well." An epigram written on Longfellow's death in 1882 shows Watson's power of condensed criticism was developed at a comparatively early age.

I have said that it is by their style that Watson's poems gain the claim they have to distinction. Style almost never deserts him; it distinguishes even those poems of his that verge on society verse and the sermon. "There can be no doubt that Style is the greatest antiseptic in literature," Watson writes, "the most powerful preservative against decay. . . . The truth is Style is high breeding. . . . It does not necessarily imply transcendent beauty. . . . What we do imply when we speak of a horse or a woman or a poem, as having Style, is a certain crowning attitude which we recognize instinctively as the result and sum of various essentially aristocratic qualities which fuse in perfect harmony and rhythm. Serenity—by which I do not for a moment mean languor or apathy, but serenity based upon strength—is one of these qualities. . . . A certain touch of hauteur is perhaps inseparable from Style in its most impressive manifestations. . . . Thus frankly democratic poets like Burns are without Style, properly so called. One of the characteristics of that order of poets is absence of reserve, whereas we have a feeling that Style always holds something back, never quite lets itself go. Probably passion plus self-restraint is the moral basis of the finest Style." Indignation, brevity, simplicity, Watson says, make for Style; "its very life and soul are its remoteness from the vulgar, the plebeian, its inalienable aristocracy of birth and breeding. . . . I cannot help reverting yet once more to Milton because he best proves the truth that in poetry Style is the paramount and invincible force. What else is the secret of his supremacy among our poets—a supremacy which no poet can doubt, and no true critic of poetry?"

Watson seldom attempts to capture the highest notes of poetry. Yet he captures high notes from many masters. He can borrow from the Poe he depreciates:

> In his immemorial fastness
> At night's aboriginal core—

and he speaks with Tennyson's accents when he writes of "Gardens of odorous bloom and tremulous fruit." Once, too, he has reflected the light that glitters through

> magic casements, opening on the foam
> Of perilous seas, in faery lands forlorn—

warming it, as he imprisons it in words, with radiance caught from Wordsworth's clear morning glow. Many more of his memorable passages are, like these, virtual paraphrases of great sayings familiar to us in the Bible, Shakespeare, Milton, Dryden, Pope, Gray, Wordsworth, Keats, Tennyson, and Arnold. Pope's greatest line reappears in Watson in "The irremediable day and final doom"; "a divine discontent" becomes "a large and liberal discontent," and echoes all are these: "Mighty from Milton's pen and Cromwell's sword," "Not to bring peace Mine errand, but a sword," "For waters have connived at our designs, And winds have plotted with us," "There is, O grave, thy hourly victory, And there, O death, thy sting." Like the eighteenth-century poets, he is again in his habit of calling a river "a wave," the Mediterranean "the southern foam"; in his predilection to critical and occasional and didactic verse, in his usual repression of exultant passion, in his narrow range of vision.

It is here that his limitations make themselves most apparent. It is not that, as Wordsworth accused the eighteenth century, Watson does not write with eye on the object—you feel he sees it; but that he does not receive an individual impression from it, that he takes impressions of some one that saw and noted it before, that perhaps his reflection upon it is his own, but that oftenest his opinion too is the opinion of some other.

Of great poets often, of "the high imperial past" of England less often, of nature and of dream-laden romance now and then, Watson has written with style but short of great. That style, though, is a distinctively late Victorian style, close always to the rhetorical, and thence largely outmoded in a time that likes simplicity and directness and discoveries about life in its poetry. It is not prose fiction that is the rival of Watson's poetry, as he thinks, but the impassioned verse of a round dozen of contemporary poets with a firm grip on life, poets not without style, but with readings of life that we cannot forget.

ARTHUR CHRISTOPHER BENSON

From 1893 to 1905 Arthur Christopher Benson (1862-1925) published six volumes of careful and unexciting verse. These six volumes he collected, with exclusions, into *The Poems of A. C. Benson* in 1909. Of all the hundred and sixty-two sets of verses of this last volume, I can recall the content of only six, "Fritillaries," "The Toad," "My Will," "The Shepherd," "The Cat," and "The Charcoal-Burner." And this despite the fact that I am interested in just the sort of little things he writes about, the pets and small deer of the dooryard, birds, and flowers both of the garden and the wild. Of these six poems "My Will" parallels "The

Choice" of Pomfret, the standard by which all poems of a home of country contentment are to be judged.

"The Shepherd" and "The Charcoal-Burner" are characters in verse. You can see them clearly both, rural figures about whom romance still clings, but rendered both with a faithful realism. "The Toad" and "The Cat" are clear thumb-nail sketches of two of the most unresponsive of all creatures. Both are done to the life. No countryman or suburbanite who has a cat but has seen her as Benson sees her:

> On some grave business, soft and slow
> Along the garden-paths you go,
>   With bold and burning eyes:
> Or stand, with twitching tail, to mark
> What starts and rustles in the dark
>   Among the peonies.

"The Fritillaries" records his regard for these outland and reptilian flowers. All these verses I have written about are miniatures of little things, but remembering Jane Austen who made miniatures of such, as well as of great things, I would not cry them down because of their scale or their intent. Their weakness, and that of all his verses, is that they are not impassioned. He has not been able to get his great care for them all into his record of them.

Benson writes a good deal of literary criticism in verse as well as in prose. Dean Swift, Collins, Gray, Cowper, Coleridge, Keats, and Fitzgerald are commented upon in sane and safe fashion, very much as he comments on Fitzgerald again, and Tennyson and Rossetti and Pater, in little prose books upon them. Pleasantness is the earmark of all that he does. It is easy to understand why he was so loved a teacher at Eton, and why his lectures and teas at Cambridge were so well attended. This same pleasantness is the best asset of such a story of his as *The Hill of Trouble* (1903) and such volumes of essays as *From a College Window* (1906). Now and then he dared to plumb into the depths of things, but generally he is too considerate to publish his discoveries. Only once has he said such a disturbing thing as this:

> He deems that knowledge, bitter sweet,
> Can rust and rot the bars of right.

STEPHEN PHILLIPS

The historical and absolute estimates of criticism pick out very different elements in the poetry of Stephen Phillips (1864-1915) by which to judge him. By the historical estimate he is written down the dramatic poet who put tragedy in blank verse back upon the stage, by *Herod* (1900) and *Nero* (1906), in the first decade of the twentieth century. By the absolute estimate he is given a little place among the poets of the race as the elegiast who wrote "I in the greyness rose" and *Christ in Hades* (1896) and "Marpessa." The effects of these three poems, as the intentions with which each was written, are very different one from the other. There is a kind of simplicity, a directness, a finality of utterance all his own in the best passages of the first poem. There is much that is his own, and peculiar to him alone, in *Christ in Hades*, but one has *Balder Dead* in mind as one reads. So it is, too, with "Marpessa." The blank verse in which it is written is individual, and new, built though it is on Marlowe's and Milton's. The very rhetoric into which it lapses at times is not the rhetoric of any earlier poet. "That were unhappy long and now are dead" has a new fall. Other passages have a color, a sensuousness, a richness of imagery found in just such a combination in none of the old poets to whom he went to school. Keats he suggests now and then, in the largeness of his figures, in the mellowness of his tone, in the sweet earthiness of his speech.

It is an eye akin to that which looked out, in imagination, with Cortez upon a peak in Darien that saw:

> All Asia at my feet spread out
> In indolent magnificence of bloom.

The plays drop honey, too, at times, in the scene in *Ulysses* (1902), for one place, in which the hero is with Calypso in her "odorous amorous isle of violets." It is upon the languor and ultrasweetness of this place that there breaks in the memory of Ulysses of his native place. Better stuff again are those passages of this play that present the meeting of Ulysses with Eumæus, though these need the stage and the actors to bring them before us in their full intensity. The one performance of *Ulysses* I saw at the Walnut Street Theater in Philadelphia in May, 1904, was far from a notable one, but Fuller Mellish so played the swineherd who recognizes his master that Tyrone Power was lifted by his fellowactor's complete possession by the part to the only great moment of his whole performance.

There were two theatrical moments in the performance of *Paolo and Francesca* by the H. B. Irving Company in Philadelphia, October 31, 1906, that I remember. The one was the portrayal of Miss Maud Milton of the awakening of mother-love in Lucrezia toward Francesca, an awakening too late to enable her to save Francesca from Giovanni's jealousy. The other was that moment, so much easier to produce, when H. B. Irving as Giovanni came through the curtains, wiping from his sword the blood of the lovers he had slain, the blood of his wife and of his brother. Whether these moments are dramatically true as well as theatrically effective, whether they are what would have inevitably happened to just such people as these in just such a moil of circumstance as this is a question. There are possible arguments both pro and con. I believe that these two situations are dramatically true as well as theatrically effective, but I can hardly claim as much for certain other situations in this play, and certain situations in other plays.

The Sin of David (1904) was to have been staged with all the Oriental splendor revealed by recent archæological unearthing in the East. That staging was to have been a visualization for the English-speaking world of a memorable story of the Old Testament. The censor, however, would not license the play because it put the Bible upon the stage. In its adapted form, with a background of Cromwellian England instead of the Old East, it had to wait long for a real try-out. In July, 1914, it received an adequate production at the Savoy Theatre in London, with H. B. Irving, Miriam Lewis, and Henry Vibert as the leading actors. Even thus produced, however, it was not a pronounced success.

Phillips was fortunate generally in the actor-managers who produced his plays. Sir George Alexander did *Paolo and Francesca* first in London, on March 6, 1902, and Sir Herbert Beerbohm Tree eighteen months earlier had had a great success with the later written play, *Herod*, put on at Her Majesty's Theatre on October 31, 1900. On January 25, 1906, *Nero* was produced by Tree at His Majesty's Theatre, London. It was withdrawn May 19, 1906, a good run indeed for a tragedy in blank verse. *Paolo and Francesca*, revived by Miss Jane Cowl in 1928, proved that it had not been outmoded by the passage of a quarter-century. *Faust* (1908) and *Pietro of Siena* (1910) and *Harold* (1916) are much lesser plays. The energies of Phillips were burned out when he wrote them. The passion that was almost his greatest strength is dead, and there is little poetry in any one of the three to lift the forced rhetoric of most of the lines.

Phillips has spared himself the necessity of the creation of character in most of his plays by choosing to dramatize stories from legend or history familiar to most of us from youth. The mere naming of their principals brings long-known men and women before our mind's eye. We have all been brought up to read the story of the fated lovers, Paolo and Francesca. Herod and Mariamne are almost as familiar as if their story were told in the Bible. The story of David and Bathsheba and Uriah the Hittite is told there. Ulysses we met in tales from Greek legend even before we read Homer. Nero and Harold as villain and hero loomed large in history, and Faust was come upon as soon as we began opera-going or college German.

It seems to me, as I have intimated, that Lucrezia in *Paolo and Francesca* and Eumæus in *Ulysses* stand out most clearly of all his characters, but that may be only because I saw the parts notably taken on the stage. The one is wholly his own creation, the other emphasized from an already created character. No one of all of the characters as limned by Phillips is as fully realized, though, as Tennyson's Becket. That character I had visualized from a reading of *Becket* before I saw Irving in the part. Whether I had so visualized Lucrezia or Eumæus I cannot remember. The fact that I cannot remember indicates, perhaps, that neither part deeply impressed me upon a reading of the play before seeing it on the stage.

The greatest effort of Phillips after that which went into his plays went into his picturing of a world beyond death. That was a life-long effort. The theme of *Eremus* (1894), that early poem in blank verse that he disowned, is very close to it. The theme is considered in *Christ in Hades*. Death, or the world beyond death, informs about a third of his non-dramatic verse, and he is concerned with either this theme, or a kindred theme, in all of his principal plays save *Herod*. In *Faust* a world half-way to Heaven is the last scene of the play. In *Paolo and Francesca* the lovers have before them the prospect of centuries of torture in Hell. In *Ulysses*, as in its original in Homer, the hero follows the way the dead must go to Hell. In *Nero* and *The Sin of David* spirits of the slain return to earth to seek vengeance on those who killed them.

All his productive years Phillips contemplated a long poem on the world beyond death. He tells us in *Literature*, in the issue for February, 1899, what he thinks about this afterworld as "a field for modern verse." He then intended to work into such a long poem his various stories of modern city life, "The Woman with the Dead Soul" and the like. This he never did, but in *The New Inferno* (1911) he did write a long poem of the life after death. It is an inconsequential attempt, nine cantos about the haunting of the dead man by the sins he sinned living. The petty upshot of it all is that "Death carries us into no higher court."

With his powers slackening in his last years Phillips could never have made a long poem that would have been worthy of these early poems he intended to include as parts of it. "The

Woman with the Dead Soul" is, indeed, notable in its way. It is in decasyllabic rhymed couplets, but with a movement, a progression, a flow, very other than that of the static epigrammatic couplet of Pope. The picture of the woman dressed with meticulous care, and moving like an automaton through the daily affairs of life, is the most biting character analysis in all Phillips. It is, too, a creation known far and wide. One can refer now to a person with a dead soul and trust that he will be understood. One can assume that all the English-speaking world knows the meaning of the phrase even if it does not know, all of it, the poem from which the phrase comes. There is no other poem of Phillips with such universality as this, even if "I in the greyness rose" and *Christ in Hades* and "Marpessa" are higher poetry.

There is no deep vision in "The Woman with the Dead Soul." Phillips sees in the original what the man in the street could see in her. He understands no more of her than that. He seizes upon the distinguishing characteristic of her, the dead soul, and presents it directly, forcibly, with no subtlety at all, and with such clearness of phrase that nobody can misunderstand him. He is not of the poets who speak in parables, but of those who out with what they have to say, like Burns and Byron, in words of the market-place. Whenever, indeed, in play or in poem, Phillips has to present the common and universal passions, he attains a simplicity of expression that goes to the heart of the matter in a few words. And the accent of the writing, like the phrasing, is familiar to our ears, though it is carried, at times, by a blank verse with a movement all its own. Phillips discovers for us few new thoughts. He reveals no new depths of life. He uses few new symbols to make us pause and wonder. He has no great shaping imagination. He is little of a seer. What is new in him is his way of handling the decasyllabic line. He has studied the pause and the shifting of accent, the change of pace and the change of pitch, until he has made himself master of his medium. His diction is that we have known from infancy, but the movement and stanzaic structure of his blank verse are new achievements.

"I in the greyness rose" is not a perfect poem. He did not work it over often enough to get out of it the stock phrases. He did not rid it, as he might have done by labor, of inversions. It is, however, a bit of life, a something of everyday experience caught in a phrase or two, so cast in words that it is safe against time. A man is looking through the chest in which are the little treasures of his dead wife. A glove and "a sheet of music torn" do not particularly move him. Then he takes up her letters. The most of these, too, fail to move him deeply. She who is dead is beyond all partings and weariness and sorrow. What he cannot endure is a letter in which he finds:

> A hurried happy line!
> A little jest, too slight for one so dead.

Christ in Hades (1896) is the first poem of Phillips that I read. He won me on this first reading of him. It was a noon hour in a crowded and noisy newspaper office that I read it. One of the staff who had just come home from a trip to England brought it back as a present for me. "You like thin sheafs of verse," he said, throwing it down, in grey paper cover, on the desk before me. I couldn't spare a minute for it until noon, and then, before I ran out for my lunch, I stole time enough to look it over. It was its freshness, its sense of spring, its suggestion of sunlight and its delight in rain that took me instantly. It was only after my reaction to these qualities that I came to realize that there was here a new treatment of Greek life. I was, indeed, eating my rice and cream in the little eating place up the street when this realization came to me. Christ, "all fresh out of beautiful sunlight," was brought into the dimness of the Greek Hades. I recalled the picture, and the line, as I can recall them now. Certain lines, indeed, fixed themselves in memory at that first glancing at the poem, and others on my reading going out home in the train, and others still on my poring over it again and again that evening. I can write some of them even yet from memory. "Trees Motionless in an ecstasy of rain" I have always retained, even to the memory of "trees" in one line, and the rest of it in the next. Others good to remember are "How good it is to live, even at the worst," "the scent of over-beautiful, quick-fading things," "The Sweetness of the world edged like a sword," and that line in which there is so much of the dawn, "A dreadful freshness exquisitely breathes."

There is blue noon in *Christ in Hades*, and breezes, and rivers, but its general effect is of the greyness of dawn in a misty world, of the greyness of dawn and dew on the grass, of the greyness of dawn and rain falling. Always Phillips is good at rain, and at the smell of earth fresh-broken by the plough, and at ghosts.

In "Marpessa" not only insular Greece and its islands rise before Phillips, but all Greece, Magna Græca, and Asia beyond that part of its western edge that was Greek. There is here that riot of Orientalism, of the color and warmth and extravagance of the Old Testament that is dominant in *Herod,* too, a Hebraism as definite as the Hellenism of other parts of "Marpessa" and so many other verses of his. There are brave words from the God as he pleads for the love of Marpessa. The words of Idas are simpler, more direct, more Greek. Yet the romantic note is sounded, too, the note found in the *Odyssey*. To Idas Phillips attempts to give lines to match:

> Was this the face that launched a thousand ships
> And burnt the topless towers of Ilium?

"Marpessa" is not all of one texture. There are arid lines in it and rhetorical lines as well as lines drenched with the dew of natural magic. The poem holds together fairly well, however. It "recites" well, particularly to music, as do many passages in the plays. I have heard such lines done both indifferently and well upon the stage. I have heard "Marpessa" done well from A to Z "in hall." There was a suggestion of the theater, of opera more particularly, in this recitation, as there is so often to me in Phillips, and in his master Marlowe so long before him.

Despite his actor's life and his love of theatrical situation and rhetorical diction Stephen Phillips is a Puritan at heart. He is troubled when he is happy; such a condition as happiness is too good to last. Of God Phillips writes:

> He, as I think, intends that we shall rise
> Only through pain into his Paradise.

Phillips acknowledges the power of the carnalities and splendors of this world we live in. Sin is savorsome, there is no doubt of that. But for sin man shall be damned. That is equally sure. Phillips has every sympathy for those who succumb to the temptation of "The baited sweetness and the honied wrong." And, yet, he is, for a poet, most orthodox in his belief.

Phillips is proud of his art, certain that he is a poet, but humble in his realization of a great gift. Poetry is to him "more than sight," a sort of divine insight, in which the spirit is "rapt in hurry to the stars." It is in *Nero* that there are the most references to his art. The artist militant speaks out boldly in his declaration that "From art to empire is too swift a drop." So have felt all the poets with pride in their art. The man of feeling cannot rid himself of an innate contempt for one not concerned with the eternal things. It was of little avail, however, for Phillips to be answering his critics here. Nero is made to say:

> I would write a play
> Lived there a single critic fit to judge it.
> Whether a dancing girl kick high enough—
> On this they can pronounce: this is their trade.
> With verse upon the stage they cannot cope.

What Arthur Symons had said about the words put into the mouths of Phillips' characters being not what they would have used but the poet's external poetizing about what was their situation had evidently gotten under his skin. That he was steadily cooling "to all things great" toward the end of his life was also regrettably true. That he should have fallen, though, into the almost complete neglect that is his to-day is not just. Stephen Phillips has a movement of blank verse all his own. He has at times freshness and beauty of phrase. There are lines of his that keep place in memory alongside of lines from the great poets.

LAURENCE BINYON

Laurence Binyon (b. 1869) is not just to himself in *Selected Poems* (1922). It would seem that his purpose here was to reveal himself as a lyric poet, to gather together those that mean most to him of the shorter verses he had published since he came before the public in *Primavera* (1890). It is not in these shorter verses that he is at his best. He cannot write impassioned verse save in the larger verse forms, in the ode, in the eclogue, in the epic in little. And even here he cannot, save now and then, in "Sirmione" and "Thunder on the Downs," in "Tristram's End," and "The Death of Adam," sustain the emotion of his impassioned speech throughout a long poem. He has, in most poems, to give you the circumstances that make him impassioned before he can rise to the impassioned passages; or, if he does begin under full tide of feeling, he is unable to keep it at the full through all of a long poem. Few English poets can. The genius of the race is for the lyric.

There are writers, like Abercrombie, who are content to be narrative poets or dramatic poets only, to forgo the lyric altogether. Abercrombie, indeed, denies that the lyric is the form of forms for English poetry. Binyon does not make that mistake, but he is not content to be judged first by his narratives and by his plays. His plays were forced from him by the emphasis of the times on drama, by the experiments of Yeats, and by the temporary success of Stephen Phillips in blank-verse plays. Binyon had no native genius for drama, and it cannot be claimed for any of his plays that they are more than pageantry adapted to the stage. They are of the very stuff of which "Porphyrion" and "The Death of Adam" are made. No one of them, even of those more largely conceived, *Attila* (1907), or *Arthur* (1923), has in it as true dramatic speech as there is in moments of "Tristram's End," which, though parts of it are cast in dialogue, makes no pretense to be drama.

It may well be that Binyon does not wish to emphasize the picture-making power of his verse, because so much of his life has been concerned with pictorial art. He was for years in the British Museum in charge of Oriental Prints and Drawings, and he is an acknowledged authority on the art of the East. His specialty has brought him to America for lectures and research three times, in 1912, 1914, and 1926. It is natural that he should want to be judged as a poet rather than as a painter of pictures in words, but he cannot escape the fact that the interest that made him the art critic he is has compelled him to be a painter in words. It is the simple truth that through all his younger manhood he was as concerned as a painter with the color and form of things. And so he is, too, only in a less degree to-day.

It is just as natural that as he grows older he should become more curious as to what lies behind the shows of things, what their spirit is, what their place in the scheme of the world. This kind of interest, however, does not necessarily lead to greater poetry than that which is concerned with the pageant of life. Shelley is not a greater poet than Keats. Binyon has quoted, in *English Poetry in Its Relation to Painting and the Other Arts* (1918), the distinction of Lessing between poetry on the one hand and painting and sculpture on the other. The main differences, Binyon writes, flow "from the fact that poetry deals with a sequence in time and involves action or movement, while painting and sculpture are stationary and present a single moment."

Certain poems of Binyon give pictures that are exactly like those of painting, pictures of just one scene, "The Paralytic," for instance. Certain other poems give pictures of a series of scenes, scenes that often go a large way toward the presentation of a story, as in "Porphyrion." His most distinctive poems are of the one class or the other, but all renderings of things seen. Pictures of everyday scenes in London and pageants of Oriental splendor bulk large among these. The "London Visions" are renderings of the picturesqueness of London, some done with the artist's eyes wide open, others when he is in half-dream; the Oriental pageants have taken color and shape before him as he has read and brooded of the pomp and splendor of the life of old time in Magna Græca and Syria and Persia. A man living in London, even if he is a poet, cannot escape present-day problems, and Binyon has determinately chosen to write often of London of to-day. A half of the poems of his young manhood are of London; but it is not London that fills his highest, happiest dreams. These are of English seashore, of Montenegrin mountain, of Syrian deserts, of pageants in Antioch and Carmanian vales, of Arthurian romance.

From his first poem of *Primavera* (1890) Binyon has been picturing landscape and ceremonials of splendid life, either for themselves or as symbols to interpret his own moods. Whatever else they contain, the succeeding collections of his verse contain many descriptions, all presented with good workmanship. Writing of the poetry of Robert Bridges, Binyon has expressed his admiration for "that structural beauty," that "wholeness of good tissue which is the pith of all enduring art." He would have art "proud, serene, and perfect." Binyon's own best poems are "proud" and "serene," "with structural beauty," but not, as he has written, built of pale words. There is no paleness in his poetry, no morning light, but the waning splendor of a spent sun in the afterglow. How he loves the time between sun-set and day's end!

> Come let us forth, and wander the rich, the murmuring night!
> The shy blue dusk of summer trembles above the street.

And how the night itself! "Liquid gloom quivered with stars Appearing endlessly." There is splendor in the description of the dead city in the rock-bound desert that Porphyrion fled, his vision peopling it with hosts "for mountain battle armed." There are amplitudes of space, of "boundless country darkening" in Porphyrion's outlook on the "great uplands dimly rolled" away to Antioch and the sea.

Binyon, the son of a clergyman, has by birthright an interest in "the storied sacred East," but it was of the landscapes of home that he first wrote, not then with many intimations of his latest power.

He was at Oxford in these days, but he writes strangely little of its old beauty, lover of all things beautiful that he is. Its "spires and towers" do loom up over the willows of "Cherwell Stream," but that is all of it we see. In *The Praise of Life* (1896) and *Porphyrion* (1898) the several poems picturing English countryside and seashore reveal his descriptive art at fuller power. There is the quiet joy of a day on the upper Thames in "The First Day of Summer;" the subject and sentiment of "The Oak" recall experiences and thoughts of happy rambles in the New Forest; "May Evening" is described as it is in every English farming country. Each of these poems is in its way beautiful, but not one of them smacks of the soil, has the home-thrust of observation that brings back to keen senses the very tang of wood and tillage. Binyon, whatever his upbringing, is in his poetry a city man. Although there is little detail, countryside and seashore are present to these descriptive poems in form and color, but taste and smell and sound are seldom used to bring very out-of-doors before us. A flower to Binyon is apt to be a thing of beauty, or a symbol of beauty, and nothing more; not, too, a primrose or a foxglove whose mention would make the definite appeal of a thing known and loved. So seldom does he name a bird that it is a real surprise to find that he does know a sedge-warbler when he sees it downweighing a tall reed, and a thrush with "dewy notes." I state his neglect of the little things of nature not as a defect, but as a limitation. It is not the way of his masters Tennyson and Wordsworth, but of his more remote master Milton, who wrote before Englishmen were wholly awake to the beauty of England, and of his master Keats, like Milton a cockney and like him a man who lived too little out-of-doors.

There is one poem in which Binyon makes a selection of symbols that brings the scenes he paints before you in their utmost beauty and significance. If each of the three scenes were a painting, you would fall to discussing whether the "atmosphere" of the first or last were better rendered. "The Driftwood Gatherers" seems to me completely to realize its intention. It is not the highest poetry he essays here, sketches of an old peasant couple at their little tasks by the Atlantic. His first presents the old man and woman gathering driftwood "along the deep shelve of the abandoned shore;" then on "their homeward path, bordered with heath and pine," then at their humble meal of autumn fare while "the low lamp kindles their old cheeks." This cottage life by the shore is of the life that Crabbe knew, but what different scenes he chose to select from it; how despairing his, how heartening this of Binyon's! "The Driftwood Gatherers" is a poem to be put beside A. C. Benson's "Shepherd"; both are bits from the heart of English peasant life, now so fast disappearing. It illustrates how happy Binyon may be in his diction. Driftwood, the word itself, and that of which it is the symbol, has every association of romance, but the picture is drawn realistically. How well the homely words are chosen! The reader's heart cannot but warm with sympathy as he reads of "heath and pine," of the "happy fire" leaping on the "swept stones," of the old songs the woman sings, of the man's feigned chiding. There is an element of narrative in "The Driftwood Gatherers" as in so many of Binyon's more successful verses, but the story of an afternoon and evening in the life of an old couple is told by a succession of pictures. It is just such a poem as a painter might illustrate without distortion.

It would seem from the record in Binyon's verse that he has had deeply happy outings in Flanders, in Portugal, in Montenegro, and in Italy, as well as in his own England. Montenegro, of foreign lands, lifts his heart highest, since there he finds three of the things he loves most, pines and mountains and free men. Binyon knows, too, something of our American countryside. He has followed the old road along the Wissahickon that Poe once trod, but he has not been kindled by buttonball trees rising with white branches out of low fog and against the green of banked hemlocks to picture them for us. He liked this bit of winter landscape, though, for he cried out "How jolly!" an exclamation that is used by Englishmen when deeply moved.

Binyon has written of many sides of London life, of many

kinds of London scenes, generally as they are summed up in a characteristic picture. Now it is a great dray rolling down the street, its giant driver guiding it triumphantly; now it is Duse as Magda; now the great golden dome of St. Paul's looming above the smoke-wrapped city; now Salvation Army singers, in whose enthusiasm the poet sees the reincarnation of the delirious spirit that fired the Dionysia's "mad, leafy revels at the Wine-God's will"; now a quiet sunset on "full-flooding Thames." Various lights illumine these city scenes Binyon chooses, but while dawn and full noon and sunset color some, London at night inspires so many that I have come to think the characteristic lights of the poems are the flickering street lamps. The most of his poems of this sort belong to the pre-electric days.

Miles out of London in the fragrant country fields he looks down on London's "endless fiery maze," where "night comes to few unanxious, happy eyes." As he wrote in this early poem so he wrote when half of his poems were "London visions." Eight of the twelve poems of the first series of *London Visions* (1896) are night pieces; four of the ten poems of the second series of *London Visions* are night pieces; "The Threshold" is of twilight, and others in which no time of day is mentioned have the dark setting of night. Of the night are "The Fire," "The Dray," "Eleonora Duse as Magda," and "The Supper" in *Porphyrion and Other Poems*.

Although "The Supper" is more or less in the manner of Davidson's poems of London, most of Binyon's city verses are very different from his, as they are different again from Robert Buchanan's and Henley's. Binyon is more intent on the picture of his subject, where Henley is as much interested in the surge and sound that accompanies the picture as in the picture itself. Henley, too, is almost always the impressionist. Buchanan cares much less for making pictures of city life than he does for telling the life stories of victims of that life. Davidson has generally a problem to propound as well as a story to suggest and a picture to paint.

Vivid in color as is "Martha," rich as are the sunset pictures of

"The Threshold," London cannot furnish material for such pageants as can the East. Before his lot was to work in London Binyon had written of the "storied East afar." It was to the nearer East of Greece, so familiar to him from his studies, that he turned for subjects when he would write verse. "Persephone" was his Newdigate prize poem. It is a far cry from "Persephone" to "Porphyrion"; the one is but 'prentice-work, the other that of a thorough craftsman. Binyon's readings in the Greek authors ordinarily considered at college must have whetted his curiosity to know the wonders of countries farther east, or more Eastern in modes of thought and life than Greece. His study of Daniell's water-colors assuredly deepened this curiosity. It is not, however, the mysteries of the East, but its splendors that captivate him. He writes sometimes of these mysteries, but his vision is always as clear as a Greek's; no matter how Oriental the subject, it is presented with Greek precision and sharpness of line.

"Porphyrion," his most ambitious poem on an Eastern subject, though it has for subject the driving-out of religious enthusiasm from a young Greek's heart by the apparition of a beautiful woman that finally lures him to his death, and though it is told by a succession of highly colored pictures, is as clearly visualized as Ulysses' return to Ithaca. "Porphyrion" is a blank-verse poem of about 1,500 lines, "suggested," Binyon tells us in a note, "by a story of Rufinus told in *Historia Monachorum*," but "adapted . . . to his own use" and having "therefore a quite altered complexion in the poem." So on a passage of Arrian he builds "The Bacchanal of Alexander," and so on Josephus Stephen Phillips builds his *Herod*.

If the doubter draw from the poem the inference that ideal beauty is after all but a chimera, there is the compensating inference that a struggle for the ideal makes life itself sweeter and keener in the living, gives a man more of the joy of "this perilous rich world." There are many of Binyon's finest lines and passages in "Porphyrion." The "purple" lines show that he has profited by his study of Keats, his Homeric similes suggest comparison with

Arnold's. The poem reaches its utmost pageantry in a passage which describes the scene of splendid revelry on which Porphyrion wandered in the first night of his return to Antioch.

In the *Odes* (1901) Binyon further pursued his studies in the pageantry of Oriental life. Five of the eight poems of this volume are on Eastern subjects. "The Bacchanal of Alexander" is most impressive of the five. The Macedonian's peaceful but triumphal progress through the Carmanian vale in Southern Persia is the subject of the poem, and when you have finished you have before you as clearly as if you were looking upon the frieze of some Greek temple the picture of the Conqueror throned and his Seven of Macedon on "Two massy ivory cars, together bound," his soldiers garlanded following him and the Carmanian harvesters looking on awed by the great spectacle.

Binyon writes at his greatest power in "The Death of Tristram," or, as he calls it in his *Selected Poems* (1922), "Tristram's End." It is of the last lie of Iseult of the White Hands and the deaths of Iseult of Cornwall and of Tristram that he writes. He is a bold man who will retell any part of the story when such masters from Gottfried von Strassburg's day to Swinburne's have made poems out of its many episodes. Binyon challenges comparison with those two poets I have mentioned, with the noble prose of Malory, and with Tennyson and Arnold, to mention only the best known of the writers that have cared so much for the great old tale that they must write of it. Binyon, as is his way, uses many pictures to tell his story, but he uses dialogue to bring before us the stormy youth of the lovers. If their recital of young days is not dramatically true, it is a brave attempt at the high old way of romance, and it results in poetry as high as the story's high passion. It was of this poem that Yeats, half-chaffing Binyon, said: "Yes, Binyon, you've written one poem, your Tristram."

In *Western Flanders* (1898), Binyon writes in prose of old cities, making us wish he had attempted impressions of them all in verse. His description of Ypres reads as if it were a transcript of a dream; a dream, he says, the moss-grown city is, a survival of medievalism where "the hours fall slowly on unrecognizing ears." Doubly valuable is it now that the Great War has had its will of the city. What it became Binyon chronicles in a sonnet "Ypres."

The Death of Adam (1904) has its scene again in the East, but there is more in it of the land that Milton dreamed than of the West Asian uplands. The poem, a long narrative in blank verse, tells of the last ten days in the life of Adam, and how in these last days the few thoughts that took shape in his dimmed mind were of his life in Eden and in those first years after he was driven out of Eden. Binyon has been even bolder here than in attempting a new version of the story of Tristram and Iseult, yet I think his boldness will be forgiven by all who read *The Death of Adam*, for the poem has the noble bearing of its high ancestry.

Binyon, like so many of the poets his contemporaries, has taken his fling in drama, but, like so many of them again, without success. *Paris and Œnone* (1906) is an eclogue of Mt. Ida given dramatic form. It is workmanlike verse, but no more. It was played by Gertrude Kingston at the Savoy Theater, in March, 1906, but it won no place for itself on the stage. Nor did *Attila* (1907), though its performance by Oscar Asche and Lily Brayton at His Majesty's Theater in September, 1907, revealed an intensity of feeling hardly to be expected in a writer of so quiet a tone as Binyon. *Bombastes in the Shades* (1915) is only a skit, a slight anti-German farce. It is in prose. In November, 1919, his version of *Sakuntala* was played in London, at an afternoon performance, with Aga Khan and the Maharajah Gaekwar of Barode in the audience. *Arthur* (1923) was written with Sir John and Lady Martin Harvey in virtual collaboration with the poet. It is an interesting and worthy rearrangement of the old legend of Guinevere and Lancelot and Arthur, of the overthrow of the Round Table, of the rebellion of Mordred, and of Arthur's death. It had a brief success in the theater.

The long concern of Binyon with Chinese art stood him in good stead in *Ayuli* (1923). Though it was published so recently, the date at its end is 1911. It has beauty in it, and it flaunts a challenge to the world, that leads to the breaking of the challengers by the world they defy. It advances the rights of youth and beauty against old age and what has been. So far as I can find out, its dramatic qualities have not been tested by presentation on the stage.

A good craftsman in all forms of letters, Binyon had done rather better than was to be expected in his plays. He has done well, too, in the large body of verse he wrote from 1914 to 1918. A sheaf of this was collected in America in 1917 as *The Cause*. Much of it is occasional or propagandist, but at least one memory, of a scene at the front, "Fetching the Wounded," has the kind of beauty you find in his many pictorial poems.

Problems of present-day life do not much concern Binyon unless they happen to be picturesque, nor do religious questions, nor the life after death whose contemplation so fascinates Phillips. Binyon is like his cousin, however, in his lament for the brevity of youth, for the brevity of life, for the brevity of all good things. Binyon, too, has a deep regret for "a girl that's dead." Binyon in many declarations holds that life is sweet and well worth the living. In "The Vision of Augustine and Monica," a paraphrase of parts of the *Confessions*, he follows sympathetically Augustine's dream of "an ampler sphere" where is "splendor past access of fleshly eye," but in "The Renewal," rejoicing in a May morning lived to the uttermost among "sun-drunken pines," by a sun-flooded sea, he buoyantly declares that men should:

> dedicate no more
> Their travail to some far imagined shore,
> Some dreamed-of goal beyond life's eager sphere,
> For lo! at every hour the goal is here.

At such topmost hours of life as were his this May morning on the sea-beach he holds that:

> in his bosom flow
> Springs of all knowledge he hath need to know.

The secret of life is, then, the very joy of living. Living is strife, not peace; like Meredith and like Henley, Binyon rejoices that it is strife, that the world,
> the immortal foe,
> To truceless war our ardour challenges.

. . . . .

Binyon has written a good deal that might be called love verse, but not one set of these verses is so distinguished as are many of his "London Visions" and of his Oriental pageants. His contemplative love verse has more charm for me than his love lyrics. His lines have seldom sing or lilt, qualities so necessary to the lyric. Nor does Binyon attain greatly as a philosophic poet, for few of his poems concerned primarily with the questions of life are beautiful. More are interesting, but these chiefly because of their self-revelation.

It is in *The Idols* (1929) that he enters most thoroughly into the question of a life hereafter for some part of what we are in the life we know. He comes to no satisfying conclusion, of course, but he falls back on what is best in what we are now in lieu of such a conclusion:
> It is now and it is here,
> The something beyond all things dear,
> The miracle that has no name!

There is high aspiration in the poem, and a consideration of our idols, the things that make life fine. The relative values of the arts and religion and science are weighed, the results of these weighings being about those which would be arrived at from a consensus of opinion among the thinking and cultivated men of our time. There are passages not a few of grave beauty, but very few passages of impassioned poetry, keenly felt as is all the discussion.

It is in his descriptive poems of English countryside and seashore, and in the descriptive passages of his narrative poems on

Eastern subjects that I find most beauty, sometimes great beauty. And this beauty is chiefly the beauty of the pictures he draws so surely and colors with such certain art. Beauty comes, too, at times, out of a preoccupation with the past of the place he is describing. In "Sirmione" the poem opens in the darkness, lake and mountains and "old olive stems" all blotted out by the coming-down of night.

> Where are those mountains far-enthroned and hoar
> Above the glittering water's slumbrous heat,
> With old blanched towns sprinkled about their feet?

There, in the darkness, thoughts come to the poet of that passionate poet Catullus, who fled to his home here from "The marble-towered magnificence of Rome." Our modern poet would summon before him a pageant of "All quick and fiery spirits that have been," and he would conjure up the future, too. The end is, as so often in poetry, that the poet is content with what is, the love and the life he knows.

"Thunder on the Downs" is another one of the long odes in which Binyon alone seems to be able to write impassioned verse. This poem opens quietly, and with description of landscape. Gradually, however, you are led to a passage in which the poet apostrophizes the downs above the sea. Later on in the poem there is a noble tribute to the England of his dreams. Here, too, is one of the few readings of life in Binyon:

> All the lust
> Of gainful man is quieted in dust.

In "The New World: To the People of the United States," is one of the discoveries that are to Binyon's work what the "readings of life" are to a Meredith or a Kipling:

> Man is older than all the things he has made
> And yet the youngest spirit beneath the stars.

"The Mirror" and "Initiation" are other long odes that lift high above the level of most of Binyon's verse but are not of "the wholeness of good tissue" of "Sirmione" or "Thunder on the Downs." "The Mirror" opens on too high a note to be long sustained:

> Where is all the beauty that has been?
> Where the bloom?

"Initiation" sags between the silvern clarity of its opening and its impassioned close. It kindles Binyon to the divination that "Blood knows more than the brain."

Binyon holds that rhythm should have "magic responses to the turns of emotion," "natural falterings," "victorious bursts." What instances of these qualities do his own verses reveal? Perhaps these lines approach closest to magic responses: "The tinge and odour of neglected time"; "All the glory of war and sounding arms"; "irrevocably lost The old thoughts that so long had sheltered him"; "A land of youth, lovely and full of sap Upon whose border trembled the wide sea"; and "Lonely and loud a sudden trumpet blew." Perhaps these are "natural falterings"; "Some lost and lovely yesterdays"; "The lovely ways of gliding leaves"; "Invisible new beauty in the air, Wings in the light, or glory in the wind." The battle pageant in the fourth book of *Porphyrion* rises almost to what is a "victorious burst" and there are "victorious bursts" in *The Death of Tristram* and in *The Death of Adam*. It will be long before I can forget the effect of that passage in *Porphyrion* that comes to its kindling close in the flaunting line, "Drank, like an ocean wind, the air of fame."

In insisting on the pictures of Binyon's poetry, in finding its chief beauty, among beauties of higher kind, in its description of pageants and places, I do not wish to call him a poet of externalities. Though it is the picturesque in London that wins him, he sometimes paints that picturesqueness not only for itself but as a symbol of the condition and mood of London's men and women. It is not always, though most often, only a city of pictures to him. Now it is the "city of strife, mother of pain," now a place of fascination so great that he can write:

> But me the turbulent babble and voice of crowds delight;
> For me the wheels make music, the mingled cries are sweet.

Both these quotations are records of moments when London picturesqueness was not the first element in his interest in London. Binyon's most constant power, however, is the power of the painter, not the power of the seer or of the singer. He is very skilful in many kinds of pictures: a shorescape with realistic detail like "The Driftwood Gatherers"; a compound of portraiture and still life, such as the sumptuous Oriental banquet in *Porphyrion;* or the greater pageant of the battle in the same poem. He has great power of painting landscapes on the largest scale. The very rarity of mountain air, the wide horizon of high outlooks is brought before us in this picture from *Porphyrion*:

> He was led
> Onward through many a city of the plain
> Till vaster grew the silence, and far off
> The noise of men; and he began to climb
> Pastoral hills that into mountains rose
> Skyward, with shelving ridges sloped between,
> Long days apart.

That last phrase is the stroke that brings home the immensity of the picture's distance.

The man that so loves mountains that his spirits rise as he climbs higher and higher and leaves the homes of men farther and farther behind is again so in need of companionship that he is lonely anywhere outside of London. It is, of course, a matter of mood. When in London he loves best the night; for at night the city is most beautiful to him, and men most companionable. Whether in London or out of London, with friends or alone, he has with him the sense of the infinitude of time, of the brevity of life. Only rarely is the brevity of life forgotten in exultant hours such as those of *The Praise of Life*, but in the unexultant hours he is seldom pessimistic, for though he is aware how short is life he is equally aware how good is life.

The poems of Binyon do not win the reader on a first reading. The pomp and pageantry seem at first sight hardly more than decorative, and in some poems that is all they are, but in his higher poems, such as "Sirmione" and "Thunder on the Downs," and "Tristram's End" and "The Death of Adam," they have their true use as the beautiful symbols of deeply poetic thought.

Binyon has always tried to write, though he has not always succeeded in writing, in the spirit of the declaration of faith he makes in his essay "The Poetry of Mr. Robert Bridges"—"Poetry is made to be known, loved, enjoyed, and the poetry which wins us with a tranquil and sure power is victorious in the end over that which thrills at first reading, and chills on the third or fourth." It is with a "tranquil and sure power" that the poems of Binyon I have praised win me. I have never been rapt clear out of myself by any poem of his, but many have grown more beautiful to me on each reading, until now I am sure that these are of the true metal.

CHAPTER IV

The Victorian Aftermath

THE fate of a poet like Francis Coutts (1852-1923) is an ironic one. Though he finds true things to say on important topics, and though he is a competent artist, he has been little read save in the years from 1896 to 1907. It was in 1896 he published his *Poems*, and in 1907 his *Heresy of Job*. Between came *The Revelation of St. Love the Divine* (1898), a long-drawn-out assertion of the inherent purity of passion; *King Arthur* (1902), a play accepted by Lewis Waller; and a chapter of high praise by William Archer in his *Poets of the Younger Generation* (1902). You would think the little noise that these made in the world would have kept his name before the reading public for another generation, but it did not. To-day he is unread, forgotten by the newspapers who wrote him up as a millionaire poet, and scarcely more than mentioned in books on the literature of the century's end. Even the fact that he was Francis Burdett Thomas Coutts-Nevill, Baron Latymer, after 1914, did not keep the press interested in him.

Even in his brief hour he sold few volumes of his verse, his public being not a great deal larger than the reviewers and his personal friends. Yet he wrote sound verse, he respected his craft, he won recognition from such fellow-poets as Watson and Stephen Phillips. Story-tellers and playwrights no better in their crafts than Coutts in his have a chance of a following, but a third-rate poet without a flair for sentimentality or melodrama counts hardly at all in public estimation. It is the ill fortune of Coutts to be not even a one-poem poet. What is best in him is not concentrated in one set of verses as in Charles Wolfe and Christina Rossetti and Francis Bourdillon, but spread thin through a hundred. Nor is there in his verse a discovery of life so true that it will keep its finder known, or any phrase that has taken its place in everyday speech. Francis Coutts is a poet, but a minor of the minors.

Edmund Gosse (1849-1928) tells us in "Philomel in London" that he heard a nightingale sing "in a poplared London Street." That incident from which he made verses is of more importance than the verses he made out of it, or than any other verses he has made out of a wide and long experience. The middleman between Ibsen and England, the commentator on Donne, the friend of Stevenson, the man associated with scores of little adventures of all sorts, never made enough of himself to be a poet. He was too busily concerned with other men's careers and works to have a strongly individual life of his own. The first book of his verse I read, *In Russet and Silver* (1894), is an old man's book. *Firdausi in Exile* (1885) I came on next and found but one set of verses there to arrest me, the sonnet "Unheard Music," and that for its opening similitude only. *New Poems* (1879) is another volume of verse such as nearly any man of letters who has gone to school to the poets could write. *On Viol and Flute* (1873) is of the same category. Sir Edmund Gosse was a personality in the life of his generation and he has given us essays that catch in some measure the charm of that personality. It is there and not in the verse that one finds the best of him.

F. W. BOURDILLON

The chief reason for mentioning F. W. Bourdillon (1852-1921) is that he wrote "The Night has a Thousand Eyes." We have all heard that song sung many times. We may be in doubt of its quality as literature, but we cannot doubt its popularity in its own time. I was given in 1899 an American collection of his verse named after this unusually appealing poem of his, *The Night has a Thousand Eyes*, reprinted that year from an earlier edition of 1891. There are other verses as good in the volume, but none other that has made so universal an appeal. There is never any freshness in his phrasing, the words are worn and tired, the images commonplace. From the first line of each set of stanzas you are aware of what will follow.

There are those who submit that he should be mentioned for his translation of *Aucassin and Nicolette* (1887). I am not sure. It seems obvious to me. It is without distinction from what he has done with it, though of course the original has glimpses of medieval life in it that no translation can much cheapen. Bourdillon is humble enough in his estimate of himself, admitting that his verses are "ill-wrought." He has sympathy for "the common human" and the public has responded to his statement of that sympathy. In "On Brighton Cliffs" he wonders of the crowds at the famous watering place:

> And what of these vain, vulgar lives?
> Have they some unheard music as they pass,
> Unlovely each, yet making in the mass
> Some God-delighting beauty, that survives,
> Serene and lovely as the silvered sea,
> Where all foul things and cruel creatures be?

These lines are from a fourteen-liner, but he habitually contents himself with eight lines, of pleasant singable platitudes.

Margaret L. Woods (b. 1856) is the woman who wrote "To be young and wise is folly." You find that in her "Gaudeamus Igitur."

NEWMAN HOWARD

Newman Howard (b. 1861) had his day from 1901 to 1913, from the time of the publication of *Kiartan the Icelander* to the gathering together of his lyrics and dramas into *Collected Poems*. For this decade he was reviewed at length and compared with the great. Now, in retrospect, it is a little hard to understand the extravagance of his appreciation, for, despite his technical competence and his whole-souled dedication to the art of poetry, he has never broken new ground. He holds to the old order of things in life as in art, and he wins my sympathy for so doing. He has dignity, high intention, knowledge of many things, and a sense of values. He has, however, made no province of life his own, he has struck no new note, he has made no music with words that was not before him, he has made no discoveries of the secrets of things. He is always on the beaten track, though he tried hard to get off of it in "The Guanches," a vagary into the Canary Islands.

He finds the material of his poetry in Icelandic saga, Italy of the Renaissance, Provence and the Greece of Constantine, Alpine flowers, and the English countryside. Had he a fresh vision of things, the old themes and backgrounds would not matter, but he has not a fresh vision of things. All his three closet dramas are well done, but *Kiartan the Icelander,* which shows "That light which Galilee on Iceland shed," is more completely realized than *Savonarola* (1904), or *Constantine the Great* (1906). *Kiartan* is all that will and work and deep sympathy for humanity can make it. It has imaginative power, too. The characters are finely conceived. It is pitched high. The final touch, though, is lacking. It never rises above good writing, good characterization and good architectonics into impressiveness of form or great portraits or pure poetry. It never takes on wonder and mystery as do the shorter plays of Gordon Bottomley on kindred subjects.

MAURICE HEWLETT

There is no more pathetic figure in all the long line of English rhymers than Maurice Hewlett (1861-1923). He tried so hard and for so many years to be a poet, and he failed by so wide a margin from being a poet. There are moments, in his prose, in which he comes within hailing distance of poetry, but in verse, despite great themes and whole-souled endeavor, there are wide deserts of words between him and the promised land. He so kindled his friends by his high intentions that some of them were persuaded he was a poet. His *Letters* (1926) reveal even so levelheaded a critic as Binyon inclining to that belief. There was never English poet had a better theme for an epical poem than Hewlett in *The Song of the Plow* (1916). It is *The Hodgiad,* the epic of

Hodge, the man with the hoe, the British laborer who has for centuries been the underling to a governing class of Norman origin. In twelve books Hewlett presents crucial moments of English history from Senlac to late Victorian times, with Hodge the man of the people always the figure in the foreground. The "envoy" sees Hodge and his erstwhile master made one, England made one, by the World War, which is worth all it cost by that happy consummation.

There are better things in *The Village Wife's Lament* (1918) than the best of *The Song of the Plow*, but they fall short of poetry by a long distance. It is the story of a soldier's wife who loses her man and her babe because of the World War. In a sense the woman's protest against war is a tract, but what you recall after the reading is over are the characteristic Hewlett pictures of the wife and her four tall sisters in their youth, and certain pictures of landscape. This that follows is as near as its author ever comes to poetry.

> When from the folds the shepherd comes
>   At the shut of day,
> The fires are lit in valley homes,
>   The smoke blue and gray—
> So still, so still!—hangs o'er the thatch;
>   So still the night falls,
> My love might know me at the latch
>   By my heart-calls.

This shows the lack of mastery of verse which mars all such work of his, his uncertain ear, his feeling for evening, a feeling he shares with so many English poets from Collins to De La Mare. There is no improvement in his art of verse from its beginnings in *The Masque of Dead Florentines* (1894) on. *Songs and Meditations* (1896) is poor 'prentice-work, *Artemision* (1909) exercises in the Greek manner. He put all his energy into *Helen Redeemed* (1913), but the poem never comes to life. *The Agonists* (1911), too, is lifeless. It is only when he has the peasant for subject that Hewlett's verse takes on a dignity that all its imperfections cannot wholly minimize. After he settled down at Broadchalke in Wiltshire in 1903, he made the simple folk, his neighbors, his chief study. Had he come to them sooner Hewlett might have found in them an inexhaustible subject for stories in prose. In verse, for all his love of his countrymen, he cannot do them justice. He sentimentalizes them, he is never wholly at ease with them, he fails to find the poetry in them that was so patent to Hardy.

EDEN PHILLPOTTS

These many years I had been reading the verse of Eden Phillpotts (b. 1862). I had read the verse with right good will, for I have always been happy in his company, in novel, in short story, in play, and in verse. Yet I could never like more in his verse, save for a phrase now and then, than its material. I never could find poetry in his verse. Then I picked up *Brother Beast* (1928). I read the first set of verses in it, "The Challenge," and I liked their material. I turned the page and came upon "The Cart-Horses." I found promise in the title. I like cart-horses, as I like most beasts I know well. I read on and came upon a picture of the two big brutes astray in the moonlight, drinking together at the side of a stream. It was not until line nine, however, that there came to me that thrill even a hardened reader knows when he comes upon poetry. Lines ten and eleven, twelve and thirteen, made me certain that here was that rare thing, a poem. The poem rose steadily to its end. It was something no man had done before:

> moonlight found their lustrous eyes and woke
> A glint of consciousness, a hint of mind.
> Now they rubbed noses, shook their heavy manes,
> Lifted their necks and neighed upon the wind,
> Then fell to whispering, their little brains
> Busy about shared interests, unshared
> By those for whom their strenuous time was spent.
> One something said, whereat the other stared,
> Then started galloping, and off they went,
> To vanish on a far, night-hidden heath.

He who wrote that is seer, and man and brother, in one, a fellow of St. Francis, of Marvell and Sterne, of Wordsworth and Hardy, of Masefield and Hodgson, and of all the rest of that goodly company of the poets that have cared greatly for dumb beasts. There are other verses that count in this late volume of Phillpotts: "The Badgers," that child and sage may both like; "The Otter" he saw "beading" in a river of Dartmoor; "Upland Birds," a pleasant gathering; and "The Water Vole," "one ray of silver pelt." In no other poem, however, is there such vision and understanding as in "The Cart-Horses." Read *As the Wind Blows* (1920), *A Dish of Apples* (1921), *Cherry-Stones* (1924), and *A Hundred Sonnets* (1929) for their blessed countryness of subjects and patient humanity, but read "The Cart-Horses" for its poetry.

SIR OWEN SEAMAN

The turn of the century was the heyday of Sir Owen Seaman (1861-1936). It was his *The Battle of the Bays* (1896) that made him generally known, and it was his *Harvest of Chaff* (1904) that showed the last widening of his powers. He was to write more amusing stuff after this, several slim volumes of it; he was to become editor of *Punch* (1906); and he was to be knighted (1914), but the full capacity of the man was already revealed. Some of the poets who were his game in the nineties and in the first decade of this century are little read now; parodies and travesties of Sir Lewis Morris, Sir Edwin Arnold, Sir Alfred Austin, John Davidson, and Sir Henry Newbolt have not the point they once had. We still read, however, Wordsworth and Browning, Whitman and Swinburne, Sir William Watson and Kipling, and Seaman's mocking but never malicious echoes of them are as good reading now as when they were written. There is more bite, perhaps, to the satire of later singers, but no such rollicking humor as we found in his earlier collections.

There are verses satiric of fads and foibles of his day in dress and manners as well as in literature and politics. Knickerbockered girls and muscular women are celebrated in "To Julia in Shooting

Togs" and "Lucy Gray." *The Yellow Book* comes in for a thwacking, and William II of Germany. Sir Lewis Morris is declared to be "master of The mediocre-obvious." Le Gallienne's love of paved streets and chimney-pots provokes Seaman to the remark that:

> London is the missus
> Of this Narcissus.

America is dealt a few knocks now and then in both "take-offs" and political satires, but our country is well treated compared to Germany and France. There are serious moments in these satires, and there are a few wholly serious poems, most of them occasional, on the deaths of writers and royalties, or on war. Seaman's verse is always well-knit, direct and cutting. There are no ambiguities in him, and no brutalities. He wields the rapier most times, the bludgeon only seldom.

ARTHUR S. CRIPPS

Arthur Shearly Cripps (b. 1869) makes his knowledge of the classics the background for his verses set to the beat of African drums. Mashonaland seems to him to lie only a little this side of Greece, and it is as surely dominated by Pan as any mountainside in Attica. He is humble before what the life of South Africa has taught him. He says of himself and his fellow-workers in the missions, "We came to teach, we stay to learn." Yet he has nothing of revelation for us of the ways of South African natives, nor any such "tone poems" as we find in Conrad's *Heart of Darkness* or in Brett-Young's *Marching on Tanga*. Cripps has traveled far in the flesh from that *Primavera* (1890) to which he contributed with Laurence Binyon and Manmohan Ghose and Stephen Phillips when they were young men in Oxford, but he has traveled not at all in spirit despite the rich experience he has had. His preoccupation is now with the country of his adoption, the atmosphere of whose veldt he has caught so well as to win the praise of Roy Campbell. There is more of South Africa, however, in Kipling's

"Lichtenberg" than in all the verses of *Pilgrimage of Grace* (1912). Perhaps it was as much as any one could ask to have two of the *Primavera* quartette "come through." Manmohan Ghose has published later in the *Garland* (1899) but his writing has not attained even to such individuality as has that of Cripps. Binyon and Phillips have their sure places of prominence and Cripps a little niche of his own.

HILAIRE BELLOC

Hilaire Belloc (b. 1870) has written delectable nonsense rhymes and a readable set of verses about the Sussex whose love he shares with Kipling and Sheila Kaye-Smith and Blunden. I have known certain lines from *More Beasts for Worse Children* (1897) ever since my eyes first fell on them. They are about the llama:

> The Llama is a woolly sort of fleecy, hairy goat,
> With an indolent expression and an undulating throat,
> Like an unsuccessful literary man.

I like his serious verse only now and then. What success it has is a success happened upon at first writing. He has himself never loved it enough to labor over it. Because I happen to care for sandy places and because they are little sung I quote:

> I never get between the pines
>   But I smell the Sussex air;
> Nor I never come on a belt of sand
>   But my home is there.
> And along the sky the line of the Downs
>   So noble and so bare.

You will find, though, passages in *Path to Rome* (1902) that are better poetry in prose than this in verse. *Verses* (1910) is an amateur's collection for all that it was published fifteen years after he began putting out books. One might quote what Stevenson said of Scott much more truly of Belloc than of its original: "A great Romantic, an idle child." And this despite an output of print that is almost Wellsian or Bennettian.

G. K. CHESTERTON

Gilbert Keith Chesterton (1874-1936) is a man of many prejudices. Without them there would be little interesting in his verse. What interest those prejudices give it, however, wanes after a second reading. It is mildly irritating, on a first meeting with his verse, to find it repeating all the familiar gibes at things American, but those gibes, read again, lose their slight sting. There is no real venom in his remarks, as there is in Kipling's, and, after all, the day has passed when the opinions of foreigners mattered much to us. We are through with all but all of Chesterton when we put down his *Collected Poems* (1932) after our rereading. There is nothing but "The Donkey" worth third reading. It is the association of the beast with Christ that gives this set of verses what distinction it has. The poet fails utterly to present the creature. The donkey is to him nothing in itself, only its carriage of Christ lends it significance. Else it is but an animal Chesterton has glanced at, not a beast known and loved. The much tooted *Ballad of the White Horse* (1911) is at once thin and wordy, a much ado about little or nothing. "To a Modern Poet" is amusing to turn to when we have a surfeit of imagism and other more boresome experimentation in verse. Chesterton is an antidote to certain absurdities of the youngest generation, but we end with calling down a plague on both their houses. There is nothing in his verse that is not in the verse of the half a dozen predecessors he follows. Even his occasional smartness only emphasizes the difference between clever verse and poetry.

MAURICE BARING

There is hardihood and a chance for life in one short poem of Maurice Baring (b. 1874). It is the "Elegy on the Death of Juliet's Owl," verses so light they are almost society verse, verses so arch and happy they rise surely to the quality of lyric. For thirty

THE VICTORIAN AFTERMATH

years and more he has been turning out stories and plays and verse of many sorts, all of it accomplished in a way, and seriously intentioned, but most of it cold and uninspired. He had, however, one lyric moment, and in it he wrote:

> Juliet has lost her little downy owl,
> The bird she loved more than all other birds.
> He was a darling bird, so white, so wise,
> Like a monk hooded in a snowy cowl,
> With sun-sky scholar's eyes.
> He hooted softly in diminished thirds;
> And when he asked for mice,
> He took refusal with a silent pride
> And never pleaded twice.

Even these charming lines sag once into amateurishness, the persistent blemish of all his writing, but their innate happiness of feeling will not be denied. In all his *Selected Poems* (1930), though, this passage is the only one of lasting delight.

What shall one say about a hundred other writers who have published one volume or more of verse well knit, freshly worded, a genuine record of experience, but in no real sense of the word distinguished? Such writers may have published prose that has won a place in literature, or only a single little volume of verse all their own but of so faint accomplishment it has made no lasting impression. One would rather mention by name none of such writers, but one wishes one's record as nearly complete as one can make it. A writer who has done such a book as *Mysticism* (1911) can afford to indulge herself by publishing *Immanence* (1912). Evelyn Underhill (b. 1875) has read her "A.E.," and she cannot divest herself of his influence. When she follows other veins than those he works she is no more original and less arresting. There is pleasantness in "Olive Song," but it might have been the work of any one of a score other writers who know their Umbria.

Havelock Ellis (b. 1859) digs out of his youth enough sonnets to make half a slim volume. He bodies it out with translations from Spanish folksong and you have *Sonnets with Folksongs from the Spanish* (1925). The sonnets are careful exercises and the material of the folksongs is a revelation of a world different from that most of us know.

Gilbert Cannan (b. 1884), the novelist, spent six years, he tells us, on *Noel* (1922) a satiric epic in seven cantos and a long prologue. There is no poetry in it, not even such pseudo poetry as he got into the prose *Miles Dixon* (1910) of his nonage, in which he caught something of the rhythm and wild-heartedness of Synge. You do follow the adventures of his South African hero with a certain amount of interest, for he, like Maugham's Philip in *Of Human Bondage*, is subjected to all the currents in politics and art and business that distinguished civilization in the days when those who are now oldsters were in their youth.

It would have been a great pleasure to have included a chapter on books of nonsense and the like. It is the exigencies of space that prevent such an inclusion. I have a very great joy in nonsense verses, and I do not believe that travesties or parodies really affect the value of what they make fun of Ridicule of any kind is powerless to affect that which is worth while. One has only to think of Meredith's test of the comic spirit, that a man must be able to see himself ridiculous in dear eyes and to correct himself by the image of himself he sees in those dear eyes to have an appreciation of the comic spirit. The verses of W. S. Gilbert (1836-1911) have been a delight to me all my days since I heard *Pinafore* as a child. I was sung to sleep when I was hardly more than an infant by the verses of Edward Lear (1812-1888). It is always with somewhat mixed feelings I recall him. In those childish illnesses that marked periods in one's young years, the visitations of chicken-pox and measles and mumps, there was always brought out in our household a set of china that was commonly known to us children as the "sick china." It had a red rim around cups and saucers, and floral designs in red and green and yellow scattered inside those bands of bright vermilion. It was always, too, in these times that

Edward Lear's *Books of Nonsense* (1846, 1871, 1872, 1877) were brought forth for our delectation. I can remember as if it were yesterday my mother singing to me "The owl and the pussy cat went to sea, in a beautiful pea green boat." That "runcible spoon" fascinated me. I never understood it, and I liked it all the better for that.

These various verses of Lear became as universal almost as Mother Goose. I have met man after man who would tell me he had never heard of Edward Lear, but who when I would quote from Edward Lear would say, "Oh, I was brought up on that." This is perhaps the greatest distinction, to have one's verses become as generally accepted as folklore. It may be that they have not weathered the years as well as Gilbert or Lewis Carroll and it may be that the nonsense rhymes of Hilaire Belloc have more or less superseded them. There is no doubt, however, but that "The Llama is a woolly sort of fleecy hairy goat" is of the very lineage of Lear. Lord Alfred Douglas has tried his hand at this sort of writing, claiming indeed that he is the inspiration of Belloc. He, too, is amusing, but it is to Lear my thoughts always revert when I read this sort of thing. The verses of Lear do not hold their own as well as *Alice in Wonderland,* but they certainly were until yesterday as generally accepted. "The Akond of Swat" is as persistent as any. Who is there who does not succumb to the sheer inanity of:

> Does he wear a white tie when he dines with friends,
> And tie it neat in a bow with ends,
>   Or a knot,
>   The Akond of Swat?
>
> Does he like new cream, and hate mince-pies?
> When he looks at the sun does he wink his eyes,
>   Or not,
>   The Akond of Swat?

CHAPTER V

The Song of Empire: Kipling and Newbolt

THERE is so much other than poetry in the verse of Kipling (1865-1936) that it is easy to forget how much poetry there is in it. People who did not care for poetry liked the vigorous measures and cubbish satire of *Departmental Ditties* (1886); and people who did not care for poetry could understand the ringing imperialism and plain and forthright speaking on known themes in *Ballads and Barrack Room Ballads* (1892). Here, too, were familiar rhythms, rhythms of the music-hall, marked, emphatic, certain, that read themselves aloud as your eye fell upon the page. Here was a poet as instant to the times as a street preacher or editorial writer. Here was a poet with none of that "music and moonlight" business that will do for sentimental moments but that is really a bit mawkish unless you are just in the right mood for it.

Meanwhile, the people who cared for poetry, and knew it when they saw it and heard it, said that there was a ballad that was poetry in *Departmental Ditties;* and that there were twenty sets of verses with poetry in them in *Ballads and Barrack Room Ballads,* and two sets of verses that were high poetry, "Mandalay" and "L'Envoi." From this second volume, the world took to heart several sayings and made them popular maxims. It quoted phrases and couplets until their familiarity began to breed contempt, but they were good sayings nevertheless. "Gentlemen unafraid" cropped up in ofter-dinner speeches. "East is East, and West is West," thus truncated, or the two lines as Kipling wrote them:

Oh, East is East, and West is West, and never the twain shall meet,
Till Earth and Sky stand presently at God's Great Judgment Seat

THE SONG OF EMPIRE

appeared as titles to newspaper editorials or brought these weighty writings to an impressive close. "The Conundrum of the Workshops" became a shibboleth of art students of all sorts. College professors abreast of the times told their classes:

> There are nine and sixty ways of constructing tribal lays,
> And every single one of them is right

applying the lines to the innumerable ways in which poetry may be written.

"The English Flag" was recited at St. George's Day banquets, and even in the music-halls. "Danny Deever" and "Mandalay" were set to music and sung by Tom and Dick and Harry to Moll and Sue and Kate.

The Seven Seas (1896) settled the business. There could no longer be any denial that a great poet had arrived. Here was the man who, although perhaps a Tory, should be made poet laureate by the Government. Yet the government made Alfred Austin, a pleasant poetaster of proper political affiliations, laureate. It did this even in defiance of "A Song of the English," in which Kipling showed that the English in our modern world, like the Jews in old time, were God's chosen people.

It was in the part of this series of songs entitled "The Song of the Cities" that Kipling said things not too complimentary about America, but we did not mind them much, for we had our own anti-foreign agitators, and an organized band of twisters of the Lion's tail, and so we properly discounted political writing parading as poetry. Then, too, he deleted the offending verses in later editions. Nor did we mind "An American," which, after all, was a rather keen analysis of our characteristics. For "An American" he made amends, after his fashion, in "The Choice," when we entered the World War. In "The White Man's Burden" he gave us advice as to what we should do about the Philippines.

All this assumption of the post of poet-prophet to the English-speaking world is better understood if we realize that Kipling regarded his function as poet to include the revelations of a seer as well as the arts of a singer. Perhaps, among his clerical forebears was a Cromwellian minister who believed he was appointed and anointed of God to lead all England into the straight and narrow path of righteousness. If Kipling could tell England what to do in world politics in "The Truce of the Bear" and "Kitchener's School" and "The Old Issue" and "The Dykes," surely he had the right to tell the descendants of Englishmen in America what they should do in their crises. Was he not, too, partly American himself by marriage and residence? All this elder-brother sort of direction was, of course, a little irritating to some of us, but it is all beside the mark. This sort of versifying is not poetry. And, at that, he atoned for a good deal of it in "Great Heart," those verses which own the greatness of Theodore Roosevelt as ungrudgingly as any verses by an American.

To many people these music-hall verses and these satires and these pronunciamentos make up Kipling. They are a part of the man surely, but they are not what make the man the poet he is. Nor do those among his verses that have to do with his art make him the poet he is. They reveal his creed, they explain what else might remain hidden in symbolic speech, but they are not what of beauty he had to give the world. I have referred to "The Conundrum of the Workshops." That is his first answer to his critics, his "apology." It had been said of his work, and it is still said of it: "It's striking, but is it Art?" And: "It's human, but is it Art?" And: "It's clever, but is it Art?" And, less often: "It's pretty, but is it Art?"

In "To the True Romance," Kipling reveals to us, as Masefield was to reveal to us later in his sonnets, that to the poet Art and Religion are almost one.

>Since spoken word Man's Spirit stirred
>   Beyond his belly need,
>What is is Thine of fair design
>   In Thought and craft and deed.

"L'Envoi" to *The Seven Seas* is another of these articles of artistic faith. The lines that end it are accepted now, I think, the world over, and in all cults and coteries and schools of art, as a truth indisputable and universal. "The Palace" is still another of these articles you can interpret in terms of everyday living or in terms of art. Interpreted either way, it proclaims stoutly the necessity of keeping the faith, of holding to tradition, of building with what has been used before in building. It is, too, a confession of the artist's inability to realize his dream. "My New-Cut Ashlar," too, is somewhat in this vein. Here, too, is summed up in a line that reaction to life that all he writes goes to prove he holds fundamental: I saw nought common on Thy Earth. This faith of his that there is naught common explains partly, perhaps, why there are so many grotesques among his verses. There is no reason, of course, why grotesques should not be good art, save that there is always a lack of serenity in a grotesque. There are verses of Kipling wholly grotesques, and these, for me, remain just verses. There are verses of his with no element of the grotesque in them, and some of these never lift into poetry. Others of this latter sort are fine rhetoric touched with poetry, like "The Recessional."

There is generally an element of the grotesque, though, even in his best poems. Among these best are "The Ballad of Fisher's Boarding House," "Mandalay," "Chant-Pagan," "Lichtenberg," and "The Return," the last three from *The Five Nations* (1903). It is not always the dialect that accounts for the grotesque in these verses. There is no dialect in "Lichtenberg." It is not always, either, a kind of offhand modernness of speech or figure that accounts for their grotesquerie. It is often due to a certain twist in the poet's mind. All sorts of old sights and experiences come back to the trooper in South Africa who gave being to "Lichtenberg." As he rode in the rain he recalled sights and experiences of his life in Australia, where, too, there was wattle, or acacia. The language, in places, is the language of the street. In other places it is the authentic speech of poetry. The vernacular diction and the diction lighted by the glow of poetry are set over against each other with sure artistry. The words of the street grow oracular in the context, the glamorous words fall into a loveliness of rhythm that holds them forever in memory. The first six lines are of the diction of the street; the last two are magical. All eight are close-packed with many kinds of meaning. There are two "readings of life" in the first six that you are not likely to forget. The one is:

> Smells are surer than sounds or sights
> To make your heart-strings crack;

and the other is:

> the big things pass
> And the little things remain.

The magical lines are:

> Like the smell of the wattle by Lichtenberg,
> Riding in, in the rain.

Between them there is that vain cry of the voices at night for what has gone on the wind. As so often in poetry, the first stanza of the poem gives in little its whole content. The four other stanzas only elaborate and apply the burden of the first stanza. Each of these four stanzas ends with a couplet that is a repetition, with slight variations, of the couplet that ends the first stanza. After you have read the five stanzas those final lines have made themselves a part of you, as does an air similarly returning in music. And these added stanzas go to prove the truth of the reading of life with which the poem opens, that:

> Smells are surer than sounds or sights
> To make your heart-strings crack.

If constant repetition to eyes and ears could make a good poem trite, "Mandalay" would be trite. We hear it on the radio, from the stage, from the lecture platform. It faces us in newspaper and anthology and the sheaf of music we are looking through. Yet we do not tire of it, or at least many of us do not. I do not, after forty-odd years. It was not quite so long ago that the truth of it was borne in upon me unforgettably. An old neighbor who had spent a year of youth in Singapore was dying by inches that hot summer. He liked to have young people sit with him of evenings on his porch, and to listen to his yarns of the East. He used to repeat again and again, "If you've 'eard the East a-callin', you won't never 'eed naught else." All the considerable success of his career lay between his experiences in Malaya and this last illness, but it was "the sunshine an' the palm trees an' the tinkly temple-bells" that had given him the chief share of romance that had come to him, and he treasured his memory of this romance above everything else now he was in the shadow of death. It is a greater tribute to "Mandalay" that it has as intimately affected thousands of us who have no memories of the East.

"Chant-Pagan" and "The Return" are closely akin. The one tells of how an irregular, discharged, has to content himself "rollin' 'is lawns for the Squire." The other does not just accept what must be. The soldier from South Africa of "The Return" philosophizes. He, too, has memories, and he tells us not only of them but of what they taught him. They taught him:

> If England was what England seems,
>   An' not the England of our dreams,
> But only putty, brass, an' paint,
>   'Ow quick we'd chuck 'er! But she ain't.

If I were to make an anthology of what seems to me best in Kipling I would include these five poems I have mentioned, "The Ballad of Fisher's Boarding House," "Lichtenberg," "Mandalay," "Chant-Pagan," and "The Return," and these eleven fellows of theirs: "The Song of Diego Valdez," "The Gipsy Trail," "Bridge-Guard in the Karoo," "Sussex," "The Feet of the Young Men," "The Way through the Woods," "Cuckoo Song," "A Charm," "The Prairie," "A Song of Travel," and "Helen All Alone." These sixteen poems are a small percentage indeed of the four hundred and over you will find in *Rudyard Kipling's Verse:*

Inclusive Edition, 1885-1932. They are the cream of the cream, each one worthy of a place in any anthology of English poetry.

If you ask me, Why not put "M' Andrew's Hymn" or "The Mary Gloster" in this company, I'll say that lyrics are nine times out of ten higher poems than didactic or narrative verses, no matter how characteristic these latter may be of their author or their time. I like very much, in their way, the out-and-out grotesques, those without any moral, like "Old Man Kangaroo and Yellow Dog Dingo," and those with a moral, like "Tommy." I like, too, such grotesque tributes as "Fuzzy-Wuzzy," but I do not pretend that any one of these three sets of verses belongs to poetry.

I would like to write in detail of all of the sixteen poems I think best of Kipling. I cannot spare the space, but at the same time I cannot pass by the twelve I have but listed without a word. "The Ballad of Fisher's Boarding House" has a restraint of starkness about it that is of a kind with the reticence of the border ballads. It is not its old story of the spite of the woman scorned, this time the lightest of light women, that gives it the place it holds in memory, or its quick killing, but the stripped bareness of it all and the irony of the failure of

> The maid Ultruda's charm—
> The little silver crucifix
> That keeps a man from harm.

The touch of sentimentality as Hans dies shows that it is not in the prose story only that Kipling has been influenced by Bret Harte. It is narrative poetry, of course, this ballad, but it has that lyrical intensity of presentation that lifts narrative into something better than itself.

I must point out that "The Song of Diego Valdez" is a lament for the lost liberty of youth. "The Gipsy Trail" is a love lyric that searches the wide world for its imagery. "Bridge-Guard in the Karoo" is a poignant echo of the Boer War, a catching of the joy the "details guarding the line" have in the mail from home and speech with the people on the train that brings it.

THE SONG OF EMPIRE

"Sussex" is the poem that gives us those two lines:

> Only our close-bit thyme that smells
> Like dawn in Paradise.

It is a celebration of the county in England that Kipling had made his home county. It is full of telling effects, instants of beauty, readings of life, but it has no other passage to put beside those two lines. There are so many lines one would quote from "The Feet of the Young Men" one ends by quoting none of them. It is hopeless to give any sense of its spaciousness, its world-wide horizons, without quoting all of it. "The Way through the Woods" has a charm of quiet in it that seems little like this man of drum and trumpets. "Cuckoo Song" would have delighted Herrick. "A Charm" takes us back to Cynewulf, but ends on a line that might be out of the George W. Russell who regards Kipling as the arch-enemy of Ireland—"Every man a King indeed!" That is not a very Toryish belief, that it is the need of England to know "Every man a King indeed." "The Prairie" is another of his many poems plangent with the home call. "Helen All Alone" is a most intense dramatic lyric.

"A Song of Travel" is Kipling's most perfect lyric. There are many sets of verses of his that are completely accomplished pieces of rhetoric. There are many poems of his that have their fine moments, but there is no other poem of his that reveals him so completely the master. It has a notable subject, and one that no man in the world is better qualified to speak upon than this world-wanderer. Emotion, images, development, rhythm, accent—all are one. The phrases are inevitable and in just accord. Stanza on stanza it develops incomparably, ending with that ringing challenge to Time that brave men have been daring down the ages:

> By our Arts do we create
> That which Time himself devours.

Space, too, man has conquered. "A Song of Travel" leaves us in that high mood in which we feel nothing is impossible to man.

Kipling is humble enough in his attitude toward his art. He knows what ups and down are his. Looking back over what he had written he must have recognized the beauty of certain lines of his and the truth of others. He must have had the very thrill he had as a young man in Vermont when he came upon, in his "Flowers," that line about our robin that is fellow to Emerson's line about the redwing and Tennyson's about the ouzel: "Robin down the logging road whistles, 'Come to me!' "

We can see the truth between the naked words, and we will admit his wide and deep experience. He has traveled all the seven seas. Bright moments and glad days have come to him wherever he has been. He has put roots down quickly in many places, deep roots in those four quarters of the earth in which he has lighted a housefire, India, Vermont, South Africa, and Sussex in England. He has a marvelous faculty for the details of places, the look of country, the scents and colors of flowers, the cries and habits of birds, the ways of maids and men. There has been hurry in such a life, necessarily. There is evidence of hurry now and then in the verses. The best of them, though, have come out of the depths of leisure. They have the fullness and breadth and serenity of great art. New as some of them seem in their impressionistic effects, these best verses hark back to old and stable things, to the prayer-book and the ballads, to Bunyan and the King James Bible. Bravely as they front the future, they are haunted with the echoes of great days gone. Kipling is Old English to the core.

SIR HENRY NEWBOLT

The patriotism of the verse of Sir Henry Newbolt (b. 1862) won it a place in public estimation from the moment of its first appearance. "Admirals All," a stirring song of Devon seamen, gave title to *Admirals All* (1897), the first of a series of thin sheaves of verse. Only Kipling has written more poems that have become part of the proceedings of public occasions in England. "Vitaï Lampada," a recitation piece in English public schools, was read to troops before action in the Boer War, and it was found still of service in heartening men in the World War. "Northumberland" is read to music when "The lads of moor and Tyne" meet to celebrate their home county. "Gillespie" and "A Ballad of John Nicholson" are part of the ritual of banquets of service men returned from India.

What Newbolt had written up to 1912 was gathered together in that year as *Poems: New and Old*. From all its two hundred and more pages are only two quotations that I remember, and both of these are from poems included in *Admirals All*, his first sheaf of verse. They are: "Play up! play up! and play the game!" and "When the strong command Obedience is best."

There is no set of verses in all Newbolt you would include in an anthology of the best in English poetry. There could be no anthology of English patriotic verse worthy of consideration did it not contain a half-dozen of his sets of verses. There is grace in certain of his lines that border on society verse, in "Imogen," for one instance. He writes himself down a servant of beauty in "O Pulchritudo," but patriotism is more to him than beauty. He is passionately proud of England, and he is only less proud of his association with certain English poets, Laurence Binyon and Andrew Lang and the late laureate. Sir Henry Newbolt might well be written down "servant of England, and friend to Robert Bridges."

CHAPTER VI

The Catholic Rhapsodists

THE poetry of Francis Thompson (1859-1907) is all but lost in its own torrent of imagery and sound and color. Now his verse is Bacchic in wild "wassail of orgiac imageries." Now its "mortal melodies" are marred by "broken stammer of the skies." Again and again the "figured descant hides the simple theme." And time on time the theme is far from simple. He can write of children with the artlessness of a Wordsworth, as in some stanzas of "Daisy." He can follow the progress of poetry through the nineteenth century with clarity, as in "The Nineteenth Century" and "The Victorian Ode." He can show the inexorableness of God's love in tracking down and capturing the soul that would elude Him, as in "The Hound of Heaven." He can write odes that many readings will not make clear, "The Mistress of Vision" and "Orient Ode" and "Ode to the Setting Sun." They are transcendental and mystical and symbolic all at once.

It is the ode that Thompson considers the lyric at its highest. In "Crashaw" he writes: "the lyric's highest form—that which is to other lyric forms what the epic is to the narrative poem or the ballad—is the form typically represented by the ode." Spenser and Crashaw and Coventry Patmore he considers the masters of the ode. It is these poets whom he follows in his own odes and ode-like poems, which make up fully the half of his verse. His most widely heralded poem, "The Hound of Heaven," is an ode, and there is no department of his poetry that does not include in its proudest attempts odes or ode-like poems. In his poems on children "Sister-Songs" is an ode, and "To Monica Thought Dying" and "To My Godchild" are similar in form. The Platonic poems in praise of Alice Meynell in "Love in Dian's Lap" are odes. There are odes on nature, "Ode to the Setting Sun," "A Corymbus for Autumn," and "From the Night of Forebeing."

Besides "The Hound of Heaven," there are "Orient Ode," "To the English Martyrs," and "An Anthem of Earth" among his religious poems. "An Anthem of Earth" is concerned, though, with so many aspects of life, it might be called as readily a philosophical poem, or a nature poem, as a religious poem. Among his poems on public affairs, "The Victorian Ode," "The Nineteenth Century," and "Cecil Rhodes" are odes. "Laus Amara Doloris" and "Against Urania," and "The Dread of Height" are odes concerned with poetry and little else. So great, though, is his preoccupation with poetry that there is hardly any poem of his that is without reference to poetry, and passages in its praise are to be come upon even more often than passages in praise of the goodness of God.

That the story of Thompson's life made good copy had something to do with the success of *Poems* (1893). That he fled to London after half-hearted and wholly vain attempts to study medicine in Manchester; that he became a wastrel of the city streets, sandwichman, purveyor of old books, and chore-boy; that he wrote verses on pieces of paper salvaged from ash-cans and the like; that he was rescued by Wilfrid and Alice Meynell from semi-starvation and the opium habit, and given the chance to become an author—all this added to the interest of his verse when it was published seven years after his coming to London. My copy of *Poems*, which I bought in June, 1894, was the fourth edition, of March, 1894. As each edition was of five hundred copies, this fourth edition meant an issue of two thousand copies in little more than three months, a good disposal of a volume of so esoteric verse for the nineties, as it would be a good disposal of such verse for to-day, for that matter.

"The Hound of Heaven" and "Dream-Tryst" and "Daisy" are here, three of the five poems of Thompson that are finished wholes. The two others—"Ex Ore Infantium," called "Little

Jesus" in *The Works of Francis Thompson* (1913), and "From the Night of Forebeing"—are found in *New Poems* (1897). There are biographical passages in these poems, but no such record of his hard years in London as you find in *Sister-Songs* (1895). In this "offering," as he calls it, to Monica and Madeline (Sylvia) Meynell, Thompson puts into verse something of the experience that paralleled De Quincey's. Thompson's Ann of Oxford Street was:

> A child . . . . a spring flower; but a flower
> Fallen from the budded coronal of Spring,
> And through the city-streets blown withering.
> She passed,—O brave, sad, lovingest, tender thing!
> And of her own scant pittance did she give,
>   That I might eat and live:
> Then fled, a swift and trackless fugitive.

Francis Thompson was luckier in most respects than his older namesake, James Thomson, of "The City of Dreadful Night." Francis was sent down into the country by his rescuers, first to a religious house in Sussex, and then to another in Wales, where he recovered his health sufficiently to write most of the one hundred and thirty poems you find in the two volumes of verse in his collected works. The volume of prose, the third volume of this collection, throws a great deal of light on his verse, by example as well as by precept. Thompson, under the tutelage of Wilfrid Meynell, wrote for *Merry England* and *The Tablet* among Catholic periodicals, and later for the *Academy* and the *Athenæum*. Some of the prose is only good journalism, but certain parts of it are as carefully written as his verse, and out of as great a delight in the subject. These parts are very like passages in his odes, fine things in themselves but none too closely related to the underlying theme, and cheek by jowl with involved and obscure passages.

It is only at intervals in this prose that his imagery gets the better of him, as it does oftener than at intervals in his verse. It gets the better of him in his criticism of Shelley, whom he elsewhere apostrophizes in verse. The light and warmth and rare air

THE CATHOLIC RHAPSODISTS 147

there are so often in Shelley's verse appealed particularly to Thompson, who, also, is intoxicated by height and sunlight. Thus Thompson writes of Shelley:

> The universe is his box of toys. He dabbles his fingers in the day-fall. He is gold-dusty with tumbling amidst the stars. He makes bright mischief with the moon. The meteors nuzzle their noses in his hand. He teases into growling the kennelled thunder, and laughs at the shaking of its fiery chain. He dances in and out of the gates of heaven: its floor is littered with his broken fancies. He runs wild over the fields of ether. He chases the rolling world. He gets between the feet of the horses of the sun. He stands in the lap of patient Nature, and twines her loosened tresses after a hundred wilful fashions, to see how she will look nicest in his song.

Thompson has here forgotten his religion for a moment in his excitement over poetry. But it is seldom he so forgets his religion. More characteristic of him is this passage from his essay on a saying of Stevenson, "A Renegade Poet on the Poet": "For poetry is the teacher of beauty; and without beauty men would soon lose the conception of a God, and exchange God for the devil: as indeed happens at this day among many savages where the worship of ugliness and of the devil flourish together." That passage, by some rare divination of what was to come, was written when there was hardly a sign of the worship of ugliness in all the arts that prevailed for a while after the World War. In his way, Thompson was of the prophets as well as of the poets.

No ode of Thompson storms along more mightily than "From the Night of Forebeing." Its sub-title, "An Ode after Easter," helps to explain some of its complexities. It is an ode to Spring.

> The great-vanned Angel March
> Hath trumpeted
> His clangorous "Sleep no more" to all the dead.

It celebrates the time when the "green spray showers lightly down the cascade of the larch," and when:

> From sky to sod,
> The world's unfolded blossom smells of God.

Light radiates through and about it, as it does through and about the "Ode to the Setting Sun," "light flagrant, manifest." There is a glow about "From the Night of Forebeing," effulgence that breaks into blinding floods of light. It is a poem of midday, but there are fellows to it with sunset splendors, fuming clouds of reds and golds and purples, a "cataract of colors." Rarer are pictures of night, when he has to endure "the abashless inquisition of each star"; or of the hours before dawn that he knew something of those nights he spent in the London streets. One belabored yet tremendous passage of dawn and early morning is that to be found in *Sister-Songs*:

> As an Arab journeyeth
> Through a sand of Ayaman,
> Lean Thirst, lolling its cracked tongue,
> Lagging by his side along;
> And a rusty-winged Death
> Grating its low flight before,
> Casting ribbed shadows o'er
> The blank desert, blank and tan:
> He lifts by hap toward where the morning's roots are
>   His weary stare,—
>   Sees, although they plashless mutes are,
>   Set in a silver air
>   Fountains of gelid shoots are,
>   Making the daylight fairest fair;
>   Sees the palm and tamarind
>   Tangle the tresses of a phantom wind—
>   A sight like innocence when one has sinned!
>   A green and maiden freshness smiling there,
>   While with unblinking glare
>   The tawny-hided desert crouches watching her.

I have quoted this long passage because all of Thompson is in it. There is imagination of the highest order here; there is the vivid-

THE CATHOLIC RHAPSODISTS 149

ness of things seen in a vision; there is the thing perfectly said in the line, "A sight like innocence when one has sinned," and there is a power of dramatization of nature in the last line, "The tawny-hided desert crouches watching her" that only the great poets may rival. There is tortured language, too, strain that results in attainment and that breaks down short of attainment. There is "lordship of language" and enslavement by rhetoric.

If it seem that what I put down here to represent Thompson be little more than a string of quotations, I can only submit that such seems to me the only way to present what he is. The strength of the man, a few poems excepted, is in lines and passages rather than in poems that are sustained wholes. He is a poet to quote from rather than to read aloud to your friends who care for poetry. It is not only that he is difficult to understand on a first hearing, but that there are long passages in all save a few poems of his that never, after many readings, take on deep significance. Dull passages, incoherent passages, weak passages crowd his poems. If you read straight through the poems, the inspired passages are obscured by the uninspired passages. You cannot get the best out of Thompson until after many readings. Puzzle out, analyze, guess, until you get the general drift of a difficult poem. Mark its great moments, its felicities, its astounding riots of imagery, its penetrations to the core of things. Then reread for the marked passages. This, of course, is not the formula for "the reading" of "Daisy," or "Dream-Tryst," or "Ex Ore Infantium," or "From the Night of Forebeing," or "The Hound of Heaven," and one or two more, "The Dread of Height" perhaps. It is, however, the best way to get the best out of most of Thompson.

"From the Night of Forebeing" is freer of obscurities than any of his longer odes, and full of fine things easy to understand. One of this latter sort is:

> Happiness is the shadow of things past,
> Which fools still take for that which is to be!

That is "a reading of life." Other passages you retain are most often picturesquenesses of phrase or lordly words rather than "readings of life." "And round and round in bacchanal rout reel the swift spheres intemperably" comes back to my mind on those starlit nights in which you sense somehow the roll of the systems through space. "For the great earthquaking sunrise rolling up beyond Cathay" of "The Mistress of Vision" becomes a parallel in your mind to a line of "Mandalay." In the prelude to his first written poem, the long "Ode to the Setting Sun," he described it as

> For Rome too daring, and for Greece too dark,
> Sweet with wild wings that pass, that pass away!

Just what makes those two lines so magical, so rousing to the emotions, so provocative of roving thought, it is hard to say, but that it does these things there is no doubt. "The liberal laugh of earth" we are aware of on days of harvest. "The blear and blank negation of all life" has an ultimateness about it that keeps it in memory;

> The stars still write their golden purposes
> On heaven's high palimpsest

is memorable as Milton is memorable.

Very different are those two lyrics of Thompson's first volume, *Poems*, "Daisy" and "Dream-Tryst," which went around the world in the poet's corners of newspapers in the nineties of last century. I was paste-pot and shears on a paper in those days, and as such it was my duty to look through all the papers that came to the exchange desk from Florida to Alaska, from Maine to California. Often as not one or the other of the two poems was printed without the poet's name, proof positive it was clipped for the verses themselves and not for the author's fame.

"Daisy" is sweet of the Sussex moor where he wandered with the child who inspired it. It is full of clarities of speech, simple and direct appeals to sentiments in which we all have a share. After the child had gone her way the poet writes:

> Still, still I seemed to see her, still
> Look up with soft replies,
> And take the berries with her hand,
> And the love with her lovely eyes.

The girl of "Dream-Tryst" is older, and the poem is a love lyric as surely as Shelley's "I arise from dreams of thee." More direct still are the lyrics of "A Narrow Vessel: Being a little dramatic sequence on the aspects of primitive girl-nature towards a love beyond its capacities." Its third poem, "Love Declared," is so far from the Francis Thompson of most of his poems that his official biographer declares it founded on fiction. That may be. At any rate, it reveals suddenly how other might all his love poetry have been had his earlier years been as those of men in the usual surroundings of youth. In "The Way of a Maid" he has the penetration to see that, under certain circumstances:

> the infinite must be
> Best said by triviality,
> Speaks, where expression bates its wings,
> Just happy, alien, little things.

In "Ex Ore Infantium" Thompson humanizes the child Christ as does another Catholic poet, our American Father Tabb, in "Out of Bounds."

There are times when "The Dread of Height" seems a fellow of "From the Night of Forebeing." It seemed when I read it at twenty-six less full of light than the longer ode, but closely knit, and packed close with truths, phrased with a happy finality. It stirred me more at forty, I find from notes in my lecture on Thompson, so many times rewritten. At sixty it seemed to me to have in it more of the tears of things than I had noted on readings when I was younger. That, I suppose, is only natural, for the tears of things become more apparent to the summed-up experience of the years.

One line of "The Dread of Height" explains much of Thompson's trouble with his poetry, his attempting of more than a man can do with words. "Ah me!" he exclaims, "How shall my mouth content it with mortality?" It is when he does so content himself that he speaks his "fellow's speech," and attains a beauty that can be clearly discerned. In another line he gives us a phrase for another of his weaknesses, "The incredible excess of unsensed sweet" in his poetry. "For low they fall whose fall is from the sky" does not soon drop out of mind, and we all confess in our candid moments our "potential cousinship with mire."

There are poets, greater and lesser, who live almost wholly in certain isolated lines of theirs. Most of the world knows only one recitation piece of Emerson, but along with it at least a dozen lines each of which expresses a truth cherished by men. There is no poem of Pope in general knowledge now, as Gray's *Elegy* is in general knowledge, but "Damn with faint praise" is even more a part of English speech than "Beauty is its own excuse for being." And "Damn with faint praise" has twenty fellows as familiar. It may be that it will be thus that Francis Thompson, too, is remembered. Certainly it would seem that the world could not quickly forget: "This essence of all suffering, which is joy"; or

> What so looks lovelily
> Is but the rainbow on life's weeping rain;

or

> I the Orient never more shall feel
> Break like a clash of cymbals, and my heart
> Clang through my shaken body like a gong.

There are those who make much of Thompson's poems on public affairs, but these were written to order, and they have not the spontaneity and large ease of the earlier odes. It is by memorable lines, scattered through all his verse, and by the five finished poems I have discussed, that Thompson is likely to be remembered. He wrote in one place that it was only his "withered dreams" that the world would care for after his death. In another and higher mood he was more confident of his future, and prayed:

> Oh! may this treasure-galleon of my verse,
> Fraught with its golden passion, oared with cadent rhyme,

THE CATHOLIC RHAPSODISTS 153

Set with a towering press of fantasies,
Drop safely down the time,
Leaving mine islèd self behind it far
Soon to be sunken in the abysm of seas.

LAURENCE HOUSMAN

Laurence Housman (b. 1865) is jack of all trades and master of one. Nobody of his day and generation can compare with him as a writer of fairy tales. He is, too, verse writer and engraver, playwright and novelist, translator and satirist. There is no one of these later offices in which he is not to a greater or less degree proficient, but what really matters is his *Farm in Fairyland* (1894) and *Blue Moon* (1904). He collected what he considered the best tales of his four volumes of fairy tales in *A Doorway in Fairyland* (1922). It is a real deprivation to the children of the race that all of these books are so hard to come by.

His moment of public response came in 1900 for *An Englishwoman's Love Letters*. This is an elaboration in prose of certain motives in the sets of verses he published in *Rue* (1899). The world passed his numbers by and in cynical mood he hoaxed it by reworking them into a series of notes from a girl to her beloved. In the end the lovers are separated by some sinister bar not of their making but dropped between them by fate.

I bought *Green Arras* (1896) when it was published, largely because of the beauty of its binding and engraving. It is facile verse but it does not stay in mind. *Spikenard* (1898), which allied Housman with Coventry Patmore and Francis Thompson, shows no strong individuality of its own. Now and then you catch echoes of his older brother, A. E. Housman, as in "1685" of *Mendicant Rhymes*. You find *A Shropshire Lad*, too, in several of the sets of verses of *The Heart of Peace* (1918). His list of over seventy books pretty nearly tells you why there is no more real achievement in his writing outside of the fairy tales. The one line of all his many verses that keeps recurring to me is "All things that shine give shade," a fellow to De La Mare's "The loveliest thing earth hath a shadow hath."

CHAPTER VII

The Decadents: Arthur Symons and Ernest Dowson

ARTHUR SYMONS (b. 1865) is better as a critic of poetry than as a poet. There are few things in life other than the arts that he can care for deeply, but he worships all the arts with a passion that is only short of idolatry. That is the weakness in all his writing, that he cares more for the arts than for the everyday little things and great things of life,—that and his lack of a sense of humor. He likes to write verse about lust; about stage pictures; about pale sunsets over water; about rain at night; about Helen and Faustus; about one dog of his, Api; about dead cities; and about little else.

Symons does not like to write robustiously about any of these subjects, but delicately. He prays for a "delicate lust" in one set of verses, but he sometimes falls into indelicacy in writing about lust. He is not original. In *Days and Nights* (1889) Browning and Tennyson are both influences, but he soon finds that his temperament is Latin rather than English, and that Rossetti is more congenial to him than any other poet among his British predecessors. Gautier and Verlaine soon displace even the Italianate Englishman as influences, however, and he makes them his masters until he is captivated by Yeats, and echoes him faintly. Whatever sort of verse Symons writes, and under whatever influence he writes, he is always a sound craftsman. And yet he has written a very great deal, practically a book a year since his *Introduction to the Study of Browning* (1886). The greater part of the writing is prose, criticisms of all the seven arts, and of the handicrafts, which he sometimes adds to literature, music, painting, sculpture, architecture, acting, and dancing to make an eighth art; and descriptions of cities; and "spiritual adventures."

The best of him by all odds is his criticism of the arts. He writes admirably of all of them. One may not agree, as I do not, for instance, with his thesis that Richard Strauss tries chiefly to express ideas in music, but one has to admit his consideration of *Thus Spake Zarathustra* and *Heldenleben* and *Todt und Verklarung* closely reasoned and intensely imaginative. I do not wholly agree, either, with his criticism of Duse, whom I have admired as much as any actress I have ever seen play, but I think his criticism of her the best I have read. I think Symons the last man, by nature and training and experience, to criticize Wordsworth, but the critic is so wholly wrapt up in poetry that he achieves the impossible and writes an illuminating essay on Wordsworth in *The Romantic Movement in English Poetry* (1909).

The very best of Symons is his criticism of poetry. He will have none of movements in the ordinary sense. In "The Tractarian Movement" he says: "a definite aim sets many minds working together, not in mere comradeship. No such thing ever happened in the creation of literature. It is each one of these poets [of the '*Romantic Movement*'] whom I want to study, finding out, if I can, what he was in himself, what he made of himself in his work, and by what means, impulses, and instincts." In these days, when a great deal of literary criticism is no more than explanation of why Poet No. 1 and Poet No. 9 are catalogued under A, and Poet No. 13 and Poet No. 29 are catalogued under Z, as fellows in this or that movement, that declaration should be announced on the housetops, and again and again and again. So, too, should this, also from the preface to *The Romantic Movement in English Poetry*: "I have tried to get at one thing only: the poet in his poetry, his poetry in the poet; it is the same thing."

Equally admirable is all the "introduction" to this volume of criticism. It is, in a way, a consensus of opinion, but it is given a unity and directness and a convincingness of presentation that could come only of so clear thinking and so deep knowledge of poetry as are Symons'. Poetry must have rhythm. Poetry must transport. English poetry almost always transforms nature, as distance in English landscape transforms nature, and the hard clarity of distance in the Mediterranean countries does not. There is a great deal to quarrel with in this "introduction" as, for instance, his declaration that the novel and the prose play are the only great prose forms, and that no one to-day knows Pomfret or "The Choice," that poem of his that so early in the eighteenth century sums all that century characteristically felt about country life. Yet there are few pronouncements in English about poetry equal to it for making clear the very nature of poetry.

Symons cannot, however, even approximate in his practice of poetry what he lays down in criticism as its cardinal principles. His is an essentially prose mind, that clear mind of the Latin that can never kindle, but that can know only the cold joy of seeing into the inwardness of art. The story of *Tristan and Iseult* (1917) that warmed the self-contained Arnold to a white glow, leaves Symons unimpassioned. Symons evidently intends his play to be bare, austere, gray as the sea that is its background. He intends, too, to have it blazing with light, as the sea blazes with light at noon, under a high sun. *Tristan and Iseult* is gray, austere, and bare, but it does not blaze with light, as it does not throb with passion. It is little of it dramatic speech either, and little of the little that is dramatic speech is at the same time poetry. It has a moment or two, but only a moment or two.

> I think that from this moment we have done
> With being happy or unhappy: all
> We have to do is only to rejoice
> Because we are together and alive

is dramatic speech, but, wrenched out of its context, it does not seem to be poetry, whatever might carry over to it of the emotion of the moment from its context. And the old doctrine, dubiously true, that is expressed in:

> Love is not love
> Unless it root up honour like a weed

has found its way into surer words than his.

THE DECADENTS

Silhouettes (1892), his second volume, is a gathering of verses of light love and satiety; of sketches of Bohemia and Dieppe; of characters, almost all girls; and of studies after Verlaine. There are unconventionalities in certain of the verses of *Silhouettes*, but little to trouble those critics of his whom Symons calls "the blameless moralists of the press." He contents himself here as a rule with such generalities as:

> Drawn blinds and flaring gas within,
> And wine, and women, and cigars.

Parts of *London Nights* (1895) are soused in sensuality. There is not much that is delicate here, and one must depart from delicate words to give a sense of their true quality. The ways of loving of his frail ladies show them true daughters of Lilith.

It is a relief when we come on verses light enough to be taken as *vers de société*, as "On the Stage," and to the country pictures, put in by sixes and sevens, when he feels we have had as many "London Nights" as we can stomach. Once in a while there is a real note of pathos, a sense of "the pity of unpitied human things" as he expresses it in the verses to Yvette Guilbert, "At the Ambassadeurs," but more often it is that unendurable thing, sentimentality over lust. Symons justifies his subjects of unsavory sort by quoting from *Modern Love* of Meredith, but what is most objectionable in such verses of Symons is not their material but the attitude of their maker and his insistence on detail. He is objectionable as Swinburne is not, or Dowson, or even "Laurence Hope" in their presentation of similar themes.

Symons is at his worst in matters of this kind in *Amoris Victima* (1897). Here there are pulings over "passion" and whinings long drawn out over the loss of the once possessed one. Worst of all is the sick satiety of body and soul that is the common end of such affairs, unless it is the doubt of the sincerity of it all that will crop up in your mind. Is it not all something to write about, after all? One remembers what Symons wrote of the hero of one of his *Spiritual Adventures*, and wonders whether "A Prelude of Life" is not self-revelation. The hero of this sketch says of himself: "I wanted to want to be good, but all I really wanted was to be clever."

Symons had been reading Blake and Wilde and Yeats and the old moralities before writing *Images of Good and Evil* (1900). There is no strong personal note in the volume and little poetry. There is carefully considered, highly intelligent, and wholly uninspired verse in plenty. There is little significance in the later volumes of verse of Symons. They are largely variations on his old themes, *The Knave of Hearts* (1913) and *Lesbia* (1920). *Tragedies* (1916) contains three plays, "The Harvesters," "The Death of Agrippina," and "Cleopatra in Judea." All are full of echoes of old plays and plays of a few years previous. "The Harvesters" tries hard to be something. Its blank verse is of good texture, but there is no surprise at all in the play, in which Mary Raven stabs her recreant lover as Nan stabs Dick Gurvil, but goes on living after. "The Death of Agrippina" looks as if it were written to go Stephen Phillips one better than his *Nero*. "Cleopatra in Judea" reveals the serpent of old Nile using her wits to escape from Herod. It is the best of the three, for Cleopatra is nearest of all the three heroines to being a creation of character.

One would be hard put to it to find one poem of power in all Symons to represent him in an anthology of late Victorian and Georgian poetry. No one stands out for me as a thing known and loved. I cannot recite from memory a single poem of his, not even one stanza of one poem. I remember one line out of "Renée," "Pallid out of the darkness, adorably white," and that she came to him from an old door, probably a stage-door, with rain in her hair. Writing that last sentence, I turned to the poem and found it was "the night in her hair," and not the rain, though there is rain in the poem, as in so many of his poems. So all I can recall exactly of Symons is two lines, one of which I care for a good deal, "The pity of unpitied human things." It is not by so little you recall even minor poets that count. It is a pity that almost the first critic of poetry of our time did not find out in the nineties that he was not a poet, and give all of himself to criticism of poetry. And yet who knows? It may be that he is all the better a critic of poetry for the plugging on at his careful and uninspired verse.

ERNEST DOWSON

There never has been more perfect workmanship in English poetry than in the verse of Ernest Dowson (1867-1900). There has seldom been a more complete realization of what a poet set out to do. His intention, however, is not always of the highest. There are times when he chooses a subject which cannot stir him to deeply impassioned writing, as, for instance, in his "To a Lady Asking Foolish Questions" and "To William Theodore Peters on his Renaissance Cloak." There are times when his writing, impassioned as it is, does not raise to dignity an ignoble subject, as "Ah, Manon, say, why is it we" or "Libera Me."

In fully half of his fourscore poems he has done fully what he intended, and at least twenty are made notable by the perfect blending of workmanship, impassioned feeling, and arresting meaning. It is only the monotony of subject common to so many of them that keeps a score of them out of the anthologies. Two-thirds of all the verses that he has written are love poems. There is no exalted love in any one, nothing comparable to the exalted love of a Yeats in "Fallen Majesty" or *The Shadowy Waters*. The most famous of them all, indeed, has in it what is sordid and ugly, and it is raised above this sordidness and ugliness only by the contrast between the poet's Cynara and the woman of the "bought red mouth." In the poet's own life was a long devotion to a restaurant-keeper's daughter who listened to his wooing but married her father's waiter. It is this beloved whom he symbolizes here as Cynara, as he symbolized her in the preface to his *Verses* (1896) as Adelaide. It was a piteous affair altogether, for the girl not only did not love him but could not at all understand his devotion and the poems that sprang of it.

Dowson is "made up" in the picture that Symons gives of him in the memoir and criticism that is prefixed to most reprints of his works. It may have been a help to the reputation of Dowson just after his death to have Symons stand as sponsor for him, but Dowson should now have the chance of being judged for what he is, and not in the light of another man's opinion of him. Resentment at this picture and at a certain attitude of patronage toward Dowson have been expressed by Somerset Maugham in *Of Human Bondage* (1915) and by Victor Plarr in *Ernest Dowson* (1914). Yet there is no doubt that, while he had the gentler side portrayed by Plarr, he "flung roses, roses riotously with the throng," that he "cried for madder music and for stronger wine." Yeats corroborates in *Autobiographies* (1927) the stories of Symons to this effect. Speaking of the restaurant-keeper's daughter, Yeats writes: "Sober, he would look at no other woman, it was said, but drunk, desired whatever woman chance brought."

The poems must have most of them been written in the quiet moods that followed Dowson's recoveries from debauchery. There is a plaint in nearly all of them. If you do not notice it at the outset of a poem, you will come upon it quickly as an underlying element of the poem. Sometimes the plaint sounds at the beginning, and rises to a moan for things that satiate and pass, that disappoint and disillusion. So constant is this sadness that we are glad when Dowson writes for a moment of something outside of himself, of other people than himself and his beloved, or of out-of-doors. Yet, just when we congratulate ourselves that he has for once chosen an objective subject, his self will intrude, as it does in "In a Breton Cemetery." For two stanzas he tells us of "fisher-folk," and "peasant-folk"

> who told their lives away,
> From day to market-day,
> As one should tell,
> With patient industry,
> Some sad old rosary,

only to have the "dear dead people" in their graves beckon to him to join them. So, too, it is in "Breton Afternoon." This poem begins "where the breath of the scented-gorse floats through the sun-stained air," but it soon strikes the elegiac note: "And why have I wept for a white girl's paleness passing ivory!"

Brittany, celebrated in these two poems, comes also into "Yvonne of Brittany." It was Dowson's best-loved part of the world, though the London docks and cabbies' midnight eating stands and Dieppe and Paris were as constant haunts of his. His way of life brought its inevitable consequences, over which, however, he never complained. "I am ready to reap whereof I sowed," he writes, "and pay my righteous debt." He paid, with sadness of spirit, and tuberculosis. All his money went, too, and he who had been brought up comfortably and sent by his people to Oxford was saved from the streets by Robert H. Sherrard, and nursed during the last six weeks of his life in a bricklayer's cottage in Catford.

Dowson is the poet of things that pass, of youth that passes, and love, and sorrow, and life itself. He has summed practically all that he had to say in the eight lines of the stanzas now prefixed to *The Poems of Ernest Dowson* (1905):

> They are not long, the weeping and the laughter,
>   Love and desire and hate:
> I think they have no portion in us after
>   We pass the gate.
>
> They are not long, the days of wine and roses:
>   Out of a misty dream
> Our path emerges for a while, then closes
>   Within a dream.

There are variations on the things that pass, but the end of many is just the passing. "A Coronal" so ends, and "My Lady April," and "April Love," and "A Requiem," and "A Valediction," and "Seraphita." Almost all the poems are on a note of futility or failure. Here are a few of their last lines: "Behold, the Weary West!" "And winter bringing end in barrenness"; "Estranged, sad spectres of the night"; "And I shall soon forget"; "Bear us on to the ultimate night"; "Sleeps the sleep which she desired"; "Beneath the drear November trees"; "Sufficient for the day were the day's evil things"; "Nor part in seed-time nor in harvesting"; "Before the great waves conquer in the last vain fight"; "Whose thorns are sweet as never roses are"; "Love's aftermath"; "Where the wan grass droops and dies"; "Yet is day over long"; "To death the host of all our golden dreams"; "And fires fade out which were not cold, Erewhile"; "The weary ways of men and one woman I shall forget"; "This is the end of all the songs man sings"; "Beneath the slow decadence of the sun"; and "Faded it lies in the dust and low." That is not all of them, but that is enough to prove how addicted he is to the gospel of defeat and death. There are men, of course, to whom such sadness is the sweetest of morsels on the tongue, but that is not the way it is with Dowson. Once, however, he does luxuriate in sadness:

> Must we grow old, and leaden-eyed and grey,
> And taste no more the wild and passionate
> Love sorrows of today!

Most often, though, the sadness of his verse is the direct reflex of the sadness of his life.

It must be that all who read have noticed how good are these lines that end the poems of Dowson. Good as they are, they are only part of the wholeness of good tissue that you find in all his verses from first line to last. I have picked out twenty-one poems that seem perfect things in their kind. Of those I care for most of the twenty-one, I have mentioned all but "Autumnal" and "Chanson sans Paroles." The music of both of these is as notable as their perfection of phrase and atmosphere and capture of mood. Dowson has been to school to Poe, but he attained to a finish that was not always his master's. He has labored hard; he has re-fused lines into a perfect stanza and re-fused stanzas into a perfect whole. His is an art far beyond any possible to the mere handler of the file.

THE DECADENTS

> Pale amber sunlight falls across
>   The reddening October trees,
>   That hardly sway before a breeze
> As soft as summer: summer's loss
>   Seems little, dear, on days like these.

All the three remaining stanzas are as this first stanza, and all fuse into one perfectly executed poem. Dowson thought that that line of Poe from "The City in the Sea": "The viol, the violet, and the vine" the loveliest line in all poetry. Dowson makes no attempt to rival it anywhere in his writing, but other effects of Poe, including a reserved use of the refrain, are to be found in "Chanson sans Paroles."

> In the deep violet air,
>   Not a leaf is stirred;
>   There is no sound heard,
> But afar, the rare
>   Trilled voice of a bird.

There is a cool monotony to that such as you find in phrases of Debussy.

And speaking of Debussy, I have always wished that he might have set *The Pierrot of the Minute* (1897) to music. Then we had had a night piece comparable to "The Afternoon of a Faun." I saw Dowson's "dramatic phantasy" played at The Little Theatre, Philadelphia, in March of 1914. Perhaps I should rather say I saw and heard it, for I had as much pleasure out of the spoken couplets as out of the stage pictures. It might have been better done, as it would have been before a more sympathetic audience, but done under such circumstances as those under which it was done, it showed a vitality on the stage I had not expected. It is not Dowson at his best, but it has charm and it is a harmonious whole, as so many structures for the stage are not.

It is, of course, a moonlit thing; but not moonlight, but a kind of half-light, is over the most of Dowson's writing. Religious as he is at times, the half-light over his poems does not suggest the half-light of a cathedral. Nor does it suggest twilight over fields greying with dew, but rather the half-light of some leafy place, such as a faun would choose to doze away noon hours. That is what Dowson always suggests, an errant faun, a Donatello moody and sad under his awakening to a half-sense of sin.

RICHARD LEGALLIENNE

In "Yellow Book" days, Richard LeGallienne (b. 1867) was experimenting in many literary forms. He did his best work, I think, in criticism, in *Retrospective Reviews* (1896), in which the young men of that time, his contemporaries, were most pleasantly middlemanned. His *Prose Fancies* (1894-1896-1900), of the borderland between familiar essay and short story, had a vogue in that time of the rebirth of preciousness. There was verse, too, in *English Poems* (1892), but it was not of such appeal as his prose. You will find "A Ballad of London" in many of the anthologies, but his later collections of verse have contributed no other poem so wholly the man and his hour. Though he later deserted London for New York, and New York for Paris, he is in his writing as resolute a Londoner as Charles Lamb. More than any other man he symbolizes the nineties, the years in which Elkin Mathews and John Lane were working so valiantly to give poetry again a hearing.

"LAURENCE HOPE"

Mrs. Violet Nicolson (1865-1904) brought "the success of scandal" of her verse to its climax in 1904 by her suicide upon her husband's grave. It is a pitiable story, that of the overstrung young wife of the old soldier, of the young Scotswoman who "went native" in her verse under the fascination of Indian ways. Hers was a deliberate attempt to become the mouthpiece of the primitive and fervid life of the East. She was silent on all the higher things of Indian religion. It was the physical side of India, the teeming fertility of its sun-smitten soil, that overmastered her. The heavy scents of tropic flowers and perfumes went to her head. The animality of the lower orders of the people was glorified in her

THE DECADENTS 165

expression of it. Cruelty was first frankly accepted, and then half-delighted in. In "Afridi Love," "At the Taking of the Fort," and "Sher Afzud" she fairly luxuriates in pain and horror. The jungle "got her" in the end.

Her records of episodes indoors are almost always vitiated by an effluvium of boudoir air that is no more distinctive, however, of the East than of the West. This atmosphere invests incidents of a sort more characteristic of the smoking-room than of print. The best of "Laurence Hope" is not, however, in these things most usual in her writing, but in her rendering of out-of-door aspects of Eastern lands. She can catch:
> the purple Indian dusk,
> With its clinging scent of sandal incense and musk,
> And withering jasmin flowers.

Descriptive poetry is seldom of the highest sort of poetry, but as we find it in "Laurence Hope" it is grateful after her over-forthright expression of the abject love of woman for her lord and master. This abject love is, indeed, the dominant motive of all three of her volumes: *The Garden of Kama* (1901), *Stars of the Desert* (1903), and the posthumous *Last Poems* (1905).

There is little in her verses that is hers alone. Outside of the Oriental prostration of woman before her beloved, her verses are largely variations on that theme Swinburne emphasized in "At a Mouth's End," a theme that left upon his soul:
> savage stamp and savour . . .
> The print and perfume of old passion,
> The wild-beast mark of panther's fangs.

There are in "Laurence Hope," too, memories of certain French stories of Africa, of Balzac's "Passion in the Desert," of Gautier's "One of Cleopatra's Nights," of Loti's Moroccan sketches. Morocco, indeed, comes into her verses as second only to India as a source of inspiration. England is so infrequently mentioned that when it is mentioned it comes as a surprise to us, as does so cool and refreshing a picture as that of the sea in "The Window Overlooking the Harbour." She is full of echoes of other English poets than Swinburne. In my copy of *India's Love Lyrics* I find I have written, by the "Song by Valgovind," "after Kipling"; by the "Kashmiri Song by Juma," "like Symons"; by "His Rubies," "à la Davidson"; and by "Kama the Indian Eros," "Tom Moore." No one can mistake the obligation of

> Maybe you were an Emperor then
> And I a favourite slave

in "Golden Eyes" to Henley's

> I was a King in Babylon
> And you were a Christian Slave

that so impressed Barrie that he "featured it" in *The Admirable Crichton*. Reincarnation is suggested in "Golden Eyes," as it is elsewhere in her verses, but it never rivals the variations on lust and love as a favored motive.

There is no questioning the success with which "Laurence Hope" fastened her verses upon the imagination of her time. She was as surely the priestess of "passion" to a generation, or at least a half-generation, as Ella Wheeler Wilcox before her. From 1902 on until the World War it was a common sight to see perfervid young women reading her in trolley-cars, and trembling and going white as they read. Her popularity lasted over into the earlier radio days, "Pale hands I loved" and "Less than the dust" being frequently on the air to wailful melodies. Even now "Laurence Hope" has almost as many champions as Mrs. Browning, but she is passing rapidly, as have passed Eliza Cook, and Mrs. Hemans, and the Hon. Mrs. Norton.

CHAPTER VIII

William Butler Yeats and the Irish Literary Renaissance

YEATS has himself suggested in *The Bounty of Sweden* (1925) that he would not even have been considered for the Nobel Prize if he had been lyric poet only. It was, he thought, because he was a founder of the Abbey Theatre, and a writer of plays himself, that his name was sent from England as that of a candidate for the Nobel honor. So it may be. England was drama-mad through all the first quarter of the twentieth century, and so great a poet and novelist as Thomas Hardy was not strongly recommended to Sweden. Sweden, too, with a realization, however halting, of what Strindberg was to the world, and envious, in a way, of her neighbor's Ibsen, was under the spell of the fashion that declared drama to be the greatest form of literature.

Though it may be his drama, or his activity in dramatics, that won Yeats the Nobel prize, it is not on his drama that his reputation rests, but on his lyrical poetry. There are only moments in his dramatic poems or in his plays in verse that are as fine as lyric after lyric. In *The Countess Cathleen* (1892), which, rewritten time and again, remains a dramatic poem and not a play, is his greatest moment:

> The years like great black oxen tread the world,
> And God the herdsman goads them on behind,
> And I am broken by their passing feet.

Those lines, great in the way lines of Milton are great, bring the poem to a close. Just before them are those other lines that will no more out of memory than the final lines:

> The Light of Lights
> Looks always on the motive, not the deed,
> The Shadow of Shadows on the deed alone.

These lines explain why Cathleen is saved, even after she has sold her soul to the devil. Her damning bargain has not held because she made it unselfishly, to buy back the souls of her people, pledged to him for food to save themselves from starving. There are other lines in *The Countess Cathleen* that are safe against the years. A peasant wife tells the devils who have corrupted her husband and son:

> You shall at last dry like dry leaves and hang
> Nailed like dead vermin to the doors of God.

That is homely and great at once, understood of all men, and as instinct with finality as death itself.

Some ten other lines and passages in *The Countess Cathleen* forced me to mark them on my last reading of the poem, my twentieth shall I say, or my thirtieth. Most of these passages made their appeal through the pictures they present, their apt putting of the ways of animals, their satire of trade, their sheer poetry.

There is little characterization in *The Countess Cathleen;* or in *The Shadowy Waters* (1900), another play as often rewritten; or in *Deirdre* (1907). That his plays are essentially patterns, or decorations, or pageants, or extensions of lyric mood, or spoken fragments of epic, has led him, unconsciously perhaps, but inevitably, to minimize character. He talks a great deal in his *Autobiographies* (1927), of the anti-self or counter-self, an objective self that enables him to escape from his subjective self. It is these two selves, however, that constitute almost all that passionately interests him, these selves and their expression in poetry. He can no more be deeply interested in another man than himself than can D'Annunzio.

There was a time when he was much exercised about ancestral memory, and when he contended that the magic of poetry was close to a real magic that put the reader of the poetry at one with the universal memory, with all the experience of the past. By this magic the reader was enabled to be a participant in old loves and old battles, in all old delights, to know all the emotions that men had known from the beginning of time. He might not, reading the poetry, be aware, consciously, of these old delights, but they gave him that thrill and rapture and ecstasy that he was so keenly aware of, but that he could not trace, consciously, to what was expressed in the poetry. In short he believed there were subconscious meanings and emotions in the written word, as well as in the reader of the written word. He has now apparently shifted somewhat from this position, being rapt away by his theory of the anti-self.

Yeats feels, unquestionably, as much as man can feel, the story of *The Shadowy Waters,* for it is a symbolic presentation of his own story. He was preoccupied with it from boyhood until he completed it in 1900, for fifteen years, we may take it. I had almost written until he had gotten it into final form. But "final form" for any of his longer poems Yeats never attains. His excuse for this constant tinkering with what he has written is that it is not really revision so much as a redreaming, after long brooding, of the poem.

Yet despite this long preoccupation with *The Shadowy Waters,* and despite the intensely personal story it embodies, there is little personality to either Forgael or Dectora. They remain figures out of faery, superhuman from one point of view, and merely such "plumed yet skinny shee" as Synge gibed at in the pictures of "A.E.," from another point of view.

Like so many poets Yeats has a quarrel with the world, with life and with death.

> All would be well
> Could we but give us wholly to the dreams

At the end of *The Shadowy Waters* Forgael and Dectora, having sent all the others homeward on her ship, drift off, alone, on his ship, into the polar mists, where death awaits them. Yeats cannot be content save with mortality.

Deirdre is a real play, with sharp conflicts and maddening moments and death. It is high tragedy, worthy of its old and noble origin in *The Three Sorrows of Story-Telling.* Why Yeats allows his heroine to try cunning to outwit Conchubar and win to the freedom of death is not wholly clear. Maybe, in his conception of the situation, she could not have stabbed herself with Conchubar's men about, and so had to demean herself to gain the moment out of their sight in which to kill herself.

Many stops are sounded in the play. It opens on doubt, on uncertainty. There follow apprehension, fear, self-controlled quiet in the face of death, panic, frenzy, studied calm, deception, the escape into death. Always there is intensity, passion, drama. Yet there is no such characterization as you meet in *Deirdre of the Sorrows* (1909) of Synge.

There are great passages in *Deirdre,* passages in which what is true dramatic speech is at the same time high poetry. One line given to the First Musician tells all the story of the love of the old king for the girl it was fabled would throw The House of the Red Branch into ruins:

> She put on womanhood, and he lost peace.

I am not sure whether that line or a line from *The Shadowy Waters* is the most memorable in all Yeats. This latter line is:

> There's nothing in the world that's worth a fear.

I dare not comment on either. What is needed is the quiet in which what is great may be taken to heart in its full significance.

There are five lines in *Deirdre* which quintessentialize Yeats as does the passage on dreams in *The Shadowy Waters:*

>   wild thought
> Fed on extravagant poetry, and lit
> By such a dazzle of old fabulous tales
>   That common things are lost, and all that's strange
> Is true because 't were pity if it were not.

The Green Helmet (1910) is a "heroic farce," a play so far removed from any life we know that it calls for some such method of presentation as that Yeats arranged for *Four Plays for Dancers* (1921), a presentation by players in masks and with such formalism as marks the Noh plays of Japan. Masks are the inevitable end of such a formalism and such a studied absence of all reality as had been having their will of Yeats as he aged. Such youth of heart as Hardy had at eighty when he wrote his mummer's play, *The Queen of Cornwall* (1923) is rare indeed. In most of us, as Yeats says: "The heart grows old."

There is sure craftsmanship in all *Four Plays for Dancers*. There is good writing, too. In *At the Hawk's Well* (1916) there is something more, high passion, what Yeats would say was sad and lonely and insatiable. In these late plays he uses musicians not only as orchestra, but as a kind of chorus. This device goes back as far as *Deirdre* (1907), but it is now developed into a system. The musicians accompany the action with drum and gong, zither and flute. They fold and unfold the shawl to which curtain and objective scenery have now shrunk. The look of the place that is background to the action is now conjured up by verses the musicians recite. There is poetry in this descriptive verse, and more characterization than is usual in Yeats. In *At the Hawk's Well* the musician chants:

> I call to the mind's eye
> Pallor of an ivory face,
> Its lofty dissolute air,
> The salt sea wind has swept bare.

I cannot help wondering whether any mask can suggest that "pallor" and "lofty dissolute air." I cannot say, for I have not seen in performance any one of his plays in the Japanese manner.

It is his aristocratic bias that has driven Yeats to this dramatic form. His art of the stage does not appeal to the many, but write some sort of drama he must. So now he writes these little plays for no more than half a dozen players and for an audience that can be gathered in a room, an audience of from fifty to a hundred.

The flair for the distinguished and aristocratic has been with Yeats from his youth, but it has grown on him with the rapidity of geometrical progression in his later years. It is natural, perhaps, in his father's son. J. B. Yeats, Sr., was not only the artist, the portrait painter, the friend of prominent men, but the scion of an old clerical stock, an aristocratically minded man with the rapture of the forward view. J. B. Yeats was one of the signers of the British memorial that recognized Walt Whitman. The older Yeats was a believer in loneliness as an inspirer of good things in all the arts, but, above everything else, in the art of life. He was a despiser of the mob. The son, who owes his father much, in encouragement, in sparks struck from the clash of their minds, in tradition and code handed on to him, is at one with his father in a belief in aristocracy. Like his father, Yeats will consort with all kinds of people, if they are interested in what he is interested in, mediums, astrologists, alchemists, students of demonology, wastrel artists and what not.

Yeats likes to think, though, of the men of his family who have played proud parts in life. He tells us much of the high heart and masterfulness of the Pollexfens, his mother's people; he likes to believe his Butler blood is from the great Duke of Ormond; and he persuades himself that his Corbets are the proper Corbetts.

Aristocracy of intellect is as much to him as aristocracy of lineage. Though in his first enthusiasm for Irish themes in Irish literature he praised patriotic poets not worthy of praise as poets, however commendable their patriotism, he soon outgrew that practice. He has never since, for policy's sake, praised in print writing that he did not admire. Nor has he written of other writers with his tongue in his cheek. He has not always been quick to recognize genius, if it was not of the kind he warms to at once. He failed to see at the outset of the career of James Stephens, for instance, what Stephens was to amount to. He recognized, on the other hand, the genius of Masefield from the beginning, and that of Sturge Moore, as earlier he had recognized the genius of "A.E." Yeats has had little tolerance for writers, however agreeable as human beings, if he has not thought them of real power. As he writes in "To a Young Beauty":

> There is not a fool can call me friend,
> And I may dine at journey's end
> With Landor and with Donne.

It is the aristocracies, Yeats writes in "Poetry and Tradition," that have made "beautiful manners." It is the countrymen who have made "beautiful stories and beliefs, because they have nothing to lose and so do not fear." And it is the artists who have made all the rest of the beautiful things, "because Providence has filled them with recklessness."

Yeats had contact with the peasant story-teller in old summers of his youth passed in Sligo. There he was well known by everybody because of his people. His great-grandfather, John Yeats, had been rector of Drumcliffe, and round about Sligo, here and there, lived others of the name of Yeats, and many Pollexfens and Middletons, of his mother's people. Place names of the neighborhood are frequent in his early writing, Ben Bulben, Knocknarea, Collooney, Innisfree, Drumahair, Lisadill, Scanavin, Lugnagall, Glencar, and the Rosses.

Both the brothers Yeats, William Butler Yeats (b. 1865) the poet, and Jack B. Yeats, Jr. (b. 1871), the painter, were well known all about Sligo before the world knew them well. I stopped at a sweet-shop in Sligo one day in the late summer of 1902 to get some bread against a climbing of Knocknarea. There was no bread. It was the wrong time of day for bread, or they were out of it, and all I could get to fortify the two of us was a piece of plumcake. Such a piece of plumcake, indestructible by man or time, reposes on a glass compote under a lid of bell-glass in every sweet-shop on the west coast. The very fellow to the one I bought in Sligo, by the bye, was thrown on to the stage during the riot over *The Playboy* on its first staging in Philadelphia, and nearly caused a quarrel between the actors O'Donovan and Kerrigan, playing Christy and Shawn Keogh, both of whom wanted it as a souvenir.

As I was buying my weighty and hard piece of plumcake in Sligo, I asked the woman in the shop, for something to say, did she know if Yeats ever lived near-by. "Which one do you mean," she answered in that counter-question reply so characteristic of the race, "Jack or Willie?" The Yeatses were certainly well known in that neighborhood.

The Irish doorman at a club in Philadelphia, on the first visit of the poet to America in 1903, knew of Yeats as a great conjurer-up of spirits, second only in power, indeed, to an eminent Catholic prelate.

It was, of course, as members of their family that the woman of the sweet-shop knew the Yeatses, but I have come on emigrants from Sligo to America who knew that "Mr. Willie" was a poet before he was announced as such in interviews in the American papers.

There were stable-boys, and men who worked in his people's pern-mill, and fishermen along the water-front, all willing to talk to the eager youth, once the mutual shyness was dispelled. It is not to be thought for a moment, though, that Yeats had Douglas Hyde's way with the country people. He was too restless and too unable to take life easy for that. Nor was he yet a good listener. One wonders is his "Biddy Hart" from life, or his "priest at Collooney," or his "woman at Ballisodare"? Later, when Lady Gregory took him about among the people near Gort, he became a better listener, but it was Lady Gregory who put into writing the stories and incidents that were told them.

There is as much from the library, though, in the first slim volume of verse of Yeats, *The Wanderings of Oisin* (1888), as from the cabins by shore and bog and mountain. The title poem, he tells us, in the notes to the edition of 1895, "is founded upon the Middle-Irish dialogues of St. Patrick and Usheen (Oisin), and a certain Gaelic poem of the last century." It tells, in a manner based on that of William Morris, of the Fenian bard's three centuries of dalliance with a woman of the otherworld. Oisin is a man in middle life, down-hearted at the defeat of his order in the great battle of Gavra, when Niamh comes to him on her horse out of faery and carries him away from his lamenting people to the island of the ever-living. But even there the "ancient sorrow of man" overcomes him, and she takes him away again, over sea again, to the island of victories, where he joys in fighting, for a hundred years, an invincible old-man-of-the-sea, an immortal demon. Then again Oisin is discontented, and again Niamh takes him away, over sea, to the island of forgetfulness, where another hundred years are dreamed away. He is lulled there by a

> bell-branch, slow dropping a sound in faint streams,
> Softer than snow-flakes in April and piercing the marrow like flame.

All these wanderings Oisin is telling to St. Patrick, in his old years, after his return to Ireland, now Christian Ireland, and much less to his liking than the pagan Ireland he had left. Yeats has left *The Wanderings of Oisin* out of his *Selected Poems* (1921). He feels, I suppose, that it is not wholly in his own manner, that it has tags in it from Mid-Victorian poetry. I am sure he would quarrel with "evening tide." Yet such a traditionalist as Yeats should remember that such phrases as that, with the associations of years about them, have far more power to move than the arbitrary symbols understood only by a little clan.

It has long seemed to me a pity that Yeats allowed his instinct for narrative poetry to be sidetracked by his bias for the drama. He took to drama partly for his love of the spoken word and partly because he felt his countrymen would not read poetry but would listen to the spoken word in plays. As a matter of fact, as the movies were to prove later, it is the action rather than the spoken word that brings audiences to the theater. It may be true, though, that Yeats did increase a love of literature in Ireland by the Abbey Theatre drama he sponsored. It was certainly an audience of more than usual intelligence, small though it was, that the Abbey Theatre gathered and developed.

Yeats early interested Arnold Dolmetsch in the making of a psaltery to which verse might be spoken. He might well have adapted the use of such a psaltery, or some other sort of lyre, to the accompaniment of the spoken tale. He might have introduced a fashion of epic chanted in hall that would have been to our day what the recitals of the bards and minstrels were to old times. It may be that such a form of the retelling of the Deirdre story, or the Grania story, would have better suited his powers than drama. He has hardly either the room or the time to bring home fully to an audience the story of Deirdre and Naisi and Conchubar and Fergus in the compass of so short a play as is *Deirdre*. Those who do not come to the theater with a knowledge of the story must have a hard time taking in its full significance in the brief hour on the stage.

The story of Deirdre is the great story of the courtly cycle of Old Irish Romance, The Red Branch Cycle. Its stories of Cuchulain are only less important. Yeats has written on several of these Cuchulain stories. "The Death of Cuchulain" was one of his earlier narratives, a narrative a little short of a hundred lines. This same death of Cuchulain, in fighting the waves of the sea, is the episode that ends *On Baile's Strand* (1904). It follows here, as it did in the earlier narrative, his killing, not knowing it is his son, of that son, in a combat like that in which Rustum kills Sohrab. Cuchulain has part, too, in *The Green Helmet* (1910), *At the Hawk's Well* (1916), and *The Only Jealousy of Emer* (1919). In none of these plays do you receive so decided an impression of the hero's personality as you do from the Old Irish epic, the *Tain bo Cuailgne*, as you find it, say, in *The Cuchullin Saga* (1898) translated by Eleanor Hull.

Many poets, as they grow older, hate to acknowledge the power of their early verses. Their pride in present accomplishment is too great to allow them, like Swift, looking back on writing of his youth, to cry out: "My God! What a genius I had then!" On one of his American tours Yeats told me that he always liked best the poem or play that he had just finished, and, after it, *The Shadowy Waters*. He did not include it, however, in his *Selected Poems* (1921), and that must be taken to show it has lost place in his estimation, to be a lesser thing than *The Countess Cathleen*, *On Baile's Strand* and *Deirdre*, there included.

He is half-tired, too, of "The Lake Isle of Innisfree," resenting, perhaps, that part of its reputation is from its praise by Stevenson. With many of his generation, he registers the extremity of the swing of opinion away from the late Victorian idol. Yeats does say, however, in his *Autobiographies*, that "The Lake Isle of Innisfree" is the first poem in which his own manner asserts itself strongly, though he deprecates the old ballad tag of "I will arise and go now." The truth is that that phrase, so familiar from "Willy Reilly" and a host of other ballads, at once awakens the sympathy of what is known and loved to every reader brought up on Irish ballads, the very audience for which Yeats believed he was writing and for which he wished to write. I have had experience on experience that proves the appeal of the known and loved. In talking to an Irish audience, an audience that would call itself an audience of intellectuals, I have had it listen with attention, but with no enthusiasm, to a discussion of Ireland's leading contemporary poets and to liberal quotation from them; and then break into spontaneous applause at the recitation of Brian O'Lynn rhymes we had all known from childhood. The appeal of the known and loved cannot be gainsaid. Nor is there any shortcoming of taste in responding to this appeal.

It had been better for Yeats had he spent more time in his youth with the country people about Sligo, and less with his spiritualistic uncle, George Pollexfen. It is the lack of the common human that prevents the wide appeal of a great deal of the rarest work of Yeats, poetry as exquisite as any English poetry. Its abstraction alienates even many to whom poetry is a large share of life. The arbitrary symbolism of much of his poetry is another bar to appreciation of it, and its distance from the daily interests of men results in many lines of it taking on a formality that affects readers as does the formality of rhetoric. As sometimes in Milton, one misses what the eloquence is about.

Rhetoric, of certain kinds, Yeats abhors, especially the sentimentalized rhetoric of the patriotic poets, but he too often only substitutes for it a rhetoric of his own, a rhetoric of esoteric things. That fine poem, "The Valley of the Black Pig," fails of its effect at the end, its "Master of the still stars and of the flaming door" ringing on the ear, in its abstract symbolism, like a stereotyped phrase, and one alien to the spirit of the poem, and to the quality and associations of the rest of the lines. The Rosicrucians and Old Irish legend lie down together no more quietly than the lion and the lamb.

Since Yeats excludes them from his *Selected Poems*, most of the verses from *The Wanderings of Oisin* and *The Countess Cathleen* volumes must no longer be considered by him of his best. He retains four poems from his first volume, and seven from his second, and he relegates to "Early Poems" (1885-1894) two poems from *The Wind among the Reeds* (1899). It is "The Rose of the World" that is the large omission from the second volume, and the title poem, *The Wanderings of Oisin*, from the first. *The Wanderings of Oisin* has a freshness of feeling and a freedom of movement and a luxuriance of imagination that are lacking from his later works. There is a frank humanity about it, too, that is not to be found again, save at moments, for, though the love story running through all his writing is human enough, its humanity is hidden by a number of devices. It is hidden by symbolism, by presentation through legends not familiar even to most readers of poetry, and by that studied abstraction upon which he prides himself. One's poetry must be austere, he holds, aloof, aristocratic, hierophantic, dressed up in what he calls "Mask and Image," that it may be understood wholly only by the elect. Like so many of the poets of his country, he harks back, consciously or unconsciously, to the riddling bards of Gaelic Ireland. It had been easy for him to "learn to chaunt a tongue men do not know."

In the poem from which I quote, "To the Rose upon the Rood of Time," Yeats almost professes himself a fellowy man. At other times he is wilful in putting off his humanity. In *Autobiographies* he writes: "As I look backward upon my own writing, I take pleasure alone in those verses where it seems to me I have found something hard and cold, some articulation of the Image, which is the opposite of all that I am in my daily life, and all that my country is." Yeats, I think, deceives himself. The Image, or as he calls it more exactly elsewhere, the Mask, is often the very reflection of the man Yeats. His abstraction at times holds him apart from all oneness with his kind. He often falls into a state of mind that is almost waking trance when he is preoccupied with some concern of his, even when there are people about. He can, however, wake up suddenly, and lay about him with characteristic Irish vigor. He has courage and address and resourcefulness in controversy, but always he delights to slip away from the usual, the obvious, the common. Too often that means from the human, too. The marvel is, with his preoccupation with art and spiritism, he continues to be as human as he is. Fortunately he has not been able to do with himself as he would. Sometimes one cannot but wonder if, after all, a good deal of this talk about Mask and Image is only romancing, just another breaking-out of national instinct. Whatever it is, one has to accept the talk as part of Yeats, it and other characteristics more or less inimical to poetry.

So one has to accept the Rosicrucianism of Yeats, all the machinery of Michael Robartes and Owen Ahern and the Judwalis and Kusta-ben-Luki, as one has to accept the peculiarities of one's friends. Where there is so much that interests and attracts, so much that delights and entrances, where there is genius in short, one must be content with more than a little that is repellent.

There are some who hold all this business of ultra-mysticism as little more than an affectation, a very different thing from romancing. In romancing you make all that is to be made out of something that interests you, you let your imagination play with it. In affectation you profess something in which you do not really believe. The ultra-mysticism of Yeats is not affectation, it is at best a vagary, at worst an obsession. What is hardest to bear in this mysticism is not that it mars his verse, as it undoubtedly does, but that it must have stifled often his writing of verse. He complains that composition is difficult to him. Composition that amounts to anything generally is. Only the greatest geniuses know the ease and sweep of the flight of the eagle, and very few of the smaller geniuses know the grace and swiftness of the flight of the swallow. With difficulties in the way of his composition at all times, the added burden of such complexities as he delights in must again and again deter him altogether from writing. "The fascination of what's difficult" too often fastens itself upon him, to the detriment of his art.

The intention of Yeats, when he began to write, had been different from all this. "When Lionel Johnson and Katherine Tynan and I, myself, began to reform Irish poetry," Yeats writes in "Poetry and Tradition," "we thought to keep unbroken the thread running up to Grattan which John O'Leary had put into our hands, though it might be our business to explore new paths of the labyrinth. . . . I was more preoccupied with Ireland, and . . . took from Allingham and Walsh their passion for country spiritism, and from Ferguson his pleasure in heroic legend, and while seeing all in the light of European literature found my symbols of expression in Ireland."

Yeats is candid enough, outspoken enough, unenigmatieal always, in his autobiographieal or critical or propagandist writing. He owns up frankly when he changes his point of view. That has been often, so we need not take too seriously declarations about his art that do not agree with his practice of it. Yet, on the whole, his shifts are not so great as they seem on our first notice of them.

In this critical and propagandist writing of Yeats there is at times, however, a vehemence and an overstatement that we have come to look for in Irish controversy, that spirit and habit of mind that make Wilde and Shaw and George Moore forget proportion and lay about them on friends and foes alike. With his usual candor Yeats admits the like of himself, also in *Per Amica Silentia Lunæ:*

When I come home after meeting men who are strange to me, and sometimes even after talking to women, I go over all I have said in gloom and disappointment. Perhaps I have overstated everything from a desire to vex or startle, from hostility that is but fear; or all my natural thoughts have been drowned by an undisciplined sympathy.

This is the confession of a man ill at ease with his fellows, unable to be his natural self, who finds it impossible to "take life easy."

Another confession in this same book, as full of self-revelation as anything he has written, tells us more openly than all other confessions of his, how hard life has been for him:

> I think the common condition of our life is hatred—I know that this is so with me—irritation with public or private events or persons.

Make all due allowance for the hypocrisy of most of us, for our suppression of what is unpleasant in our lives, our wilful blindness to the way things are, our instinctive putting of the best face on things, and such a declaration as this would yet be an exaggeration of the situation as it is with most of those who have prospered at all. It sounds like a complaint of youth, or of the unsuccessful man. Yeats is neither young nor unsuccessful. It must be a revelation of excessive sensitiveness, or of an unworldly expectation of having things as one wants them. Perhaps now that he has a house, and family, and an acre to play with, the heart-easing hours will grow more with the years.

Despite all these difficulties and these irritations, and despite a long struggle for pounds, shillings, and pence, Yeats has been constant in the service of art. His dallyings with spiritism and Rosicrucianism have turned him from his art only for a time. His strength and his weakness have always lain in his devotion to his interests, his art of poetry first among them. Indeed his devotion to his interests might be said to have given him little time to live. For a man who all his life has been a public man, he has had a narrow experience of life. He has traveled far, but he has never gotten away from himself. He has met many men and many women, but he has not known well many women or many men. He can hardly interest himself in his fellows if they are not artists or Exhibits A or B or C of spiritism.

Yeats was for all his youth and young manhood and full manhood as constant in love as in his art of poetry. And yet the critics of poetry have had little to say of his devotion. The very human love story that runs through all his verse has been more or less lost sight of in the legendary and symbolic character of much of that verse. The great lady who gives her name to *The Countess Cathleen* is imagined from this love of his. The restless heart of Maire Bruin in *The Land of Heart's Desire* (1894) was the restless heart of his beloved. It was to grow "out of fashion," this love, "like an old song." In the end it had become to him a

> monstrous thing
> Returned and yet unrequited love.

Between 1892 and 1917 this passion made itself a part of more than forty poems and plays, a good few of them among his most notable achievement. In *The Countess Cathleen* you feel that the protest of the bard Aleel against the selling of her soul by the Countess, for Ireland's sake, is the protest of the poet against his lady's giving up of her personal happiness for her country's sake.

In *The Wind among the Reeds* there is reference to her in "Aedh Tells of the Rose in His Heart," "Aedh Laments the Loss of Love," "Michael Robartes Bids His Beloved Be at Peace," "A Poet to His Beloved," "Aedh Gives His Beloved Certain Rhymes," "Michael Robartes Asks for Forgiveness Because of His Many Moods," "Aedh Tells of a Valley Full of Lovers," "Aedh Tells of the Perfect Beauty," "Aedh Hears the Cry of the Sedge," "Aedh Thinks of Those Who Have Spoken Evil of His Beloved," "The Poet Pleads With His Beloved for Old Friends," "Aedh Pleads with the Elemental Powers," "Aedh Wishes His Beloved Were Dead," and "Aedh Wishes for the Cloths of Heaven." I have listed the poems with their original titles, in which appear the names of Aedh (Hugh) and Michael Robartes. In *The Collected Works* (1908) and in *The Selected Poems* (1921), Yeats has substituted "Lover" or "Poet" or "He" for the names of his imaginary anti-selves, or other selves, that he first used. The words we know, in place of the symbolic figures we can understand only with difficulty, make the poems more human under their later titles.

There is a certain unreality, a dreaminess, even a kind of make-believe at times, about these earlier love poems. The poet has still a joy in the sorrow of defeated love. The lady is not his, but she is not, after all, another's. One wonders, to use his own words about Spenser crossed in love, "if his lamentations come out of a broken heart or are but a useful movement in the elaborate ritual of his poetry, a well-ordered incident in the mythology of his imagination." After all, out of his disappointment, he was able to build a "sorrowful loveliness," just as surely as "Out of the battles of old times." No one of them has a clearer beauty, and more untroubled, than that he now calls: "He Wishes for the Cloths of Heaven," a perfect lyric of eight lines. It is that in which he beseeches his beloved, since he has spread his dreams under her feet, to "Tread softly because you tread on my dreams."

Yeats can dramatize his beloved with a certain amount of objectivity in *The Shadowy Waters* (1900), that icy dream of all-for-love-and-the-world-well-lost. It is his lady's grand air, the embodiment of her country's ideals in her mien and carriage and bent of mind, that inspire his *Cathleen-ni-Houlihan* (1902). His lady here is not only his beloved but very symbol of Ireland. There is no clearer likeness of her than that which is given to Cuchulain as his description of Aoife, the Amazonian Queen of Skye, in *On Baile's Strand* (1904). Even as late as 1907, when he draws his Deirdre, in *Deirdre,* after her image, he can keep himself out of the picture. She breaks into his poem "The Old Age of Queen Maeve." In her courage, in her leadership, in her pride, in her power over words, she was of the lineage of this great Amazonian Queen of Connacht, the gray cairn of whose fabled burial-place rose on Knocknarea, that mountain across Sligo Bay from Drumcliffe and the Rosses, where Yeats spent so many days of childhood and youth.

After her marriage to another; her neglect by her husband;

her unhappiness; her loss, in a degree, of her dignity and position; it is no "ritual of his poetry" you find in his verses about her, but cries out of a sore heart.

There is a series about her in *The Green Helmet* (1910), "A Woman Homer Sung," "That the Night Come," "The Consolation," "Friends," "No Second Troy," "Reconciliation," and "Peace." The first of the series gives us, by its title, a phrase to describe women of all time, from Helen to Dona Rita, that have heroic mould, and fated beauty, and fascinations, "A Woman Homer Sung." The strong human call sounds in "The Consolation," in which he wonders if his love had prospered, would he

> have thrown poor words away
> And been content to live.

We know that Yeats would never have "thrown poor words away." In his youth he wrote "for words alone are certain good." That belief, in its right interpretation, is his to-day, as it was fifty years ago. He will write on to the end, more and more austerely, perhaps, and with that hard sureness of phrase that has grown on him with the years.

The sequence of love poems continues in *Responsibilities* (1914). "A Memory of Youth," "Fallen Majesty," "Friends," "The Gold Heaven," and "That the Night Come" carry on the story. The sequence all but ends in *The Wild Swans at Coole* (1917), with "Memory," "Her Praise," "His Phoenix," "Broken Dreams," and "A Deep-Sworn Vow." It must be he met her again as she was ageing. Yet he went on singing her praise, "stubborn with his passion.... When age might well have chilled his blood."

The end is as ironic as the most modern heart could wish, and as natural, and as human, and as right. He married a young woman in 1917. A daughter and a son were born. The poet had something better to leave his old ancestors than a book! Out of this new life as a married man come the volumes of verse, *The Tower* (1928) and *The Winding Stair* (1933). The old building, tower and farmhouse in one, with its mounting steps, that gives title to these little books was near Ballylee in Galway, that western land he came to know so well in his middle years. The tower was near the site of the cottage where once lived Mary Hynes, the woman of a hundred years ago whose beauty is still a living memory in the neighborhood.

We see this new life in his later middle years beginning to affect his poetry in *The Wild Swans at Coole* (1917), in "Men Improve with the Years." He makes Robartes say of him, Yeats, in "The Phases of the Moon" that he has

>   chosen this place to live in
> Because, it may be, of the candle light
> From the far tower, where Milton's platonist
> Sat late, or Shelley's visionary prince.

Though Yeats may have had some such reasons as those here hinted at for choosing the tower at Ballylee for his home, the results, as far as his poetry is concerned, were much those you would expect in any domesticated man. He had been interested in insects and birds and the lesser beasts from his young years, and he now wrote about them with a new interest because they inhabited his own acre. There was no mention, however, of a badger, his favorite among the animals. It was not secluded enough, I suppose, for that retiring fellow. Yeats wrote about those who were once neighbors here: Mrs. French, whose serving-man brought her "an insolent farmer's ears" which he had clipped off, in a little covered dish; and Mary Hynes, the peasant beauty; and Raftery, the blind poet, who made a great song on her. He writes, too, of "an affable Irregular, A heavily built Falstaffian man," who passes by; a starling by his window; a water-hen and cows; honey-bees; children in a convent school; and his own children and their mother. There were echoes still, in "A Man Young and Old" and in "The Tower" of his old love story, one grouchy and one agonized. Nor did he free himself of Robartes and Ahern and the Rosicrucian incubus, but the larger part of these books, old man's musings though they be, are about things that many people can interest themselves in.

I had wondered, as I read the poems of Yeats in which he told of the great love of his life, and the poems in which, in age, he told of his disappointments in life, had he thought of Dante and Beatrice and of the exile of Dante. In 1918 as I was reading the verses anticipatory of *Per Amica Silentia Lunæ*, I knew that he had. These verses, called "Ego Dominus Tuus," are a dialogue in which speak "Ille" and "Hic." To the latter are given the lines:

> The chief imagination of Christendom,
> Dante Alighieri, so utterly found himself
> That he has made that hollow face of his
> More plain to the mind's eye than any face
> But that of Christ.

All through the writing of Yeats you will find passages in which he girds at the world and himself. In *In the Seven Woods* he resented being "thought an idler," and in *The Tower* he shows how strangely sensitive of opinion he must be at heart, he who seems to be, and should be, by his life, as sure of himself and as independent of spirit and as indifferent to what people think of him, as ever man was. He who has been first a public man to Ireland evidently had cherished some secret dream of being even more of a public man than he has been. Yeats is to Ireland the founder of a school of literature which has given modern Ireland a place in the literature of the world. All men who read the papers know him to be that, whether they are indifferent to literature, or whether they disapprove of the kind of plays his theater, the Abbey Theatre, puts on its boards. He is the inspirer of Lady Gregory in her work of translation from the old Irish legends, as well as in her work in farce. He is the discoverer and encourager of Synge. He brought George Moore back to Ireland. He gave Dunsany his first chance on the stage, even if he tried to bend his genius in a way not natural to it. And if his candidature for the Nobel Prize originated in England, he was the first Irishman to win it.

Yeats has spoken on the Irish drama, and on the Irish Renaissance generally, in Great Britain and America and Sweden, as well as at home. He is known in France, and in Italy. He is better known throughout all the world than any Irish writer save Shaw, and he has the standing of a poet, while Shaw, an expatriated man, has only that of the satirist and propagandist. And yet his position fails to satisfy Yeats, not only because human ambition is unappeasable, but because, maybe, he has a feeling, deep down in him somewhere, that he failed to win the love of his youth because he was not a man of action.

Yeats vindicated the position of the poet in *The King's Threshold* (1904), as one who should sit at the high table of the king with druid, brehon, and warrior. He has never overcome the feeling, however, that the man of letters is not, as such, recognized as of the first rank of men when compared with millionaires and warriors and statesmen. Such a feeling is not his alone. Another distinguished poet told me that he was given a place at table at the banquet of the graduates of his college below the places of his fellows successful in finance and industry and government. Civilization in English-speaking countries had been slow to recognize the place of the artist. It is not so strange after all that Yeats is disappointed, in a way, with his career.

Poem on poem of Yeats proves that he loved the physical Ireland, the look of the land, places in forests where there is "pale green light" under beech-trees; brown bogs where "dews drop slowly" at twilight, and curlews call; "the cromlec on the shore" and "the grey cairn on the hill." Yet he has always minimized description of landscape, made it only the background for mood or action, never painted it for its own sake. So often is it the landscape under twilight that he alludes to, that those who called the school of verse he inspired "the twilight school of poetry" had here justification for the term, as well as in his book of sketches, *The Celtic Twilight* (1893). The word "twilight" itself occurs again and again. There are "twilights of dew and of fire," "twilights of rest," "druid twilight," "grey twilight," "odorous twilight," and many of the like. There are even more descriptions of the hour itself, descriptions perfect in kind. As often, almost, as you come under the spell of twilight in the poems of Yeats, you hear the wind in them, slipping by in the faintest murmurs, rustling the leaves, moaning about the house-corners. Yeats loves the wind and hates the wind. Man is, he says, in one place, "a hater of the wind." In another he cries: "There is enough evil in the crying of wind." Yet at another time, he finds dream more blighting than the wind:

> No boughs have withered because of the wintry wind:
> The boughs have withered because I have told them my dreams.

Yeats praises the wind, though, in "Running to Paradise," whether in his own person or dramatically you can take your choice. Yeats is never better than in such songs as this "Running to Paradise," songs of irresponsible men, fools, jesters, and beggars. "The Cap and Bells" is another of the kind, "The Happy Townland" a third, and "The Song of Wandering Aengus" a fourth. There is a new music in these verses, and magic, and surprises in the imagery that freshen the mind and restore its youth. You must say the same about the poems of twilight and of the wind. And you must say the same about the few lyrics of *In the Seven Woods*. "The Withering of the Boughs," "Under the Moon," and "Red Hanrahan's Song about Ireland" are a trio you would have to make part of any anthology of the best in English verse. In that anthology you would have to place at least every other poem of the thirty-seven of The Wind among the Reeds, eighteen of them surely. From *The Countess Cathleen* you must choose "The Rose of the World," which its author leaves out of his *Selected Poems*, possibly because it does not belong wholly to his "canon." You must choose, too, "When You Are Old," "The Sorrow of Love," "The Lake Isle of Innisfree," "The Two Trees," "The Rose of Battle," and "To Ireland in the Coming Times." From *The Wanderings of Oisin* "Ephemera" must be included; and "The Falling of the Leaves," Tom Moorish though it is; and "The Meditation of the Old Fisherman"; and "Down by the Salley Gardens"; and "To an Isle in the Water."

There are fewer poems to be chosen from the later volumes of lyrics. For years after 1903 drama absorbed most of the energies of Yeats, perhaps to the lessening of the number of lyrics that he wrote. *The Green Helmet and Other Poems* (1910) shows tendencies toward epigram and satire, almost certain signs that lyric feeling is drying up. Of its twenty-five poems, "A Woman Homer Sung" and "No Second Troy" stand out among the eight love poems, all very much of one tone. The shorter poems from *The Green Helmet* are reprinted in *Responsibilities* (1914). Among the new poems added there is "Running to Paradise" and, perhaps, "September, 1913," to add to the anthology of the best of Yeats, and hardly another one. *The Wild Swans at Coole* (1919) gives its title poem to such an anthology, and "Broken Dreams." I can find no third of the standard of his best up to 1903.

I know those, generally very young men, who think very highly of the verses of *The Tower* (1928). I like certain kinds of hardness, as well as any man, what I call the right kinds of hardness, such a hardness as you find in the form and finish of Frost; and I like austerity; but I like also a light of dream or of passion that transmutes hardness and coldness into beauty. I like what Yeats himself describes when he refers to his desire to write

> one
> Poem maybe as cold
> And passionate as the dawn.

I do not like, however, that kind of hardness and coldness that leaves lines, intended as poetry, rhetoric only.

There are many single lines and couplets in the verses of *The Tower* that arrest you and fix themselves on your memory, but there are few poems that have wholeness of such tissue. There is querulousness here, Job-like lamentation over the approach of old age, even an echo of a contemporary poet, which Yeats himself acknowledges. There is a catching, for the first time by Yeats, of the quality of eighteenth-century poetry, in a very beautiful picture of a formal garden, a passage that Pope would have liked.

I shall not forget, either:

> only an aching heart
> Conceives a changeless work of art.

That is an axiom very close to many in his father's letters to the poet. I shall not forget, either, "the cold snows of a dream," it so accurately describes so much of the writing of its maker. I like "Those winds that clamor of approaching night." It is a fellow to the menace of "winter and evening coming on together" of Frost, which I have long liked.

The artist's scorn of the world, its pettiness, its indifference to beauty, its low scale of values, a scorn he has held from the beginning, has grown on him with the years. Once expressed with a cold and detached hate, it now drives him to acrid scolding and now to delight in death. The world is a "pragmatical, preposterous pig of a world," and wonder descends upon him to question:

> Is every modern nation like the tower,
> Half dead at the top? . . .

These themes are recurrent in *The Winding Stair* (1933), a volume that is remarkable for a severe and ascetic art and for a thinking unblunted by age. *The Winding Stair* breaks no new ground, however, it achieves no tones unachieved before, all its notes have been already sounded in *The Tower*. There is a humanity, a right softness of mood now and then, that had been rare in his writing except when memories of childhood informed it. Yet in the end of all he questions, in verses appended to *The King of the Great Clock Tower* (1934):

> Why should I seek for love or study it?
> It is of God and passes human wit;
> I study hatred with great diligence
> For that's a passion in my own control,
> A sort of besom that can clear the soul
> Of anything that is not mind or sense.

A Full Moon in March (1935) is but a rewriting in verse of *The King of the Great Clock Tower* published earlier in the same year. Another rewriting in verse of *The King of the Great Clock Tower* follows "A Full Moon in March." There are some lyrics rewritten and a few new ones added.

The binding and printing of *The Winding Stair* is as beautiful as those of all the books of Yeats from *The Wind among the Reeds* onward. Its cover design, like those of several of its predecessors, is by Sturge Moore. None of us can be indifferent to the format of the books we read, and Yeats has been fortunate in nearly all his editions. His *Collected Works* (1908), with portraits of him by his father, J. B. Yeats, Sr., by Shannon, by Sargent, and by Mancini, is surpassed by no collection of any English poet. In all his endeavor Yeats has always been a devoted servant of beauty.

Yeats has been to his time, too, as great an inspirer of genius as Coleridge in his time, a hundred years earlier. His labors in behalf of Ireland were recognized by his choice for the upper house of the Free State parliament. What matters most to us, though, in a consideration of English poetry, is the nearly fifty lyrics of his that could be kept out, with difficulty, of an anthology of the best poems in English. Throw out half of these fifty, and there remain more poems of his to be included than of any other poet save Shakespeare and Wordsworth and, possibly, Browning. Despite the lack of fellowliness in Yeats, despite his Rosicrucianism, despite his symbolism, despite the unfamiliarity of the names of the Irish heroes and heroines in his poetry, he has given us as many lyrics of high beauty as any other English poet. The sheer poetry there is in the man absorbs and sublimates and transmutes, in fully half of his poems, the unpoetical elements he insists on putting into them. Did he not insist on all this detritus of study and speculation there would be no poet of his century to transcend him.

G. W. RUSSELL ("A.E.")

Yeats is more than a poet. It were enough were he a poet only, but he is more. He is the inspirer of a school of drama; he is the discoverer and encourager of poets; he is an interpreter of art. He is, too, in a way, a public man in Ireland. Yet after all is said nine tenths of what matters in Yeats is his verse. It was far otherwise with George W. Russell (1867-1935). One tenth of what mattered in "A.E." was his poetry. Another tenth was his painting. Eight tenths of what mattered in him was his service to Ireland in governmental activities and public service. That service was over, however, several years before he died. For years, though, "A.E." was not only Sir Horace Plunkett's right-hand man in the Irish Agricultural Organization Society, but the interpreter of Ireland to the world, the man whose middlemanning did most to explain Ireland politically and economically to itself and to other countries. It was he who answered what he regarded as Kipling's slur on Ireland at the outbreak of the World War. It was he who was striving to tell America what a blessing to the world was the experiment in government going on in the Free State.

Russell had tried to be, and for a number of years he succeeded in being, to Ireland what Emerson was to America and to a large part of the world elsewhere, the friend and aider of those who would walk in the spirit. "A.E.'s" service as an editor of magazines, as a discoverer of genius, and as a reconciler of warring factions was for years a notable service. It was the personality of the man that enabled him to perform so many differing functions. He had such a way with him, so great an influence at one time that his aid was almost necessary to the successful exploitation of any new project in Ireland. Perhaps time will adjudge his advocacy of coöperation in agriculture, his methodizing of new ways of marketing crops, as his greatest service. He wheeled over large areas of Ireland on his bicycle, meeting thousands on thousands of people personally and winning them to modern methods by his gifts of persuasion.

So, too, "A.E." could win people to a belief in the value of his poetry by his personal charm and by his perfervid reading of his verses. He persuaded many that he was a prophet and many that he was a poet little short of greatness. He so persuaded me, but he has failed to hold me to that admiration I had for his poetry when

I was young. Much that once lifted me to a kind of mazed ecstasy lifts me no longer, but leaves me on earth and cold.

The colors of it all were full of glamour for me. Now most of it seems to me highly colored, indeed, but hard. There is softness only about his twilight scenes. Those that would repeat sunset and dawn, moonlight on the mountains and the star-studded dome of heaven, seem garish or stereotyped or frigid to me, and one and all hard and a little pretentious. There is an old adage that it is dangerous for artists to paint sunsets. It is just as dangerous, I think, for poets to dally with them, or to attempt other prodigalities of color in the skies, rainbows or auroras or the wonders of dawn.

The typical poem of all his volumes from *Homeward* (1894) to *Midsummer Eve* (1928) lifts from a description of nature to some sort of spiritual ecstasy. So it is in "The Great Breath" in the first book, so it is in "The Forge" near the last. It is beauty that concerns him in the early poem; it is prophecy of a world rule for his countrymen that he rises to at the end in the later poem. In Ireland "The earth juts up her bones," but

> Here in her secret forges
> Grows stern through storm and cold
> The will for the world masters
> Of aeons yet unrolled.

The flashing colors and the wild lights have died out of his later poetry, but the poetry is none the better for their absence. Of secondary value as they were, they were the larger part of the verses. Later as he looked at the sky it was not rayed in diamond streamers or bejewelled with colors like those of the peacock's tail. "The sky is cold as a pearl Over a milk-white land."

> Out of a timeless world
> Shadows fall upon Time,
> From a beauty older than earth
> A ladder the soul may climb.
> I climb by the phantom stair
> To a whiteness older than Time.

That is the tone of the writing of his age. In his youth such lines as these were characteristic:

> Its edges foamed with amethyst and rose,
> Withers once more the old blue flower of day.

That is, of course, of Ireland, but Babylon or India is just as close to him when dream is dominant. It has always been, as I have said, in his verses that come to him softened by twilight that he is at his happiest. Such a one is "Memory of Earth," and "The Unknown God," and "Dusk," and "Babylon." This last poem has in it that overleaping of space and time so easy to those who can revisit the bodies they dwelt in in previous incarnations. He walks "the ways of ancient Babylon," Babylon of three thousand years ago, and brings back a beloved "Babylonian maid" from that towered city to the Ireland of to-day.

Russell always felt that there was an old and irreconcilable war between art and spirituality.

> The gay romance of song
> Unto the spirit life doth not belong.

Certainly he had not labored unremittingly enough to perfect the technique of his verse. Nor had he enough concerned himself in his verse with all the many phases of life that so interested him in his contacts with people. And because he had not been preoccupied with art and life they revenged themselves upon him for his lack of devotion. Despite his sense of beauty and his powers of imagery his verses tend toward formula, become stereotyped, cold, hard with a kind of artificial glitter. They still remain, though, many of them, as important as Holy Writ to certain "come-outers" in religion. I have seen *The Earth Breath* (1897), *The Divine Vision* (1904), and *Voices of the Stones* (1925) on parlor tables where a generation ago you would have found the Bible. "A.E." was spiritual leader as well as prophet to fairly large groups of people. Outside of such groups his verses tended with the years to become more and more a part of the ritual of an outworn creed.

LIONEL JOHNSON

Lionel Johnson (1867-1902) had four compelling interests in his life: the church of his adoption; the rehabilitation of Ireland's independence, spiritual, intellectual, and physical; his old school of Winchester; and the Greek and Roman and English classics. It was not, though, in the way of Crashaw and Patmore and Francis Thompson, the way of the Catholic rhapsodists, that he wrote about his religion. It was not in the way of Yeats or Russell that he wrote about Ireland. It was somewhat in the way of Arnold that he wrote about Winchester. It was very much in the way of Arnold that he wrote his verses critical of literature. An Arnold perfervid in faith instead of agnostic, an Arnold of an eighteenth-century formality instead of a very Victorian tolerance—that was what Lionel Johnson was.

I am not sure that it is not Johnson the crittic in verse that wears best with the years. I have been reading him since 1894, and though I should have, in all honesty, to write down "Glories" and "The Age of a Dream" and "Bagley Wood" as his best poems, I should have to admit that "Oxford Nights" and "The Classics" are more of my life than these lyrics I should choose for an anthology. There is rhetoric in all his verse, it is chanting rather than speech, speech that should be simple and loved through use and wont. There is a grave augustness about his critical verses that is very like the grave augustness of his prose in *The Art of Thomas Hardy* (1894). Than the passage in which he gives his vision of Hardy's works we have no better Latinical prose in late Victorian times. A like gravity, a like pomp and circumstance, are to be found in the critical verse. "Homer, grand against the ancient morn" gives you the keynote of "The Classics." In "Oxford Nights" Johnson unbends a little, in contemplation of those "dear, human books" that were his companions through many sleepless nights. This unbending is with an eighteenth-century urbanity. He loves Lamb, but he cannot bring himself to chat as Lamb does. He would subscribe heartily to Bacon's "It is good a little to keep state," but he would hesitate to agree with that same philosopher's "It is good a little to be familiar." He is familiar in "Lines to a Lady Upon Her Third Birthday," but only with effort and the most precise ceremony.

There is the beauty of carving in marble rather than of the girl "Glories" celebrates in that cold poem. You see no "Roses from Pæstan rosaries" or the girl in her bloom that was "more goodly red and white." You must content yourself that now, in death:

> She hath a glory from that sun,
> Who falls not from Olympus hill.

The octave of "Bagley Wood," a full-voiced chant, has a sort of frozen grandeur, and "The Age of a Dream" is only less august. Both are cold, marmoreal, and, it must be confessed, close to rhetorical. "Magnalities and splendors" he admired and hoped to attain. He did attain to them at moments, often at the expense of the humanity of the passage.

It was Yeats who won Johnson to a deep interest in Ireland. Johnson wrote the "Prologue" to the first year's performances of "The Irish Literary Theatre" in 1899. There are poems on Ireland in *Poems* (1895) and his second volume he called *Ireland with Other Poems* (1897). As you read these various poems on Celtic themes now in the *Poetical Works* (1915) they seem to lack spontaneity and to suffer more from their eighteenth-century verbiage than do the critical verses and those about Winchester. Johnson is better in his verse about the English countryside, in "In England" for sample. The countryside of south England was familiar to him from childhood in Kent and in Hampshire; and on west into Hardy's country in school and college days. His family was Cromwellian Irish and Protestant, and had Englished itself largely through the services of members of it in the English Army. There is no intimacy in any set of verses that Johnson wrote about Ireland. He is not one with the people or the landscape or the institutions of Ireland. He is the English public schoolboy of his time. He came to intellectual maturity very easily. He wrote his best verse while an undergraduate at Oxford from 1886 to 1889. It is England he writes of in:

> The night is full of stars, full of magnificence:
> Nightingales hold the wood, and fragrance loads the dark.

There are no nightingales in Ireland. Detached, though, this poem, "Bagley Wood," is, as nearly everything Lionel Johnson wrote was detached. Save in "The Precept of Silence" I feel as if he were writing of what happened to some one else rather than to himself. He is writing of himself, but so impersonally that what he writes seems wholly objective. For all his sympathy with the medieval church, with "Black armour, falling lace, and altar lights at morn," Lionel Johnson was from childhood a middle-aged eighteenth-century gentleman, with his face to the past and only an academic interest in romanticism, Celticism, and Wordsworthian concern with dalesmen and their speech. By his death in 1902 English criticism suffered a loss, but not English poetry. He had done what was given him to do in verse in his twenties.

KATHERINE TYNAN

Katherine Tynan Hinkson (1861-1931) was the first of Irish women poets of late Victorian and Neo-Georgian times. There was something of the amateur about nearly every other one of them, but she was all but always the artist. She began writing before Ireland was very instant to its poets as the truest inspiration of their poetry. She began in 1885 with *Louise de la Valliére,* a volume of Pre-Raphaelite verse. She worked away from the influence of Rossetti as the years went on until in *The Wind in the Trees* (1898) she found herself, a poet whose power lies in the exquisite transmutation into tender lyrics of moments of delight in garden and orchard and meadow. Her moods have been many from the early sheaf of verses to the later. The moods most often recurring have been those in which love of God, of St. Francis, of her fellow-men, of nature, and of Ireland have been now one and now the other dominant.

As far back as 1894 Mrs. Hinkson had published a "miracle play" in *Cuckoo Songs*, and she included six little plays of like sort in *Our Lord's Coming and Childhood* (1895). One part of a *Lover's Breast-Knot* (1896) is devoted to poems of child life, but the greater part of this last-named volume is given to a wife's love of her husband. Mrs. Hinkson had married H. A. Hinkson (1865-1910) in 1893 and taken up her residence in England, where she was to remain until 1911, when she returned to Ireland. The most and the best of her verse had been written in England, and a good deal of it on the English countryside. When she did write of Ireland in London or in country places in its outer environs she saw the home places all the more clearly for the distance. What was unessential had faded out, what she remembered was more native, more of the soil, of richer flavor. In *The Wind in the Trees* (1898), a volume published five years after she left Ireland, she writes most particularly of the home landscape. In "Spring Longing," loom up "the mountains, fair and dim" above her father's farm southwest of Dublin; and in "The Grey Mornings" again rises before her the vision of the "grey meadows" of home below "the grey mountains new-waked from slumber." It is England, though, I take it, that she is writing about in "Drought," to me her best poem. I praised it writing about her poetry more than a quarter of a century ago, and it is as much to me now as it was then. She is looking at a quiet landscape through half-shut eyes, of trees yearning after a dry spell for the coming of rain:

> The sky is greyer than doves,
> Hardly a zepher moves
> Little voices complain;
> The leaves rustle before the rain.

Her eyes are open wide, though, as she writes "Poplars":

> The blinding sky's unkind,
> The day has dust and glare,

> The poplar keeps the wind
> In her cage of light and air.

These two quotations prove her power of picturing and hint at the music of her lines. More musical still is her "Children of Lir," written in the memorable measure of "Love in the Valley."

> Dews are in the clear air, and the roselight paling,
>   Over sands and sedges shines the evening star,
> And the moon's disc lonely high in heaven is sailing,
>   Silvered all the spear-heads of the rushes are,—
> Housèd warm are all things as the night grows colder,
>   Water-fowl and sky-fowl dreamless in the nest;
> But the swans go drifting, drooping wing and shoulder
>   Cleaving the still water where the fishes rest.

That is Mrs. Hinkson at her average in verse, a little careless of inversion, a little too easily satisfied with her rhymes, but most musical and picturesque. She has always fresh phrasing, even when her material is familiar, and an air of distinction lifts about every third set of verses well above the best of most minor poetry.

There are no new effects in her later collections. There are poems of as good texture and of as warm an appeal in *Innocencies* (1905) and *Experiences* (1908), in *Irish Poems* (1913) and *Herb O'Grace* (1918) as in *The Wind in the Trees* (1898) and its predecessors, but they do not widen her scope or bring any sort of fresh beauty our way. There are war poems, to be sure, which she had not written before, but the best of these are, after all, only poems of motherhood, such as she had long written, presented from a slightly different angle. The one that moves me most is "Alienation," in which she writes of a boy's desire to go to war against his mother's will. It is its refrain, of more general application than to the case instanced in the poem, that comes home to the heart:

> God pity mothers when their sons
> Grow cold, that were their little ones!

Her *Collected Poems* (1930), published with a foreword by A.E., deepen for me the impressions of a life-long reading of her poetry. There are more good sets of verses than one's memory had listed; her command of the music of English words is more sure; and the frequency of lines to quote more noticeable. Above all the transfiguring touch is here. What she writes is made beautiful by her art, even if its material seems commonplace to those lacking in imagination and fretful for new effects. She has the lyric heart and the gift of melody, powers for which no scholarly curiosity or seeking after strange effects can compensate.

THE HON. EMILY LAWLESS

In her life-time the Hon. Emily Lawless (1845-1913) published one volume of verse, *With the Wild Geese* (1902). After her death another volume was privately printed, *The Inalienable Heritage and Other Poems* (1914). It was a great and difficult subject that she essayed in *With the Wild Geese*. "The Wild Geese" were those Irish soldiers who, driven into exile after the surrender of Limerick to the armies of William III, took service in the armies of France and Austria and Spain and wandered homeless through Europe until death ended their longing for Ireland.

Miss Lawless, historian as well as novelist and poet, knew well their story, as she knew well the stories of all the classes and races who make Ireland the bundle of contradictions it is. Ireland is to her "the western land of sad renown," and the exile of "The Wild Geese" its most romantic spectacle. Brooding over their hard fate, she writes of them with a kind of cold passion, which sometimes lifts the rather rhetorical writing to poetry. It is only in "Fontenoy" that she succeeds in sustaining both her mood and the expression of it to the end of the poem, but even "Fontenoy" is rhetorical.

She has her happiest moments in the division of *With the Wild Geese* concerned with the Aran Islands. She was, indeed, the first worthy exploiter of Aran life, writing admirably of it in *Grania* (1892) long before it was written of by visitors like Lady Gregory or Synge, or by a native son, like Liam O'Flaherty. She sees Aran as "the last verge of a worn-out world," "a little . . . sea-girt world," where there is

> Some lurking legacy from dead pagan days,
> Bloody, and secret, dark, unnameable,
> Branding the spot and its unhallowed stones
> As with a martyr's curse.

There is nothing sinister though, to "The Wild Geese," in the picture of the west country that rises before them far from home. The sounds of home are as instant to her as its sights. She is keenly aware both of:

> barren moor lands, waste and bare,
> And distant moan of sullen Celtic seas.

To her "The sea sobs to the gray shore, the gray shore to the sea." There are times when it seems:

> Sad as when from green hills one plaintive bleat
> Wakens the silence with its homeless note
> And listening plovers wheel.

There are other times, though, when the very loneliness of the landscape of Ireland is seen as a boon to men:

> . . . where unblackened rivers race
> And skylarks sing.

> . . . where, remote from smoke and noise,
> Old Leisure sits knee-deep in grass.

"ETHNA CARBERRY"

Anna Johnston MacManus (1866-1902) is remembered for one slight volume of verse, *The Four Winds of Erinn* (1902), which she published under the pseudonym of "Ethna Carberry." Among the verses collected here, one set, "The Passing of the

Gael," had that decade of popularity that is the life of most writing catching the note of the hour, but that fails of beauty and distinction. There are arresting phrases, musical and melancholy, in other poems too, especially in those descriptive of Donegal, her home in her brief marriage with Seumas MacManus. "In Donegal" conjures up:

> a purple moorland where a blue loch lies,
> Where the lonely plover circles, and the peewit cries

She was dead before she could write the half of what the northwest meant to her.

NORA HOPPER CHESSON

To the many who read of her death on April 17, 1906, Nora Hopper (b. 1871) Chesson was only a name. To the readers of English and Irish magazines in which, for twelve years, her verses frequently appeared, she was a facile verse-maker, who could rhyme pleasantly on any subject. Even to those who care greatly for poetry it is improbable she counted for much, for she wrote in so many manners that she dissipated her very considerable power. Three subjects she was mistress of, the otherwordly romance of the Celt, the pity of beautiful things vanished with the years, the joy of woman's surrender to love. In the days when the Celtic Renaissance was just begun she made her reputation with *Ballads in Prose* (1894), but for all the beauty of her work whose subject material is Celtic, she struck the other notes with more distinction. Very often it was the pity of Greek myth gone with the morning of the world that she chose to celebrate; and it is here that she completely achieved. The best of her later verse, however, was on the third subject, and had she lived to write better things even than the good things she did, it would seem it had been in personal lyrics of the kind of which "Southernwood" is the most distinguished.

Nora Hopper Chesson seemed to have more in her, for all her Irish and Welsh ancestry, of glad Greek than of dream-rapt Celt.

Perhaps had she lived in Ireland, her father's country and always before her inner eye, her Celticism would have had deeper roots. As things were, her knowledge through her father's talk and, brief as it was, her own visiting, taught her much directly. I have heard a distinguished exponent of the Gaelic Revival dismiss her shortly as a pleasant imitator, now of Yeats, now of Katherine Tynan Hinkson, and now of "Moira O'Neill." It is easy to find likeness between lines of Mrs. Chesson's and lines of these writers, but it should always be remembered that Yeats and Mrs. Hinkson went to the Pre-Raphaelites, as did Mrs. Chesson, and that such likenesses are largely due to the masters the three had in common. "The King of Ireland's Daughter," with its "gray sails sailing west over gray water," is Pre-Raphaelite in tone but its music is its maker's, as is the music of "April in Ireland," which Mrs. Chesson conceives in "gown of mist and rain-drops shot with a cloudy blue." The *Ballads in Prose*, from which I have been quoting, is a first book, but it contains, I think, with the exception of "Wild Geese," Mrs. Chesson's most original verse inspired by Ireland. In her later Irish verses her obligation to "Moira O'Neill" is often very direct.

More impressive than the lyrics of this first volume are the prose tales that give it title. In many of these is an incessant call of the sea, a call that is symbolized in "The Sorrow of Manannan," a tale told as if it were of old time, and perhaps suggested by some one of the many similar myths of the Celtic past. Her later shorter tales of like sort show that she could not regain at will the power that made "Aonan-na-Righ" a tale of old-time savagery so stark that you must turn to match it to the sternest of the tales William Sharp told in his rôle of "Fiona Macleod." Mrs. Chesson, so successful in the ballad in prose, succeeds indifferently in the ballad in verse. "The Strangers" has very evident power, but it has not the clearness of outline the ballad must have to hold fast, while its story is told, the attention of the reader; nor do the several other ballads in *Under Quicken Boughs* (1896) or *Songs of the Morning* (1900), attain notably.

It is in *Under Quicken Boughs* you will find her best verses of the "Greek convention," though this stanza comes from *Songs of the Morning:*

> Sad sobs the sea forsaken of Aphrodite;
>   Hellas and Helen are not, the slow sands fall,
> Gods that were gracious and lovely, Gods that were mighty,
>   Sky and sea and silence resume them all.

The music of that is the music of Swinburne, but it has a fall all its own. Earlier than this stanza is "Helen of Troy," which has sung itself into my memory, where it recurs more often than any poem of hers. Here is its onset:

> I am that Helen, that very Helen,
>   Of Leda, born in the days of old;
> Men's hearts were as inns that I might dwell in:
>   Houseless I wander to-night, and cold.

Aquamarines (1902) reveals still further Mrs. Chesson's versatility, but no poem of a new beauty. It brings back again the wish that she had not tried so many kinds of poems—lullabies, love songs, fairy songs, war songs, odes, descriptive verses, lyrical ballads, ballads—and that she had not used so many kinds of material—Celtic, Greek, Scandinavian, and the flowers and seasons of England. It is her own experience and personality that are really valuable. Some of the above forms and materials are not especially suited to her treatment and she gets from them only the ordinary stock in trade of the minor poet. But final judgment of a poet, fortunately, must be by the best the poet has done, and judgment by her best ranks Nora Hopper Chesson high. Let him who has not read her get *Ballads in Prose, Under Quicken Boughs,* and *Songs of the Morning,* and read "The King of Ireland's Daughter," "April in Ireland," "A Connaught Lament," "The King of Ireland's Son," "Helen of Troy," "Southernwood," and "The Chrysoberyl"—which last I have not dared to praise—and he will have a new delight, the delight of meeting a new personality expressed in a new music of words.

DORA SIGERSON SHORTER

Dora Sigerson Shorter (1866-1918) was very un-Celtic in that it was in the detail of technique and in phrasing that her weaknesses lay and not in architectonic power. In the underlying framework of all her verse she was strong. Her ballads are akin to their progenitors of the Border in stark power and in constant concern with the supernatural. They achieve, however, few new effects, they break no new ground, they strike no new note. They are very generally tragic, and many of them have in them an element of the supernatural. "My Lady's Slipper," to be found in *Ballads and Poems* (1899), is the best of them. It tells the story of O'Roork of the Lake, who is tricked by the woman he loved. She, now his foe's wife, asks him to take her away from her husband. He carries her off to his old manor house in the woods, in a half of which lives his closest friend. O'Roork sees her "flit up the long steps."

> Red was her cloak, and her face like a flower
> Dear to behold;
> Little red slippers she wore in that hour
> Buckled with gold.

That was his last glimpse of her. He sought for her, but in vain. He then sought for his friend who lived in the other half of his house. He was gone away. O'Roork stood his sorrow as best he could. The story, as I have followed it, is muttered by O'Roork, now an old man, crouched by the fire in the old house, entering the door of which he last saw his love. As he recalls the bitter past, his young hound comes bounding to him, little red slipper in mouth. The pup gambols away to where he had found it, followed by the old man. The way leads to a turret room, behind whose wall and with an entrance from his friend's part of the house, he finds a secret room of which he had not known before. There are the lovers:

"Huddled and crumbling, stretched on the ground,
Mould and decay,"

and by them a phial that tells how they died.

This is as finely accomplished a poem as Mrs. Shorter was capable of, a poem of arresting subject, clearly imagined, brought before us simply, but for all its poignancy not a ballad of the first order. It remains, at the end of all your thoughts of it, a good story, but somehow unacceptable as fact.

Other ballads of possibilities, but not completely realized, are "The Little Black Hound," "Earl Roderick's Bride," and "The Woman Who Went to Hell."

Her lyrics are many of them too long drawn out. "The Kine of My Father," "Last Eve," and "A Vagrant Heart" are well enough in the reading, though they do not remain long in memory. From her first volume *Verses* (1893) to *The Sad Years* (1918) the same phenomenon is presented, good verse that might have been made into something better than good verse by longer brooding over it, by a better technique, by a willingness to work it over and over again.

She was so vivid a personality herself, so beautiful, so enthusiastic, and of so fated a mien that all who met her could not help but read into her verses more of herself than she took the trouble to imprison there. She was so passionately attached to Ireland that Irishmen who felt about their country as she did read into her patriotic poems a passion that she was unable to express there. The best of these poems is "Ireland," a poem the feeling of which carries you across certain obviousnesses so rapidly that you scarcely notice them. She sees Ireland as "the dream of a God" that broke "To this beautiful land." She so fired the imagination of those about her that they one and all took her high intention for a high accomplishment. That must have been the way of it. Otherwise it is impossible to understand how she could have been praised so highly by Swinburne and Meredith, Francis Thompson and Katherine Tynan.

WINIFRED M. LETTS

It is natural that I should care more for the verses of Winifred Letts (b. 1881) than what there is of poetry in them warrants. A good few of them are of County Wexford, and it was from County Wexford came Lawrence Kelly, my childhood's mentor in things Irish. Her pictures in *Songs from Leinster* (1913) of

> The women at the well with dripping pails,
> Their men colloguing by the harbour wall,
> The coils of rope, the nets, the old brown sails

are pictures that Lawrence used to draw for me along with others of inland scenes, of turf-cutting, of cobbling, of "tethered goats that wait large-eyed and still To watch you pass." He, too, was full of such sayings as she mosaics into her lines, "sober as a cardinal's cat," "she's a right To be aisy now she's dead," and "Don't cock your little finger, Pat." And though Lawrence was a most proper and God-fearing man, he could rejoice in such pleasantries as those of that slum portrait, "The Retort Courteous."

"The Old Wexford Woman" talks, too, just as Lawrence used to talk, about the younger generation of forty years ago:

> The way they are now they're seeking their pleasure,
> The days are too slow.
> They'd look twice at a spade were they hunting for treasure,
> It's towns that they want, and evenings of leisure
> To streel to and fro.

Mrs. Verschoyle is as good at the Dublin slums as she is at the Wexford fishing villages. She is good, too, at the Wicklow Glens and at English countryside. Her second volume, first issued as *Hallowe'en and Poems of the War* (1916), was republished in 1917 as *The Spires of Oxford and Other Poems*, taking its new title from the title of the poem in it that was in a trice on all lips. That is a very poignant poem and so musical and easy to learn by heart that it will run through your head time and again.

There is little of Ireland in this second book of verse, but though she disappoint you by not following what is her forte she compensates somewhat for this by giving us her poetical credo. She would have her readers,

> hear the call
> Of all things sad, neglected, small;
> Thrill to the magic of the wind,
> Love country, town and your own kind,
> Sinners and saints and sea and sky
> Just as they are.

She herself holds to these things, and writes of them, with humor, with sympathy, with music.

EVA GORE-BOOTH

Eva Gore-Booth (1871-1926) was the maker of "The Little Waves of Breffny." She published many verses in her several volumes, but, though I read faithfully each succeeding collection from the 'prentice-work of *Poems* (1898) on to the end, only that one poem, found among the cold abstractions of *The One and the Many* (1904), has remained in my memory. It is of the order of "The Lake Isle of Innisfree" of Yeats, and not so good, but it has its place. Set to music, it has been widely sung, in parlor and hall and "over the air." It is a poem of loved places, places that will not cease their calling. "The little roads of Cloonagh go rambling through my heart," she tells us, but "the Little Waves of Breffny go stumbling through my soul." Like De Vere and Allingham, like Emily Lawless and Yeats, Eva Gore-Booth never forgets the west country:

> . . . a twilight land in the west,
> Where old unquiet mysteries
> And pale discrownèd spirits dwell,
> And the world's will is laid to rest.

Led to a study of Plotinus and Porphyry through her discipleship to "A.E.," she came to worship an austere ideal. It could not, however, kindle her to any such felicities as could her homesickness for the west country. In "Reincarnation," for all her preoccupation with the Neo-Platonic ideal, the lure of the home places breaks through her dreaming, and brings her back to earth:

> O Earth! green wind-swept Eirinn, I would break
> The tower of my soul's initiate pride
> For a grey field and a star-haunted lake,
> And those wet winds that roam the countryside.

"MOIRA O'NEILL"

It is not hard to carry in mind all the verses that "Moira O'Neill" has made. There are only the two slim volumes of them, *Songs from the Glens of Antrim* (1900) and *More Songs from the Glens of Antrim* (1921). There are twenty-five songs in the earlier volume, and twenty-two, without the sixteen translations from the Italian, in the second. Her reputation rests on the songs from the earlier volume, all but all of them concerned with homesickness for her loved corner of Ulster. There are sixteen more glen songs in the second volume, and a six from Northwest Canada, but while the latter broaden her scope a little, none of either group, or of the translations, break any new ground. She stands or falls by the early songs. None of them are long, and all of them can be understood and be fully felt on a first reading. They were popular in *Blackwood's Magazine* and in *The London Spectator* from the moment of their first appearance. My *Songs from the Glens*, the ninth impression, dated 1903, shows how immediate and how wide was the appeal of them collected.

Mrs. Nesta Higginson Skrine (b. 1871) writes of her native Antrim as it looms to her in exile on the plains of Alberta, on a ranch by the River Bow, with the Rockies white in the offing in their "inviolate snows." The home call is what is strong in these verses, but they concern themselves with other tried and proven motives. There are the partings of lovers; wooings and weddings; birds, babies, and cottage interiors; the salt dividing sea; the reflections of age. The best of them all are "Corrymeela" and "Lookin' Back." There is real lyric cry in both of these, music, and picturesqueness of phrase. There is longing rising to passion in:

> Wathers O'Moyle, I hear ye callin'
> Clearer for half o' the world between,
> Antrim hills an' the wet rain fallin'
> Whiles ye are nearer than snow-tops keen:
> Dreams o' the night an' a night wind callin'—
> What is the half o' the world between?

STEPHEN GWYNN

It is only in a few poems that the verse of Stephen Gwynn (b. 1864) sloughs off rhetoric and rises to impassioned poetry. Three such are his version of "The Woman of Beare," "Ireland," and "Mater Severa," all to be found in *The Queen's Chronicler and Other Poems* (1901), and reprinted in *A Lay of Ossian and St. Patrick* (1903). In 1923 there appeared his *Collected Poems*, but that volume added no new treasures. What matters is the three printed first in *The Queen's Chronicler*, and "The Ash Walk," also from that earliest volume. Of the ash trees he writes:

> See how, like conscious creatures, they
> Breathe in the blue soft Irish day,
> And the delighted air receives
> The lovely answer of their leaves,
> To the soft wind among them playing
> In ceaseless gentle motion swaying:
> As when a woman fond and fair
> Feels on her wealth of loose-piled hair
> Her lover's hand, and, sweetly bent,
> Whispers a sigh of mere content.

"The Woman of Beare" is as stark and cruel as this is gentle and kindly. The two descriptive poems of Ireland occupy a middle ground, and both have the very quality of the moors and mountains and ocean shores they picture.

SEUMAS O'SULLIVAN

The verse of Seumas O'Sullivan (James Starkey, b. 1880) is very definitely of "the twilight school" of Irish poetry. Yet it owes more to "A.E." than it does to Yeats, and it yields passages parallel to those in other poets, poets as different as Poe, A. E. Housman, Stevenson, Newbolt, and Emily Dickinson. His best poem is "The Sheep," which he puts, wisely, almost at the forefront of his *Poems* (1913).

> Slowly they pass
> In the grey of the evening
> Over the wet road,
> A flock of sheep.
> . . . . .
> Ah, what memories
> Loom for a moment,
> . . . . .
> Of the white days
> When we two together
> Went in the evening,
> Where the sheep lay.

He is good at all things of the evening, home-coming herds, and poplars with long shadows, and dreams. He is a sure craftsman, he finishes all his little poems perfectly. They carry out to the last letter his intention in writing them. There is, however, a dimness about them, a dimness that settles down over them and clouds them in memory. There is no great urge in any of them, no heartbreak, no overwhelming joy. They are studies in greys and mauves and soft purples. You remember scarcely a one of them individually. It is only as an effect you remember them at all, an effect of evening hues, save that one of the sheep. You miss the human touch in them as you miss it in "A.E.," and there is no glamour of the otherworld and no Miltonic largeness of conception to compensate for its absence as there is in Yeats. Starkey seems to feel the danger of missing human appeal in his verses but he cannot help missing it.

> Therefore guard well thy heart.
> O earth-born, harbour thou there
> No vision but earth can give,
> No rapture but earth may share.

What philosophy of life there is in his verses is rather negative. He is content, on the whole, to question things but slightly.

> O friend, I think they are the truly wise
> Who take, and take, and never analyse,
> For still a wise acceptance seems to be
> The very crown of all philosophy.

He is in no sense a beginning, as Ledwidge is, and in their little ways Strong and Higgins and Austin Clarke. He is a follower of the founders of the Irish Renaissance and practically all that he is is included in what they did before he wrote at all.

JOSEPH CAMPBELL

In the preface to *Irishry* (1913) you will find the point of view from which Joseph Campbell sees the pageant of Ireland. "Artists are fortunate in that the color of Irish life is still radiant. One hears on all sides of greyness, emigration, degeneracy, but one has only to look about to see that the cry has no mouth." So, from all quarters of the country he conjures up his portraits of people:

> Shepherd, plougher, pensioner,
> Scholar, priest and labourer.
> Symbols of the god in man
> Since the tale of time began.

Line three of these four proves him a stout follower of "A.E.," but the painter that is deep-seated in Campbell gives him eyes with which to see for himself. Like his work with the pencil, much of his work with the pen is in black and white. I remember his shepherd "dark against the stars" and "The Gombeen" who "like a spider sits" behind "a web of bottles, bales, Tobacco, sugar, coffin nails." Clearer in memory are such poems as "Loafers," with its lyric lift:

> A lark trilling, a butterfly
> That mounts and falls and flutters by;
> My Thoreau open at *Walden Pond;*
> Blue hills of mystery beyond;

and such a narrative as "The Newspaper-Seller," the record of an interview with an old Irishman one winter's night in New York City. All is simply and directly told, so directly and simply one is apt to lose sight of what art there is in the telling. All is leavened by sunlight and rare air, and by a kind of bitter humor. It is the Orangeman most often sets him agog, the Orangeman of "that barbarous nook, Belfast, my own calf-ground." There are many moods caught in poems of such diverse subjects, the quiet moods caught with most art, I think. "The Old Woman" is one study in quietude, and "The Osier-Sellers" another. I am not sure which I like better of the two. Both are good, both leave pictures in the memory. In his prose, too, Campbell strikes the lyric note. There is a wail as of the keen in *Judgment* (1912), his play, and many of the passages of *Mearing Stones* (1914) have the accent of speech. You hear a man talking in "The Peasant in Literature":

It has been said before that there is "too much peasant" in contemporary Irish literature, especially in the plays. The phenomenon is easily explained. Ireland is an agricultural country, a country of small farms, and therefore a nation of peasants; so that a literature which pretends to reflect the life of Ireland must deal in the main with peasants and the thoughts that peasants think. And peasants' thoughts are not such dead and commonplace things that I, who have learnt practically all I know from them, can afford to ignore them now. The king himself is served by the field. Where there is contact with the unseen in this book, with the mysteries which we feel rather than understand, it is because of some strange thought dropped in strange words from a peasant's mouth and caught by me here, as in a snare of leaves, for everyone to ponder. Impressions, with something of the roughness of peasant speech in them and something of the beauty, phases of a moment breathless and fluttering, the mystery of the sea, the thresh of rain, the sun on a bird's wing, a wayfarer passing—those are the things I sought to capture in this book.

This passage explains not only the purpose of *Mearing Stones*, but of all his books of verse, and it lifts at the end to poetry.

HERBERT TRENCH

Herbert Trench (1865-1923) made the stiffest texture of words for his thoughts of any poet of his generation. Even his shortest verses were brocaded as if they were odes, and made to move with eighteenth-century pomp and parade. You find "Come, let us make love deathless" and "She comes not when Noon is on the roses," in many anthologies, just why it is difficult to understand. They are formal, unoriginal, memorable in no way. Both of these lyrics are in *Deirdre Wedded* (1900), his first collection of verse. It had a good press, partly perhaps for the vogue of things Irish in that day. The title poem, which fills more than half of the little book's one hundred and one pages, is better than the lyrics. There are some fresh images in it, and a sense of high and tragic issues. We are told of this Deirdre:

> Tall as a rush is she,
> Sweet as the glitter of the netted lakes.

On the whole, though, she is the least human Deirdre that we have, in no wise comparable as a figure to the Deirdres of Yeats and Synge and Stephens.

We are not told that "Deirdre Wed" was written as a program poem for music to be composed upon it, but it may well have been, as Trench confessed of the leading poem of his second volume, *New Poems* (1907), "Apollo and the Seaman." That is a lesser thing than "Deirdre Wedded."

In 1924, one year after his death, all his verses, and his play *Napoleon* (1919), were gathered together in *The Collected Works of Herbert Trench*, and enthusiastically reviewed. He had the gift of making friends, and his directorship of the Repertory Theatre in London had brought him prominence. As with many another writer, what the man was among his fellows counted as much toward his reputation as his writings themselves. The simple truth is he is no more than a rhetorical poet.

THE LYSAGHTS

It is something for a poet to have given a man on the other side of the world from himself a chart to steer by. It is something more if he have given that man a poem to turn to as he turned to the secluded garret that comforted his sore heart in childhood, as he now turns to a hill walk that brings heartsease, or to a face that spells home to him. Sidney Royse Lysaght has done these things for a friend of mine, a man who counts in life, and for that reason I would honor him, even if there were no other reasons so to do. "To My Comrades," the dedication to *Poems of the Unknown Way* (1901), is the poem that has meant so much to my friend. It is, in a way, a variation of the old theme we find in the earlier verses of Whitman, "To those who've failed in aspiration vast," and in the later verses in the "Dedication" to *Salt-Water Ballads* (1902), of Masefield.

Every thinking man must be aware of his own insignificance, must know that, but for a half-dozen people, it makes little difference whether he live or die. It is not every thinking man, though, who has the courage to own to himself that he is only an average man. Lysaght has that courage. He hails as comrades men who would give all to the world but of whom the world has "no need," men "who heard the voice of God and disobeyed," men "who desired no laurel of the race." This is the man speaking, whether dramatically or for himself, who once so interested Meredith that he gave him a letter of introduction to Stevenson, whom he visited in Samoa. Lysaght made an impression on Stevenson, who mentions him not only in a letter to Meredith, but in another to William Archer. "There was a sort of geniality and inward fire about him," wrote Stevenson, "at which I warmed my hands." He was the kind of man Stevenson wanted to tell things to.

Three sorts of experience have moved Lysaght profoundly. The first is that acquired on the voyage around the world that took him to Samoa. The second is his emancipation from formal religion and his advocacy of the religion of humanity. The third is his joy in the Irish countryside he has known as child and man. His verse on all three topics suffers from a lack of concreteness. He notes "Magellan clouds," "the wild-rose of Antarctic skies," "radiant southern stars," and "the moonlight shining on the folds of silver reefs" of Pacific islands, but there are few definite and clear pictures of landfalls and departures, few human figures, and no place-names at all. Place-names are much in themselves, and when they are, in sound, what so many place-names in the Pacific and Ireland are, liquid music, his failure to use them is a wanton throwing-away of effects that would greatly have increased the appeal of his verses. As they are, nearly all of these verses suffer from a sort of vagueness and irrelevancy.

In *Horizons and Landmarks* (1910) is a series of condensed stories, "The Spirit and the Flesh," that arrest and move us, but they are not bitten in. There are some discoveries about life in Lysaght, but most of them not very profound. He has said nothing more memorable than:

> The child is not the dreamer; but the youth.
> No dream can lend enchantment to the truth
> In childhood, and no glamour from afar
> Can make its paths more wondrous than they are.

There is incisiveness, too, in:

> But she was not of those who make the slip
> And miss the fall, like many a merry dame.

Yet this sort of writing is rare in his verse. Of his prose I know only the novel *Her Majesty's Rebels* (1907), about a sort of pseudo-Parnell, which gets down to things as they are.

Lysaght has been for more than a century a name in Irish literature as well as among Irish landlords. To Edward Lysaght (1763-1810), wit, song-writer and *bon vivant* of Dublin at the end of the eighteenth century, is attributed, without authority, "Kitty of Coleraine." A century later comes along another Edward Lysaght with a book of verse, Edward E. Lysaght with *Irish Eclogues* (1915). He is the son of Sidney Royse Lysaght. The verses of *Irish Eclogues* are slices of life, but pleasant slices. They have to do with the common experiences of a strong farmer. They have to do with plowing and harvesting and the care and sale of cattle. They appeal strongly to me, who, too, know what are vigils with calving cows and horses with colic, and what the ways of laboring men. This is life, everyday life, seen as a beautiful thing, and good to live. He farms at one of the family estates in County Clare just across Lough Derg from Goldsmith's country. Sidney Royse Lysaght lives at another near Mallow, in County Cork, in that part of Ireland where Spenser lived in Kilcolman Castle. Both son and father are artists, the one with the temper and outlook of a farmer with vision, and the other with the outlook and temper of an emancipated Anglican clergyman.

JAMES STEPHENS

They are songs of innocence, these verses of James Stephens (b. 1882), and songs of experience, but the most of them songs of innocence. The modern minstrel pipes his songs down valleys wild, as did his countryman Blake who sponsors them, or down valleys which, if not wild, are far from the troubled ways of men. He pipes them, too, as Blake did less often, down the troubled ways of men. This song is made as Stephens is crowded between a car and a tram, but it is a song of the stars, the stars he sees as he looks upward from his narrow place of refuge. That song is made as the poet strays along goat-paths in the sunny quiet of a hillside almost within hail of the upland pastures of Theocritus. The two poems tell almost all that Stephens is. He is the poet who looks up, no matter where he is, no matter what he is writing about. He is the poet who is always bringing us word of pastoral places quiet in the sun, or of a simplicity as delightful as that of the pastorals, even though it comes from a room with one window four flights upstairs from a mean street of Dublin's slums.

In his first slight collection of verse, *Insurrections* (1909) Stephens does not sing so bright a world as that characteristic of him from *The Hill of Vision* (1912) on to *A Poetry Recital* (1925). The first poem you meet on opening *Insurrections* is about a girl refusing to go on dancing for men in some low hall while her husband lies dead. The next poem is of a back street with stews. The next but one is "What Tomas an Buile Said in a Pub." This is the first poem of the book that is arresting. It tells you how God stayed his hand when he was dissatisfied with the world and about to smash it with a blow of his fist. It has affiliations with "The Blessed Damozel." As this poem suggests Rossetti, so the first and second poems suggest Davidson, and the third Emerson. This is as you would expect. The young poet is apt to begin in the vein of poets whom he admires.

Elsewhere in *Insurrections* are passages that make you think of Hardy and Browning and Blake. There are a few that are in a new vein, of the quality we now recognize as that peculiar to Stephens. "Chill of the Eve" is such a one, and "The Tale of Mad Brigid" and "Fossils" and "Seumas Beg." So clearly did I remember the background of *Insurrections* as colored with the blacks and greys of evening over sea and shore and with the dreary mirk of night in mean streets that I was surprised at the blaze of sun in *The Hill of Vision*. In his second collection of verse Stephens is busier with memories of his days on the road than with memories of Dublin byways. You meet here Mad Patsy, and a light-o'-love, rough wooers and gentle, a sootherer, a spalpeen, an old beggar, and a tinker and her brat—in short, many characteristic figures of the roads. Most of them are presented in the measures and with the time-honored effects of English poetry, and with gladness in the heart of the poet.

There is no imitation of Yeats in Stephens, or of Tom Moore, or of the Gaelic poetry revealed by Dr. Hyde in his *Songs of Connacht* (1894-1906). Later, in *Reincarnations* (1918) Stephens was to give us a book based on the verses in Irish of Raftery, O'Rahilly and O'Bruadair, but even in these "translations" only the material is Gaelic. The verses are all, metrically, in the English tradition. Nor is their spirit wholly the spirit of the originals. The personality of Stephens is so dominant that there is more of him in these poems than of the originals. So it is, too, in his "translations" from Sappho.

Stephens is an Irish Nationalist of the following of "A.E.," who discovered him and gave him his hearing as a poet. He has, from the time he began to publish, used the life that he lived in Ireland as the material of his writing, but he has never made such an attempt as Daniel Corkery has made to Gaelicize his form and style. It may have been instinct rather than judgment that led Stephens to use the art of the center on the material of his province, but whichever led him to the choice so to write, it was a wise choice, and he has followed out consistently the methods he had mastered by 1912.

Meredith is obviously a great influence on his prose. In lyrics of landscape, in descriptions of character, in epigrams that are readings of life, and in philosophizing, he shows the influence of Meredith. And Meredith, let us always remember, was proud of his Irish blood, if never sentimental about it, as he was about his Welsh blood.

It may be that Meredith has something to do, too, with the optimism that you find in all Stephens after *Insurrections*. When he had gathered together the verses for this little book Stephens no doubt noticed that on the whole they were not particularly highhearted. At least so it would seem that he felt from the verses now printed as a foreword to the collection:

> What's the use
> Of my abuse?
> The world will run
> Around the sun
> As it has done
> Since time begun,
> When I have drifted to the deuce.

That his refusal to emphasize the ugly, the dispiriting and the unhappy is conscious is proven by what he says in "A Prelude and a Song" at the forefront of *The Hill of Vision:*

> Weary indeed I know the whole world is;
> Then do not sing to me a song of woe,
> But tune your pipe to every merry bliss
> Ye can remember, and I will not miss
> To join in every chorus that I know.

Stephens does not avoid themes that lay bare the secrets of things, but he carries so stout an optimism to the seeing that the nature of things cannot daunt him, the world cannot be ugly, or dispiriting, or heart-rending. In "The Fulness of Time" even Satan is guided into Paradise and seated by the side of Christ.

You do not look for a systematized philosophy in the elliptically minded poet. You will not find such a philosophy in Stephens. *The Crock of Gold* (1912) and *The Demi-Gods* (1913) both exemplify the truth that the earlier formulates into "Virtue is the performance of pleasant actions." We must remember, of course, that this, as a declaration of Pan, represents only a third of life, the "blood" of Meredith's "blood and brain and spirit." If, however, you take the sum total of all that is said by the Philosopher, who represents "brain," and all that is said by Angus Og, who represents "spirit," and add to this the various declarations of Pan, you will have a code that is as frankly pagan as that indicated in the quoted declaration of Pan, though it would not be so completely materialistic.

"The Prelude" to *The Hill of Vision* may be taken as conditioned by the "nymphs and dancing satyrs" with whom it is here concerned, but it represents, for sure, something of the poet's own belief:

> Good and bad and right and wrong,
> Wave the silly words away:
> This is wisdom, to be strong;
> This is virtue, to be gay:
> Let us sing and dance until
> We shall know the final art,
> How to banish good and ill
> With the laughter of the heart.

There is no more poetry in this verse of Stephens than in its parallel passages in his prose. For years, indeed, I felt he was a better poet in prose than in verse. One passage particularly I was always quoting, from *The Crock of Gold*, to indicate that he finished these little lyrics in prose as carefully as if they were sonnets. It is this:

The sun was shining gloriously. There was scarcely a wind at all to stir the harsh grasses. Far and near was silence and warmth, an immense cheerful peace. Across the sky a few light clouds sailed gently on a blue so vast that the eye failed before that horizon. A few bees sounded their deep chant, and now and again a wasp rasped hastily on his journey. Than these there was no sound of any kind. So peaceful, innocent and safe did everything appear that it might have been the childhood of the world as it was of the morning.

There are others as good as this from *The Crock of Gold;* the description of Mary Makebelieve in *The Charwoman's Daughter* (1912); the portrait of Mary MacCann in Book I of *The Demi-Gods;* Deirdre in the moonlight in Chapter IX of *Deirdre* (1923); and the changing of Etain in Chapter XIII of *In the Land of Youth*. It was not until I read *A Poetry Recital* that I began to waver in my opinion, and to wonder if, after all, some of the new verses here were not so fine as any of his prose. Now I am not sure. He himself, I shouldn't wonder, is in doubt, though he wrote in my copy of *In the Land of Youth:* "I'll say that the second part of this book is about the best thing I have done." It is here that he, most strangely, prints, just as if it were prose, the verse of the death song that Midir sings to Etain.

It is the innocency of Eden days that Stephens would have us emulate. He is as modern as the next one in his revulsion at cruelty. For witness, read "The Snare." If you would know his sympathy for that other virtue of modern times, freedom, read in his *Green Branches* (1916) his threnody on the men who fell in the uprising of Easter Sunday, 1916. In one poem he will quarrel with intolerance, in another with injustice. His kindliness, his large-heartedness, his sunniness of temper, his health of mind, are writ large on all his verse and prose. He is entirely content that it takes all sorts and conditions of men to make up the world. He never forgets that humor is one of the royal roads to truth. He laughs at everything, even love. Make an anthology of his love poems, and you will find laughter in nearly all. List them for the pleasure of the memories you have of them: "Fossils," "Light O' Love," "The Brute," "Mount Derision," "Nora Criona," "The Girl I Left Behind Me," "Afterwards," "The Daisies," and "The Red-Haired Man." Among these you will find a set of verses hardly more than society verse, several grotesques, lyrics of Elizabethan tone, moments of insight, and songs of experience.

It would seem that Stephens regarded the twenty-two sets of verses of *A Poetry Recital* as his "selected poems." Eight of them I cannot find in any of his previous volumes. The fourteen others include one from *Insurrections;* one from *The Hill of Vision;* four from *Songs from the Clay;* two from *The Rocky Road to Dublin* (1915); and six from *Reincarnations.* It was from this sheaf of poems, not yet gathered in *A Poetry Recital,* that Stephens chose what he wished to represent him in his readings on his tour of America in 1925. Six of them are based on Irish originals, but these are all but one of those he has made wholly his own. Among those that are Stephens chiefly are the wild grotesque, "Righteous Anger," a rendering of the famous "Coolun"; and versions of Raftery's "Mary Hynes" and "Peggy Mitchell." He chooses, too, as of his best, "The Paps of Dana," of the genre of Emerson's "The Mountain and the Squirrel"; and "The Fur Coat," also a semi-grotesque. "The Centaurs" is here, a most spirited poem, and of the many that show his sympathy with the various strange races between man and the beasts, fauns, satyrs, and the like. "The Daisies" is here, a lyric at one with the morning its background, and with that morning song of the reign of Elizabeth.

Among the group of poems unpublished before are several that illustrate theories of verse that Stephens described in his American readings. The rhythms of these poems have close relationship to their material. The rhythm of "The Rose in the Wind" dips and swings as does the rose described. "The Main Deep" tries to catch the long roll of the waves in mid-ocean. "Away! Far Away!" is designed to drag slowly, and it does. It seems to me, however, that the note at its end, telling us how we are to read it, is a confession that its measures do not compel us to read it as slowly as Stephens would have us read it, and as he reads it himself. "Chill of the Eve," reprinted from *Insurrections*, of sixteen years earlier, proves how long Stephens had practised what he was preaching on his American tour. He prints the verses a little differently in *A Poetry Recital*, but the movement is the same. It is, indeed, an old practice in English poetry, to have the verse move with its sense, a practice that Campion did a good deal to develop.

A poet's theories of his art are seldom so important as his performance of it, and they do not always really account for the performance being what it is. The theories are sometimes arrived at after the performance, as were Poe's theories about "The Raven." It does not matter very much one way or the other. It does not matter to me at all whether "On a Lonely Spray" is a result of the theories of Stephens or a cause of them. It matters a great deal that it is a beautiful poem, in some ways his most beautiful poem. Were it not that the first two lines of its last stanza are not wholly clear, I would write it down without hesitation as his most beautiful poem. You can interpret these lines, but you cannot be sure that your interpretation is the poet's. It is a poem apart, with no fellow at all like it, in my reading of English poetry. It is in rhyme what free verse is trying to be without rhyme. It has one beauty of imagery, and another beauty of rhythm, and you cannot say if either is its first beauty. It builds up, line on line, into a perfect whole. From its opening to its close, there is nothing, unless it be those two uncertain lines, that you would have other than it is. This is its opening:

> Under a lonely sky a lonely tree
> Is beautiful! All that is loneliness
> Is beautiful! A feather, lost at sea;
> A staring owl; a moth; a yellow tress
> Of seaweed on a rock, is beautiful!

And this is its close:

> Where is an eye, is beauty! Where an heart,
> Is beauty, brooding out, on empty air,
> All that is lonely, and is beautiful.

There are certain other poems of Stephens that I wish he had included in *A Poetry Recital*. One of these is "The Goat Paths." I have very personal reasons for liking this poem, but I do not think they are the only reasons, or even the first reasons, why I like it. An old Irishman, now with God, with whom I had a chat nearly every day in years long gone, was always telling me about goat paths above Fedamore, and the beasts and men that followed them. Other reasons why I like the poem are its music and its pictures and its light, its air as of the heights. Still another, and a potent reason of my liking, is that it is symbolic of its maker. There are "crooked paths" in his mind, quick turns, sudden reverses, steep falls, precipitous climbs. That is what you find in certain parts of his mind. In other parts you find "quiet sunniness" and "sunny quietness." And if you are not in the mood for

YEATS AND THE IRISH RENAISSANCE 225

symbolic interpretations, the place described in the poem, with its heather and furze, with its bounding and staring goats, may bring contentment to you.

"George's Street," too, I would have in any "poetry recital" from the verse of Stephens. In what other poet of to-day do we find so Elizabethan a ring as in:

> Listen! if but women were
> Half as kind as they are fair,
> There would be an end to all
> Miseries that do befall.

I miss, too, another favorite, "Blue Stars and Gold," the psalm to which I have referred, which he sang "standing between a car and tram" in a Dublin street and looking up at:

> Blue stars and gold, a sky of grey,
> The air between a velvet pall.

I miss still again in *A Poetry Recital* certain child verse I like very much in "The Adventures of Seumas Beg" in *The Rocky Road to Dublin*. It is all Stephens' own, fit to stand comparison with any of the memorable child verse in our tongue. Think of any maker of child verse that you wish, Stevenson, William Canton, Riley, De La Mare, Milne, and Stephens will hold his own as you put him side by side with each. In utter poetry only De La Mare can rival him. You meet all sorts of delectable creatures in this child verse of Stephens, a giant, the devil, a man blown across the sky on a carpet, an angel, a witch. You meet the wind as the enemy of the child as you have so often met it as the enemy of the old man.

Than its *"Boh, Little boy!"* you could not have a better illustration of the retention of the child's imagination into manhood. There are a hundred little ways, in this series of poems, in which you are made aware of how consistently this child's attitude is retained. In no way is it more apparent than in his presentation of animals. Dogs, cats, hens; donkeys, horses, goats; cows, spiders, crows: one and all they awaken his solicitude.

The survival of the child in the poet even through his middle and old years has often been pointed out. This survival is developed more fully by De La Mare in his lecture on *Rupert Brooke and the Intellectual Imagination* than in any other writing that I know. It is certainly true in the case of Stephens. The world and all that in it is has to him still the freshness and wonder and nearness to heaven that it had when he was "Little James." There is nothing better in his poetry than these qualities. Such profundities as mark certain pages of his prose are rare in his verse. You have one or two in "The Lonely God," among them that which describes the prostration of the intellect before "The insolent vacuity of Time," the impossibility of finding even "The fringes of the Infinite."

Ecstasies are common to both prose and verse. They never lift higher than in "A Prelude and A Song." The "Song" of this poem is, in fact, an orgy of aspiration for the perfectibility of man. It is an unorthodox and poetic version of a getting of religion such as is common in certain evangelistic sects. This "Song" has curious affiliations to both Milton and Blake. It has the sense of space that is Milton's and the perfervidness that is Blake's. About the practicability of these Blake-like reactions to "the despotism of fact," about the practicability of following their lead away from the complexities of to-day, there will be differences of opinion. There will be less difference of opinion about the stimulating quality of his protest, and about the beauty of his dreams of Eden. They ring long in our ears, such lines as:

> Cure the world of good and bad,
> And teach us innocence anew.

LORD DUNSANY

The contrivers of the well-made play said Dunsany (b. 1878) was no dramatist. He proved by *If* (1922) that he could achieve a commercial success on the stage, as he had proved earlier by *The Gods of the Mountain* (1911) that he was master of the one-act play. The more facile romancers found fault with his *Gods of Pegana* (1905) and his *Time and the Gods* (1906), but all the world now admits that the romantic tale has never been better handled in English than in "The Avenger of Perdondaris" (1919), or the modern fairy story more simply told than in "The Coming of the Troll" in *The King of Elfland's Daughter* (1924).

It may be that Dunsany will go on to show that the strictures of the poets on his verse are equally ill-taken. As things are now, however, after he has collected fifty sets of verses in *Fifty Poems* (1929), he is written down an amateur poet, as amateur as his friend, Dr. Oliver Gogarty. Yet there are plenty of good things in the half-century, the very first set of verses among them. "Art and Life" has fresh imagery. "The line of some queer old thatch Against wintry sky" arrests you at once. The underlying thought of it all holds you,—the richness of life, the thousand things to catch and to preserve through art, the short time we have between birth and death to make beautiful things for others to enjoy. There is, it must be admitted, a certain awkwardness about it all, as of an early version of a poem, a version that might have been worked over into what would have finality. It has not finality, this "Art and Life." It is something more than improvisation, but it is not perfected verse.

I heard Dunsany say once in a reading that all beautiful things are done easily. That is a challenging statement, the offspring of an attitude of mind that has nothing but scorn for the labor of the file. As a matter of fact his own verses have often need of that labor. The repetition of the idea of "haunting" twice in this short poem of seven stanzas is just carelessness. "Old willows standing like witches Haunting a stream" is followed at only six lines' distance by "All sounds that sigh upon seas Or lands that are haunted."

Dunsany is restive under criticism, but he must know in his heart that his verse has not the art of his prose, that his best poetry is in his prose. Scorn of his critics breaks out in verse that is not itself impeccable, in his "Ode to a Dublin Critic." Here he thus justifies himself:

> Through steely gaps that I have known
> In mirage mountains, upon wings
> Has my imagination flown
> To bring you news of magic things.

Such news Dunsany has unquestionably brought us, but oftener in his prose than in his verse. There are five sets of verses about Africa in *Fifty Poems*, "The Hunter Dreams in His Club," "A Song of Wandering," "Evening in Africa," "Night," and "In the Sahara." They are chiefly memories of things seen, bits of landscape, a bull rhinoceros, the Milky Way, "some crumpled-rose-leaf-mountains." A fair sample of these African poems is:

> . . . . all Sahara's blue
> Bursts into little waves of pink
> That fade as dreams at morning do.
> . . . .
> Like sparks these glories I have known
> Shall flash, though faintly, from my pen.
> What was not given for me alone
> Shall shine years hence for many men.

So, let us hope, it shall be. Certain it is that the picture Peterboro left on his mind has "shone" for me ever since I first heard it over the radio. Dunsany, apostle of yesterday, over so modern an institution as the radio was an anomaly, but the lines "Under Mount Monadnock" came to me as clearly from New York as "The Old Brown Coat" (1919) he had read sitting beside us a few nights before. It may be that my partiality for New Hampshire affects my liking, and the measure of "Love in the Valley" in which "Under Mount Monadnock" is written. It is, I think, though, very Indian summer in the Northland.

Like a flame the maple blazes with the oak leaves;
All in windless weather the huge apples fall.
Sunset and twilight; birches haunt the evening,
Walking in the wild wood slender and tall.

More of Dunsany's verses find their genesis in the World War than in any other subject save Africa. There are trumpets in "A Dirge of Victory" and shawms in "To the Fallen Irish Soldiers." Nothing in either sonnet stirs me, though, as does the romance of "The Riders," a poem whose last line reveals what the poet took as "the tip of Quixote's spear" is in reality the newly risen "evening star." Dunsany has, indeed, a soft spot in his heart for "a large low star." I like, too, the spaciousness of "The Watchers," with its refrain "Come again in a million years." That is a thought that quickly snuffs out all the ugliness of our dwindling modern world. The imperturbability and aloofness and timeliness of the stars have never been driven home upon my consciousness more forcibly than in the two lines:

All of that time Orion twinkled;
Nothing changed in the Milky Way.

I like, too, and very greatly, the idea of "A Heterodoxy," which brings the poet's dog to him in heaven, and the idea of the bat of "Affairs," who is not jealous of man flying, because to him are entrusted "the high affairs of the bat."

For all his preoccupation with yesterday Dunsany can rejoice in Caruso's voice forever "safe on the gramophone." There are only moments, though, in his verses, as in his stories, and as in his more characteristic plays, that he is concerned at all with modern things. What Dunsany really loves are:

the slopes of Fairyland
Above the fields of yore.

FRANCIS LEDWIDGE

You come to a rereading of Francis Ledwidge (1891-1917) with a quiet happiness. You sit and think of him with the book unopened in your hands. You remember certain lyrics very clearly, "Behind the Closed Eye" first, with its pictures of his birthplace, Slane, in that English-looking county of Meath. You remember "The Homecoming of the Sheep," the background of which is Greece. You remember "A Little Boy in the Morning," and you are in Ireland again. Then you find you can recall no other lyric by name. It is difficult, too, to recall any lines save:

> The sheep are coming home in Greece,
> Hark the bells on every hill!

You find that you have not all the lines even of this one poem in your memory. You cannot go on from the opening, but you recall lines toward the close of the poem:

> And the moon comes large and white
> Filling with a lovely light
> The ferny curtained waterfall.

You thought you would never forget this poem, so way-off and sleepy it was, so intimately of the evening, so soft with moonlight. Yet you have forgotten most of it. You have had in your mind, from the moment that thought of Ledwidge rose there, that he was killed in Flanders. You are thinking now of what might have been, of what he might have written had he lived. You remember that Dunsany called him "the poet of the blackbird." You try to call up a line in which he praises the bird, or a line in which he catches its song. "The mellow ouzel fluted in the elm" of Tennyson comes to you, and "the boxwood flute" that Henley said the blackbird blew, but not what Ledwidge heard him whistle. You were too old, perhaps, when you first read Ledwidge to have lines stick in your memory as they did in the twenties. Or is there a lack of incisiveness, a lack of emphasis, in the phrasing of this peasant Keats? Is it that you delight in the soft rhythms as you read, but that the images are not hard enough to cut into what of you remembers and remain clear and sharp against the effacing years?

You remember what pleasure you had in reading Ledwidge, how many "purple patches" there were, and you open the book, thinking you will hunt for them first. You find yourself, however, turning the pages, looking for "Behind the Closed Eye." You find it is the second poem of your book. This book is *The Complete Poems of Francis Ledwidge* (1919). It comprises *Songs of the Fields* (1915), *Songs of Peace* (1916), and *Last Songs* (1918). You thought "The Homecoming of the Sheep" came next of your favorites, but it does not. "A Little Boy in the Morning" came next. These two are from *Songs of Peace*, and as you read through the three collections you find this second collection contains most of his best poems. They were written, no doubt, after he was a soldier, but before he had a good deal of his vitality sapped by his service in the East. The verses written in Londonderry in 1916 and in France and Belgium in 1917 have a tired air.

You marked, of course, the lines you liked on your first reading, and you found others, on your second reading, that you had missed on your first. Now, on what is perhaps your seventh reading, you are finding others, as is always your experience in reading poetry that really counts. Dunsany, in his preface to *Songs of the Fields*, had called your attention to the first lines you marked. They are the lines in which Ledwidge praises his beloved blackbird:

>   And wondrous, impudently sweet,
>   Half of him passion, half conceit,
>   The blackbird calls adown the street
>   Like the piper of Hamelin.

Turning back to the "Contents" for the "B's" you wrote in for reference to the blackbird, you find there are sixteen poems so marked. As there are one hundred and twenty-two poems altogether in *The Complete Poems* there can be no doubt at all of how large was his concern for this bird. The blackbird is, indeed, to the British child what our robin is to the American child. Both are yellow-billed, and thrushes, and the friendliest of birds. They are both our familiars of lawn and garden, and they are both thieves of strawberries and cherries. Both run on the ground and listen for earthworms with heads cocked to one side. Both are cheery singers, the blackbird perhaps something more. The blackbird has been praised time and again by the poets. He is:

> The ousel-cock, so black of hue,
> With orange-tawny bill

that Shakespeare sings. He is sung at length by Richard Jago, Cornishman and friend of Shenstone, in that mid-eighteenth century, which no matter how formal its poetry and its gardens, still felt neither complete without the presence of "feathered songsters." William Barnes and Thomas Hardy, Dorset men both, said their say about the blackbird in verses that all who read poetry have nearly by heart. Not so well known is Bourdillon's "Blackbird." "The night has a thousand eyes" has gone around the world, but not these lines:

> O Blackbird, who hath taught thee
> The heartbreak in thy song,
> In the shadowing after sunset
> When April days grow long?

Most familiar of all the tributes is Stevenson's "Birdie with the yellow bill," but we may well doubt that Ledwidge met these lines in childhood. In his youth, when he was writing his poems on Irish legend, he must have come across the many references to the bird in the translations that he read. In the first song that Finn made he praised the blackbird, and in a score places else in *Gods and Fighting Men*, or whatever version of the old stories you are reading, you will come on the mention of the bird and his song.

How do the lines of Ledwidge in praise of the blackbird stand comparison with those of other poets, of old time and of to-day? The lines I quoted above give the fullest description we have of the song in all English poetry. I was tempted to say the most exact, too, but the songs of birds of the same species differ a good deal, and not only in quality and pitch and tone, but even in the phrasing. Hardy has told us that the blackbird whistles "pret-ty de-urr" in Wessex, and "purrity dare" in Ireland, a difference of phrasing as well as of tone.

In the first poem of *Songs of the Fields* is the first reference of Ledwidge to his bird of birds:

> And the sweet blackbird in the rainbow sings.

In "A Rainy Day in April" we find:

> And sweet the little breeze of melody,
> The blackbird puffs upon the budding tree.

In May, "only in spasms now the blackbird sings," but that song is so clear in his memory that he can hear it when he will. He can make it sound again in his ears. He hears it in "river voices," which are "sweet as rainwater in the blackbird's flute." Walking the paved streets of Manchester he thinks of Meath, "where Peace shuts the blackbird's wings." He notes with joy the singing of the bird after its first singing season is over:

> I heard a blackbird whistle half his lay
> Among the spinning leaves that slanted down.

He carries with him memories of blackbirds seen against backgrounds that made little wonders of composition:

> The blackbird in a thorn of waving white
> Sang bouquets of small tunes.

At war, Ledwidge longs for peace and Ireland, and the chance to be writing once more down by the Boyne:

> And when the war is over I shall take
> My lute a-down to it and sing again
> Songs of the whispering things among the brake,
> And those I love shall know them by their strain,
> Their airs shall be the blackbird's twilight song,

Their words shall be all flowers with fresh dews hoar.—
But it is lonely now in winter long,
And, God! to hear the blackbird sing once more.

It is curious how fully symbolical the song of the blackbird is of the verse of Ledwidge. It is not one of the rare songs, it is not one of the complicated songs, there is no bravura in it, no coloratura. It is a simple song, a homely song, but sweet and rich and clear. Every second poet speaks of its flute-notes, and rightly, but it is a very simple flute it suggests, a flute that is cousin to a penny whistle, that is not far from the old straight flute of village bands, —in short, a peasant flute. And all this that I have said of the blackbird's song might be said of the verse of Ledwidge. The imperfections of his verse are the imperfections of the blackbird's song. Says John Burroughs, describing the song as he heard it in England: "It was the most leisurely strain I heard. Amid the loud, vivacious, work-a-day chorus it had an easeful *dolce far niente* effect. . . . It constantly seemed to me as if the bird was a learner, and had not mastered his art. The tone is fine, but the execution is labored; the musician does not handle his instrument with deftness and confidence." With the exception of the "labored," this description of the song of the blackbird fits admirably, as I have said, the verse of Ledwidge. And so, too, does the comment of W. H. Hudson, who after quoting the above words of Burroughs, goes on to say: "Perhaps it may be said that, of all the most famed bird-songs, that of the blackbird is the least perfect and the most delightful."

The song of Ledwidge was becoming more perfect with the years. Had he lived, and known the leisure of peace, a future of the richest attainment was before him. Dunsany, in the excitement and sorrow of the death of Ledwidge, said, according to the London *Times* of August 9, 1917, that "if Ledwidge had lived he would have surpassed Burns, and Ireland would have lawfully claimed, as she may do yet, the greatest of peasant singers."

Ledwidge is more than just the poet of the blackbird, though to be that in itself would be a good thing. He is the poet of other birds, over thirty of them, "this poor bird-hearted singer of a day." He was out-of-doors all a happy childhood, and though he went to work young, and spent some time in a grocer's shop in Dublin, he never could stand for long any job that kept him away from the countryside by the Boyne. He knows the birds, his "masters in song," as few poets know them. A Hodgson or a Frost is as exact, but not many others. When he is not sure of a bird, as in "Evening in England," he calls it "a marsh bird," and when he cannot recognize a song, as in "Autumn Evening in Serbia" or "The Lure" he refers to its singer as "a strange bird . . . singing Sweet notes of the sun," or to the song as "music of a foreign bird." So it is that when I read of "a brown rail" in his verses in one place and of a "corncrake" in another I put them down as different birds, as water-rail and land-rail; and when I read of a "thrush" and a "throstle" I believe him to be distinguishing between a stormcock and a song thrush.

He knows skylark and robin, linnet and sparrow, goldfinch and yellowhammer, owl and cuckoo, swallow and martin, swift and nightjar, kingfisher and woodpecker, crow and magpie, woodpigeon and stock-dove, quail and curlew, lapwing and bittern, heron and swan, wild geese and duck, cormorant and seagull. Only in his reference to these last four is there question as to the variety mentioned. He is just as exact, too, in his reference to flowers. The birds have few poems to themselves, but they come in, as do the flowers, to add the beauty of little things known and loved to poems intimately human in feeling and conception.

Ledwidge writes about his home places in the countryside of the Boyne, Crewbawn, Crocknaharna, Currabwee and Faughan. He writes about his art of poetry; and love; and Celtic legend; and city scenes; and death; and vision; and country customs. "All Hallow's Eve" is a glimpse of what store of folklore he had, folklore as much English as Irish. His poems on Celtic legend are none too good. His poetry, like his name, is English. His place-names are Irish, but the poems in which we meet Faughan and

Crocknaharna are English in quality. It is true not only that the Englishman's house is his castle, but that the village where he lives is holy ground, from which he can see now and then a vista of Paradise. So it is with Ledwidge. The light that never was on land or sea invests these little places by the Boyne. Places, indeed, as I once heard Masefield point out, have inspired almost as many English poems as love.

Writing to Katherine Tynan Hinkson from Belgium on July 20, 1917, just eleven days before he was killed, Ledwidge says of the loved places of liquid name that he has celebrated in his verse: "I would give £100 for two days in Ireland with nothing to do but ramble on from one delight to another. . . . I want to see again my wonderful mother, and to walk by the Boyne to Crewbawn and up through the brown and grey rocks of Crocknaharna. You have no idea of how I suffer with this longing for the swish of the reeds at Slane and the voices I used to hear coming over the low hill of Currabwee."

It is the old, old stuff of English poetry that you find in Ledwidge, freshly felt and freshly phrased, and put in the old proved way that has come down to us from Spenser, and that has been followed by poet on poet who has held the old proved beauty best. It is loveliness that Ledwidge is concerned with first and last, a kind of childlike loveliness, a loveliness of tender and gentle things; and there is no attempt made to avoid sentiment. He does not fall into sentimentality in what Dunsany has given us of his writing, but we, speaking of this kind of poetry, are in danger of so falling. It is moments of beauty that he writes about, moments of beauty awakened for him by nooks and corners that he loved, by flowers and bird voices, and by girls.

It is easy to cull good phrases from Ledwidge, good lines, "purple patches" that are gray and white and blue in their colors. "Bright eyes and twilight hair," "The blue distance is alive with song," "grey twilight hushed the fold," I find marked in the earlier poems. In "Music on Water" is a passage of which Keats would not have been ashamed:

> In the red West the twisted moon is low,
> And on the bubbles there are half-lit stars:
> Music and twilight: and the deep blue flow
> Of water: and the watching fire of Mars.

I marked a line in "In the Dusk" on an early reading of the poem, but it is only lately that it has begun to knell slowly in my ears whenever I think of its maker, "Always beyond the dark there is the blue." And here is a fellow to it which also, as Yeats puts it, "articulates sweet sounds together":

> And lifting slowly on the grey evetide
> A large and lovely star.

The loss of Ledwidge was, to my way of thinking, the greatest loss English poetry suffered through the World War. It must be remembered that he had had no trained criticism of his verse until he sent some of it, at twenty-one, to Dunsany in 1912. There was not much help from others until he came to be a little known in Ireland for his *Songs of the Fields*. *Songs of Peace* was an advance on the first collection. And if *Last Songs* merely marked time, that is easily understood. Poetry for all his love of it could not be first in his life while he was fighting. Nor can a man bled of strength by such experiences as were Ledwidge's in the East be at his best even in such moments of rest as he had in France and Belgium.

There are many kinds of attainment presaged in his early work. In "A Dream of Artemis" Ledwidge tells of some of the things he loved, somewhat after the fashion of Rupert Brooke in "The Great Lover." Many of the things here listed he had still to write about. And, all the time, as the world opened before him, there were more and more things to write about. He liked the strange landscapes of Serbia and Greece, and they moved him to new effects in his poetry. At twenty-four he had felt:

> A hundred books are ready in my head,
> To open out where Beauty bent a leaf.

He was writing down to within a few days of his death, writing under the most forbidding conditions. There was never a young man with a greater impulse to create beauty. He who is a minor poet might well have been a major poet by now had the war spared him.

OLIVER GOGARTY

One who should know tells me that Dr. Oliver Gogarty (b. 1878) is the third poet of Ireland. "We have Yeats and 'A.E.,'" he said, "and Gogarty." I should rather say that Gogarty is the man who wrote "Golden Stockings." That is as winning a poem about a child as we have in all English literature. One thinks of "Noble Lovely Little Peggy" of Prior, and of "Lines to a Lady upon Her Third Birthday" of Lionel Johnson as of its company, but one cannot say that either is a better poem. "Golden Stockings" is about a child racing around in a meadow of buttercups. There is sunlight in it, and breeze, and the spring:

> Golden stockings you had on
> In the meadow where you ran;
> And your little knees together
> Bobbed like pippins in the weather
> Where the breezes rush and fight
> For those dimples of delight;
> And they dance from the pursuit,
> And the leaf looks like the fruit.

The picture of the child in the meadow is good enough in itself. It is made better than good by the simile of little knees bobbing up out of the buttercups like golden pippins tossed out of their leaves by the wind. That is a figure as fresh and fetching as an air of Mozart. It contents us as do all discoveries of beauty. It does not dissipate its effect by carrying us away to other things. It keeps us concerned with what it images, with the child in the meadow of buttercups. The poet makes us, reading, feel as he felt in the seeing, that this is a sight would last through years of blindness.

An Offering of Swans (1923) takes its name from the last set of the twenty-three sets of verses that make up the thin volume. "To the Liffey with the Swans" is hardly worthy of the circumstances that begot it. Kidnapped by gunmen, and imprisoned in a warehouse by Liffey's side, just above Dublin, Gogarty escaped by the river, and made his way to England. When it was safe for him to come back to Dublin to live he gave two swans to the river that aided and abetted his escape. Yeats tells us this version of the story in his preface to *An Offering of Swans*. There are other versions. What is surer than the correctness of his version is his judgment of the poems in the book. Though he has children of his own, you would not expect Yeats to care greatly for "Golden Stockings." That is outside the sorts of poetry that he admires most. Of those sorts are the three all but perfect lyrics he lists as his favorites, "Non Dolet," "Begone Sweet Ghost," and "Good Luck." Where his sympathies are enlisted, Yeats's judgment of poetry is unerring. As I have never heard Gogarty read his verse, I hear in the voice of Yeats those two lines so direct and august with which "Non Dolet" begins:

> Our friends go with us as we go
> Down the long path where Beauty wends.

I suspect that Gogarty's voice would be warmer, that the genius for comradeship there is in the man would color his tones, as it colors his written words. Very human, and a little like Carew, is "Begone Sweet Ghost," in which he adjures the lady who haunts him:

> O do but clothe you in the dress
> Whereby was young Actæon killed.

In the very vein of the Cavalier lyrists is "Good Luck." The first stanza is the best stanza of the three, as the first stanza of songs, from the days of the Elizabethan songbooks, is so apt to be the best of all. Stanzas two and three of "Good Luck" are, however, only less good than stanza one because that is perfect. The couplet that ends "Perfection":

> Yet, for all the faults of her
> Than Perfection perfecter

is an echo of Francis Thompson's

> Then for her faults you'll fall in love with her.

There is very little, though, in Gogarty, save his fellow-feeling with the Cavalier lyrists, that suggests any other poet. It is only the poetasters, as Dunsany says, that are like each other. The poets are each of his own kind. It is all his own, this style of Gogarty, these clarities, this fall of words. No one else has, to use his own phrase, so "bland" an air, so cool a sunniness about his poetry.

There are several such two lines as these that end "Perfection" in Gogarty, but not all of them are rhymed into couplets. One that haunts me is:

> Old causes God, in guiding Time, espoused
> Who never brooks the undeserving long.

And another:

> Poppæa's hair was golden amber:
> Historian, is not that a fact?

And a third:

> Where is the leaf that would carry beyond her
> The spendthrift gold of the fallen leaves?

A fourth, a real couplet, confesses a sentiment that perhaps explains why most of these verses of Gogarty are not so good as their best moments:

> Teach us to save the Spirit's expense
> And win to Fame through indolence.

In the second little gathering of Gogarty's verse, *Wild Apples* (1929), you come upon fresh things with that delighted surprise that is so rare an experience in the reading of minor poetry. His imagination leads him all over the world. At one moment he is in "a sweet air of Persia." At another he is in some "safe Roman croft." At the next he is in "Old days of glory" in Erin. The kinds of beauty Gogarty loves are often aristocratic, "the limestone lordly houses" of yesterday so many of which have been burned since 1916; ladies whose portraits he presents with startling clarity. It isn't often a whole poem of Gogarty is as good as its best parts. It is a bit here and a bit there that you enjoy on turning his pages. You savor the lines that catch and imprison yearning and beauty. "There's hope in the masts at the end of the street" haunts you, and every time you look at poplars after you have read "Sandymount" you recall his "votive poplar trees." There are correspondences between thoughts and moods of his and thoughts and moods of Yeats, but the accent of the writing and the fall of words in Gogarty are always his own. He echoes the code that has been growing stronger and stronger in Yeats of admiration for austere and kingly days of old time, and he does not balk at a certain substratum of savagery in them. In "Castle Corrib" Gogarty tells us, "The men around regret the sword." In "To Death" he questions:

> But for your Terror
> Where would be Valour?

When it so happens that a poet cares greatly for many of the things for which you, reading, care greatly, you are perhaps prone to set his value higher than less prejudiced sympathy would. Gogarty cares greatly for a damson plum in blossom:

> Out of the dark of sleep I come
> To find the clay break into bloom,
> The black boughs all in white!

His care is my care. His experience is my experience. Every time I pick him up I find some image that has always been a delight to me. So when I read him I am always expecting old adventures of this sort. That makes reading him a gentle sort of excitement and perhaps unsettles the critical judgment. I put this down because I am not quite sure my enthusiasm for his verse is justified.

Had Gogarty lived with these verses of his longer, redreamed and redreamed them; spent his spirit, and his art as a craftsman, upon them, we might have a sheaf of verse from him as memorable in its way as *A Shropshire Lad* in its way. As things are it is remarkable that the busy doctor, the light-hearted wit and the honored statesman should have found time to be the poet he is.

PADRAIC COLUM

You cannot but wonder why Padraic Colum (b. 1880) called his first volume of verse *Wild Earth* (1907). Ireland is an old country, a very old country, with many memorials of human occupancy from prehistoric times. Cromlechs and stone circles are widely distributed throughout its counties, great stone forts and great earthworks make the Aran Islands and County Meath places to visit, and round towers and the ruins of religious houses are found in many different parts of the island. It may be that Colum was in revolt against all the talk of Ireland in the twilight of the "twilight school of poetry" originated by Yeats, of a tendency among his countrymen to look back to old times rather than forward to new.

Perhaps it was only that "wild earth" is the best phrase of the best line of his best poem. This poem, "A Poor Scholar of the 'Forties" tells us that of the life-time's teaching of the scholar all that he can hope will remain in after years is:

> in rustic speech, a phrase
> As in wild earth a Grecian vase.

That is an arresting image, and there are others only less arresting here and there in his verses. You remember his poems for their subjects and for these images. There is hardly one of them a completely accomplished poem, a fit setting for the memorable phrases, a fit embodiment of their motives. "An Old Woman of the Roads" is a prayer of a tinker body for a house with:

> heaped-up sods upon the fire
> The pile of turf against the wall.

"The Drover" has the appeal of all poems of wayfaring and wanderlust. There are pictures of Ireland in it—"Brown bogs with black water," the stir of fairs with:

> Loud words and dark faces
> And the wild blood behind.

There is nothing in the slight volumes that have succeeded *Wild Earth* to compare with its best. *Dramatic Legends and Other Poems* (1922) has the material of poetry in it, but that material has not been fashioned into poetry. There are verses informed with Irish feeling and verses that attempt to open vistas into the past of lands older even than Ireland, but there are no finely wrought poems. *Creatures* (1927) is as disappointing as *Dramatic Legends,* certain of whose verses on animals it reprints. There is knowledge in it of otters and asses, of swallows and pigeons, and good writing about them, but no poetry. It would seem that in verse, as in the prose drama, Colum came to maturity in youth, and did what there was in him to do then. It was not the transplanting to America checked his growth. He had ceased to develop while he was hardly more than a boy in Dublin. So it has been with more poets than we care to admit.

L. A. G. STRONG

The quickest way to put L. A. G. Strong (b. 1896) in his own little niche is to say that he is the poet of the short poem. It would not be proper to say the poet of the epigram, because, while some of his short poems are epigrammatic only a few of them are true epigrams. They are some of them pictures, some of them sayings, some of them readings of life. They are seldom antithetical or plays upon words. "Winter," with its black trees, like sweeps' brushes against the sky, shaking "a crowd of sooty rooks" into the air, is a picture. "Zeke," too, is a picture of an old man going "tappy tappy up the Haisle." "Washerwoman's Song" and "A Memory" are sayings. "The Old Man Advises His Son" is a reading of life, telling us as it does, "Ye'll do well not to trust the deceivin' moon." "Outside the Abbey Theatre" is an epigram. A little group of four-liners is listed as "Epitaphy." Short stories are condensed into "A Lament" and "The Old Man at the Crossing."

Every set of verses that I have referred to, save "Winter" only, is from *Dublin Days* (1921), his first book of verse. That is by far his best book, prose or verse. Like so many writers of Ireland, he skims the cream at his first try, leaving skimmed milk only thereafter. *The Lowery Road* (1923) is pleasant verse, with an occasional flash of power, as in "Talk at an Inn," but far below *Dublin Days*. *The Lowery Road* offers little that is new, it is not individual, it leaves little for the memory to recall and delight in. *Northern Light* (1930) is a collector's item, signed by the author on the reverse of the title-page, but with none of the sharp grotesquerie that signs as his very own a half-dozen sets of verses in *Dublin Days*. *Northern Light* is a record of a vacation in Scotland over against the Hebrides. There is good writing in its verse, fresh images, but little that scores.

There are few poets, unfortunately, that have the courage to stick to the vein in which they "struck it rich." They wish to show that they can write more than one sort of poetry, that they are versatile, that they have several sorts of power. It may well be, of course, that Strong thought people would tire of the rich vulgarity of the best verses of *Dublin Days*. Perhaps they would, though I have not tired of "The Brewer's Man" in more than a decade, or of "Old Bridget" or "The Bait Digger's Son." Not one of these is high poetry, but each one is a grotesque of power, and poetry of a kind. Moreover these three, and "Outside the Abbey Theatre," "The Old Man Advises His Son" and "A Memory" are all his own, of a new kind of poetry, and persistent in the memory. Strong should have stuck to his last.

JAMES JOYCE

The artistry of James Joyce in verse is a prose artistry, of the order of the prose of his pre-Ulyssean days. In *Chamber Music* (1918) and in *Pomes Penyeach* (1927), he almost never attains to poetry. There is a certain intensity of mood underlying each little set of verses, but it hardly ever buoys up the words and sets them singing. He records things seen, and felt, and remembered, in vignettes of a cold clarity. One or two of them count for something, but the others are so empty of any real passion that they do not count. The pathological condition that had been so evident in *Dubliners* (1918) and from *Dubliners* on, is to be found, too, in the verses. It mars *Pomes Penyeach*. Ireland, Adriatic lands, and Switzerland are background for these verses or are the very stuff of the verses themselves. There is freshness of phrase and directness of utterance in some of them, but they do not hold in memory. It is impossible for the normal man to have any sympathy with several of them and those that do touch a normal and common human experience do not bite very deep. You, reading them, have a feeling that they are variations on themes and not poems that would not be left unsaid. The experience in them is generally dimmed and made faint by distance in time and space. They are never better than in "Tutto E Sciolto":

> A birdless heaven, seadusk, one lone star
> Piercing the west,
> As thou, fond heart, love's time, so faint,
>   So far,
> Rememberest.

Monk Gibbon (b. 1895) has an individual note. It is usual to compare him to W. H. Davies, and there are poems of his so like the Welshman's in subject and in cadence that the comparison is justified. Again, a poem will be his not only in material and point of view, but in cadence as well. The best of Gibbon is the capture of first love waking in a girl. The feeling is right, keen, "like arrows pointed—Green blades under an April sky." Often he does not quite get said all he feels and thinks about what he wants to write about. Many of his verses are only intimations, stabs at expression, 'prentice-work. Always, though, he writes of what he has seen with his own eyes, or felt, or experienced. He is always guessing at the whys and wherefores of things; he would like, if he could, to be plumbing the depths.

Though Gibbon writes himself down a wanderer, he likes many things treasured by stay-at-home folks of simple farming sort, cockcrow, children, dunghills, cherry-blow, stone walls, beasts feeding. Though he was in the World War there is little of it in his writing. It is with the happy and beautiful things, he holds, a poet should be concerned. He never writes unless he has something to say, and his verse has interesting comment on life even when it falls short of lyric. Read "Forbears" in *For Daws to Peck At* (1929) if you would know him at his best.

RICHARD ROWLEY

It is in "To a Poet" that Richard Rowley gives us his own measure. In upbraiding Yeats for preferring a high dream and "over-curious skill" to a song "sweet as life, and strong as death" he betrays his own preference for sentimentalities over the discoveries every poet worthy of the name makes for himself. There are no discoveries in Richard Rowley. We know no more of life after we have read him than we knew before, we hear no new music of words, we have seen no beauty of a kind other poets have not already brought us.

Rowley is a competent writer of verse. He takes a definite point of view and he is consistent in it. He is of the city rather than the country. He tries to write of machines and their tenders as Gibson writes of them. He has a gift for weaving place-names pleasantly into his verses. An Orangeman, he is no bigot, and he can laugh as well as sentimentalize. He is at his best in his grotesques. Of all the poems he collects for *Selected Poems* (1931) "The Piper" is the most original. It has an abandon and wildness that show the Belfast man can playboy it as well as his compatriots from Connacht. The spectacle of Moses and Aaron peeling off their coats:

> And hopping about on the kitchen floor,
> Like a couple of mountain goats

is a delectable one. I like next best "The Bachelor-Man." It has a bracing irony and a sardonic pathos that, somehow or other, blend happily. His protagonist is not the only unmated oldster who has found out:
> That life's a dreich job at the best
> Wantin' women an' drink.

In the sort of verse Rowley writes oftenest there is not much chance for characterization, but he has well caught, and in three lines, in "Reticence," the Scotch-Irishman's refusal to let on what he feels.
> A'll go un'er the mould
> Wi' a hantle o' things in my heart
> That hez never been told!

That is as true a thing as Rowley has said and as near to a discovery as he can come.

AUSTIN CLARKE

There is no question but the later work of Austin Clarke (b. 1896) is making for new effects in verse. By vowel rhyming, as he writes in the notes to *Pilgrimage and Other Poems* (1929), "lovely and neglected words are advanced to the tonic place and divide their echoes." One misses, though, in the verses of this volume and of the *Cattledrive in Connaught* (1925) certain of the more familiar and traditional effects of English poetry that delighted him in *The Vengeance of Fionn* (1918) and in *The Fires of Baäl* (1921). It is for the betterment of all poetry in English that the range of its technique be widened, but experimentation such as Clarke's almost inevitably leads to the dissipation of power. If there shall in the end come out of his studies in the effects of Gaelic measures in English verse an art individual and full of force we will hold the experimentation well worth while. If, however, that experimentation fails in bringing about such a perfection, we will have to lament an expenditure of energy that, employed as it was in his earlier verse, might have resulted in a real modern epic on a hero tale from old Gaelic legend.

Neither of the epic fragments in *The Sword of the West* (1921), "Concobar" or "The Death of Cuchullin" is as successful as *The Vengeance of Fionn* or *The Fires of Baäl*. Clarke, indeed, seems to shy away from the full-scope epic. Perhaps it is he feels a long epic poem is incompatible with our day, a thing readers will avoid, or perhaps he has not the patience or the architectonic power to carry through so stupendous an affair. It may be that the epic episode, dramatically conceived, is most native to his genius. The first part of *The Vengeance of Fionn*, the visit of the old leader of the Fianna to Grainne and Diarmuid, a creation of Clarke's youth, is what in all his work is most arresting. This poem has everything needed for epic but architectonic power. The heroic note is here, the large accent and grand style that Arnold demanded of great poetry. Here, too, is imagination, lordship of language, characterization, the gift of landscape painting and the power to give body and force to the pageantry of high life we have known from the time of Homer.

Clarke is just as much at home in the Orient in *The Fires of Baäl* as with the west of Ireland in *The Vengeance of Fionn*. The vivid color and magnificence of Eastern life is caught as surely as the wild and stormy greyness about Beann Gulbain and Knocknarea:

> Great branching cedars
> And massive walnut burnished by the wind
> Of autumn time before the swallows haste

> Sorrowing from the north, shaded the vales
> And from the silver tops of aspen trees
> Rose lowly hills speckled with juniper,
> Crushed sweetly by the Asian caravans
> Jangling bronze bells among their creaking loads,
> When, laden with purple luscious grapes, green gourds
> Still unmatured and ripe red apricots,
> Or gorgeous bales of damasked tapestries,
> Guarded with spears and moon-edged scimitars,
> The desert dromedaries from the glooms
> Of mountains slowly wind through starlight swamps.

That is a picture of Moab under the mountain into which Moses was to go up to die. Here is a picture of old Fionn on Beann Gulbain:

> He stood knee-deep in ferns; boar-like, his eyes
> Glinting. He saw above the forest's verge
> The black blunt precipice of Gulban rear
> Skyward, the clouded mountain tops and three
> Eagles in the high blue air like flies
> Flickering around a solitary peak.

There is, for all its stricter form, more than a suggestion of Dr. Hyde's translations of *The Love Songs of Connacht* in this "Blessing" which you find in *The Cattledrive in Connaught*:

> O Woman of the House, no sorrow come
> From the dark glen to leave your floor unswept,
> When I was tired you gave me milk and bread
> And I could sit down by the fire and dream
> Of her who crazed my heart; when dew began
> Behind the door and the lazy candle was lit,
> I made this rann for sleep: no mouse creep out
> Nor evil thing, O Woman of the House.

FREDERICK ROBERT HIGGINS

There is freshness of point of view and freshness of phrase in the verse of Frederick Robert Higgins (b. 1896). There is revolt in his poetry against the tenets of Yeats. He seeks to express what he calls "The racial strength of a Gaelic aristocratic mind—with its vigorous coloring and hard emotion," and he succeeds in a measure in doing what he attempts. There are horsemen of the kind we first met in Borrow in his verses, wild mountainy men, high-blooded fellows that know no restraint. There is no such gallery of portraits as one meets in Joseph Campbell's *Irishry* (1913), but there are portraits, "The Horse Breaker," "Cleopatra," and "The Ballad of O'Brudir."

Better than the portraits, better than the cry of wild blood, better than the vignettes of landscape here and there are certain images Higgins is the first to use in poetry in English. "A.E.," in his preface to *Island Blood* (1925) has picked out the best of these in this first volume. In "Old Galway" he writes of a girl with "high combs in her castled hair":

> She in the deeps of whose wild eyes
> The lost Armadas stir.

Perhaps that will the more easily be realized in all its significance if we recall the legend of Spanish blood left in western Ireland on the wreck of King Phillip's galleons seeking their way back to Spain after their defeat by Drake.

A young cow Higgins looks upon is "Fat as a snail in the moontide and silked like the seas." That is individual, and so is:

> Over one dim green hill,
> The grass-slim moon has grown
> So full that soon she'll spill
> Wet light on many a stone.

He uses his own eyes, and in the mind back of them there are few memories of old poets. I like too,

> Her movements are softer
> Than kittens' paws.

There is more of the moon in his writing than in that of any poet I know, twenty-four references all told to it in the forty-seven poems of *Island Blood*. It is frequent, too, in the imagery of *The Dark Breed* (1927), which shows, however, no advance upon *Island Blood*, and no such store of fresh images.

There is an advance again in *Arable Holdings* (1933). Higgins has here relied more on the old verse of the peasant bards of Ireland than in either of his previous volumes. The genius of these bards is, indeed, akin to his. They are wild-blooded and bitter-spoken, and so is he. They have the gift of fresh perception of nature and of the common facts of life, and so has he. They comment for themselves and make picturesque phrases, and so does he. He approximates to certain of their ways of verse, to internal rhyme and assonance. He blinks no truths, no matter how upsetting; he is direct, downright, naked, and unashamed. Family ties are strong in him. For all his stout individuality he assents willingly to a patriarchal system of society. No verses in this new volume are more appealing than "Father and Son."

> Yes, happy in Meath with me for a day
> He walked, taking stock of herds hid in their own breathing;
> And naming colts, gusty as wind, once steered by his hand.
> Lightnings winked in the eyes that were half shy in greeting
> Old friends—the wild blades, when he gallivanted the land.

Best of all his powers is that of lifting the common to distinction by sheer intensity of presentation. A wake, its reek of "sad tobacco," and huddling couples of young folk, is made notable by no exclusion of sordid detail. The triumphing realization of what Padraic O'Conaire was in life dominates all and transfigures all into nobility.

CHAPTER IX

A. E. Housman

ALFRED EDWARD HOUSMAN (1859-1936), Professor of Latin at Cambridge, is the most laconic of the poets of our day. He published in his lifetime only two brief volumes of verse, *A Shropshire Lad* (1896) and *Last Poems* (1922). There are, in all, in these two volumes, only one hundred and four sets of verses of a total of twenty-one hundred and twenty lines. If he had followed the Tennysonian precept of a line a day, Housman could have written all his poems in somewhat less than six years. As a matter of fact he seems to have written a very large part of them in two orgies of composition, one in 1895 and the other in 1922. It is in the short preface to *Last Poems* that Housman tells how his verses were written: "I can no longer expect to be revisited by the continuous excitement under which in the early months of 1895 I wrote the greater part of my other book. . . . About a quarter of this matter (*Last Poems*) belongs to the April of the present year (1922), but most of it to dates between 1895 and 1910."

There is a great deal told in the few words of this preface, and there is more to be read between the lines. Housman, a man of thirty-three in 1896, was still deeply rooted in Shropshire, though he had been thirteen years in London as government clerk and teacher of Latin in University College. These thirteen years had been years of exile, and there had been three years at Oxford before them that were only better because they permitted of easier visits to Knighton, and those other so loved places "in valleys of springs of rivers" and among those "hanging woods and hamlets" over against Wales.

It was not only the countryside of Shropshire that called him.

That countryside did call him strongly. There called him, too, and just as strongly, his memories of childhood, of fellowship with his comrades, of fairings into Ludlow, of mayings with "rose-lipt maidens," of memorials of old wars on the Welsh Marches. We all know how the home-place rises before us after years of absence from it, how clear it is and how beautiful to the mind's eye. Time has blotted out what was unessential in that place and its life, what was ugly, what was hard to bear. Only that remains which is food for the spirit. Much of this is little things, which mean more and more as the years pass; partly because they are, after all, first things, appreciated with a wonder and a freshness of feeling that after-years are hard put to duplicate; and partly because they are things long lived with and so loved through very familiarity; and partly because of the enchantment that distance proverbially lends.

Shropshire haunted Housman, no doubt, so instantly, so insistently, so poignantly, that there was no way out of his preoccupation with it save by saying out from his heart all that it meant to him. Some ghosts can be laid only by letting them have their will. It is a noteworthy roll-call of poems in which he praises Shropshire. Even when they are descriptive, they are more than descriptive. This one has in it his lament for the short while we have to enjoy the beauty of the world. The next one is the catching of a mood evoked by the landscape. The next involves an incident as simple as any out of folklore.

It is now as "a western brookland" where "poplars stand and tremble By pools" that he sees Shropshire. Now it is a bit of it he sees, where "the aspen heaves Its rainy-sounding silver leaves." Again it is an out-of-the-world spot where you can hear the beech-nuts rustle down and where you can see the pale purple of the autumn crocus. Shropshire is again a place of

>   glittering pastures
> And empty upland still
> And solitude of shepherds
> High in the folded hill.

Most often, however, it rises before you as a tumbled hill country, under April skies and washed sweet by April air, where:

> Loveliest of trees, the cherry now
> Is hung with bloom along the bough,
> And stands about the woodland ride
> Wearing white for Eastertide.

There are various veins in Housman. There is the vein in which he writes of Shropshire, though more austerely, as Herrick writes of his kindlier Devonshire. "March" and "The Lent Lily" and " 'Tis Time, I think, by Wenlock town," and "With rue my heart is laden" are in this vein. There are other verses which have about them certain qualities that recall Propertius. These are often elegiac. Among them are verses to Shropshire lads who have taken the Queen's shilling, who have gone overseas to fight her battles, and who have left their bones in alien soil. So heavy a toll has death taken of those he knew in boyhood that he would make the most of those still "men alive." He would help them to whatever it is they wish. He would stand by them in trouble. The verses in which he records these feelings are most of them stoical, but now and then one is high-hearted in fronting the future, or exultant in the joy of comradeship.

Housman shows his concern with the Shropshire of yesterday in "The Welsh Marches." In this poem, a long poem for this man of short poems, Housman considers the old wrongs that were done in the wars of Celt and Saxon. In "On Wenlock Edge" it is the further past of Roman times that rises before him. It is this concern with Roman times of Housman that has so influenced Masefield, one of the many juniors of Housman who have learned to look at England as he has. Laurence Housman, as ready to write as Alfred Edward to refrain from writing, has been influenced by his elder brother, as he has been by many other contemporary poets his elders. Wilfred Wilson Gibson rescued himself from pseudo-Pre-Raphaelitism by suddenly seeing his northern fell country somewhat as Housman had seen his western hills.

The methods of Gibson are far from Housman's, but it was Housman taught him how much there was to write about in humble lives. In a way, they all derive from Wordsworth, but the epigrammatic and gnomic quality which came in with Housman, and which is found in the younger men, shows that some of them derive from Wordsworth by way of Housman. Flecker has owned coming under his spell; and W. H. Davies, original as he is, found his way to his own brevity partly by the model of brevity set up by Housman. The characteristic poem of Housman is of four stanzas of four lines each, or sixteen lines in all. Many are shorter, of twelve and eight lines only.

It is *A Shropshire Lad* that I have been generalizing from so far. In it is nearly all that is best in Housman, and practically all that has influenced later writers. What it was to large numbers of people was revealed when orders began to come in for *Last Poems* on the announcement of its forthcoming publication. The first edition of *Last Poems* was of four thousand, and, before this edition was on the street, a second edition of four thousand was arranged for. Thus eight thousand copies of *Last Poems* had been ordered before the book was actually published.

Last Poems has good writing in it, but it is in the main little more than an echo of the earlier book. An old man's outlook obtrudes itself now and then, but there is little of the mellowness age so often brings. *Last Poems* is remarkable, indeed, for its many recapturings of the moods out of which *A Shropshire Lad* was written. It is so much of a part with *A Shropshire Lad* that we might think it, had we not the author's testimony to the contrary, largely made up of verses that he had rejected for that book. We are glad to have these *Last Poems*, but we look in vain among them for lyrics we would put in an anthology of his best. There is the old point of view, the old stoicism, the old epigrammatic quality, the old effects of rhythm, the old clarity of thought and utterance, the old bright light of April over all. There is even something of the old love-longing. There is a plaintiveness here and there that we had not in the earlier book. There was wistfulness there, but no such note as that we find in "The West," the very first poem in *Last Poems*. In younger years he was not afraid to own:

> In all the endless road you tread
> There's nothing but the night.

Now, however, he cries out

> Comrade, look not on the west,

the west of setting sun, and salt dividing sea, and death.

There is the old sure artistry of phrase but little of freshness of phrase. Perhaps there could not be. You cannot surprise a generation with a second revelation of what on its first revelation was a thing of a new beauty. I find three felicities only in *Last Poems* to place against two-score such in *A Shropshire Lad*. All three are bits of out-of-doors. One is "Past hawthornwood and hollow"; another is "The sloe was lost in flower, The April elm was dim"; and the third is "The plum broke forth in green, The pear stood high and snowed." How accurate is this last description will be known only to those who are aware of the differences in the blow of European, American, and Japanese plums. The Japanese plum breaks forth in so greeny a white it looks an utter green in certain lights. There is an occasional grandiloquence, such as was wholly absent from the first book. Of this sort are the two lines:

> The chestnut casts his flambeaux, and the flowers
> Stream from the hawthorn on the wind away

that are the opening to IX, but the Housman we know comes back in the following pair:

> The doors clap to, the pane is blind with showers,
> Pass me the can, lad; there's an end of May.

Epigrammatic Housman was in the first book, but never there a writer of epigrams. That he is now, in the new book, I should say in the two quatrains of XXII that match each other with the lines, "The hour for lies and him," "The hour for truth and her." The saving humor of *A Shropshire Lad* is still with him. He has stood the years well. They have not, however, added to his stature as a poet.

There is no volume of English verse of its size, of sixty-three poems, that has more poetry in it than *A Shropshire Lad*. Its nearest rival may be that even shorter volume, *Poems*, of Ralph Hodgson. Or, if you wish to go back to earlier times, the thin sheaves of Gray or Collins might be compared to *A Shropshire Lad*. Surely it may be said, in all reverence to the past, that the anthologies of the future will contain more lyrics of Housman than of either of the eighteenth-century poets. Nor is it presumptuous to look forward to a day when the lyrics, "Loveliest of trees, the cherry now," "In valleys of springs of rivers," and "With rue my heart is laden" will have as sure a place in the affections of men as the "Elegy Written in a Country Churchyard" itself. Already they are as well known and as well loved as anything in Collins.

Saying after saying in *A Shropshire Lad* is memorable.

> To look at things in bloom
> Fifty springs are little room,

once taken to heart is yours forever. It is a saying to put over against many of a very different philosophy of life in Housman. His mood changed from time to time in that fit of writing in the spring of 1895. It was optimistic at times, but it was more often pessimistic. There is the doctrine of "Gather ye rosebuds while ye may" in "Oh see how thick the gold-cup flowers" with its:

> Ah, spring was sent for lass and lad,
> 'Tis now the blood runs gold,
> And man and maid had best be glad
> Before the world is old.

Pessimism is dominant in:

> Wonder 'tis how little mirth
> Keeps the bones of man from lying
> On the bed of earth

In like Hardian mood Housman cries out:

> Ay, look: high heaven and earth ail from the prime foundation;
> All thoughts to rive the heart are here, and all are vain:
> Horror and scorn and hate and fear and indignation.
> Oh why did I awake? When shall I sleep again?

It is the Shropshire lad's belief that though friendship and love, like all things human, are frail, you must needs hold to them; to friendship to keep you brave, to love to keep you clean. Housman accepts the ironic as natural, but at times it is so overpowering that he cannot smile it out. The tears will spring, the wounded heart bleed.

To the man who thus sees life, it is inevitable that external nature, the hills, the trees, the skies, should bring forgetfulness of human pain only for the moment. The old feuds of the Welsh marches, the wrongs done down all the ages, will make themselves known through hundreds of memorials. The wanderer about Uriconium or Clungunford, no matter how beautiful the countryside to-day, will have his thoughts brought back to "what man has made of man" by relics of old wars unearthed by plough or rain. And then the "blue-remembered hills" of Shropshire are themselves symbols of his vanished youth, and suggestive of personal memories. So it is unlikely that the poems sprung of memories of these wanderings will escape certain notes of "the ancient sorrow of man."

Humor, now kindly and now grim, helps to vary the tone from one poem to another. All oldsters will rejoice in the declaration:

> But I was one-and-twenty,
> No use to talk to me.

And men of all ages will agree with the doctrine that:

> the feather pate of folly
> Bears the falling sky,

and shrug, and accept its corollary:

A. E. HOUSMAN

Think no more; 'tis only thinking
Lays lads underground.

It is in the inspired doggerel of "Terence, this is stupid stuff" that Housman records more readings of life than in any other of his poems. The poet believes, of course, that worthy things can run the gauntlet of laughter. Here are three straight from the shoulder:

> . . . malt does more than Milton can
> To justify God's ways to man.
>
> Ale, man, ale's the stuff to drink
> For fellows whom it hurts to think:
>
> Look into the pewter pot
> To see the world as the world's not.

And here are another three in another six lines:

> Therefore, since the world has still
> Much good, but much less good than ill,
> And while the sun and moon endure
> Luck's a chance, but trouble's sure,
> I'd face it as a wise man would
> And train for ill and not for good.

There is evidence in plenty here of a Puritan ancestry in the thinking of Housman, but there is little evidence here, or elsewhere, of his literary ancestry. I have mentioned Propertius and Herrick, but there are in Housman no direct obligations to either. Places are the inspiration of many of his poems, as they have been to many English poets before his time. It is in his own manner, though, that he writes of places, a manner that seems born with him. All of his work is singularly of a texture, and there is no 'prentice-work among it. If there were juvenilia he had put them behind him before he collected his verses into *A Shropshire Lad*.

Housman is one of the beginnings in English poetry, the striker of a new note. It is these facts of his originality and of his influence that make him of different caliber than most minor poets. If it were not for these, we would write him down as a fellow of Stevenson and Clare, of Gray and Collins, of Cotton and Marvell. As things are we have to say he is of the order of Arnold and Landor, Herrick and Donne.

CHAPTER X

The Penetration of Thomas Hardy

THOMAS HARDY is a great poet by reason of his power of penetration to the realities of things. He has no overmastering music or verse with which to intoxicate us, no Shakespearean lordship of language, no rush of splendid images with which to take us by storm. He writes, in his most appealing poems, in a speech founded on that of his native Wessex, but with all difficult provincialisms left out. He refines his southern dialect as Wordsworth refined his of the north, but he retains the simplicity and downrightness of folk-speech. The sympathies of Hardy are those of the people from whom he sprang, countrymen of the lower middle class. He has none of the tricks of the literary fellow, none of the antics of the professional wit, none of the false pride of the intellectual, none of the cant of the artist to whom his craft is more than life.

Hardy loved ale and good company, but he had little in common with the writers who gathered at Cheshire Cheese, or coffee house of Queen Anne, or Mermaid Inn. There was in him no quality of Grub Street or Fleet Street. He had a strongly individual point of view, a personality all his own, but he had the fatalism of his country kind, and, despite a vigorous resentment against the injustice of nature, he had the resignation of a people long accustomed to make the best of what is, from untoward seasons to vagaries of government. He accepted realities, despite vehement protest against them, as do the folk.

These realities, stripped bare to him because of his intense interest in them and his sharp vision, hurt him in the seeing, many of them, and he could not forbear hurting us in his retelling of them. He retained until late in life that common weakness of youth, the desire to hurt by telling the truth. Even well toward the end of his life, when he was determined not to tell all he could see of the inwardness of things, he rather resented his self-imposed restraint.

> And if my vision range beyond
> The blinkered sight of souls in bond,
> —By truth made free—
> I'll let all me,
> And show to no man what I see.

There was a propagandist purpose, too, at times in his telling of the truth about things. He owned to this bias in the prefaces to his later volumes. When you realize that his verse of the most mastery of language was written after *Tess* (1891) and *Jude the Obscure* (1895) showed him succumbing to such purpose, it is remarkable that more of his memorable poems are not overburdened with propaganda. Two of his most deeply seated characteristics saved him, his interest in his people and his native candor. If he would preach against the system of things because of an observed fact that made for injustice, he would realize that this observed fact was perhaps at variance with many of its fellow-facts. There might not be enough of such observed facts of like import to prove that injustice is a law of nature. Then, too, even if life dealt unjustly with a man, that man had had happiness before the injustice overtook him, or had found early days so savorsome despite the injustice of nature that the injustice was only of secondary importance. Or the spectacle of the man's bravery under his fate was so bracing that, by comparison, his suffering sank into insignificance.

The Early Life of Thomas Hardy (1928) reveals to us that Hardy was preoccupied with poetry from the time he began to write about 1860, that his novels were all of them written only because it was through them that he could get a hearing and make a living. From 1860 onward, through all the time of his novel-writing, he was writing verse, too. Before *Wessex Poems* (1898), however, only four sets of verses of his were published. Hardy did not have the benefit of the reaction of public and critics to his poetry that enables a poet to find out whether his work is felt and understood as he intended it to be. Few men have been masters of an art practised wholly in secret. Even Emily Dickinson is not a perfect example of the exception to that rule.

There are verses of a new beauty and of a new music in the first and second volumes of Hardy, but the beauty and the music seem to be stumbled upon rather than achieved. There is not the mastery here that there is in the novels or that there is in the later published poetry. *Poems of the Past and Present* (1901), reread now after the manner of Hardy in verse is well known to me, reveals more poetry than it did on my first reading of it. When I first read it I found little of magic in it, little of music, little of lyrical cry. Now I find more lyrical cry, but the volume, like its predecessor, seems still to me to be wanting, save for a few poems, in music and magic. There was more of these qualities in *Time's Laughingstocks* (1909). There had been in the earlier volumes passages with the old familiar falls, in "The Alarm" and "The Dance at the Phoenix." There had been "Lizbie Browne," first of a series of poems about girls, some of them "livers in levity," that will not out of mind, but "Lizbie Browne" betrays an imperfect mastery of verse. Hardy cannot yet speak, in verse, in such words as he would use. There had been, too, the grave music of "Retrospect," with that beginning, "I have lived with Shades so long," that has so seventeenth-century an accent.

Time's Laughingstocks, however, has poem on poem of a wholeness of good tissue, poem after poem in which Hardy was able to say straightforwardly and simply and memorably what he would. In narrative there is "A Tramp-woman's Tragedy," jog-trot ballad to the ear, but a joy to one's inner being from the moment of first reading. There are here, too, lyrics to treasure from first word to last, "The House of Hospitalities," "Bereft," "Shut Out That Moon," "Her Father," "The End of the Episode," "The Rambler," "She Hears the Storm," "Carrey Clavel," and "Julie Jane," a group of nine not to be matched in either the first or the second volume.

It is a new world that we enter here, that is, a new world of verse. The world of his novels is, of course, one with it, the poetry of passages of their prose being fully as great as the best of his poetry in verse. No poet before Hardy presents a world much like it. There are notes here and there that recall certain notes of Campion. There are likenesses to Donne in the introspective verses. There is a common choice of country subjects with Herrick. There is a fidelity to fact that equals Crabbe's. The color of Hardy's verse, though, the tone it borrows of the man who made it, the point of view, the philosophy of life, are all met with for the first time. Irony is the predominant quality of this verse, and its distinguishing characteristic a predilection for country themes, a joy in the look of Wessex and in the ways of her folk. In background and in theory of art Hardy is, of course, nearest to Wordsworth of all English poets, but his philosophy of life is so far from Wordsworth's that one hardly ever associates the two.

It is usual to place A. E. Housman in comparison with Hardy, and Masefield, too, and both do certainly present likenesses to him. Housman cannot be said to have gone to school to him, as *A Shropshire Lad* (1896) was published two years before the world knew Hardy as a poet in verse. It is written out of a knowledge of country life such as Hardy had, however, and there are as many records, proportionately, of lives gone wrong in it as there are in Hardy. There is irony in Housman, too, and a somber view of things, but his pessimism is more forthright than is Hardy's, and his point of view, a young man's point of view, sharply differentiates his verse from the elder poet's. Masefield has gone to school to Hardy, but there is so little protest in Masefield against things as they are that it is only in material and method of characterization that there are similarities between the two.

There is no propaganda in Masefield. Hardy half-confesses to propaganda in the preface to *Late Lyrics* (1922), in a long "apology" for his verses. Hardy writes: "For—while I am quite aware that a thinker is not expected, and, indeed, is scarcely allowed, now more than heretofore, to state all that crosses his mind concerning existence in this universe, in his attempts to explain or excuse the presence of evil and the incongruity of penalizing the irresponsible —it must be obvious to open intelligences that, without denying the beauty and faithful service of certain venerable cults, such disallowance of 'obstinate questionings' and 'blank misgivings' tends to a paralysed intellectual stalemate. . . . And what is today, in allusions to the present author's pages, alleged to be 'pessimism' is, in truth, only such 'questionings' in the exploration of reality, and is the first step towards the soul's betterment and the body's also."

Fortunately the characteristic and prevailing moments of Hardy are not so burdened with moralizing. Before this that I have quoted was written, Hardy had written as an artist, and after this had been written he wrote again as an artist. Nor was he always so sure of his views, or so sweeping in his generalizations about life and letters as he is in this preface to *Late Lyrics*. In the preface to *Poems of the Past and Present* (1901) he writes: "the road to a true philosophy of life seems to lie in humbly recording diverse readings of its phenomena as they are forced upon us by chance and change." Nearly twenty-seven years later, when he wrote the preface to *Winter Words* (1928) he declares that "no harmonious philosophy is attempted in these pages."

The heyday of Hardy in verse was late, in *Time's Laughingstocks* (1909), and in *Satires of Circumstance* (1914). He was sixty-nine when he published the one, and seventy-four when he published the other. It is impossible, though, to say that these best verses were written late in life. Some of these later published poems, he tells us, were written years before they were printed, but in only a few instances does he tell us which. In the "apology" to *Late Lyrics* (1922) he refers to "a freshness" in the "unusually far back poems" which is "now unattainable." We can only guess, however, at the presence of this "freshness." There is no sure test that can determine its presence. "Freshness" to him and to us may not be one and the same thing.

It is no wonder that there are not so many arresting moments in the later volumes, *Moments of Vision* (1917); and that *Late Lyrics* (1922), *Human Shows and Far Phantasies* (1925), and *Winter Words* (1928). Though they show his intellectuality unimpaired, they have not the brightness and the music of the verses published earlier. It is a wonder, though, that *The Queen of Cornwall* (1923) revealed a passion almost youthful. Such a passion is hardly to be looked for in a play published when its author was more than eighty.

His earlier faults of propaganda and prosaic passages do not often recur in the later volumes. These are burdened, however, with "seconds," verses put aside when earlier collections were made, and with verses written in tired moods of old age. We are glad, of course, to have all that he has written. At his most pedestrian he is always dealing with life at first hand out of as great an experience and understanding of it as any English poet has possessed. So, even if the emotion of the moment of writing has not been of enough intensity to lift that writing into high poetry, it still has great value as a record of life.

At his best Hardy is a great poet. For all the simplicity of utterance of his verses, the absence of lordly language and of splendid figures, for all the almost folk point of view of many of them, they are not all of them to be fathomed on a first reading. Such as are not are so weighted with experience, so full of the gravity of life, so deep-thoughted, so analytic, so questioning, that we must read them many times to understand them completely and to realize their portent. A wide and deep experience of life is needed to take to heart the full significance of his verse. There is no obscuring of thought or expression by imagery or exuberance of language. There is no cleverness at all in Hardy, only the greatness of the man who sees and who understands all that man can see and understand, who sympathizes with all, who has the power to write down clearly all his knowledge and vision.

Hardy knows all the great central things, in art, in philosophy, in history, in the countryside, in the lives of men. He knows the Bible; the Greek tragedians; Shakespeare, Wordsworth, Tennyson; Voltaire, Schopenhauer, Von Hartmann, Einstein. He knows local folklore and the campaigns of Napoleon. He knows the songs of "the little fifers"; the ways of hedgehogs and of sheep; the wheel of the stars through the skies. He knows, none better, love and hate, lust of power and the burden of memories. He never postures, or flaunts it, or shows off. He is unobtrusive, quiet, a very part of nature. "A Jog-Trot Pair" gives the key on which he lived. He was "just folks," as we say in America. He was commonplace in conduct. No allowances had to be made for him because he was a genius. He never found everyday doings boring. He was for all this "happier than the cleverest, smartest, rarest."

There are so many poets whose verse is far from the everyday things of life that it is a great relief to have a man like Hardy to turn to, one who is deeply interested in all that happens in a neighborhood, one who sees all life so imaginatively that there is little in a thoroughly known neighborhood but may be transmuted into art. As the church was content to leave the best tunes to the devil, so the majority of poets have been content to leave the best subjects to the popular versifiers, men with a flair for appealing subjects, but with no powers of the poet for their presentation. Too many of the poets are more interested in their art of verse than in its material, or fond of material which, in the nature of things, can appeal only to the few, often only to a coterie.

Hardy's ability to get at the heart of a situation amounts almost to divination. It is partly the result of an universal and inexhaustible sympathy, a sense of oneness with his kind that includes all men as brothers, a keen realization that their innate humanity makes all men interesting and companionable if you have the wit to understand them. One of his poems records an incident that must have happened to every approachable and neighborly man. Two brothers call, "in their usual quiet way." They talk:

> awhile
> Of ordinary things,
> Till spread that silence in the room
> A pent thought brings.

Those last two lines touch universal experience. We are not surprised, any of us, to learn that it is death the brothers have come to announce.

What appeals to Tom, Dick, and Harry appeals to Hardy. And these ordinary things appeal to him no less because everything else there is in the world appeals to him, too. In "Great Things" he sings the praises of cyder, the dance, and love, holding them among the greatest, just as surely as soul itself. Hardy is of Wessex, of the very fiber of its folk, bone of their bone, slow, long-suffering, with a sort of angry patience of what must be. In "A Wet Night" he complains of the hardship of a foot journey across a moor on a rainy evening. Then he thinks that his people must have often endured such nights in the old time before him, "In sturdy muteness," and he is comforted and quieted. What they bore he, too, should be able to bear. In "Wessex Heights" he writes:

> There are some heights in Wessex, shaped as if by a kindly hand
> For thinking, dreaming, dying on, and at crises when I stand,
> Say, on Ingpen Beacon eastward, or on Wylls-Neck westwardly,
> I seem where I was before my birth, and after death may be.

Here, in the so well known and so loved countryside he has lived long years, all his life save for some early sojourns in and about London. Here he built himself a house, and planted the place about it. "At Day-Close in November" he can say:

> Beech leaves, that yellow the noon-time,
>   Float past like specks in the eye;
> I set every tree in my June time,
>   And now they obscure the sky.

There is more of his love of nature in "Afterwards," perhaps, than in any other poem of his. Here he reveals himself, his interest in out-of-doors, and here he wonders will any one after his death recall that he loved "the leafing trees"; "The dewfall hawk"; the hedgehog that roams the dark, "mothy and warm"; the full-starred heavens of winter; the bell that tolls for a funeral.

Again and again is sounded his love of the simple things that are the eternal things. In "Any Little Old Song" he tells us that he only needs "the homeliest of heart-stirrings," that "any little old song" will do for him. He refers once to "The Mockingbird," and we are led to wonder did he know many of our American songs, our "Old Black Joe" and "Tenting Tonight on the Old Camp Ground" and "Aunt Dinah's Quilting Party." Had he known them, doubtless he had liked them, as he did so much that was Mid-Victorian, whether hymns or dances, gowns or poetry. In his verses, "On an Invitation to the United States," he said he shrank "to seek a modern coast," but he would have fitted in well here, as, indeed, anywhere in the world. He would have found his very people here in New Hampshire, speaking his Old World speech, playing such Old World tunes as he would have recognized, and stepping to the old square dances he knew so well in Dorsetshire. Here he would have found just such stories as he knew at home. He would, indeed, have found here more stories than people, for the West and the cities have claimed the people. The stories still linger, in the memories of the few oldsters who hold on to the old acres. Hardy could not, however, have been happy anywhere but in his home-place, where he was so deeply rooted, where the generations of his family have lived before him.

There is testimony in poem after poem of his love of old church music, a love that inspired so much of *Under the Greenwood Tree* (1872). He liked old ritual, too, old dances, old furniture, old houses—"all that art had wove in antique style." He liked all things of yesterday, but no writer is more abreast of all issues of the hour. His philosophy of life, too, is very different from any of the philosophies that were accepted in old time. Perhaps it was that he looked backward in things of the heart, and forward in things of the mind.

The fact that he and his brothers and sisters were the last of their line impressed him profoundly. Ever-present consciousness of it burdened and oppressed him. He laments:

> I the last one—
> Outcome of each spectral past one
> Of that file, so many-manned.

In a moment of depression, in the old home of his youth, he wrote himself down:

A pale late plant of your once strong stock. . . .
A thinker of crooked thoughts upon Life in the sere,
And on That which consigns men to night after showing the day to them.

The constraint of thought in these lines reduces their rhythm almost to the rhythm of prose. So it is, elsewhere, all too often, in his verses.

There is much of the night and the dark in Hardy. He is keenly aware of the stars:

> the Lady's Chair,
> Immense Orion's glittering form,
> The Less and Greater Bear.

The moon chills many of his verses. But it is the dark without the moon or stars that is most often recurrent in them. He knows what it is to have "the country darkness" clasp him; what dread men have of the dark for itself and for its way of bringing back memories it were better not to recall; what prophecies of ill to come whisper in your ears as you sit alone, or even with companions about you, in silence, in the black night.

The dark weighed upon Hardy, but not so seriously as the thought that he and his family were the last of their line. The insistently recurrent thought of that was one of the several contributing factors to the somberness of his outlook on life, that after him there was no seed. Again and again he writes of the brief remembrance there is of all who have peopled the earth. Only the few distinguished by beauty or power, sorrow or genius, chance or infamy, live in memory longer than the lives of the youngest who knew them. Fifty years suffices in most cases to blot out all memory of the dead. The dead, Hardy had a feeling, are in some way aware of their existence in memory. They dread the death of those who give them, through remembrance, a sort of second life.

A realization that the temporary is the all, of which Hardy writes in the first set of verses in *Wessex Poems*, is another cause of this somberness. That realization, I sometimes think, is at the very root of the irony that so flourishes in all that he writes. And yet Hardy is not primarily a gnomic poet, but a narrative poet. He is a narrative poet who sees in the story that he is telling an illustration of the irony of existence. There are in his writing fewer lines that are aphorisms or epigrams or readings of life than you would expect. And the striking phrase, while more common, is not to be found upon every page. Some of these phrases are self-revelation, one or two unintentional self-revelation. He speaks of "my somber image," and declares "No Answerer I." No answerer, but a questioner, he is almost always in his poetry. Some of his lines that I recall oftenest are: "And the sun was white, as though chidden of God"; "Yellow as autumn leaves, alive as spring"; "The years have gathered greyly"; and "All smalling slowly to the grey sea-line." Of a sort rarer in his verse are: "The power, the pride, the reach of perished Rome." There is alliteration there, alliteration very like that of Old English verse. It is common in Hardy, and productive of some of his best effects. You find it again in: "On the rugged ridge of Waterstone, the peewits plaining round." Combined with assonance it lends emphasis to the thought expressed in "Mind-chains do not clank where one's next neighbor is the sky."

Out-and-out readings of life are: "When might is right no qualms deter"; "Those house them best who house for secrecy"; and "He who goes fathering Gives frightful hostages to hazardry." The mordancy of its satire takes away, perhaps, some of the impressiveness of:

> After two thousand years of mass
> We've got as far as poison gas,

but it is a couplet not easy to forget.

The philosophy of Hardy has already forced itself into consideration in relation to other phases of his poetry. It is, of course, the philosophy of his novels, the philosophy of a man who sees about him everywhere the war of natural instincts with the laws that man has made for man. Nature punishes man for the instincts that nature has planted in him, and often society adds its punishment, too. There is no justice in the system of things. So man after man has discovered, from Job to William Dean Howells. What distinguishes Hardy's statement of the injustice of nature is his keen perception of the irony there is in the relation of man's hopes to their non-fulfilment. In poem after poem the ironic note is emphasized. You hear it, as I have said, in "The Temporary the All," at the very outset of his first volume, and you are never out of the sound of it as you turn page after page of volume after volume down to the last poem of *Winter Words*, "He Resolves to Say No More." Fortunately he never tries to formulate his philosophy into a system, but is content with Exhibit A and Exhibit B and Exhibit C of the irony of life.

When Hardy can free himself of irony, and speaks simply, it is often at the expense of the quality of his writing. His gnomic poems flat without it. And when not in ironic mood he is apt to moralize, to make stabs at a system of philosophy. It is then he tries to interpret his attitude towards life as distinctly meliorist. In "To Sincerity" he declares:

> —Yet, would men look at true things,
> And unilluded view things,
> And count to bear undue things,

> The real might mend the seeming,
> Facts better their foredeeming,
> And Life its disesteeming.

He speaks even more clearly in "In Tenebris," owning himself outcast for his clarity of vision and for his candor. In a poem inspired by a visit to the garden in Lausanne where Gibbon finished *The Decline and Fall* Hardy quotes with stern approval Milton's

> Truth like a bastard comes into the world
> Never without ill-fame to him who gives her birth.

The irony, in Hardy's case, is not that of the man who expected too much of life and, disappointed by what it brought him, found solace in girding at human nature and the system of things. As he wrote in *Winter Words*, "He Never Expected Much." Yet, such is human nature, Hardy was keenly aware, at least in the lives of others, how far short of expectation was most realization. Even God finds, in one of Hardy's poems, that he could build less well than he intended:

> That I made Earth, and life, and man,
> It still repenteth me.

For all his somberness and irony Hardy is not the pessimist that many make him out to be. You can quote passages from him of the deepest pessimism, like his question:

> Has some Vast Imbecility,
> Mighty to build and blend,
> But impotent to tend,
> Framed us in jest, and left us now to hazardry?

Yet you have to put over against such a passage this declaration of his, made at fifty:

> Still I'd go the world with Beauty,
> I would laugh with her and sing,
> I would shun divinest duty
> To resume her worshipping.

As Hardy is always insisting, most of what he writes, even when he writes in the first person, is not necessarily his personal experience or belief, but often as not impersonative, dramatic, what this man or that girl feels or has suffered. The first person is used by Hardy to make what is said more instant, and more vivid.

Hardy has a very keen sense of the brevity of life, he sees "That Sportsman Time but rears his brood to kill." That other favored theme of the poets, almost as much written upon as the quick passing of life, the crassness of trade, provokes him into rating:

> the Market's sordid war
> As something scarce worth living for.

There is a good deal of the loneliness of age in his verse. He had his share of human companionship. Family ties were strong with him; he had close friends in his youth; he was a good neighbor; "two bright-souled women clave to him." And yet he is lonely, and eager no more.

It is in *The Dynasts* (1903-1908) that Hardy is most subtle in his thought, most analytical of the system of things. *The Dynasts* supplements the many guesses of his other verse at the riddle of existence. It is most valuable for its furtherance of our knowledge of his philosophy of life. It is interesting, too, as an experiment, one of the greatest experiments in English letters. It is only in spots interesting in itself. Its reading is not a joy, which every other book of Hardy is for its art, even if, like *Jude the Obscure*, the story hurts you beyond endurance. *The Dynasts* cannot be called great literature. It is a closet drama on the largest scale, in his own words "an epic-drama of the war with Napoleon, in three parts, nineteen acts, and one hundred and thirty scenes." It presents a vast panorama of Europe, from the Bay of Biscay to Moscow, from Rome to Wessex, during the ten years 1805-1815.

It presents hosts of characters, and the principal ones rather intimately. This Napoleon is not only the Napoleon we have read of in history, but a man we know as we know a man several times met. Marie Louise, poor Josephine, Pitt and Wellington, Ney and Kutuzof, Nelson and Captain Hardy, Sergeant Young of Stourcastle and Captain Dalbiac's lady are all given more or less personality. There are few characters that are not more than lay figures, though they can none of them, of course, not even Napoleon himself, be presented in detail.

Played, in part, at the outset of the World War, *The Dynasts* revealed these figures in bolder outline. It left the impression that there had passed before the spectators a pageant of England at war, and of England saving the world. Though many of the scenes were of foreign places, and many of them without English personages in them, there was a sense of England dominating all.

The reading that went to the making of this drama is stupendous to think of. But there is much more than reading that went to its making. There is in it the oral tradition of a countryside. Hardy was born and brought up in that part of England most threatened with invasion by Napoleon. Men of Hardy's ancestry, direct and collateral, were summoned to the defense of the shore when it was rumored Napoleon's transports were on the sea. Captain Hardy, Nelson's Hardy, was born near where Thomas Hardy was born, and of his stock. Napoleon was already, in Thomas Hardy's youth, a sort of ogre in local folklore. Veterans of the Spanish campaigns and of Waterloo were familiars of Hardy's childhood. The whole spectacle that is Napoleon was before Hardy all his life, and when he was fifty-seven he set himself down to present that spectacle in *The Dynasts*. If we are to take his preface literally, the stupendous task was finished in 1903, in six years. Its three parts were published in 1903, 1906, and 1908, and they were gathered into one volume in 1910.

Hardy's grip of the wide-flung campaign of Napoleon is marvelous. All the many scenes are held together, and, so far as one so little versed in history as I can tell, properly coördinated. And all are realized with sharp intensity. Yet one has the despairing feeling as one finishes one's reading, and one's second reading, that it is largely waste effort. It was not what Hardy was best empowered to do. Poetry was, his life through, what was in his heart to do, but such poetry as he could attain, here in *The Dynasts*, is not of his best. It is not so great, any of it, as the poetry in prose of the novels. There is no passage in all its hundred and thirty scenes as thrilled with poetry as the description of Egdon Heath in *The Return of the Native*, or of Talbothays in *Tess*, or the lament of Marty South in *The Woodlanders*. There is no passage in it comparable to the best poetry in verse that I have praised and quoted in support of that praise.

There are moments of insight in *The Dynasts*, or it would not be Hardy's. They are few relatively, though, to the great bulk of the drama, and they are few of them phrased as are the best in his gnomic and lyrical and narrative poems. There is an epic sweep about *The Dynasts*, a sense of large issues nobly pondered, a wrestling with destiny. Yet *The Dynasts* is not great poetry, or great drama, or great literature of any sort. It is, for all its magnificence, a failure in art, like *The Ring and the Book*, and most of the plays of Yeats, and the cataloguing poems of Whitman that were supposed to give us the very breath and being of America. Hardy could compass the material of *The Dynasts* in his brain, but not in his heart. The great provincialist failed with the subject of the center, but not because it was of the center. Even a genius of the center like Goethe would have failed in such an undertaking. *The Dynasts* was an attempt at the impossible.

As you turn your mind from *The Dynasts* to the simple subjects of Hardy's provincial poems you are aware again, as you have so often been aware, that the little things of life are the greatest things. The countryside as it changes from season to season, its flowers and trees; the fruits of the earth; the beasts of farm and wild; the birds of garden and orchard, of wood and heath; man in this rural setting; his loves and ambitions; his daily concerns and his thoughts of the beyond; his reaction to work and play, to his friends and foes; his troubles over money and his soul-stirrings: these are the things that Hardy set down in

THE PENETRATION OF THOMAS HARDY

their truth and beauty. These are the great things. He puts things in their proper relation in the poem he entitles "In Time of the Breaking of Nations":

> Yonder a maid and her wight
> Come whispering by;
> War's annals will fade into night
> Ere their story die.

No poet has been more concerned with death than Hardy. From youth on it has been to the fore in his thoughts as one of the great subjects of poetry. All the circumstances of his life have deepened his interest in death. His study of church architecture, involving as it did visits to many churches, kept the spectacle of mortality always before him. The illustrations in *Wessex Poems* show as conclusively as the verses that his brooding over death gave a ghoulish quality to his thought as it did, more emphatically, to the thought of Maeterlinck. In "Reminiscences of a Dancing Man" we are led to the query, curious in such a poem:

> Whither have danced those damsels now!
> Is Death the partner who doth moue
> Their wormy chaps and bare?

"I have lived with Shades so long," "Julie Jane," "The Dead Quire," and "Friends Beyond," are four notable poems on death and the shadow of death. A class of allied poems is that inspired by ghosts and phantoms. He can conjure up the dead easily from places associated with them in life, as well as set them talking with him or with one another in their graves. "Intra Sepulchrum" is of the latter class. Of the former are "The Woman I Met," and "The Old Neighbor and the New," and the score of poems in which memories of his dead wife so overmaster him that he can all but feel her with him again. Most of his phantoms and ghosts are not, of course, ghosts believed in, or pretended phantoms, or hallucinations, but a device of the poet to give immediate presence and body to his imaginings of people dead and gone and to his memories of people intimately associated in the past with a place he is visiting. In "Paying Calls" he finds all the people he visits at home, for they are in their graves.

Places to Hardy are generally worthy of description because of some human association with them, often in old time, often in the poet's youth, often only yesterday. Description of countryside for its own sake has little place in his verse. There are touches in plenty with the tang of place in them, but they are methods of approach to human drama, or settings for such drama. In "On Sturminster Foot-Bridge" the description is a frame for the portrait of the loved one; and in "Overlooking the River Stour" the protagonist's concern with the detail of nature out-of-doors costs him knowledge of what was happening behind his back indoors that would have made for his happiness.

Hardy loves England, the look of the countryside, as only one of a stock rooted in the soil for centuries can love it. Not a place he visits in his Wessex but has associations with this or that member of his family. He loves the countryside as much in winter as in summer. He loves the coast, the cliffs with their crying seamews and such stretches of sand as those in Lulworth Cove, as he loves the inland heaths and dairied valleys and apple-orchards. He loves his share of England in the summer, especially "open drouthy downland thinly grassed," and throughout all the changes of the seasons, which he follows as curiously and as lovingly as any poet since Chaucer. His England is an England you reach by footpath and by stile, an England "beyond where bustle ends." It is rural England, agricultural England, the kindly southland along the channel, where, until his youth, something of Merry England lingered still. There are airs about it like those that wandered the Forest of Arden, and that waken in him echoes of the music of Elizabethan songbooks. In this England "a shepherd stands by a gate in a white smock-frock." It is an England, where in the long summer evenings you see "swart bats, whose wings, be-webbed and tanned" whir "like the wheels of ancient clocks."

Hardy has the English love of dogs. He celebrates his own "Wessex" in life and in death, and he has written another set of verses on a dog that is too harrowing to particularize. He has the English love of country life, and of raising things, but he has not the English love of those kinds of sport that involve killing things. He has the English love of old buildings, with the architect's knowledge to deepen that love. Yet, though architecture was his means of livelihood for a decade of his young years there is comparatively little about it in his verse, not nearly so much as there is in his novels.

There is little criticism of other poets. He pays tribute to Shakespeare and to William Barnes, to both of whom he owed much, and to Meredith and to Swinburne, to neither of whom he owed anything. Hardy agrees with Matthew Arnold that the real function of poetry is "the application of ideas to life," but, fortunately, he does not often write in conformity with that theory. He quotes Wordsworth twice with whole-hearted approval, and he shows, now in prose and now in verse, a deep interest in Milton and Coleridge, in Shelley and Keats. He was a lifelong reader of poetry as well as a lifelong writer of it, and yet he writes little of his art. In "The Abbey Mason" he tells us that the artist in stone:

> did but what all artists do,
> Wait upon Nature for his cue.

He thinks the artist should be humble:

> Can a man welcome praise and pelf
> For hatching art that hatched itself?

He knew well that

> art can but transmute;
> Invention is not absolute.

They will tell you that there is little music in the verse of Hardy, few "natural falterings," no magical lines. That is hardly true. There are lines of perfect phrase and of lilting fall, music of the sort time-honored in English song. There are other phrases and falls that one must train one's ear to enjoy as one has to train one's ear to enjoy certain of the measures of Yeats. The long line of "Friends Beyond" seems only a jog-trot measure until after many readings it takes on the sonorousness and impressiveness of a chant. The solemn and delaying rhythm of "Thoughts of Phena" is attuned to your ear slowly. You are not fully aware of the sing there is in "I was not he" until you have it by heart. There is the old music that we all have long known in "Stars wore west like a slow tide flowing"; "The thrushes sing as the sun is going"; "I hear not the contralto note of cuckoos hid on either hand."

More of Hardy's poems are about women than about any other subject. There are two main groups of these. One group is a series of portraits of girls, not to be surpassed in kind anywhere in English poetry. The other tells how "autumn wrought division" between the poet and his wife. It is a series of poems as notable a record of the alienation of lovers as *Modern Love* (1862). There is not the analysis in Hardy that there is in Meredith. What we have in "Veteris Vestigia flammæ" is a series of memories of moments in the lives of the two so long allied, moments of accord and of division, moments that had never seemed so significant as they do now that she who shared them is dead.

Hardy writes of the suddenness of her going; of her last drive; of her absence from the little walk they had taken so often together; of the place in the west where he met her as a girl; of her haunting of the places that are lonely to him without her; of the "air-blue gown" she wore that far day he first saw her; of vision after vision of her, as a girl "Fair-eyed and white-shouldered, broad-browed and brown-tressed"; of her in later years, "bright-hatted and gloved," with "nut-coloured hair and gray eyes, and rose-flush coming and going." We do not learn why it was that after summer brought them "sweets," "autumn wrought division." It is at St. Juliot, near Lyonnesse, where he wooed her, that he sees her in imagination oftenest, most times as she is riding or driving, with the terns swooping about her and the sea close by. She was a large share of life to him, she who opened to him "the door of the West," "the door of Romance," "the door of Love"; and who now, dead, opens to him "the door of the past."

Away back in the nineties, when Hardy wrote "The Division," whatever it was divided them had already been some time there. Gossip, of course, had an explanation of the division. It lay, said gossip, in the relationship behind the old story of *The Poor Man and the Lady*, recorded in his first and never published novel. The lady in life had broken the rule laid down in "A Question of Marriage," "We dine our artists; but marry them—no," but she could not be content with him as he was. She wished to make him over again in the image of her class, and he could not be other than Tom Hardy. Mrs. E. L. G. Hardy could not become Mrs. Thomas Hardy. She had labored loyally to help him in his novel-writing, but he would not please her by caring for social recognition. His faithfulness to ale when he should have grown to prefer port showed how hopeless it was to change him. Hardy was as painfully middle-class as if he had been an American, she lamented, and unregenerate in his middle-classedness.

There is no such mordancy in these poems that are inspired by his love of his first wife, as in the love stories of the series that gives title to *Satires of Circumstance* (1914). No sonnets that I know of in the whole range of English poetry contain as much condensed life as these twelve- and fourteen-liners. They strip life bare with a poignancy that makes them unforgettable, and they tell as much about human nature, the half of them, as many a novel that passes for great.

The poems on women are many of them notable for their pithy sayings. "Love is lame at fifty years" says as much as has ever been said in six words of verse. And more could hardly be said in two lines than is said in:

The Ten Commandments in one's prime,
Are matter for another time.

There are light touches in these poems, lines that are tender, caressing, fresh as first love. Of this sort is "Pink faces, plightings, moonlit May," but mordancy is often not far off. There is none of it, fortunately, in that group of poems of lovers meeting in which he makes much of the pit-pat of the girl's feet as she runs to meet her lover. Hardy is not at all averse to emphatic sex. He likes to chronicle:

> Seven buxom women abreast, and arm in arm,
> Trudge down the hill, tip-toed,
> And breathing warm.

He likes buoyant girls, with sprightliness of body and soul, like the Louie he remembers in several songs. He has a soft corner in his heart for "sweet hussies." Among such he celebrates are the heroine of "The Chapel-Organist"; the "she" of "At Wynyard's Gap"; Eve Greensleaves of "Voices from Things Growing in a Churchyard"; the girl of "The Dark-Eyed Gentleman"; and Julie Jane, "girl of joy," who died young, and "chose her bearers before she died from her fancy-men." It was Julie Jane who, face to face with death, said:

> But how can it matter, so soon to be dead,
> What one does in life?

There are a score of portraits of such warm-hearted girls, too avid of life for their own good, and terrible temptations to youths who would walk in the straight and narrow way. I have had occasion to mention several of the poems in which we meet these girls, for they are among the best poems of Hardy. I would mention seven of the girls together now, to set over against an equal number of gracious girls in the novels. In the novels we have Fancy Day, Elfride, Bathsheba, Eustacia, Grace, Tess, and Avice Caro; and in the poems Lizbie Browne, Carrey Claval, Julie Jane, Rose Ann,

Retty, Louise, and Lady Vi. There are more in both novels and poems, Phillis and 'Melia crying loudly for admission to the latter group.

I have dwelt on many concrete illustrations of this excellence and that in Hardy, but in the long process of picking them out and discussing them, I have fallen far short of proving the greatness of Hardy as a poet. There is a sense of largeness and luminousness about all his verse. You feel, in reading it, that you are in the presence of a great nature, of a nature of the broadest tolerance and of the deepest insight, a nature large-hearted and all compassionate. Hardy, you feel, knows the whole of life, and he finds, clear-visioned and somber as he is, that life is interesting through and through, and inexhaustible. There is no limit, in his presentation of it, to its infinite variety, no possible completion of experience of it. The samples of life that are his poems are presented with absolute lucidity. You remember them without effort as you remember things that have happened to your neighbors. They are, from your first complete realization of them, as much a part of your life as if they were your own experiences. Your last thought of them is your first. Hardy has penetrated to the realities of things, and he has rendered his discoveries so clearly and so largely that you refer to him as instinctively for knowledge of life as you do to Shakespeare.

CHAPTER XI

Charles M. Doughty, Sturge Moore and Gordon Bottomley

THERE is not nearly so much poetry in the verse of the epics and dramas of Charles M. Doughty (1843-1926) as there is in the prose of his *Arabia Deserta* (1888). The book of travel has the proportions and structure and unity of the epic. It is dominated by the long-suffering Nasrany, Khalil, as the Arabs called him, a figure as truly heroic as that of any famed warrior of *Iliad* or *Song of Roland* or *Volsunga Saga*. The journeyings of Doughty, his changing adventures day by day from the November of 1876 to the July of 1878, his patient determination, hold all the divergent elements of his material together, center all the interest in him, write him large against the background of wild life in high desert and teeming oasis.

There is place in this background for a hundred sketches of character, preserved as worthy of remembrance, and freshly recorded, many of them on the spot, in notebooks, but all duly subordinated to the main content of the book. There is room, too, for a hundred little lyrics of very varying emotions and subjects, of people and beasts and birds, of night and its stars, of the effects of light or season on wady and harra.

Doughty regarded *Arabia Deserta* as only a by-product of his life, the real purpose of which was the restoration to England of a poetry based on that of Chaucer and Spenser. He ignored practically all poetry after Milton, and he owed almost nothing to him; or to Shakespeare, for that matter, unless it be in the handling of the elves and fairies he is so fond of introducing into his writing. Doughty lived so apart from the literary world of his own day that he had never heard of Hardy until he saw mention of *The Dynasts* in a review of his own epic, *The Dawn in Britain* (1906-1907).

The writing and the getting published of *Arabia Deserta* (1888) occupied all his time from 1879, a few months after his return from the East in December of 1878, until the book left the press in 1888. In 1889 Doughty settled down with his wife, whom he had married in 1886, at Bordighera, on the Italian Riviera, where he lived nine years. All these years, we learn from Hogarth's *Life of Charles M. Doughty* (1928), were spent in preliminary studies for his epic on the forming of Britain, and in writing at it. It was first called *The Utmost Isle* by its author, but he changed the title to the more explanatory *The Dawn in Britain*, when it came to be published in 1906-1907, his publisher's reader, Edward Garnett, objecting to that first chosen. It was not finished until 1903, when Doughty had been five years in England, having returned from Italy that his two daughters might be educated at home. Two years after his return, the Boer War inspired him to *Under Arms* (1900). It was published at his own expense, by the Army and Navy stores. There is here first sounded that warning of a greater war to come, that, repeated in *The Cliffs* (1909) and *The Clouds* (1912) gave Doughty, after the outbreak of the World War, the reputation of a prophet. All three reveal their author as prophet first, and poet second, though both *The Cliffs* and *The Clouds* have passages of true poetry in them. As in all his long poems, whether he calls them epics or plays, Doughty is weak in the architectonics of these two books, a fatal weakness in either form.

The Dawn in Britain, the most ambitious of them all, is weakest of all, save *The Titans* (1916), in its plan and in the execution of its plan. It is longer than any other English poem known to me, save Bailey's *Festus* (1839), but it can be read, as *Festus* cannot be, at least by me. *The Dawn in Britain* cannot all be read with pleasure, however. The mere fact that I am discussing its length before any of its poetical qualities shows that its author has defeated his own ends by letting it wander on to such interminable extent.

I shall never forget my disappointment over the first two volumes. I had the books ordered by our University Library from advance notices, and I requested they be reserved for me as soon as they were catalogued. I could hardly wait for their arrival, and I badgered the Library staff to put them through quickly for me. I had read *Arabia Deserta* entranced, with more zest than I had read any book of comparable length, novel or what not. I looked through the first volume of *The Dawn* going out in the train. It didn't look succulent as I turned over the pages. I opened it further on at hazard, and came on unhelmeted warriors paying reverence to the dead. That was dull chronicle. I was afraid I was not going to have an evening lost in antiquity as I had anticipated. The volumes were worse than I had anticipated. I found only few passages of high poetry in either Volume I or Volume II. I hadn't the courage to tackle the remaining volumes when they came in, and ten years afterwards they were hard sledding for me, though I found more passages I liked than in the first two volumes. The basic trouble with it all is that the stories which compose it have not been made a part of himself by Doughty. They are a jumble of loosely related incidents, outside of him, unabsorbed, all more or less illustrating the long struggle between Rome and Britain. We meet Cæsar and Christ, Caractacus and Messalina, Joseph of Arimathea and Manannan, Son of Lir, but few familiar figures loom large in the story, and none of the invented figures have personality enough to fix themselves in memory. Nor has Doughty always been able to make his heroes grand. Too often they remain grandiose, more grandiose, even, than the heroes of Macpherson's *Ossian*. I should much like to know what those two poets Dr. Robert Bridges and Squire Wilfred Scawen Blunt, who wrote Doughty such appreciative letters about *Arabia Deserta*, thought of *The Dawn in Britain*. I know that Blunt liked the white cattle that swam with the wain after them from Belgic shores to Britain, as I liked them because they suggested the white oxen of the Campagna, and the Chillingham cattle, the survivors of the wild cattle of Britain. I suspect that he liked, too, if he read far enough to meet them, the ferocious sow, big as a bison, that Titus slew, and that talking raven that the witch-wife fed on rowan berries and the flesh of men. I wonder what Dr. Bridges found to like.

Adam Cast Forth (1908) has its moments, moments that recall now the prophetic books of Blake and now certain of his illustrations. Other passages recall the declamation of some of the oratorios. Satan is Miltonic even if his conception owes nothing to Milton, but he is, I have to say it again, grandiose rather than grand. The whole conception of the poem seems but a reimagining of Khalil's own wanderings in Arabia, but with himself blind for a time, and with a woman in tow. There are passages of tenderness, and bits of description like crude friezes from primitive temples. These have little of the dignity and Greek grace of related friezes in Sturge Moore. There are few lyric passages, and the raptures are carefully restrained. It is only rarely that there is music. Indeed music is rare everywhere in the epics and dramas of Doughty. There are a few chants of pomp and circumstance, some lamentations unto the Lord, more brass than woodwind. There are pipes, however, now and then, once even in *Adam Cast Forth:*

> The beasts have shelter and the birds have nests.
> The Lord giveth us an hollow cliff, to house,
> Flits in the chiddering swallow, and white dove;
> And the sweet honey-flies, they lodge with us.

In these words of Adama, there is none of the cluttering-up of the verses with adjective on adjective, and less of inversion and the archaic use of words than is his wont. As is usual in long poems without largeness and solidity of design, the lyrical interbreathings are the best parts of Doughty's. Here is a characteristic one, a cross section of his *Mansoul,* which shows how like he was at his best in 1920 to what he had been in 1908:

I slumbered till a turtles' gentle flock,
That feared not yet Man's shape; folding from flight
Their rattling wings; lighted on vermeil feet;
Jetting, with mincing pace, their iris necks;
With crooling throat-bole; voice of peace and rest;
All round about me, at that drinking place.
    Thence faring upward, toward that water's source;
Which, full of sunbeams, gurgles from hid grot,
In ivy-embowered mossy steep above:
And sunk oft up, reneweth as oft her course;
In channels clear; surging from gilded sand:
I stayed, where pleasant grassy holms depart;
Those streaming water brooks, bordered all along;
With daphne and willow-herb, loose-strife, laughing robin;
With woodbine garlanded and sweet eglantine,
And azure-hued in creeky shallows still,
Forget-me-nots lift our frail thoughts to heaven.
    Broods o'er those thymy argots drowsy hum;
Bourdon of glistering bees, in mails of gold.
Labouring from sweet to sweet, in the long hours
Of sunny heat; they sound their shrill small clarions.
And hurl by booming dors, gross bee-fly kin;
Broad-girdled diverse hued, in their long pelts:
That solitary, while eve's light endureth,
In Summer skies, each becking clover-tuft haunt.

Sound critics like Edward Thomas and Lascelles Abercrombie have praised Doughty to the skies. Abercrombie, of course, found in Doughty chapter and text for his preachment on the superiority of narrative and dramatic poetry over lyrical poetry. It is difficult to find in Thomas, however, any prejudice that explains his wholehearted praise. I can only explain it by saying that he must have taken the will for the deed, that the figures and movements of men against that background of myth and prehistory must have fascinated him as they fascinated Doughty in the making of his poems.

    There was never poetry higher in intention than this of

Doughty. *The Dawn in Britain* and *Adam Cast Forth*, *The Cliffs* and *The Clouds*, *The Titans* and *Mansoul* are largely conceived, but they are indifferently planned in detail, and they are often poorly executed. The archaisms and the eccentricities are less irritating after you become used to them, and begin to read on without noticing them, but they have to be gotten over each time you return to the reading of Doughty after a lapse of years. There is lofty imagination in the man, if he cannot always get lofty imagination into his poems, and a sweep of vision over wide areas of the earth and of time. The poems stand out in memory, however, as new ruins rather than as old, and new ruins have, somehow, a rather artificial impressiveness. They are like low fortifications of Mid-Victorian years half blown to pieces by target practice, rather than like Stonehenge with rude shafts and trilithons lonely against the sky.

I find more in *The Cliffs* and *The Clouds* than in the earlier epic and the earlier drama. *The Cliffs*, save as prophecy, is not imposing on the whole, but it has parts that arrest and delight. The reviewers, as a rule, did not praise it, largely because of what they were pleased to call its jingoism. The pastoral at its outset is to me the most appealing poem in all Doughty, the pastoral of John Hobbe that ends with his killing by the German aëronauts who have descended on the headland on which he is herding sheep. *The Cliffs* is drama in form, but in structure it is a conglomeration of several sorts of poetry. Hobbe is, of course, Hodge the peasant we have known in one guise or other from Langland to Mary Webb. This particular peasant gives his life for England, as he has in the past given everything else he had to give, the best of his young years, what energy his wounds have left him, and the lives of two of his sons. Could his devotion and his sacrifices and his faithfulness have been summarized in a short poem with those simplicities and that music which catch the popular ear, Doughty might have succeeded in rousing England to the German menace in 1909. But as part of the formless mass of *The Cliffs* the symbolic pastoral of Hobbe passed almost unnoticed.

The Cliffs is thoroughly "up to date" with its airships and submarines. The man who had never heard of Hardy knew what the German war lords were planning. Those years on the Riviera, with their many meetings with foreigners of all sorts, gave Doughty a knowledge of doings on the Continent that stay-at-home Englishmen could not bring themselves to consider. There is not invasion in *The Cliffs*, only naval action off shore, and the threat of invasion. In *The Clouds*, however, England is invaded south and north by German armies, and London itself invested. Only the timely arrival of help from the Five Britains overseas saves the Motherland from catastrophe.

Doughty saw what was to happen in certain aspects of the fighting in the world war with startling accuracy of prevision. He foresaw how large a part submarines and airships were to play, he foresaw the purpose of the German North Sea fleet, and he foresaw the German frightfulness. He foresaw conscription, and he foresaw the welding of the discordant elements of class and faction in England into one whole to meet the threat of the war. The fact that his mother's people, the Hothams, were navy people, and that he was intended for the navy in his youth, no doubt supplemented those talks at Bordighera in making him aware of the intentions of Germany.

There is an interesting passage about the literature of England in *The Cliffs*, and a damning of the literature in the present day. It comes out in a dialogue between the two German officers of the airship which has descended on the Sussex cliffs.

> Lieutenant Wise. "Is not their literature great?"
>
> Baron. "Some hold it was, if something barbarous.
> 'Tis now a putrid petrifying corse,
> Soul-withering, as the Medusa's head:
> The voice of hunch-back Spirits and blighted hearts.
> They imitate now each other, till they dwindle,
> Like the images of opposed looking-glasses,
> *Barocco* too! to inane nothingness.

'Tis nigh not credible, how they are untaught,
In their own tongue. They seem to think it hath,
Nor dignity nor honour!"

The last lines show that though it is the German Baron speaking the opinion is Doughty's. He, of course, knew too little of his country's literature of his own time to pass an opinion, but he had always the courage of his prejudices.

Doughty refers to Chaucer and to Spenser every now and then in his verse. In *Mansoul* (1920-1923) he holds the latter, whom he calls Colin:

Erstwhile most tuneful shepherd on these wolds;
Whose heaven-breathed chants, whose lay empassionate,
Aspiring raptures, like pure lovers' flames;
First the rude ore refined of Britain's verse.

Chaucer is second only to the master:

Quaint antique tome lay open, in this one's hand;
The scripture azure, with vermilion limned.
The Title character was, in Sun-bright gold;
DAN CHAUCER'S MERRY TALES, in Temple of Fame,
Most worthy name, for aye to be enrolled:
For the right-wise humanity of his verse.

He cannot, however, approve of all that Chaucer wrote, "too oft he speaketh too large." Spenser he praises without reservation:

Edmund, my lodestar . . . .
(Whose Art is mine endeavor to restore.)
He who descant sang, among his shepherd peers;
As lavrock doth, which lifted up of Love;
In spires exulteth in the Element;
Devoid of all offence of groundling flesh.

This moral distinction shows that Doughty was willing to forgive in Spenser what he would not in Chaucer. Consistency is, of course, the pest of little minds.

Mansoul was the preoccupation of his old age. It was first published in 1920, and then worked over, despite ill health and the weakness of his years until 1923, when its final version came out. It is that I own, with Doughty's crabbed but legible signature in it. It is the most marked of my Doughtys, though I would not claim it, for that reason, the best of him. The subject of the epic is "The Riddle of the Universe," and it may be said at once he has no solution for the riddle. Yet a man of his experience in earlier years and of his long brooding in later years has much to say on the Whys and Wherefores and Whither of life. As Hogarth quotes him in a letter to Edward Garnett, "What of this very old solar Earth-planet . . . ? How came it into being? What of man's later World therein; and what of aught beyond? has long been to me the Question of questions." Mansoul goes all over the world, and under the world, with a Merlin's glass that enables him to see through solid earth. In the abodes of the dead he encounters and questions Zarathustra (Zoroaster), Buddha, Kung (Confucius), and Socrates. Socrates helps him as much as any one with his observations on the constitution of things, but he does not help very much at that. Returning to himself from a trance, Socrates cries out:

> live in Faith of the Eternal Good.
> Who dares impeach His Justice! No man knoweth;
> To what intent Gods made and marred the World.
> Nor whether Gods made men, or Man made Gods.

On the whole, however, Doughty is no safer a guide in religion and philosophizing than he is as a critic of literature. It is for his power over words that conjure our emotions, and for his descriptions of the external beauty of the world, that those who love literature will go to him in the years to come. His prophecy of the World War will have a page in history, and certain passages of his will have place in the anthologies of those poems that catch and preserve the beauty of English countryside and the faithfulness of English men.

His descriptions of birds and of their ways and of their songs were a measurable part of my joy in *Arabia Deserta*, and the certainty that I would find similar descriptions in his long poems has made the reading of them all less tedious than that reading would otherwise have been. It interested me in *The Dawn in Britain* to find him going a little beyond the "jug-jug" description of nightingale song conventional from Elizabethan times. The song is there rendered "jug-jug-occhy-occhy," as if he had heard it for himself. In *The Clouds* is as painstaking a description as ever Hudson attempted, a description that must have been made, after many listenings, to one particular listening to the bird:

> But hark! 'tis that self gentle bird, whereof
> We newly spake, that gurgles in his trance;
> On some fresh spray, in the moonlight amidst
> That hawthorn grove, which borders nigh this place.
>   *Itchu, swat swat;*
> *Chu-chi chu-chi chu-chi chu-chi:*
> *Occhi wocchi wocchi wocchi wocchi!*
> Though but of worms he eat; like reed melodious,
> He hymns love's bliss, with that small warbeling throat
> Of his which in fowls' tongue, seem clepe to us;
> *Breme winter past, is comen in the feast,*
> *On Earth,* of Summer-gladness! (Earth where scant
> Men's raven-spirits find aught but discontent.)
>   *Chu-ti-ti, Chu-ti-ti, chutiti, toti!*
> *Toti, wi-chu wi-hi; owih, hi-hih!*
> (Wherein each hour our brethren fall in death,
> For Britain's Life!) *Hih-hi hi-hi!*
> *Owih, huit-huit, churru; Zdj-Zdj!*
> Such the bard-bird's descant: whilst dreamed our hearts!

There is perhaps more of the scientific spirit than of poetry in that rendering, but the description will keep its place, I think, among the most famous descriptions of bird song in our tongue. In *Mansoul*, in a passage written later than this passage from *The Clouds*, there is a description more like that you will find in the poets. This, too, has its place, but it will not bear comparison with the nightingale of Keats, or even with that of Wordsworth, who did not have the bird in his native north.

> A spring-tide nightingale's last blissful note,
> I hear; that awaked with his empassioned lauds,
> And nocturn's chant, neath stars, the dew-steeped Night:
> Embayed amidst green flickering leaves; where shrouds
> Her, cherishing their fledgeling birds, his mate.

Master Edmund would have liked that, and Dan Chaucer, and voted Doughty for it a modest place among the poets.

STURGE MOORE

It is the proud distinction of Sturge Moore (b. 1870) that a poem of his so fastened itself on the imagination of Yeats that the Irish poet thought one of its images his own, and used it in "The Tower." Yeats owns up gallantly, just as Francis Thompson did when he made a similar borrowing from Coventry Patmore. In the notes to *The Tower* (1928) Yeats says of "The Dying Swan": "I often recited it during an American lecturing tour, which explains the theft." It is all the more courteous of Yeats because he, too, is a specialist in swans. He calls one of his collections in verse *The Wild Swans at Coole* (1918), and he has another poem, "Leda and the Swan," beside this poem in *The Tower*.

As Yeats says, "The Dying Swan" is "one of the loveliest lyrics of our time." There are, though, in Moore, nearly twenty as lovely and they are of many sorts, and Moore has written narratives as good, and eclogues and dramas. If it were not for a curious kind of choked rhythm that he falls into all too often, he would have long since been acknowledged as one of our master poets. At the worst this habit of his results in dissonant prose, lumpy and involved, but at times it leads into felicities of speech such as a child sometimes chances on unawares. No poet of our times sees all life more freshly than this wood-engraver who stumbled on poetry at twenty-six, and published his first volume, *The Vinedresser and Other Poems* (1899) at twenty-nine.

If one may be permitted a bull, one can say of Moore that he wrote some of his best lyrics by happy accident before he had learned to write poetry. In this first volume are to be found "The Dying Swan" aforesaid; "Chorus of Greek Girls," who were "older than most sheep Though not so old as the rose-bush is"; "Summer Lightning," the last line of which is that questionable declaration, "No girl had loved unless she chose!" "To Slow Music," a thing of a beauty as rich as Keats's, but cool; "The Panther," a far echo of Blake's "Tiger" with a color all its own; and "Tempio di Venere," a memory of a ruin seen on Naples bay, and recorded most musically.

The title poem of *The Vinedresser* is not a lyric. It is rather a summary of beautiful elements in Greek life in Sicily. "At Bethel" is out of that Old Testament in which the imagination of Moore dwells almost as fondly as in the Greece of legendary times. "At Bethel" is as memorable for its picture of Rachel as "The Vinedresser" is for its recipe for wine such as is made in Cos. There is perhaps a sly humor in the giving to the angel Gabriel such an eye for a girl's beauty as he here reveals in his talk with his brother angel Abdiel. Gabriel tells Abdiel that he saw Rachel "young and strange" to Jacob, in Jacob's mind, as Jacob recalled her:

> Her lips breath misted; and, dimpled about with shade,
> There, like a rounded pebble glowed her chin.
> Long loose sleeves swaying wholly cloaked her arms;
> While, brown, in green grass-woven sandals cased,
> Her feet advancing filled her vesture up
> With something like the music of her form,
> Audible to the folds it set to move
> In grave impressive measures.

In this first volume are to be found most of the motives and subjects with which Moore was to concern himself in his subsequent writings. There are, beside the two poems on Greek themes to which I have referred, several others of similar inspiration: "Semele," "Daphne," "Niobe," "The Home of Helen," and "A Chorus of Dorides." In this vein Moore was to write later *Aphro-*

dite against Artemis (1901), *Danaë* (1903), *The Centaur's Booty* (1903), *The Rout of the Amazons* (1903), *Pan's Prophecy* (1904), *To Leda* (1904), *Theseus* (1904), *A Sicilian Idyll* (1911), and *The Sea is Kind* (1914). There are on Biblical themes in *The Vinedresser*, besides "At Bethel": "Judith," the forerunner of *Judith* (1911) the play; "Chorus of Maidens on Gilead," "Two of the Lord's Anointed," "In Elah," and "Jonathan." Close upon these Biblical studies followed the chronicle play *Absalom* (1903). The play *Mariamne* (1911) and the narrative *Judas* (1923) show how persistent has been this preoccupation of Moore's with the East of the Bible.

Here in *The Vinedresser* we find, too, such poems on art, and such poems on animals, as he was to continue to write. Later was to come that interest in children which is responsible for *The Little School* (1905). Moore is very happy in his verses about children and for children. "Beautiful Meals," with that memorable onset, "How nice it is to eat!" is already a classic; and "To Cook," in praise of her plum puddings, is as taking as an old nursery rhyme. This last poem contains a simile to savor. "As a calf careers round a cow" proves that Moore, if not countrywise, has used his eyes when he has been in the country. "Wind's Work" is another charming child lyric, and "Lubber Breeze" still another.

The legendary past of Greece Moore sees as if through clairvoyance. These pictures are of very Hellenism; this light, so full of the sun and yet so cool, is that of Olympian days; this absence of self in the contemplation of beauty is of pre-Renaissance objectivity. There is a stripped beauty of form about *Aphrodite against Artemis*. Phædra and Hippolytus are, of course, the characters that stand out, but neither of them is presented with personality. Both remain but pawns in the game that destiny plays. Thoe, the old Amazon who chores in the farmstead of Theseus, is more clearly rendered, but she is just a type, the faithful old servingwoman who would save Hippolyta's son from Phædra and fate. What is freshest in the drama is the playing of the girls of the house about Hippolytus to make him notice them. Their words and behavior as they dance about him with kilted skirts is arch and winsome. It is a presentation of a Greek life we have never met in the scores of varying presentations of Greek life in English poetry from Milton to Stephen Phillips. We feel it is antiquity that is being presented, but it is antiquity brought so close to us by a telescopic lens that all that happens is as instant to us as if it were just now going on in some farm in the hills beyond Athens. So, too, does the harum-scarum of *A Sicilian Idyll* seem to be no longer past than yesterday afternoon.

The other passage of high poetry in *Aphrodite against Artemis* than this teasing of Hippolytus by the girls is their lament, and that of the bearers of the body of Hippolytus, over him dead in his bloom:

> of the sweet in the honeycomb
> He hardly dreamed; his joys
> Were horses, dogs to pet.

Moore delighted in centaurs even before Dunsany. You meet them in the early *Centaur's Booty* (1903), and in the late *Blind Thamyris* (1920). The freedom of movement and the speed, so much greater than man's, is one of their qualities that please him most. Similar qualities in the faun that enable the creature to bound like a gigantic frog over a hundred miles as if they were not more than ten, Moore celebrates in *The Rout of the Amazons*. This poem, an eclogue-like narrative, is Moore in complete mastery of picture and pageant.

There is a high and adventurous beauty in *The Rout of the Amazons*, nobility, largeness, a note of majesty, that are rare in so perfect an accord. The spectacle of the slaughter of the women warriors by the men of Attica is presented through the eyes of the faun, but a faun made almost human by the pity of the girls stricken in their beauty. It is as firmly drawn for us as if it were modeling on a temple wall:

> A thousand rode together, poising darts,
> Behind them those with other arms came on;

All flaunting down a green-sward valley, came
Between Arcadia's gentle holted hills.
It was for beauty like a fleet at sea,
Or like an hundred swans
Sailing before the breeze across a lake!
Their vests of daffodil, or pallid pink
Or milky violet! Their saffron caps
And hoods like birds for sudden wing-like flaps!
Their white and piebald mounts! the rich green sward,
The morning light, the blossoming hawthorn trees!"

That I quote for the picture it is. These two lines that follow, of the same Amazons, for their "grand style" and "large accent":

For splendid purposes had these been trained,
And had the aspect of untiared queens.

And these three lines and a half that follow I quote for the way in which their beauty searches out all the feeling there is in us about the fall of night:

And it grew cold
And the damp spring-tide evening settled in;
Between the tall sad trunks the light grew grey,
And green gave place to blackness in the grass.

There is a primitiveness of mind in Sturge Moore, or perhaps it is a power of imagination, that makes it entirely natural for him to accept a world in which centaurs and fauns, sea nymphs and Pan, Aphrodite and Artemis are as like to be met on highway or byway as a shepherd or a farmer, a sailor or fisherman. The sea and the hills are always in his writing, and swimming more than other play or sport. There is deep feeling for long-known and long-loved places, and equally deep feeling for strange seaways and new horizons. In that eclogue, *The Sea Is Kind* (1914), Eucritos tells us:

The welcoming silence of still virgin strands,
Islands none have sailed to,

Unentered estuaries,
Untalked-of birds and beasts and folk remote,
Whose speech perplexes those who know most tongues. . .
All that lies out of reach for anchored hearts
Calls and inveigles and bewitches mine.
How can a rover promise his return?
Ulysses after twenty years came back,
But could he rest?
Penelope died lonely.
Unwilling he departed that first time;
The second time his reason could not bind
An impervious will to go.
Travel begot the taste in him:
In me desire enforces
Travel.

From the record in his verses it would not seem, though, that Moore is a great traveler. The Alps and Italy he knows, but he knows more of the Greece of legend than of the Europe of to-day.

The life of his people from the Bible is less intense, less vivid, less fully realized than the life of his Greeks. We can see the farmstead of Theseus more clearly than the palace of David. The reason, perhaps, is that Moore was more familiar with the Bible, that its people were too distinct to him from familiarity with them, in church and Sunday-school, for him to be able to visualize them and their surroundings for us as he could those whom he had created more largely out of his own imagination. The Greeks are clearer because he had to create them wholly, the Biblical folk less clear because they were dimmed for him by many presentations by others. In *Mariamne* (1911), a play on a theme allied to Biblical themes, but not built up out of the Bible, he has more freedom for his imagination, and he profits by it. In *Judas* (1923) he is not so fortunate.

Moore is interested in the lesser forms of life as well as in man. He can play as if he were a child with a ladybird, and make it fly away home. He has Medea picture on the cloak for Glaucë

"The silent polecat, fierce red ant, the wasp." The swan is his best-loved bird. There are many other references to it in *The Vinedresser* than "The Dying Swan." In "The Home of Helen" we see women bathing in Eurotas, "while gravely Swans sail in and out among them." This poem is, indeed, a fore-study for "To Leda," and "Agathon to Lysis" is another treatment of the same motive. Moore loves the white "bosomed prow," the "white insinuating neck," the "plumage like a governed storm of snow." His bird of birds is "the imperial swan with ardent eyes." So preoccupied with thought of swans is he that he sees a mouse's chin as "wool-white as down of swans." Moore likes "The silken bluefox stealing forth," "The blinking seal in furry vest," and the panther's yawning "wide-hinged python jaws."

The poem about beasts upon which he has lavished himself most wholly, however, is *The Gazelles* (1904). *The Gazelles* is a thing of an almost perfect beauty. The grace and fleetness and timidity of the hunted antelopes; the litheness and fleetness and cunning of the cheetahs that hunt them; the Persian lords and ladies that follow the hunt; the sheen on the tall grass of the plains—all is rendered by a master hand, the hand of one who is painter as well as poet. What emerges from all this consideration of the gazelles is wonder at "the meaningless beauty of their lives." It is strange, and a little distressing, to find a semi-moral at the end, an "as this with the animals so its parallel in human affairs."

Such an attempt is rare, though, in Moore. Art is to him, he tells us in *Altdorfer* (1900), "the discovery and revelation of the beautiful." The "how" a thing is done is all important to him. The "what" it is done with is a minor consideration. He sees beauty attacked everywhere, but Time is its greatest enemy. Year by year beauty wastes away.

>Look you,
>To destroy beauty
>Is what the year doth.

Art is not a reflection of nature to Moore, but the creation of a something better than nature. All that he himself has made he has made out of the life of the imagination, a life fostered by reading, and by the talk of artists. He has made almost nothing out of any direct observation of life. I do not know the circumstances of his youth and young manhood, but these poems of Greece must, I think, have been written in a place where there was no great beauty of Nature to divert his attention from the beauty he made in his mind by brooding over the much he had read of eastern Mediterranean lands.

When Moore falls short of his best it is generally because he has failed to work out the poem completely. In "Hands," for instance, he has a subject particularly fitted to his powers. He is thinking of the beauty that can be made, not by the white deft hands of ladies, but by "swart male hands." Nothing could be better than the poem's opening:

> Sing, for with hands,
> One thumb and four fingers apiece,
> They built the temples of Egypt and Greece!

Moore has not carried out his purpose. The poem is not fused into one whole of inevitable and illuminating phrase succeeding inevitable and illuminating phrase. It does not drive home meaning, and catch mood, and fall into cadences that haunt like old songs.

Nor is Moore, good poet that he is, prone to readings of life. "Nothing is pitied of the Gods and fates" is close to such, and so is "Nothing is silent when the heart will hear." Closer, perhaps, is:

> Near things alone are real,
> Now is the whole of time,

and

> Linger o'er the lovely; soon, full soon,
> The morning hours lose charm, and it is noon.

It is for the freshness of all his writing, for his new vision of Greek life, for his kindling over beauty, for the sureness of his architectonics, that we value Moore. His poetry is always what Wordsworth demanded poetry should be, emotion recollected in tranquillity. Only his lack of working out and finishing his poems costs Moore a place among the first rank of English poets.

GORDON BOTTOMLEY

The aim of Gordon Bottomley (b. 1874) in poetry is humble enough. In a note prefatory to his *Poems of Thirty Years* (1925) he states that "to add a page or a phrase to the national achievement is worth a lifetime of its pursuit." It is not often that he adds such a phrase, for it is not in verbal felicities his power lies, but he does add now and then a page, or two pages. "The End of the World" is such a two pages. It is, for all its quietness and remoteness, a poem that evokes terror, picturing as it does the snuffing-out of life, to the last bird and beast and man, as the earth cools and snow falls endlessly over all. It is eerie, soft, deadening. It is endurable only because you cannot bring yourself to believe it possible truth.

Other two pages that are memorable are epistles to Edmund Gosse, Edward Thomas, and Sturge Moore, partly friendly chat and partly discussion of the arts and life. All three are dedicatory to plays, the form in which Bottomley is most at ease and surest of his effects, and in which, alone of the forms he has tried, his gift for the creation of character and its development in action has a chance to show itself fully. He dedicates *Britain's Daughter* (1921) to Gosse, *The Riding to Lithend* (1909) to Edward Thomas, and *King Lear's Wife* (1915) to Sturge Moore. This last dedication tells us most of the three about its author. From it we learn of the life of Bottomley in his "northern valley" above Silverdale, on the coast of Lancashire between the mountains and the sea, and not far from Wordsworth's country. Here Bottomley tells us:

> For twenty years and more than twenty
> I have found my riches and my plenty
> In poets dead and poets living,
> Painters and music-men, all giving,
> By life shut in creative deeds,
> Life force and insight to my needs.

Elsewhere he tells us of his "sick isolated years," and his lifelong "quest of beauty by word and sound."

A good many of his poems are concerned, in one way and another, with his art, but it is "A Hymn of Form" that has the fullest expression of his credo. It is a difficult poem, but it will yield its meaning clearly to all who are willing to take the trouble to understand it. Form is the all in all, and its perfecting can alone bring peace to the artist. It brings more than peace, it brings rapture:

> Form comes, peace comes; the heart stands
> still, then reels;
> . . . .
> One moment, as when ousels pause for rain,
> A bloom is on the air, until it feels
> As if, after all, God is and is about to speak.

The joy of creation has never been more fully expressed by any poet, nor the exaltation of art that brings it so close to religion.

Bottomley began in 1896, with *The Mickle Drede*, one hundred and fifty copies of which were published at Kendal. Small editions were the rule of the succeeding volumes of verse, *Poems at White-Nights* (1899), *The Gate of Smaragdus* (1904), *Chambers of Imagery: First Series* (1907), and *Chambers of Imagery: Second Series* (1912); and of the plays in verse, *The Crier by Night* (1902), *Midsummer Eve* (1905), *Laodice and Danaë* (1909), *The Riding to Lithend* (1909), and *King Lear's Wife* (1915). All these volumes were reviewed with high praise by such men as Edward Thomas, Abercrombie, Herford, Masefield, De La Mare, Drinkwater, and Gosse, and yet it was not until the publication of *King Lear's Wife and Other Plays* in 1915 that Bottomley began to have any general reputation. Even then, however, he hardly sold at all. It may have been the war, which dulled the effect of so many things, that slowed down the spread of his reputation. One copy of the American edition of the plays was bought by a Philadelphia bookshop I frequent. It remained there unsold for seven years until I bought it, half in shame that I had read from it so often without any recompense to author and bookseller.

Poems of Thirty Years (1925) was published at a forbidding price. It was argued, I suppose, that Bottomley could never be popular, and that only the libraries and his friends would buy him. It is a beautiful book, printed at the Chiswick Press, with binding from a design by Charles Ricketts, and a frontispiece portrait of Bottomley by Charles Shannon. It has beautiful poetry in it, but poetry that is more of it beautiful to the eye than to the ear. There are two differing sorts of poetry in Bottomley, as there are in so many poets. There is in him a poetry that he developed under the influence of Rossetti, a poetry that is akin to painting in its effects; and there is in him a poetry that appeals as songs and ballads have appealed down the ages, whether in hall or under the lamp, a poetry that must be carried to you by the voice to make its appeal.

Gemma's Song from *A Vision of Giorgione* (1910), "Pale Ilaria, Beauty's daughter," moves to music; and "A Carol for Christmas Day before Dawn"; and "New Year's Eve, 1913," which celebrates the Cartmell bells you can hear across Morecambe Bay from Silverdale. It is not often that you find in him a stanza whose thought is so arresting as that of the sixth stanza of this last poem:

> But many deaths have place in men
> Before they come to die;
> Joys must be used and spent, and then
> Abandoned and passed by.

That gives expression to one of the truths it has always been hardest for aging men to reconcile themselves to.

"The Slave Market" is a characteristic poem of his other mode. It is beautiful, but it is clogged with too much richness of phrasing and weighted with too much imagery. That devotion to beauty that dominates his writing finds expression here, a beauty that is an ache and a burden. He cries out here, as he has cried out in other poems:

> ... all things that men have made by passion,
> Are curst with the old restlessness of beauty,
> The loneliness of beauty, the aloofness.

It is beauty that is dominant, too, in the plays, sometimes a malevolent beauty, as in *The Riding to Lithend,* in which, as in the old saga, Halgerd lets Gunnar be killed that his death may add to the toll of men her beauty has taken. *Midsummer Eve* is a dewy thing of "mothy curfewtide," with girls in it that are sisters to the dairy-maids in *Tess*. *King Lear's Wife* presents the younger years of Shakespeare's hero, and nothing further need be said of it than that its daring in the choice of subject, and the inevitable comparison that subject leads to, do not make it ridiculous. Goneril is a figure against the sky, as was Halgerd. Gruach is a third.

You meet other great ladies of legend and history in the poems of Bottomley, Helen and Cleopatra, Bathsheba and Joan of Arc. There is a firm sense of heroic life in his handling of these characters, a largeness and sweep of style that make you wonder he has not tried his hand at epic. It is the lure of the stage, I suppose, that has led him to the dramatic form, and his love of action. John Drinkwater produced *King Lear's Wife* at His Majesty's Theater, London, on May 19, 1916; and Stuart Walker played *The Crier by Night,* in several places in America this same year. Both plays stood the test of the stage well, but neither won more than a success of estimation. Gordon Bottomley seems destined in all his manifestations to be a poet of the few.

CHAPTER XII

Alfred Noyes

ALFRED NOYES (b. 1880) has many of the gifts that go to the making of a poet. He has a natural ear for the rhythms of verse, he has ease and prodigality of utterance, and he has a keen sense of the picturesque. He has been a jolly young soul from his youth, with pipe and bowl and fiddlers three all at his command when he would summon them. There was still a good deal of the child in him when he pulled a strong oar at Oxford, and when, shortly afterwards, he published his first volumes of verse. You feel the note of make-believe in "A Triple Ballad of Old Japan" in *The Loom of Years* (1902), and, more strongly struck, in *The Flower of Old Japan* (1903). There was a great deal of young days and of youth in all the volumes of the next five years, *Poems* (1904), *The Forest of Wild Thyme* (1905), *Forty Singing Seamen* (1907), and *Drake: An English Epic* (1908).

Noyes was collected in 1910, at thirty, and already a classic of a sort, and he has grown no older in all the seethe and change of the succeeding years. He is, in his verse, the breezy and sophomoric person, wholesome and hearty, optimistic and merry-Englandish, that all the world likes. Nothing could be more refreshing to our time, self-conscious in its pretense of being jaded, than such a sunniness and sense of the open air as is his. He has given us verses that sing themselves into our memory, recitation pieces many of them, and the grotesques that are the best of him. He is known most widely, of course, by "The Highwayman," a good thing of a boyish kind, and by "The Barrel Organ," a better thing of a young-mannish kind, with realities in it that stir us more than the stock romance of "purple moors," "coats of claret velvet," "black-eyed daughters" of inn-keepers, "yellow gold," hoof-beats on roads that are "ribbons of moonlight," and sudden shots out of the night.

The refrain of "The Barrel Organ," "Go down to Kew in lilac-time," is so musical, so catchy, so pleasant in the ears, that we forget it is to the grave music of "When lilacs last in the dooryard bloomed" and of "When the lilac scent is on the air and the Fifth Month grass is growing" but as a music-hall song to Brahms. Whitman, not Noyes, is the poet of lilac time.

If you cannot remember any poem of a poet unless it has a story in it, you can put it down, nine times out of ten, that that poet is not of first power. The stuff of poetry is found in the lyrical qualities of a poem, in its readings of life, in its divination of the innermost being of men and things, and this whether the poetry is of the world of romance, or of the world of reality. Outside of his narratives, I can recall but little of the verse of Noyes, and many of the narratives themselves but vaguely.

"The Barrel Organ" is one of the exceptions. Its references to known and loved things in music, to *Il Trovatore* and *La Traviata*, are a part of the reasons why I remember the poem. I happen to like Verdi, even the early dance-music tragedies, as well as *Otello* and *Falstaff*. I have seen people affected by this music as Noyes sees people affected. The poem's slight indications of characters, you can hardly call them sketches, are another reason I like it. The thief, the "portly man of business," the "very modish woman" with clenched hand, the "rowing man," the stricken laborer, the demi-rep, humanize the poem and give it an interest far in excess of his highwaymen, and Sherwood forest folk, and Elizabethan roysterers and poets, and pirates, and young intellectuals.

Other men have tried their hand at the barrel organ as material for poetry. Arthur Symons, for one, has such an attempt in *Amoris Victima* (1897), but "The Barrel-Organ" only reëchoes for him the cry of his own heart, which is "harsh with a broken string." Earlier than Symons, Henley wrote "In the Dials," a sonnet in which the youths of a slum jig "to 'Garryowen' upon an organ ground" and the oldsters "look on dispassionate—critical—something mused." The best rendering I know of, though, of this institution of the city streets is in prose, in Gissing's *Thyrsa* (1887). This has genius of place in it, and a reaction to the music in a crowded tenement section that most of us forced to frequent cities must have observed many times.

What I like best in "The Barrel Organ" of Noyes is the element of grotesquerie in it. I like "the owls that ogle London," the rose that "pouts," "the gaudy busses" full of "weary feet" keeping time to Verdi's rhythms, the "butcher of a soft reposeful tone," and "the sooty city." There is more grotesquerie in "The Forty Singing Seamen," a grotesquerie that reaches its climax in "a red and yellow unicorn is dancing round a tree." There are other worthy companions to the unicorn, "a Polyphemus" whose "battered mooneye" winked "red and yellow through the dark"; a devil-like fellow with a "golden crown" who turns out to be Prester John; "a hollow ruby Big as Beachy Head"; "a crimson leopard" and "a seagreen lion."

There is abroad a belief that poetry is only a serious sort of thing, that there is no place in it for tomfoolery, or larking, or nonsense, or the grotesque. Like Vachel Lindsay in his very different way, Noyes gives the lie to this belief. He cannot, though, storm along with a power of clowning comparable to that of Lindsay in "The Congo," just as he can never attain to the power of vision that accompanies the clowning in that astounding poem. It is not, perhaps, by "The Forty Singing Seamen," or "The Tramp Transfigured," or "Bacchus and the Pirates," or "The Lord of Misrule," whatever of symbolism there may be in this poem or that of them, that Noyes would like to be judged. And yet, I think, they are his most distinctive work, about the only poems of his, which, with their fellow "The Barrel Organ," might not have been written by any of his imitators.

Only Swinburne, of the English poets of the past hundred years, has such a rush of words and such a galloping rhythm as Noyes. It is his music alone which freshens his verse at all. All its materials are old, and its figures and its images are many of them reproduced in almost the very words of poets who were before he was. Sir William Watson's "sunlight, dew and flame," from *Wordsworth's Grave*, becomes his "dew and flame" in "The Mayflower." "The Shining Streets of London," recalls Henley's "London Voluntaries." "The Little Roads" is reminiscent of Kipling's "The Way through the Woods" and of "The Little Waves of Breffny" of Eva Gore-Booth. His "stern of a baboon" inherits obviously from Stevenson's ape that "skipped upon the trees of Paradise." "The Passing of Summer" is a sort of variation in verse of "The Pageant of Summer" of Richard Jefferies. His "Heine's Dream" recaptures certain effects of Stephen Phillips.

Noyes has not, of course, consciously set about reproducing images and phrases and falls of sound from his elders. Nor is his exactly such a case as Maurice Hewlett says is his own, a using of "other men's art and wisdom as a springboard," that is as that which gives him the impetus for "stuff of his own." Hewlett thinks this practice is so universal that he goes on to claim that "any poet can say the same." Nor is the case of Noyes exactly the case of Sir William Watson, who holds "singer's selves" "to be very part of Nature's greatness," and counts "Their descants" not the "least heroical of deeds." Noyes, in going to school to the masters, has remembered too much of the detail of their teaching.

Noyes has made few discoveries about life. He does not delight in that "fundamental brainwork" from which such discoveries come, and the architectonics necessary to the building-up of a great poem. He is not an artist caring to work and work over what is new has come to him, to sift out from this new what is worn and old. He is unconsciously retentive of what he has read, and he is facile in reproducing what of it is adapted to his own uses. He is not a great natural force which absorbs from all literature that comes his way what he needs in his writing, and revamps it with the stamp of his own personality upon it, as does a Shakespeare or a Burns. He cannot absorb his reading, digest it, refashion it in a more perfect form and raised to a higher power than it had in the original. There is nothing Titanic about Noyes.

So it is that his later work marks no advance on his early work.

What was in his power to do he had done by thirty. He did as good things later in *Tales of the Mermaid Tavern* (1913) and in "Dick Turpin's Ride," though we had met the latter before in Harrison Ainsworth's prose. Noyes did no better things, though, of the kind he did well thus early, and he did no things of a better kind.

There has been for Noyes what is a prodigious labor of reading in collecting from history material for *The Watchers of the Sky* (1922), for *The Book of Earth* (1925) and for *The Last Voyage* (1930), parts one and two and three of *The Torchbearers*. There has been here, however, no labor of the creative imagination in shaping certain aspects of the development of science from the time of Copernicus to to-day. There is, in fact, little imagination in Noyes. He illustrates admirably the difference between fancy and imagination. Fancy paints with pretty color and meticulous ornamentation old counters that have done service time and again. Imagination dares the unexplored and seizes symbols and images as yet unappropriated by the poets. Noyes is a man of fancy. Francis Thompson is a man of imagination.

There is pleasant fancy in some of the early verses of Noyes, in *The Flower of Old Japan* particularly. That poem is wistful and tender, without any false sentiment and any maudlin "coming down to the level" of children. Reminiscent as it is, *The Flower of Old Japan* is not exactly a mosaic of the Japanese material used by his predecessors. It may develop suggestions from Gilbert's *Mikado* or Henley's "Toyokuni Color-Print," but it is not a blend of them, or in a vein that is composite of their veins. Nor, as child's verse, can it be said to be a descendant of *A Child's Garden of Verses*, though it is akin in certain ways to it. It has no such grip on children as has "The Pied Piper of Hamelin" or *Alice in Wonderland*.

The Forest of Wild Thyme is not so successful as *The Flower of Old Japan*, though more native in subject. It is always difficult for any writer to do the second thing of a kind as well as the first of that kind. The effects of the first fairy-tale were old, of course, a judicious selection from the best sources, and the later fairy-tale was "a second" in that other sense in which the phrase is used in the shops. *The Forest of Wild Thyme* has its bloom brushed off by pathos. A real pathos such as that induced by the surviving children in their seeking of their dead playmate, Peterkin, is alien to the genius of the true fairy-tale. There are echoes of all fairy lore here, of Shakespeare and Mother Goose; of the Grimms and Hans Christian Andersen; and of those latter-day recapturers of the spirit of child's play, Stevenson and Riley and Eugene Field.

It is a far cry from fairy-tales of this sort to the incredible romance of *Drake* (1908). Noyes tried to make *Drake* a modern epic of England. That he did not do. Only Doughty of our contemporaries had the spirit and attitude of mind necessary to such a creation, and he failed because of his medium, that strange speech he imagined was the fit diction for poetry. Noyes did make *Drake* a romance in verse, largely planned, but overburdened with the old trappings and properties of its kind. It is luscious at times, full of what the American slang of its day called "honeycoolers." It is stirring where not too long drawn out, and it comes to a close with a defeat of the Spanish armada off the coasts of Great Britain that has all the effects of Italian opera, of the early Verdi of whom "The Barrel Organ" showed Noyes so staunch an admirer.

There is never a surprise in *Drake* from A to Z. It is just what you expect it to be from the opening pages. There are pleasant passages, and passages a little more than pleasant, in the good old manner. You hear

> the ringing call
> Across the splendors of the Spanish Main
> From ever fading, ever new horizons,
> And shores beyond the sunset and the sea.

Even here, he manages to work in his pet word of all words "elfin." Drake, ashore with some of his men for water, climbs a cliff and sees far below him in a bay "his elfin-tiny" ships. Noyes gets it, too, into one of his titles, *The Elfin Artist and Other Poems*

(1920). It is easier to sympathize with his other most dearly beloved word "thyme." That to him is always suggestive of that part of England, though he is Staffordshire born, which he loves best, the Sussex downs. This, too, it will be recalled, is Kipling's county, "Sussex by the sea." "Thyme," too, Noyes has given a place in one of his titles, *The Forest of Wild Thyme*.

Drake never disappoints you, or shocks you, or agitates you unduly in any way. It almost keeps up your interest to the end—on a first reading. A second reading is harder, much harder than a first. You have always the feeling that the writing is outside the author, that it never possesses him, save in certain moments of patriotic feeling, that it was to him, on the whole, just a grand *tour de force*.

Noyes was not, in his early years, though, a poet of empire. He was an advocate of peace. He was hard set against the policy of the mailed fist. The Great War, of course, somewhat shifted his position. It stirred him through and through, but it could arouse him to no such impassioned writing as "August 1914," for impassioned writing is only rarely possible to Noyes. His love verse is always that of a gentleman, but its lack of passion and of insight prevents its being notable. Nor is his occasional verse of much power, not even that in commemoration of other poets, a Francis Thompson, a Meredith, a Swinburne. It is in this sort of verse, that his rival in reminiscent passages, Sir William Watson, scores so heavily. Nor does his own art of poetry inspire Noyes.

There is a good deal of the religion of humanity in Noyes. Time was, in *Drake* (1908), that he could see in England's defeat of Spain in the overthrow of the Armada "That last Crusade of Christ against His priests." Now, however, formal religion seems to be gaining a firmer hold upon him. This is not to be wondered at, seeing that he has made himself the chief opponent in verse of the orgiac young intellectuals whose voices are loud in the land these days. His opposition to them is driving him further and further each year to the position of the orthodox.

If you are a believer in tradition you will sympathize with

Noyes in his satire of these intellectuals, yet you need not, at the same time, believe him possessed of all the powers of "The Man Who Was a Multitude." It does not necessarily follow that his song, because it is an old song, "shall shine like rubies," or that "it shall ring like gold," or that it shall "thunder like the sea." And it is a little strange to read his attack couched in numbers that owe a good deal of their march and verve and easy roll to that singer of the "roses and raptures of vice," who is also a patron saint of many intellectuals, Algernon Charles Swinburne.

Noyes is more impassioned in his satire than in any other kind of writing. "A Victory Dance" jolts him fighting mad. He cannot accept such an orgy, as he sees it to be, as an honor to boys killed in France:

God, how that dead boy
Gapes and grins
As the tom-toms bang
And the shimmy begins.

There is some passion, too, in the descriptions of England out-of-doors by Noyes. He kindles, as do nearly all English poets, when he comes to describe the places where he lives and which he loves. There are many poets who kindle more, but for Noyes his descriptions of countryside are almost impassioned. He has many preceptors in such writing, Keats, Tennyson, and Meredith among them.

Noyes has put something of the beauty of our American countryside, too, into verse. His American wife, his many readings of his poetry throughout the States, and his professorship at Princeton from 1914 to 1923 all contributed to his knowledge of our out-of-doors. He is just as much at home in a description of Thomas Bailey Aldrich and his saltwater environment near Portsmouth in New Hampshire ("The Crags"), as in that of Connecticut back country ("Mountain Laurel"), and as in that of pepper-trees near Los Angeles ("In Southern California") and of the pines of the Sierra Madre about the great telescope on Mount Wilson ("Prologue" and "Epilogue" to *The Watchers of the Sky*).

The Grand Canyon of the Colorado, too, he has described, in *The Book of Earth,* Volume II of *The Torchbearers,* in great detail at full noon and at night; and less fully at dawn. In this last passage the invisible playmate of his childhood, Shadow-of-a-Leaf, gets between the poet and his writing, as so often in his later verse.

Once in a long while Noyes writes with a faithful realism. "The Conductor" is one such poem. Its story, for, as almost always in Noyes, it is a poem with a story, is that of the outing of a consumptive on a London bus. It takes the man out of town, with his buxom wife and two little children, who can with difficulty pilot him about, so weak is he. The conductor, an irascible soul, gives the consumptive an orange he has treasured, with the words *"Like oranges, friend?"* It is obvious, this poem, and sentimental, sobbing with pathos under what purports to be restraint, but it is human, and, what is rare in Noyes, a subject other than stock, a something seen for himself, a bit of life. It is not high poetry, but it is better than nine out of ten of his sets of verses, for it is wholly his own and freshly seen.

Once in a while, too, Noyes can say something that is memorable in other than a picturesque or grotesque way. In "The Death of a Great Man," he tells us "Grief is for near and little things." If there were more such writing in Noyes he would approach nearer than he does to the full stature of a poet. He trusts to the music of his verse to give it a long hearing, declaring in "The Inn of Apollo":

> For the music that masters the ages,
> Be sure, is the music that sings!

That is true as far as it goes. Only it is always to be remembered that analogies between music and poetry need careful scrutiny. In poetry the music is music of human speech, in which the meaning of the words is as integral a part of the effect as their sound. Sound and sense must be wedded for the supreme beauty. Music and meaning must be at one, in perfectly modulated and imperishable words.

CHAPTER XIII

John Masefield: Apostle of Beauty

A GENERATION ago the finger of scorn was often pointed at the man who talked much about beauty. Gilbert parodied such talk in *Patience* (1881), and soon Wilde and his cult were being laughed at not only up and down England, but throughout the whole English-speaking world. That parody, richly as it was deserved, hurt the cause of beauty in art, and threw certain of the more restrained elements, who should have remained loyal to the cause of beauty, over into the camp of those who asked that art have a message.

Now, however, that John Masefield (b. 1878) has championed beauty in nearly every other poem, we do not hear so much foolish talk about the effeminacy of beauty as we did in the eighties and nineties of last century. Masefield's record at sea and on the battle-fronts put clearly before the world the fact that a servant of beauty, a man sensitive to all the manifestations of beauty, can stand the gaff as well as any man. The spectacle of the death of Brooke helped, too. So did the sacrifices of Edward Thomas, and Wilfred Owen and Charles Sorley, and the service of Siegfried Sassoon and Robert Graves and Robert Nichols. Many poets proved themselves staunch fighting men.

None of these other men are, however, so much concerned with beauty as Masefield. His devotion to it was just as much in evidence in the last-written sonnets included in *Selected Poems* (1922), as it had been in all his writing from his first book of verse, *Salt-Water Ballads* (1902). It was principally by example that he showed in these earliest verses his devotion to beauty. He began to add precept to example in *Ballads and Poems* (1910), and in *Sonnets* (1916) more than half of the poems are out-and-out discussions of beauty. In the sonnets first published in *Selected Poems* Masefield saw Englishmen in old time:

> masters of the arts of men,
> Poetry, music, painting, building.

So he laid it down in the first sonnet. And thus he followed on in the second:

> Over all England beauty was like June
> Deep in men's spirits, when we made these things.

In the fourth sonnet he chants his faith that England will rebuild the beauty that it has allowed to fall into decay:

> Rebuild in beauty on the burnt-out coals,
> Not to the heart's desire, but the soul's.

Beauty may be, however, he holds, in little things as well as in great things:

> All beauty in a little room may be
> Though the roof lean, and muddy be the floor.

Masefield found beauty in the lives of the rough sailing men he celebrated in *Salt-Water Ballads*. In the introductory verses to this volume, "Consecration," he tells us that his songs shall be fashioned and his tales be told of "Not the ruler . . . but the ranker, the tramp of the road." This "ranker" he further specifies as sailor and stoker, and he finally adds to his list, "the dirt and the dross, the dust and scum of the earth." So Masefield justifies, far in advance of his writing of them, the tales of rough life that were to come into being in 1911 and 1912, *The Everlasting Mercy* (1911) and *The Widow in the Bye Street* (1912), and *Dauber* (1913) and *The Daffodil Fields* (1913).

You would suppose, from his preface to the poems of *The Poems and Plays of John Masefield* (1918), that the general idea of *The Widow in the Bye Street* came to him before the concrete woman, of whom, and her son, he writes. "I wished to write of conversion, of a turbulent man suddenly made gentle. . . . When I had finished the story, I felt that I ought to write something unlike it, that as I had shewn one thing, which often happens in life, the seemingly unworthy man made happy, for no apparent reason, so I ought to write the opposite, the seemingly worthy woman made heartbroken, for no apparent reason." So it may be the two poems came into being, but already, in *The Everlasting Mercy*, are a Jimmy Jaggard and his mother who seem very like the older Jimmy Gurney and his mother of *The Widow in the Bye Street*. There was a good deal that was concrete, that was remembered from life, in the material of both poems.

There is little doubt, I believe, that Masefield works from the observed character and incident, however much both may grow in becoming part of his imaginative life. In those days of his youth when Masefield was before the mast he was fellow to the originals of the men we meet in *Salt-Water Ballads*. There is escape from shipwreck here; and death by fever, as recorded by the shipmates of the victims; and drink and girls ashore; all told with a vivid violence of phrase. These are verses that hold our attention, that "recite" well, that have patter and go, and a suggestion of accompaniment by mouth-organ, or jew's-harp, or accordion. That is, the ruck of them have this suggestion. There are others of them poetry in the old tradition, the four, certainly, he retains in *Selected Poems*, "Trade Winds," "Sea Fever," "D'Avalos' Prayer," and "The West Wind." I am sorry he retained only these four poems from his earliest volume, and none of the ballads that give it title. I bought *Salt-Water Ballads* in 1903, because of a review of it I came upon in *The London Academy*, and for all the years since I have rejoiced in "Evening-Regatta Day" and "A Night at Dago Tom's." " 'N'arterwards there was sweet songs 'n' good Jamaikey rum," and "Your nose is a red jelly, your mouth's a toothless wreck" seem to me of a grotesquerie that there is too little of in poetry.

The service to beauty is just as surely in evidence as the grotesquerie. It is to be found even in "A Night at Dago Tom's." The references there to old songs, "Lowlands No More," "The Shaking of the Sheets" and "Pipe the Watch Below," the dancing, the yarns, the praise of the hooker "Spindrift," are part and parcel of what Masefield calls "the rough, bawdy beautiful world." There is an excitement in such high jinks ashore that, properly rendered by a poet who knows them as Masefield does, can be transmuted into poetry. I think Masefield has so transmuted them, in all simplicity and directness in "A Night at Dago Tom's." "Evening—Regatta Day" is a presentation, equally faithful and direct, of the orgiac ecstasy that sport arouses. It has its place in poetry just as surely as the infinitely more beautiful rendering of the joy and picturesqueness of sport in *Reynard the Fox* (1919), one of the greatest of our English narrative poems.

The kind of beauty more traditional to English poetry you find, as I have said, in the four poems retained in *Selected Poems* from *Ballads and Poems*; and in at at least nine fellows of theirs: "The Golden City of St. Mary"; "A Wanderer's Song," with its echo of Kipling's "Feet of the Young Men"; "Cardigan Bay"; "Sorrow of Mydath," with its cadences as of Yeats; "Vagabond"; "Vision"; "Personal"; "On Malvern Hill," which is, in a way, after Housman; and "Tewkesbury Road," in which the music of words that Masefield was the first to discover sounds with no uncertain voice.

I have deliberately let this list run long, for I wish to stress the fact that from the beginning of his writing Masefield has been the servant of beauty. Nor have I hesitated to parallel work of his with work of the others to whom he went to school before he found that particular beauty of his own that he was destined to find. The whole of the man as he then was, and nobody else, is in "Tewkesbury Road." What we call the natural man is here, and the man who is the servant of beauty, and the fellowly man, and the eternal vagabond that is deep-seated in all of us, and the man with his roots in the soil who is almost as universal. It is good, surely, "to be out on the road" in the long summer evenings, "When the stars are mellow and large at the coming on of the night." And it is good, surely, too, as he tells us, to come upon, at such times, the lights of an inn, and the promise of food and shelter.

There are forty-three poems in *Ballads and Poems* (1910), six of them reprinted from *Salt-Water Ballads*. Of the thirty-seven new poems Masefield chooses ten for his *Selected Poems*, rejecting, and rightly, I think, several that are popular in one way or another. We hear "Captain Stratton's Fancy," one of the omissions, about as frequently over the radio as "Mandalay" or "Out of the Night that covers me." We can less well spare "Laugh and Be Merry," for it is, more than any other one poem of his, his credo. Perhaps for that very reason it seems doctrinaire to him, or preachy, or too insistent on its text. That text, "Laugh and be proud to belong to the old proud pageant of man" is all Masefield in a line. If ever there was a poet who accepted things as they are it is Masefield. He is on the side of right, of all things honorable and of good report, a man who goes out of his way to do a kindness. He can be indignant at "some yoke of priests or kings," but the visible world is, on the whole, so good that he can see it as the shadow of "eternal beauty's everlasting rose."

Masefield exalts beauty almost to a religion in very much the way Kipling similarly exalts romance. That being his feeling about beauty, Masefield resents strongly the lack of welcome beauty meets with in the world. He is proud to have been "the pen" which has expressed certain phases of this beauty. So indifferent to beauty is the crowd, though, that in one town a dog and the "I" of a sonnet are "the only two" there who knew her. That was the dog, "dog-minded, with dog's eyes," which was "damned by a dog's brute nature to be true," as are not, inferentially, certain humans. The instability of man's humanity is a trouble to Masefield always:

> Here in the self is all that man can know
> Of Beauty, all the wonder, all the power,
> All the unearthly color, all the glow,
> Here in the self which withers like a flower.

But despite that last line, and a score others that reveal weaknesses, Masefield is "proud to belong to the old proud pageant of man," and finds in man the dream of man's own self raised to the highest power, which man has called God:

> There is no God, but we, who breathe the air,
> Are God ourselves and touch God everywhere.

Masefield is very contradictory in respect to his belief in a future life. Now he persuades himself that there must be a future life. Now he has little hope that there can be. That deep-seated feeling he has of the presence of the dead near the places they knew in life seems almost proof to him now of even the survival of human personality after death. Whether there is a future life or not, life is an incomparable gift. "Even if we cease life is a miracle."

It is beauty everywhere that makes life such a miracle. At times Masefield almost identifies beauty with all that makes for righteousness, as in Sonnet LVII of *Sonnets* (1916). In Sonnet LIX Masefield calls beauty "breath of the divine." The series ends with this stoic reflection:

> Let that which is to come be as it may,
> Darkness, extinction, justice, life intense,
> The flies are happy in the summer day.

There are those who find in such agnosticism as this a direct contradiction of what he said in "A Creed" in *Ballads and Poems*, which expresses a belief in reincarnation. I heard Masefield read this poem and say of it that the belief it expressed was one to which he no longer held. Masefield divined early in his career that the quest of beauty, in the large sense in which he uses the word, was to be the purpose of his life. Nothing could be clearer and more definite than the expression of this quest in "Roadways," a poem in this same volume of *Ballads and Poems*. And when the beauty that he worships is found in "The Gentle Lady," he has the words of old courtesy and present-day sincerity in which to praise her.

The Tragedy of Nan (1909) was all there was between Salt-Water Ballads (1902) and The Everlasting Mercy (1911) to show a development in the art of Masefield. There were lyrics of a new music in his first book, and lyrics, perhaps a little better finished, in Ballads and Poems, of this same new music. There was no widening of the scope of his poetry. Nan, of course, was in prose, but it was a prose that was as fit a medium for poetry as the prose of Synge it was built upon. It must be again recalled that Synge had said in the preface to his Poems (1909): "It is the timber of poetry that wears most surely, and there is no timber that has not strong roots among the clay and worms." Masefield took this saying to heart.

In the rhythmic prose of Nan Masefield put these precepts of Synge into practice, and, even more forthrightly, in The Everlasting Mercy and the three other realistic narratives that immediately followed it. Perhaps Masefield does not himself realize just how much he owes to Synge, to whose companionship he refers in "Biography," when he speaks of "That lively mind and guttural laugh of his." Later, in With the Living Voice (1925) Masefield, writing an apology, in the old sense of the word, for his kind of poetry, shows that he still holds to the theory of poetry Synge laid down in that preface written in December of 1908. Not all the paper, of course, is a development of Synge's ideas. Masefield begins, indeed, with ideas of his own as to why it was that English poetry ceased to appeal to the crowd after the snuffing-out of the old drama in 1642.

"The greatest of the channels by which poetry could reach the hearts of men," Masefield writes, "was henceforth to be closed, or almost closed, to the poets of this land. Poetry, of a kind, was still spoken up and down the land in taverns and by firesides, but those who liked this kind of poetry knew very well that those with taste condemned it. . . . The poets who used to speak or sing their ballads about the country took to writing songs for pedlars' song books."

Masefield after a while turns his attention to the elocutionists.

For them he has blame and praise. They made poor poetry popular, but they broke the way for the reading of exciting poetry by the poet to large audiences. Such poetry had to be exciting poetry or it could not appeal to large audiences. The elocutionists, he says, "were swaying thousands where the poets of their time were swaying how many? In this land of twenty million thrillable souls were even half a million thrilled even by Tennyson? the most popular poet of two centuries."

Masefield thinks that the poets failed to find an audience because they "had given up for too long the advantages of speaking their work." Masefield himself, following in the footsteps of Yeats and Noyes, came to America to read his poetry, and attracted large crowds. I was present twice when he talked and read to such audiences, to some eighteen hundred people in a church, and to three thousand in a great hall. He had not the elocutionists's or actor's art of "throwing his voice," but his voice was of so appealing a quality and he received such attention that every one could hear and understand every word.

I am not sure that this explanation of his does account for the lack of vogue for poetry. I am not sure that the non-reading part of the public, surely more than half of the public, can be won to poetry even if that poetry has excitement in it. His adaptation of the theory of Synge gets very much nearer to the root of the matter. It is while blaming the printing-press for its effect on poetry that he lets drop his observation that the printing-press gives "importance to work which uses too little of the poet." That, of course, is just an orientation of Synge's saying that Villon and Herrick and Burns used "the whole of their personal life as their material."

Burns put all of himself into his poetry, and half his fellow-Scots read him, and at least one American out of every four, from 1800 to 1850 or thereabouts. Scott, too, was widely read for his metrical romances; it may be for the vividness of their stories or for the picturesqueness of the life against which the stories were played out, rather than for their poetry, but Masefield himself may well be read for similar reasons. Scott, it is true, did not put all of himself into his verse. He did not feel his humor could be reconciled to the other elements in his rhymed stories. Its inclusion in his prose tales is what marks their superiority over *The Lady of the Lake* and *Marmion*.

Byron put nearly all of himself into his poetry, and he was read in England as widely as Burns was in Scotland, and as widely as Burns in America. Burns, Scott, and Byron were all three more widely read by the English-speaking population of their times than Tennyson in his time, though the great increase of population in England and America in Tennyson's time may have given him a greater total of readers.

In speaking of Gray, Blake, Coleridge, and Keats, Masefield says: "Those four beautiful intelligences were not using the whole of life as their material. . . . Those poets who shrink from the life about them, however skilfully they may invent or imagine, will appeal in the main, not to the world, but to those few who, like themselves, cannot or will not face the world."

Not only these four poets, but all who worked in their tradition, write, says Masefield, "with a restricted sense of what is poetical. They cut out, as not poetical, much of the work, and many of the things, which man's use has dignified. . . . They have shrunk, in nearly every instance, from one large element of happiness in life, from fun and laughter."

The proof of Masefield's wisdom in following the suggestions of Synge is the success as art and the human appeal of the four realistic narratives. Said Synge in this same preface to *Poems:* "When men lose their poetic feeling for ordinary life, and cannot write poetry of ordinary things, their exalted poetry is likely to lose its strength of exaltation, in the way men cease to build beautiful churches when they have lost happiness in building shops." *The Everlasting Mercy* is poetry of ordinary things ending on a note of exaltation. So is *The Widow in the Bye Street*, and *Dauber*, and *The Daffodil Fields*. The exaltation in *The Everlasting Mercy* is brought about by a village tough "getting religion" and by an impassioned joy in the beauty of the countryside in Herefordshire. The exaltation in *The Widow in the Bye Street* comes from a mother's devotion and an impassioned joy in the beauty of "Shropshire uplands of late hay." The exaltation in *Dauber* arises from a man's devotion to duty and to his triumph over fear and from an impassioned joy in the beauty of the sea and of the handling of a sailing ship. The exaltation of *The Daffodil Fields* springs from the sense of life at full tide in it and from the tragic fate that tracks down and destroys in their bloom the two youths and the girl, and from an impassioned joy in the beauty of Shropshire and of the Argentine pampas.

I heard Masefield say once that more great English poems had their origin in places and men's love of places than from any other inspiration. Certainly it is true that a place and what happened there is at the back of more poems of his than any other motive save that beauty which he exalts into something close to a religion. Often it is beauty suggested by a place that he celebrates. Often the two motives blend into one.

Some English institution, too, is celebrated in nearly all of his long poems. Boxing lends a large part of the interest *The Everlasting Mercy* has. A village fair makes possible the entangling of Jim in *The Widow in the Bye Street*. The handling of a ship, seamanship, and bulldog overcoming of failure dignify *Dauber*. All the passionate futility of *The Daffodil Fields* revolves about a stock-farm where Hereford cattle are bred. Fox-hunting is the whole of *Reynard the Fox*, and the steeplechase the whole of *Right Royal* (1920). The traveling circus makes picturesque *King Cole* (1921). In these last three, the institution is more important than the story involved, or as important as the story. In the four earlier poems the story is more important than the institution involved. There is no such full characterization in the later stories as in the earlier. We know Saul Kane; and Jimmy Gurney, and his mother, and Anna. We know the dauber, and Lionel Occleve, and Michael Gray, and Mary Kier, as we do not know the fox of *Reynard the Fox*, or huntsman, or master of the hounds, or any of the members of the hunt, clearly as all are hit off. We are not with the latter long enough to get to know them. Nor do we get to know so well the horse or his rider in *Right Royal*, or King Cole or any of the show-people in *King Cole*.

In *King Cole* Masefield is just as determined to have things end well as in *The Widow in the Bye Street* he is determined to have them end ill. *King Cole* must end well because it is a fairy-tale. It begins on a note of dispiritedness, and ends with the traveling circus transfigured with a glow beyond that of human things, and with the showman's son returned to his mother and father. It turns from a dull and grey to a bright and glittering thing. It has aid and comfort for the down-hearted all the way through. No poem of Masefield has in it more memorable lines. It includes trifles beloved of children, things cosy and snug; phrases that fall on the ears like a benison; and deep readings of life. The Prince thinks a cat's fate happier than his. There is magic in "Lovely as evening stars o'er seas in trouble," and the thing perfectly said in "The nightly mercy of the eventide." It is a heartening thought, if not true in all instances, that "A man's ill fortune passes, like the night." It is only too true that "Life hurts everyone," but Masefield sees also "Life that is speed and color and bright bliss." He is all of him with his King Cole when the old piper says "Trust still to Life, the day is not yet old." The kindliness of spirit investing the poem only serves to increase its pathos, and you read at times with a film in your eyes and a choke in your throat. But all comes right in the end, as I have said, as things must in fairy-tales. His intent here is to soothe. He adjures for the nonce the desire he so often has to purge our feelings through pity and terror.

Masefield has me in his power much as Hardy has. What happens to his people hurts me deeply. Jimmy Gurney, the widow's son, and his mother, and shepherd Ern's children watching, with their noses against the window-panes, for the fairings their father fails to bring, have a way of returning to my mind and troubling me, and outraging my sense of justice. And the dauber, the boy who had staked everything on becoming a painter of the sea! How my heart goes out to him, for the hard life behind him, for the hard life about him, for the death you fear, from the start, is to end all before his ship knows landfall. And Lionel and Mary and Michael, poor devils all, caught in a net that fate has cast so blindly about them. There is wild blood in many of these characters when we meet them, and they all have rejoiced in wild blood, and suffered for it in the past. They are wild-blooded all, these young men, Saul Kane, Jimmy Gurney, Michael, and the girls they love warm-blooded and sweet-blooded, like the women of Hardy.

In all your thinking about Masefield's people your mind will carry you back to Hardy. Both writers are concerned with southern England, rural England, an England whose air is free of factory smoke and of the grim life of the north. Life is hard in Wessex and on the Welsh marches, but there is a kindliness of external nature that is not in the north, and an absence of that keen competition that industrialism forces on the north. Like Hardy's people, these youths and girls and few oldsters of Masefield are very close to the soil. They yield swiftly and disastrously to impulse, they love and suffer, almost without will of their own, because nature will have things so. Nearly all come to their deaths in youth, and the oldsters left alive are not the happier for living. They all of them win our deep concern somehow, even when they are but slightly sketched, and they are made picturesque by the background against which their fated lives burn out so quickly. Old ways are about them, and old places, villages of sharp-pointed roofs, and high downs where lapwings tumble and cry, and where the sun blazes white on sharp flints.

It is people of the lowest classes we meet most often in the earlier narratives, farm laborers and the like, or people of the farmer class who are not doing too well on their farms. In the later narratives we meet people of all the classes. Even in *The Everlasting Mercy*, however, we meet the Quaker evangelist, Miss Bourne, and the Anglican rector, a purple puffing parson, who gives us that satisfying saying of humanity:

> We're neither saints nor Philip Sidneys,
> But mortal men with mortal kidneys.

All strata of society meet in *Reynard the Fox* (1919) and *Right Royal* (1920), but the accent in both is on the upper middle class. If we read all seven narratives from *The Everlasting Mercy* to *King Cole,* one after the other, we have a sense of all English country life unrolling before us. Preacher and light-of-love at the town's end, tavern-keeper and police sergeant, strong farmer and retired navy man, lawyer and parson, squire and lord of the manor, all pass before us, a memorable pageant.

Nowhere else in so short a compass can we find so complete a presentation of country life as in *Reynard the Fox*. Here the art of characterization, that first interested Masefield when he turned his hand to plays with *The Campden Wonder* (1907), has reached its fullest development. There was admirable characterization in *Nan* (1909), and a revelation of the power to hit off a man in a line in *The Daffodil Fields* (1913). In the last-named poem Michael is described as "Young April on a blood horse, with a roving eye."

In *Reynard the Fox* (1919), in the gathering of a great crowd of all sorts and conditions of men for the hunt, Masefield presents us with seventy characters. That is as many people as most of us get to know well in our allotted span of years. Nearly every one of the seventy is clearly limned, some in a line, more in two or three lines, several in from ten to fifteen lines, and a few at greater length. Women and men are drawn with equal surety. The women we see with the clarity with which we see Shakespeare's women and Meredith's. Square Harridew, a man of "small brain, great courage, mulish will," and his three daughters are presented. Carrie is the fairest:

> Queen Helen had less golden hair.
>
> . . . . .
>
> A rosebud need not have a mind.
> A lily is not sweet from learning.

Masefield gives us his people, many of them, both inside and out, spirit, mind, and body all three, and done in phrases easy to remember. Are any of us likely to forget Old Bennett, the farmer, who sat on horseback "Just like an axehead on its helve." That is as perfect a simile as English poetry knows.

Pete Gurney had
>   the russet-apple mind
>   That betters as the weather worsen.

English character is at its best in Robin Dawe. He is miles asunder from the John Bull of Squire Western type that many would have us believe the typical man of the shires. Miles asunder is he, too, from the glorified peasant of the Cobbett type, bull-dozing, hortatory, blundering, honest, good at single-stick. Different, too, is he as may be, from any of the figures in blue jeans, and black-handed, that seem, in these days of the supremacy of cities, so much nearer the typical Englishman. Masefield is not afraid to find beauty in the mind and in the character of the huntsman:

> So, in Dawe's face, what met the eye
> Was only part, what lay behind
> Was English character and mind,
> Great kindness, delicate sweet feeling,
> (Most shy, most clever in concealing
> Its depth) for beauty of all sorts,
> Great manliness and love of sports.

Reynard the Fox is Masefield at his best. He did admirable work before it, in the lyric, in "Sea Fever"; in the play, in *Nan;* in the realistic short story in verse, *The Everlasting Mercy;* in the condensed novel in verse, *The Daffodil Fields;* but there is a wider scope to *Reynard the Fox,* more people, more beauty of countryside, and the best description of a fox-hunt in all English literature. Being what it is, there is not so much chance in it for those observations on life he can put in a line, as he can put character in a line. Nor is there chance in it, of course, for moments of dramatic intensity, but in every other respect it gives Masefield the opportunity to achieve the many different sorts of effects of which he is master. It has humor, energy, picturesqueness, sympathy with all sorts of men and all sorts of beasts, lyric moments—above all the powers of story-telling and pageant-making. Under and about it all is a depth of knowledge of rural England such as only Eden Phillpotts among living men may rival, and such as only Hardy of recent writers has surpassed.

Although we know the fox-hunt as a social institution in certain parts of America, we cannot claim that it has the place in our life that it has in England's. There have been hunt-clubs about Philadelphia since the eighteenth century, but even hereabouts the fox-hunt does not sum up the whole life of any countryside as it does in England. It is true that baseball literally fills the thoughts of many American men during all their waking hours for at least six months of the year, but it has little hold, despite some resolute "fans," among our women. Not even baseball, though, has the power that several English sports have, of taking on, in the minds of devotees, something of the sanctity of religion. We cannot understand how an Englishman feels when he says of a man: "He is the sort of man would shoot a fox." Remember for a moment how the neighbors of Major Yeats felt toward him in *Some Experiences of an Irish R.M.* when they thought he was ridding his place of foxes, and then raise their resentment to the nth power, and you will be within hailing distance of the true-blue Englishman's ire against the fox-shooter.

Reynard the Fox is in two parts. Part I is the gathering of the hunt, obviously modeled on the prologue to *The Canterbury Tales;* and Part II is the run of fox and hounds, horses and men. We are all glad, I think, that the fox pursued so far across country, and prevented from taking to earth by his earths being stopped, is "crossed" by another fox and escapes. We are all, I am sure, in the highest spirits at the finish, from hours in wind and sun. We are content as the tired hounds pad home before the tired horses and tired men. "Hunting," writes Masefield, "makes more people happy than anything I know. When people are happy together, I am quite certain that they build up something both beautiful and divine, which weakens the power of evil things upon this life of men and women." Was I wrong when I said that sport is almost a religion in England?

Beauty is the recurrent word in the introduction that Masefield wrote for the illustrated edition of *Reynard the Fox* (1920). He finds beauty in the gathering of the hunt, in people and horses and hounds, in the countryside through which they run, in the loping of the fox leading them. "That leisurely hurry, which romps away from the hardest trained and swiftest fox hounds without a visible effort, as though the hounds were weighted with lead, is the most lovely motion I have seen in an animal."

Masefield thinks the fox-hunt will persist, despite the breaking-up of the great estates, and the filling-up of the country. "Even if the small holding system were to prevail, it would hardly prevail," he writes, "over the sporting instincts of the race. Beauty and delight are stronger than the will to work." Here again (am I too insistent in pointing out?) is that regard for beauty which I find to be the leading motive in all the writing of Masefield.

In *Reynard the Fox*, as everywhere in Masefield, is that interest in animals, that affection for animals, that delight in animals, that is part of the inheritance of mankind. That, indeed, is a test of a man that all the countrywise unconsciously apply to him in judging him. Does the man like beasts? That is, of course, if he has had the opportunity of knowing beasts. If he does not like beasts, look out for him! There is something wrong in his make-up. Hardy likes beasts. Galsworthy likes them. Hodgson likes them. Davies likes them. Looking further back, we note that Wordsworth liked them, and Scott, and Gray, and Shakespeare, and Chaucer, and whoever wrote the riddles we call the riddles of Cynewulf. Does the man we are judging warm, like Burns, to the "Wee, sleekit, cower'n, tim'rous beastie"? Masefield certainly does. There is no creature that recurs more often than the mouse in his writing. Dogs, horses, cattle, all the domesticated beasts you find there, and the wild sorts, too, fox and badger, hare and rabbit, and all birds from wren to rook.

All times of day and night are described with loving particularity by Masefield, and in all sorts of situations, on sea and on land. It is most often, however, that some country place, in the Berkshire of his present residence or in the west country of his youth, is the scene, at whatever hour it is described. He loves the full flood of the sunlight at noon on high downs, "earth that smells of honey in July"; but it is nightfall and the small hours after midnight that seem most to appeal to him. He likes the time when the cats begin to prowl and the owls to come out. Such a time he generally describes from a point of view outdoors, but the midnight hours from the standpoint of a man up late with indoor work, or awakening in bed. Now it is a death-tick that engages his attention, now little scuttlings of mice, and now sounds hard to account for from any known creature rightfully busy at such hours.

It is this concern with little things that wins for Masefield the regard of children. They like these prowling cats and mitching mice and friendly dogs. They can hardly understand why Bill Tall and Ell and Mirtie Key were afraid of the fox hound pack. I know nothing better about dogs anywhere than the long description of the fox-hounds. Its most searching comment is that in which he refers to:

>Their noses exquisitely wise,
>Their minds being memories of smells.

There are some who hold that England, and what England stands for, are better summed up in "August, 1914," than in *Reynard the Fox*. It may be that they are. "August, 1914" is a great poem, the greatest of all that were inspired by the Great War. Its nineteen stanzas sum up more of what England is than the thirty-two of Gray's "Elegy," the other English poem nearest it in kind. I am not of those who hold, with Mrs. Meynell, that the "Elegy" is not of the first order of poetry. I think it is of the first order, but I do not find it so impassioned as "August, 1914."

Right Royal, too, is said to be fellow to *Reynard the Fox*. To me it is not that, for all it has to do with the steeplechase, another English institution. It is too much like a reproduction, on a smaller scale, of *Reynard the Fox,* in which, by the bye, its hero, Charles Cothill, is introduced to us. *Right Royal,* fine thing that it is, is of the same kind as *Reynard the Fox,* but a lesser thing.

"August, 1914" stresses the motive that returns in Masefield almost as often as beauty, the presence in life of the unknown generations of dead men. In every cottage, in every field, in every road and barn and mill, Masefield thinks not only of the men who are now present there, but of those who worked in these places in past times. This down above the cold hill-spring, quiet in the sun, was once "grim with sacrificial fires." That was in pre-Celtic times. Thoughts of the Roman soldiers once on these roads of Shropshire are frequent in him, as frequent as in Housman. Thoughts are ever present, indeed, to Masefield of all the people from Roman times until to-day, who "were most lovely and unhappy" in this loved place or that he frequents.

Here in America, for all our love of things of yesterday, we have been brought up on the belief that life is for the living. Sometimes in youth we have felt that we were still governed by laws made by men long dead, but if we have felt that to be true in later years, we have most of us felt it to be for the best. In England, as in all old countries, the sense of what has been done by men now dead is more instant than in America, especially in country places in England where change is slow. John Burroughs found the suggestion that the land had been long lived in the greatest difference between the English countrysides and the American countrysides he knew best, those of the Catskills in New York, and those about Washington. It seems to be the profound and unchanging belief of Masefield that:

> Wherever beauty has been quick in clay
> Some effluence of it lives, a spirit dwells.

Nothing is commoner than for city people to think that country people do not care for the beauty of places where they live. The city people are wrong in most such instances they cite. The countryman of English stock, of north European stock generally, does not wear his heart on his sleeve. If you have worked with country people, and if you have the country heart yourself, you will find out that more of them care for the beauty of out-of-doors than do people of the towns. Their love of the beauty of the place in which they live, and not use and wont alone, is what has kept them in the country when money was to be come upon more plentifully in towns. Masefield knows, of course, that country people do so care. Looking out on the Berkshire downs when he was writing "August, 1914," he thought of all the people who had lived in this countryside and had loved it down the generations.

A late development in Masefield is his taking-up of the Arthurian stories. Like most poets, he has wanted to hear his words spoken and his dreams given objective reality on the stage. So, after taking subjects from the rural England of yesterday in *Nan* (1909), and from Roman history in *Pompey the Great* (1910), and from the clash of England and Spain in *Philip the King* (1914), and from the Samurai life of Japan in *The Faithful* (1915), and from the Christ story in *Good Friday* (1916) and *The Trial of Jesus* (1925), Masefield tried still another field in the hope of stage success by writing *Tristan and Isolt* (1927). It was hardly a happy experiment. Indeed, since *Nan*, Masefield has never been at his best in a play, although there is unquestioned nobility in *The Faithful*. In *Tristan and Isolt* Masefield gives us a presentation of an Arthurian story from the peasant point of view. We have much of a swineherd, his wife and son, and of the most unknightly knights of King Marc. The high old story is obscured by the setting, and there is only one moment of exaltation, in Isolt's lament, almost at the play's end.

Nor can it be said that Masefield is much happier, save in "Midsummer Night," in his Arthurian narratives. This poem, which gives title to the *Midsummer Night* (1928), is the old legend of King Arthur's Court meeting for this one night every year in some great cavern of the hills. Here the verse lifts to poetry in the old authentic way, and the characters are worthy of Masefield and of the legend out of which they come. Arthur speaks, and Gwenivere, and Lancelot, and Gwenivach and Mordred. At the close Arthur speaks again, prophesying his return, as fabled of old, in the hour of England's need. In one of the stories, "South and West," there is a nice boy, Kradoc, who steals the wings of ladies of the upper world, or goddesses if you will, who have doffed them for dancing. You learn of what happens to him and the last goddess to whom he returns her wings. There is a sort of land over wave, or beyond the grave, where are dogs even nicer than the boy, and the very dog and very mare and very mother whom the boy had lost in Berkshire long before. "East and West" has its moments and its close is impassioned poetry, but not of the otherworld. It is Berkshire in spring that brings the magic.

Masefield has written a very great deal, fifty books and more, including his hackwork. He has written on a great diversity of topics, from the roistering of sailors to the life after death, from Ledbury slums to Christ on the Cross, from England at war to King Arthur's return on Midsummer night. He has written on men and things all over the world, from sheep-pastures in Shropshire to the pampas of Argentina, from upstate New York to Gallipoli, from Japan to France. He has had his say on Helen of Troy and Pompey the Great. He has reached back into the legendary history of England for the story of Tristram and Iseult; he has considered Phillip of Spain and his lost Armada; he has followed the fortunes of a tyro in painting on a voyage around the Horn; he has recorded talk with Synge in Bloomsbury; he has caught many of the phases of the English countryside; he has praised dogs and horses; he has conjured up Roman soldiers in camp by the sides of roads they made in Britain. He has celebrated beauty in every guise in which beauty is known to man. He has written of nearly everything under the sun, save of "the headache life" of towns.

Masefield apprenticed himself to great masters. Synge gave him his theory of art, Hardy pointed out the material congenial to him, and Chaucer handed on to him his vividness of portraiture and quick movement of story-telling. There are minor obligations to Kipling and Yeats and Housman, but Masefield has had a music of his own, from the *Salt-Water Ballads* of 1902, and a spaciousness of manner and a great style in realistic stories since 1911. No extraneous influence, save that of Shakespeare in *Sonnets* (1916), has been observable in his writing since *The Everlasting Mercy* revealed him as a major poet. Masefield has been for his whole writing life the devoted servant of beauty. During that time he has brought into English poetry more of the external beauty of the world than any other English poet and as much of the beauty of imagination as any other English poet. He has made many discoveries about life and such revelations as come only to the man of vision. He is disappointed that he has not been able to do more for beauty than he has done, that he has not made more that is a reflection of beauty. He fears that he is less susceptible to beauty than he was in youth, that what he is doing now is to remember "The beauty of fire from the beauty of embers." His devotion has not slackened, though, and he prays still, as he has long prayed:

> Let me have wisdom, Beauty, wisdom and passion,
> Bread to the soul, rain where the summers parch.
> Give me but these, and, though the darkness close
> Even the night will blossom as the rose.

CHAPTER XIV

Realists of the Countryside

WILFRID GIBSON (b. 1878) is a lesser sort of Crabbe. He is a sentimentalist, which Crabbe is not, but his material, the everyday sufferings of humble life; his direct method of narration; his bare and undistinguished diction; his sympathy with the underdog; place him of themselves among the poets of to-day where Crabbe was among the poets of the late eighteenth century. The poetry of Crabbe is, in the right sense of the word, hard, the poetry of Gibson is, on the contrary, characteristically soft. It is soft not only in temper, because of its lack of stoicism, but it is soft, in spots, in its very texture, in its choice of material, in its imagining, and in the technique of its execution. There is hardly one of the narrative poems that does not have a weakness of feeling, or taste, or imagery.

This weakness is often the weakness of obviousness. As soon as you have read the first lines of "The Brothers" and find that the young men are quarreling in a mine pit, you know what the end will be. You know they will die together. They do, of course, with the note of the pathos of childhood sounding in our ears. You read "The Lighthouse" with tears in your eyes. It is the account of a father's saving of his son after shipwreck. The very opening of the poem introduces them to you, saved. You are spared the agony of doubt as to the outcome of the swim through the cold sea and of the climb up the slippery cliff. All that is narrated after they are snug in the lighthouse with the keeper who tells the story. What the following account of swim and climb serves to do, if you read critically, is to make you skeptical about the story. However, your questioning does not do the damage now it would have done had the poem opened with what you found hard to swallow. It is artful of Gibson to dump the pair in upon you through the breaking glass of the lighthouse window so early in the poem. That is an occurrence easy to believe. After acceptance of the presence of man and boy in the lighthouse it is harder to believe that they could not have got there. Gibson is afraid, indeed, that you will not credit the story, so he bolsters it up by the reflection:—

> But they who live beside the sea
> Know naught's too wonderful to be.

That helps, of course, and if you are sentimentally inclined, and we most of us are, you may accept it all as what has happened.

We are all moved by these tales, and by the eclogues and plays of Gibson, but it is as we are moved by melodrama in the theater. The tears come readily to the eyes, but no ache is left in the heart.

It is true, of course, that a poet is to be judged by his best, and not by his worst, or even by his average. The trouble is that there is hardly a tale or an eclogue or a play of Gibson without some such flaw. Take "The Money," for instance. A woman is found starved, with a bag around her neck in which is "four-pound-seventeen-and-five." The explanation is that it was the money found years before on her lover when he was burned to death in a coal-pit. It was the money he had saved up for them to marry on. Now this is good material for Gibson's kind of poetry. Gibson, however, has to use coincidence, the memory of a story told to the narrator long since, about the finding of this same sum on a burned miner, to explain why the woman starved to death with money at hand. Worse than this abuse of coincidence, when there was no reason why the story should not be told straightly, from the omniscience of the poet, is what an absence of a sense of humor does to the narrator. These are the opening lines of the poem:

> They found her cold upon the bed.
> The cause of death, the doctor said,
> Was nothing save the lack of bread.

It is true that a poet is often the best parodist of himself, as Swinburne is, for instance, in "Heptalogia," but it is not often that a poet is so successful in an unwitting parody of himself.

Take, too, a sample of non-narrative verse, the lines explanatory of the purpose of *Fires*, printed at the outset of that volume, in lieu of a preface. It is from this book, on the whole his best, that all these citations have been taken. In these prefatory lines the poet dreams before the fire. All kinds of "flickering fancies" rise, but what he sees at the end of his reverie is the figure of "The man who hews the coal to feed my fire." Well and good, but between the first fancy of "Amber woodland streaming," and this last line just quoted, occurs "Passion's crater yearning." There is nothing to be said of such a line. It is an unpleasant duty to have to point it out.

These prefatory lines to *Fires* might be taken as descriptive of Gibson's poetic progress. He began as a belated Pre-Raphaelite with *Urlyn the Harper* (1902). He was just as fluent in the series of dramatic lyrics that a minstrel sings about his queen as he is in the annals of the poor. Already there are signs, though, of that habit of portraiture that he was to develop so fully in *Neighbors* (1920). In this portraiture there is already, too, that exaggeration of the severity of labor that runs through all his poetry of this sort. In "The Ploughman" he writes:

> His white share spills in dust the hot grey soil,
> A hanging smoke about him as he goes:
> Yet, stumbling, almost blind and parched he knows
> Calm ends the unending furrows of his toil.

May one, who has had his ribs soundly rapped by the plough-handles when the share nosed into stone after stone of glacial drift on a northern hillside, say that while ploughing is hard work it is too much to speak of it as "blinding," and that it is no more "parching" than much else of the heavy labor of the farm. One wonders if Gibson himself has gone through much heavy labor, whether he knows at first hand of the mining and quarrying and foundry work and machine-tending and farming and droving that he writes about. There is no question about his sympathy with all who are driven and dulled by heavy labor, but there is a question about the intimacy of his knowledge of it. He has some dramatic power, and it may be that he relies on this. Even dramatic power, however, will not make wholly believable emotions and situations that have not been long familiar and long pondered over by the poet. It would seem that much of Gibson's work had been written off out of first thoughts, or from the surface of his mind.

The Queen's Vigil (1902), *The Golden Helm* (1903), and *The Nets of Love* (1905) mark no considerable advance upon the first volume. *Stonefolds* (1907) is the first of many short plays of the shepherds of Northumberland, the home county of Gibson. It has to do with peasants who lead narrow lives, who suffer, who have pride and hardness of heart and wild passions. We have known such folk ever since we first met them in Wordsworth's "Michael." We meet them to-day in the plays of Abercrombie, Gibson's friend and fellow-contributor to *New Numbers* (1914).

There is not much variation in the characters in Gibson, whether you meet them in eclogues like those of *Daily Bread* (1910), or in narratives like those of *Fires*, or in plays such as *Womenkind* (1912) and *Lovers' Leap* (1924). A young man of wild blood, a middle-aged woman of a biting tongue, a doddering old man, and a young girl wronged by her lover are characters constant to his writing. He writes more of shepherds than of any other country people, and he knows more of shopkeepers than of any other class of townsmen. He has, however, gone the round of all occupations and trades, and he has written, too, of the people of the roads, of beggars, tramps, and horse-copers.

Gibson is never better in his eclogues than in *Daily Bread*. They are too alike in their grey wretchedness for you to remember them the one from the other, but they are on the whole free from the lurid melodrama of the longer plays such as *Kestrel Edge*. They read, many of them, as if they might have been worked up from reports of welfare workers or from the newspapers, but some of them, like "The House of Candles" and "The Garret," are evidently discoveries of his own. There is little revelation of hidden things in them and an infrequent awakening thought and almost no poetry at all, but some of them have a kind of scientific verity about them that is impressive in its way.

Gibson is never better in his narratives than in *Fires*. "The Shop," with its tinkling bell and its yellow primroses from Cornwall, is one I can remember. "Flannan Isle" has an eeriness that is a little like that of certain of the Border ballads, which this modern Borderer so seldom echoes. "The Hare" has about it some of the freedom of the fells, as "The Lodestar," too, in lesser degree. The one with most bite is "Red Fox." It tells how a man was deterred from shooting his successful rival for a girl's hand by meeting a family of foxes, dog-fox, vixen, and cubs, the night the girl's baby was born. "Red Fox" was what the man with murder in his heart called his red-bearded rival.

In many readings of *Daily Bread*, I marked only one reading of life:

> And toil is something more than happiness;
> 'Tis life itself.

That is about the most memorable thing that Gibson has said. There is nothing like it, and only a few picturesquenesses of phrase, in *Fires*. I find about a half-dozen passages marked in my copy of the book, and I wonder now, as I look over the book, why I marked some of them. This is one:

> eyes that looked beyond all happiness,
> Beyond all earthly trouble and distress,
> Into some other world than ours.

REALISTS OF THE COUNTRYSIDE

A cottage window light is "A warm red star of welcome in the night." In "The Flute" Gibson tells us what are:

> The things I care to hear about,
> The little things that make up life.

The plays are not so good, I think, as the tales and eclogues. Irony, a quality unusual in Gibson, tones down the melodrama of what is, perhaps, the best of them, *Womenkind*. Here the curtain falls on a bridegroom, deserted alike by bride and by the girl who is the mother of his child, muttering of women, "They're a faithless lot," and his old mother feeding him to the same tune, "Aye, we're a faithless lot." Whatever happens men must eat. Things certainly happen in these plays. Parting of lovers, deaths, and the falling of madness upon its victims are to be found in plenty. "Lovers' Leap" is the most extreme of them, "Kestrel Edge" as effective as any.

Though Gibson has appealed most to his time as a writer of tales and eclogues and plays, it is not in these, but in his short poems descriptive of people, or "characters," and in his short dialogues between people, that his best work is to be found. Once in a while there is an echo of our Americans Frost and Masters, in *Neighbors*, for instance, but its best poems are wholly Gibson's own. "Henry Turnbull" has a touch of the macabre. "Jaunty Jack" is memorably unsentimental. "Ralph Lilburn" just misses being a thing of beauty. This last-named poem recounts how a lover and his lass drove out together one night in a cart with sealed hives behind them, taking the bees out to the heather. The taking of the bees to summer pasture was a never-failing topic of an old German I knew years back in the Poconos of Pennsylvania. As a boy he had gone, summer on summer, with other boys, and with girls and old men and women, up into the Bavarian Alps, taking the bees and cows and goats to better pasture. The journey with bees on the wagons that the cows drew, and with the goats driven ahead; and those weeks of picnicking on the high pastures, were romance to that old man, now so far removed in space and years from the experiences of his youth. How he could conjure it all up for you, the beasts and bees and humans, all, in a sense, on holiday. You could see, as he talked, the fresh grass and the thick-studded flowers that sprung up in the wake of the retreating snow. I mention my Bavarian's bee story to say how much better a piece of artistry it was than Gibson's in his little poem. Again and again he thus fails to realize the possibilities of his material.

Neighbors, on the whole, however, is interesting reading. There are freshness and surprise in these dialogues and monologues and sketches of character. The very pick of these verses is the grotesques. There are other grotesques in that earlier collection *Battle and Other Poems* (1916), and in that later collection *I Heard a Sailor* (1925). In "The Question," a man in Flanders, in the trenches, wonders whether the old cow died or not that was "gey bad" when he had to leave home. In "His Father" another soldier, who forgot to put the spigot in the barrel, is thinking how angry his father will be if he the son is "reported dead, Before he gets me told about that beer." In "The Puffin" an old man laughs at himself for having his finger cut to the bone by a puffin's bite as he pulls it out of its nesting hole. In "The Parrot" there is something better than the grotesque, an opening of a window in the mind, maybe, and the glimpsing of a sight come down through ancestral memory. In "The White Whippet," the snow-white dog seen in "the ring of the street-lamp's gusty flame," is made the symbol of the secret dream of the pitmen gathered about waiting for the tavern doors to open. Only those, perhaps, who know what the racing dog is to Englishmen from the north country will realize this poem to the full, but all can enjoy the sharp contrasts and sudden beauty of it. In "The Weazel" a long story with a quick surprise in it is told in thirty-six lines. It is always, indeed, to the advantage of Gibson's writing when he compresses it. "Sabbath," too, has its jolt of surprise, of a sort unusual to Gibson. We have in America, too, many of us heard:

REALISTS OF THE COUNTRYSIDE 343

The cheerful Christians in their chapel scream
There is a fountain filled with blood. . . .

There is no breaking of new ground in his later work in *The Golden Room* (1928), *Islands* (1932), and *Fuel* (1934). There is no excelling here of old effects. There is no falling-away from his best. Set of verses after set of verses is just more of what we have had before, save that he is now more concerned with short sets of verses than long ones. Those short poems are some of them lyrics, and some of them "characters" or renderings of incidents. In "The Plum" he puts in seven lines as much that happened as he often puts in seventy. He owns to a liking for jazz and tells us of his broadcasting, but he returns most successfully in the end to his fells and their shepherds.

Gibson gives, too, foregatherings at "The Old Nailshop," in the west country, with the Frosts and Abercrombies, Rupert Brooke and Helen and Edward Thomas. It was the golden room where the parties were held that gave title to *The Golden Room*. *Islands* is a collection of verses largely about places and the experiences of travel. *Fuel*, among much reportorial work, has one poem of unrealized possibilities, "The White Hound," but still memorable, and "Ernshaw," a play in his characteristic manner.

Gibson is given the space he is given here because, after all is said, he has presented, in however crude and obvious a fashion, a good deal of life. He is made somebody by his material. He does not bring this humble life with which he is concerned before us with any great power, but by just plugging at it, at the rate perhaps of a poem a day when things are going well, he finally gets something of it before us. He is always clear, and he is always easy to understand. There is never any pioneering thought, any plumbing of depths, anything that is bothersome because unencountered before. It would not seem that Gibson wrote out of a great mass of material accumulated through the years, as was Scott's for instance, but that he went seeking the stuff out of which poetry is made, and used cannily what he found.

It is usual to say that most of the writers that count have written a great deal, that certainly all the major poets have written a great deal. This is true of a Tennyson and a Browning, a Morris and a Swinburne, a Kipling and a Yeats, a Hardy and a Masefield. It is often, however, that a writer is undone by writing too much. Noyes is such a one and Gibson such another. If Gibson had not such a fluency of expression, and such a desire to be writing all the time, his verse had unquestionably been better. He would not then be repeating himself so often and so often be recounting the obvious. Nor is his writing itself sufficiently considered. It is not tested by any high standard of taste. It is not submitted to the scrutiny of a laughing mind. It is judged by Gibson at its face value, and let go at that. The writing of Gibson is not of the sort which was easy to write and hard to read. It is of that less usual sort that was easy to write and that is easy to read. It is not, however, easy to remember, because it came out of no depths, because it has in it little of what is profound or magical or of a new music.

W. H. DAVIES

The sturdy beggar has been a figure in English life and literature from early days. He has been the envy of the settled men from whom most of the poets have sprung. The sight of the beggar afoot on the road, when the air turns warm in May, free to go where he will; to meet all the adventures of the road, little or great; to see the beauty of the world under all changing lights from dawn to moonrise: has irked farmer and cleric, shopkeeper and landowner, and all others with responsibilities that keep them day in and day out in the one round. No writers from these settled classes, even when they have been men of real dramatic power, who could see things from another's point of view, and be that other in the seeing, could express the beggar's life, for they had not had the knowledge of the road and the detail of out-of-doors in all weathers that come to the "true travellers."

That sturdy beggar has at last found expression in poetry in W. H. Davies (b. 1870). Davies is himself, of course, a human being of individuality, a man like no one else, clown or lord, but he is, too, the beggar articulate, the rough man of the roads, the happy-go-lucky wanderer, the man who will have a free foot if he has nothing else. We have had the traveling scholar articulate in Borrow, the tramp-printer articulate in Whitman, the poor-gentleman-on-the-road articulate in Synge, but in Davies we have for the first time the real tramp poet. And wonder of wonders, the tramp poet is as golden-voiced as Herrick.

In an admirably succinct biography Davies tells us that he "became a poet at thirty-four; been one ever since." His first book of verse was *The Soul's Destroyer and Other Poems* (1905), published on the proceeds of his hawking of "small articles through England" as a peddler. Edward Thomas, Edward Garnett, and Bernard Shaw were its sponsors, and it was quickly before the public. It was, being what it was, with such friends, and their publicity, a success. It had in it none of the poems on which the reputation of Davies now rests securely, but its verses were interesting biographically, and freshness of outlook and simplicity of expression were found in them here and there. The belief of Edward Thomas that it would lead to even better things is a proof of his critical perspicacity. He warned Davies of the danger of a man writing himself out, but a second collection came along after only two years in *New Poems* (1907). There are better verses in *New Poems* than any in *The Soul's Destroyer*, but it was not a success with the public. The novelty of a book of verses by a tramp had worn off, and there was in it less that was interesting biographically.

In this same year, nineteen hundred and seven, came *The Autobiography of a Super-Tramp*, prefaced by Bernard Shaw, an account in prose of those years of the nineties during which Davies was a tramp in America and a cattle-boat man on ships from America to England. This book was a nine days' wonder, but it is more than that; it is one of the most notable human documents of our time. It did him the service, too, of arousing a curiosity about him in circles wider than those of readers of contemporary poetry. The readings of their verse by Noyes and Masefield, Frost and Vachel Lindsay, that were to build up a large public for poetry of the day, had not yet begun. Yeats had read his verse in America, but that verse could not be, in the nature of things, of large public appeal on a first reading, and it did not immediately break the way for readings by other poets.

The stage was set for *Nature Poems* when that volume appeared in 1908, and *Nature Poems* was equal to the occasion. It did not disappoint the audience waiting for it, and it had in it certain of the lyrics that are as surely permanent as anything that Davies has written. I think nearly all of us who know our Davies would put "The Rain," "Truly Great," "Early Morn," and "A Lovely Woman" among his ten best poems. From all his books later than *Nature Poems*, I would choose only "Leisure," "Sweet Stay-at-Home," "A Greeting," "Sheep," "No Master," and "The Hour of Magic," six poems from twelve books of verse, to set over against the four from *Nature Poems*. It was a new note, surely, this struck in "The Rain." Its material is known to us all, but this known thing, this thing so familiar to ears and eyes, this phenomenon so recurrent in experience, and so long cherished in memory, is now become a music of words, a pattern of images, a creation of art, to take place in memory alongside of "With lisp of leaves and ripple of rain," and a score other such passages. You visualize the poet, perhaps, snug in bed, under the thatch of a timbered cottage, listening to the gentle rain falling on a tree just outside his casement—you, who love the rain and take to the attic on a stormy night to hear it on the shingles just above your head. It is unfortunate that Davies cannot keep up to the level of this opening stanza in its fellow. For four of the six lines it is good, though not so good as the first stanza, and then it drops, thud, into a couplet that is all obviousness.

> I hope the Sun shines bright:
> 'Twill be a lovely sight.

Davies has been betrayed by his own simplicity. He tells us that he tears up five poems for every one he keeps. That proves his richness of inspiration. It indicates, also, that it is apt to be hit or miss with him. The pity is that it is only once in a long while that a poem of his is a perfect whole. The pity is that so many more of them might be perfect with only a little added care and artistry.

We must content ourselves with things as they are, remembering what is fine in the poems and forgetting the rest. That is about what time does. There are, of course, poets who are remembered for lines rather than for whole poems. As great a poet as Emerson is of these. With Emerson, however, you have the compensation of lines that change the world for you. Davies seldom disturbs the depths. What Davies sees are little wonders, and he has seen very many of them, at least a thousand and one. In "Rags and Bones" we find a like confession. Once, however, he rises in defense of his attitude toward profundities:

> I hear men say: "This Davies has no depth,
> He writes of birds, of staring cows and sheep,
> And throws no light on deep eternal things,"
> And would they have me talking in my sleep?

That is a good answer. Guesses at "deep eternal things" are often no more than babbling in one's sleep. It is the privilege of the poet, too, to be concerned only with the pageant of things, and not with their whys and wherefores. The poet need be only singer, not seer at all, if he has a mind to.

"Truly Great" is a well-sustained poem of country contentment. It is one in sentiment with a dozen others of its kind in many and diverse sorts of poets, from "The Choice" of Pomfret down to our day. Davies, for all his confessed addiction to trance, is no dreamer. He sees things as they are. There is a vein of hard practicality in him, a vein more usual, proverbially, in the Scotsman than in the Welshman Davies is.

Perhaps it is enough to say of "Early Morn" that De La Mare chose it for *Come Hither* (1923), his anthology of English poetry of all time. "Early Morn" is a picture of the world at sunrise, all fresh and dewy and golden. "A Lovely Woman" is one of the uneven poems. Its onset takes your breath away, but it breaks down a little more than half-way through, dissipating its effect with forced and far-fetched images.

Farewell to Poesy (1910), *Songs of Joy* (1911), *Foliage* (1913), *The Bird of Paradise* (1914), and *Child Lovers* (1916) were collections of verse of varying excellence, but, on the whole, showing a sustained invention and a gradually widening scope. There were narratives of a new power in them, such as "Nell Barnes" and "The Bird of Paradise." The five stanzas of the former are as packed with action as a Border ballad. They tell you the story of Nell, parted from her husband, and how she taunted him with her men; of her sickening and death when he went overseas. "The Bird of Paradise" gives the delusions of Nell dying as recounted by Kate Summers. It is not ironic like so much of "Nell Barnes."

There are not many of these episodes in Davies, but all there are are etched in mordantly. "A Woman's History" follows Mary Price from five years to five-and-seventy. The six stanzas present her as tender-hearted child; ruined girl of fifteen; hardened widow of thirty-five; and harridan of seventy-five, "skinning eels alive." There is fancy, pretty fancy, and plenty of it, in the man, but that fancy must not be mistaken for sentimentality. When the fancy is not present in his writing, as it is not in "A Woman's History" and "Two Women," the instancy of all to the realities of things is revealed. Characters of his, like his episodes, have this same stark reality, "My Old Acquaintance" for one, and "One Thing Wanting" for another. You believe these stories of Davies, as you do not always believe the stories of low life of Gibson, similar in some respects, but recounted at much greater length.

Davies tells us several times that people take to him and trust him, girls from the country just come to town, beggars and the like. In "Nature's Friend" he tells how others than humans regard him—horses, cows, mice, birds, moths and bees.

REALISTS OF THE COUNTRYSIDE 349

He is always compassionate of animals, of sheep on a cattle-boat crying when they no longer can smell land; of a particular sheep that had been a child's pet and was now on its way to the slaughter-house; of a sad-eyed ox that stares at him over a fence; of "poor cows That miss at night the calves they licked by day"; and of birds injured in one way or another, though he admits, ofttimes their private lives are not what they should be. It is not often that there are touches of humor of this sort in his writing. In "Heaven" we find a more forthright humor, which culminates in jibes at the Scot's love of argument.

The collection by Davies, in 1916, of the best of his verse from the eight little volumes published from 1905 to 1916 brought home to all who keep their eye on literature that here was a new poet to reckon with. Before *The Collected Poems,* from *Nature Poems* in 1908, Davies had been acknowledged by fellow-craftsmen and critics of insight, but now came general recognition. *The Collected Poems* were advertised in the streetcars, and reviewed at length here, there, and everywhere. Since 1916 Davies has published *Forty New Poems* (1918); *The Song of Life* (1920); *The Hour of Magic* (1922); *Collected Poems, Second Series* (1923); *Secrets* (1924); *A Poet's Alphabet* (1925); *The Song of Love* (1926); *A Poet's Calendar* (1927); *Ambition* (1929); *Love Poems* (1935); and *The Birth of Song* (1936). These publications have sustained, rather than advanced, the reputation Davies won in 1916, as a result of the first series of *The Collected Poems*. Married, and on the threshold of old age, Davies is leading a more stay-at-home life than in old days. In *Later Days* (1925), chapters of autobiography in prose that supplement *The Autobiography of a Super-Tramp* (1907), Davies tells us of a home in Sussex that seems like a realization of this ideal expressed in "Truly Great."

In a sense all of the verse, as all of the prose, of Davies is autobiography. He has written all of his verses about his own experience, very little of it about his dream. There have been few reticences. The man stands revealed to us in his writing. He has stripped his life bare and he is ashamed of little of it. He weathers this self-stripping as well as the next of us. Very sensitive superficially, there is a hardness of core to the man that nothing can hurt. He is very like a child in this, like the child who will cry his eyes out over his dog that has died and then have fun in playing mourner at the burial.

Davies is particularly sensitive to the external beauty of nature. He responds quickly and easily to all the aspects of landscape. He is a keen observer. He notices the "side-leaps" of butterflies; how fast lambs' tails wag when they suck from their dams; how "the coward dog" rubs noses with "mangy curs, And fearful says, 'Come play, not fight'"; what time of year it is "When Bats wait not for Stars ere they take wing"; that a three-pound babe, "stripped at home, Looks like a rabbit skinned." It is strange that with all this feeling there is little ecstasy in the poetry of Davies. So, too, it is with Herrick, though Herrick, of course, has always sure artistry to delight you when you begin to wonder why there is so little high rapture in his verse.

There are discoveries about life in Davies. They are not many of them profound, but they are his own. One is:

> What we enjoy, and not possess,
> Makes rich or poor.

Another is:

> A poor life this if, full of care,
> We have no time to stand and stare.

It is strange, too, to note how little effect his wanderings in America have had on Davies. There are little vignettes in "Sweet Stay-at-Home" and "The White Cascade" and "The Power of Music" which seem to show an acquaintance with our southern cotton-fields and the Yosemite and the Grand Canyon of the Colorado.

Speaking of W. H. Hudson, Davies refers to his own "love of birds, which probably exceeded his (Hudson's) or any other man's." Yet he has no poem to wood-thrush or mocking-bird or bobolink, or to any other American bird. It would seem that only that which Davies had lived with a long time could make much of an impression upon him.

Davies is best as a writer of little lyrics about out-of-doors and women, lyrics as simple as songs; and as a maker of two-line readings of life that you accept as you would accept popular adages heard among the folk of a long-settled countryside. His freshness; his spontaneity, his directness, his naturalness; his first-hand treatment of birds and flowers, clouds and stars; his frank paganism: set him apart from all other poets of our day. Davies is simple, sensuous, and passionate; he has all the essentials, save ecstasy, of a lyric poet of the first power. That he would be, had he such artistry as is that of a score of lesser men his contemporaries.

LASCELLES ABERCROMBIE

Lascelles Abercrombie (b. 1881) is a difficult poet. He is primarily concerned with philosophical problems, or psychological problems, which may be carried by a thread of narrative, or of drama, but which, when they are so carried, strain the thread to the breaking point. And whatever he is concerned with he is concerned with at length. He is not the man to flash a revelation on you and have done. He would analyze and derive, he would discuss and debate. Had he been born in the eighteenth century he had been wholly at home, with Pope and Young and Dr. Johnson. Had he been born then, however, he would surely have been more explicit and simpler and more direct in expression. He seems to have put himself to school to all the crabbed writers from Donne to Doughty. Browning and Meredith he knows intimately; but, for that matter, he knows intimately all the poets of the world, the Greeks and Romans, the Old Testament men, Dante and Chaucer, Shakespeare and Racine, Milton and Goethe, Whitman and Hardy. He is one of the most learned of our poets. He quotes from all poets, and not only from the passages known generally, but from many that he has discovered for himself by the most careful reading. His knowledge, his judgment, his understanding as a poet unite to make him the best academic critic of

English poetry since Matthew Arnold. His *Idea of Great Poetry* (1925) is a book that no student of poetry can neglect.

In an age in which the lyric and the realistic narrative poem are of most appeal among the many kinds of poetry, Abercrombie writes long reflective poems and plays in verse that are surcharged with analyses of states of mind. The plays are easier to follow than the earlier reflective interludes, to which you must return again and again, and always with a fresh mind, if you are to understand them fully. Generally you find in them what pays you for your trouble.

The Sale of St. Thomas (1911) is the most praised poem of Abercrombie. It is a narrative concerned with the doubting apostle on the eve of his sailing to India. Prudence, rather than fear, makes him change his mind about sailing. So Christ, in the guise of a "noble stranger" tells the sea captain with whom Thomas had been debating his passage that Thomas is a runaway slave, a carpenter. Carpenters are in great demand in India, so the captain is glad to buy Thomas. The captain will turn him over to that ruler in India who is desirous of building a great palace of souls. Christ tells Thomas, when the captain is gone to have irons made for his carpenter, why he has acted as he has:

> Now, Thomas, know thy sin. It was not fear;
> Easily may a man crouch down for fear,
> And yet rise up on firmer knees, and face
> The hailing storm of the world with graver courage.
> But prudence, prudence is the deadly sin.
>
> . . . .
>
> For this refuses faith in the unknown powers
> Within man's nature: . . .
>
> . . . .
>
> But send desire often forth to scan
> The immense night which is thy greater soul;
> Knowing the possible, see thou try beyond it
> Into impossible things, unlikely ends;

And thou shalt find thy knowledgeable desire
Grow large as all the regions of thy soul,
Whose firmament doth cover the whole of Being,
And of created purpose reach the ends.

That is a sample of the hard texture of his writing, but easier of apprehension than the characteristic Abercrombie of the earlier poems. His writing seldom softens. There is a moment of what the Puritan calls carnality in "Odours and wines and slim lascivious girls," and a moment of exaltation in "I am a torch, and the flame of me is God." *The Sale of St. Thomas* is a better poem than any in *Interludes and Poems* (1908), or *Mary and the Bramble* (1910). In the first poem of *Interludes,* "The New God: A Miracle," there is a lyric note now and then. The love of the hills, hidden deep in Abercrombie's heart, wells up and flows into sudden felicities. "I'm thinking of a little tarn, Brown, very lone" is one such, but others of its kind are far to seek here, as in all Abercrombie. There is power in "Blind," a half-tale, half-interlude, of a mother's long training of her half-witted son to kill his father. At the end she would have stayed his hand, but she could not. She had not thought of the man who deserted her growing old. Always he was before her in the insolent strength and attractiveness of youth, and the sight of the broken man excites her pity, but too late. The trained innocent has been set on the trail of his victim, and he seizes that victim unerringly and strangles him.

It must be, I think, the fundamental brainwork in these interludes that wins them the praise of Bridges and Masefield and Edward Thomas. *Emblems of Love* (1912) is a fellow to *Interludes and Poems* in the difficulties it puts in the way of the reader. Pre-Roman Britain, Bible lands, and the Jacobite rebellion of 1745 furnish the background for these studies in the development and nature of love. It is a very modern Vashti that is driven out by Ahasuerus, and a Judith that talks worn brands of feminism before she takes the head of Holofernes.

There is a partial clearing of the style of Abercrombie in *Deborah* (1913). *Deborah;* and the plays its successors, in *Four Short Plays* (1922), *The Adder* (1913), *The Staircase* (1914), *The Deserter* and *The End of the World* (1914); and *Phoenix* (1923): all have a definiteness and surety of meaning that is lacking in the early deliberative poetry. *Deborah* loses some of its effectiveness by heaping horror on horror. In *The Adder* there is only the one horror, sensed as inevitable from the start, but shocking us none the less when it does come. There is, too, a kind of splendor about *The Adder,* the splendor of hot blood, the splendor of sin that the old-time evangelists loved to describe before they cast it and its victims into the outer darkness. Of these six plays all but *Phoenix* are of the English countryside.

The Staircase is the best thing that Abercrombie has done. It tells a story very like that of Gibson's *On the Threshold.* It is concerned with the return to the home of her youth of a woman whom life has broken. She has been turned out of doors some time back by her parents who now are dead and their old home deserted. She had brought disgrace upon the family and she had been punished with the cruelty traditionally proper in such cases. She comes back the doxy of a tramp. In the house is a young carpenter singing at his work and dreaming of who will be the first to occupy the house he has again made habitable. He knows the story of the girl who was driven out. He has romanticized the story, idealized the girl, made himself her champion. She, now the disillusioned woman, is angered by his blather over what she once was, and tells him that she is the woman of his dream. He will not believe it at first, but he has to in the end. Her man follows her in. Disappointed of food, he would beat her, but the carpenter prevents him. The tramp is outraged by such interference with family discipline. He is hurt to the quick, too, and thus admonishes the joiner:

Have I to down you first before I tan
My woman? Do you call that fair? It's low.
I'm hunger-starved and done—just enough heart

Left in me for lathering her; and you
Push in, you with your belly crammed and good:
It's low! Stand off and be an Englishman.

Torn out of the context, the irony of this seems to miss fire, to be nothing more than bad taste, but read in its place in the play, it is part of the tense whirl of it all, and dramatically true, what would come to the lips of such a waster. Police, pursuing the tramp for rick-burning, now come in and drag him off to jail, his mate going with him, as much out of kindness to the joiner to take herself off his hands as out of her habit of following her master.

The End of the World is an orgy. It uncovers as much ugliness in English country life as the novels of T. F. Powys, but you are in better company during the operation. Abercrombie does not rejoice in human weakness and misfortune as does Powys.

Phoenix is a tragicomedy of a king's house in northern Greece in the time before the Trojan War. It laughs grimly at the conventionalities. Rhodope, the young courtesan who makes all the trouble, is a new character, a creation, a girl so free of morals that she gives no more offense than would an animal. You remember her as you remember the charcoal-burner and his daughter in *The Adder;* the joiner and the tramp-woman in *The Staircase;* the sinister Luther of *The Deserter;* and Deborah, who suffers through so many years. It is the people of Abercrombie, indeed, that you remember longest, and certain scenes in his plays, like the father holding his girl's arm for the snake to bite, and not passages from the poetry, either of lyric loveliness or "readings of life."

ALFRED WILLIAMS

It must be that every one with any large experience of life must have come on an uneducated man with a gift for turning rhymes. There was in the days of my youth a "flagman poet" in Philadelphia, and in my old years I came to prize the friendship of a "fish-peddler poet" many miles from Philadelphia. No man of such origin since the days of John Clare, with the exception, of course, of W. H. Davies, has been reviewed at such length and so widely as Alfred Williams (1877-1930) of Wiltshire. A forgeman of Swindon, Williams taught himself Greek and Latin as well as the traditional measures and manners of English poetry. Fluency he has, and ease of expression, and the urge to carry through long sets of verses. Discussions and transcripts from nature delight him most. To me, however, his *Wiltshire Village* (1912) in prose is much more of an achievement than any of his verses. He began with *Songs in Wiltshire* (1909). Then followed *Poems in Wiltshire* (1911), *Nature and Other Poems* (1912), and *Cor Cordium* (1913). His later activity in letters was in a very different field. Once in a while he returned to the Valley of the White Horse or retold some Eastern tales.

It is a habit to say that the basic quarrel with pastoral poetry is its artificiality. Here, however, is pastoral poetry without artificiality, simple, direct, unprettified, but yet, somehow, flat and unprofitable. Williams manages to get the light air of the downs into his verses, and meetings there of boy and girl, and memories of what old times saw happening here. The trouble is that what he writes is inconsequential. It goes in one ear and out the other. He has read all the poets, translated Pindar, Horace, and Ovid, taken to heart Chaucer and Shakespeare, Spenser and Sidney, Fletcher and Milton, Wordsworth and Tennyson, but all to little avail. What he writes has the tags of poetry about it, but it is not poetry. He praises his home county of Wilts, and the Jefferies that made it known to the world; Salisbury Cathedral in its water meads lifting its spires lark-high to heaven; Sevenhampton fields; "Edward Slow: the Wiltshire Dialect Poet"; and the "Druidical Remains at Avebury."

An inhabitant of the village of South Marston, he went to work as a boy. "I have driven the plough," he writes, "milked the cows, made hay, and harvested the corn with the farmer and his men, and I have toiled and groaned long years at the furnace and steam-hammer, in the midst of ten thousand workmen; but

REALISTS OF THE COUNTRYSIDE

though in it, I was never of it, and, try as I will, I cannot find many good words to say for the manufacturing life." So it is that he has not been interested in singing a "Song O' Steam." He is not desirous of expressing his time, and its burdens.

Williams quarrels with the many whose writings are:

> crowded with distress,
> And crying from the dreary wilderness
> Of much-abused life, and souls self-stirred,
> Unheeded, and unpitied, for unheard,
> Or, if attended, only by the few,
> For niggard recompense is sorrow's due.
> Comfort of life's the treasure of our kind,
> And he who seeks for ill deserves to find.

That is a fair sample of Williams in reflective mood. In lyric mood he is less quickly put before who read. "All Things Delight in Sleep" is as good a lyric as he can write. Stanza by stanza it is not so bad, but its five stanzas build up to no definite end. The best of it is its onset:

> All things delight in sleep,
>   Morning to eve inclines,
> Slowly the purple-woven shadows creep.

It is when he is translating Ovid, who gives him material, that he has anything like sustained power. Now that his verses have been before us for a quarter of a century we can but wonder at the stir they once made in England. As a phenomenon they are remarkable, but their intrinsic merit as poetry does not seem what it once seemed to critics in high places.

EDWARD THOMAS

It is easy for me to overestimate the verse of Edward Thomas (1878-1917). It so happened that I was reading a collection of his verse, the half of it yet unpublished in book form, in that Easter of 1917 in which he was killed before Arras. I had taken it with me on a few days' visit to a remote farmhouse in New Hampshire. There was still a good deal of snow about though it was mid-April, three feet in the woods, unmelted piles even higher on the north sides of houses and barns, and at least a foot's coating everywhere else, save in places on the roads. At sunrise the first morning the world was as I had never seen it before, a glow of old rose and lavender, mauve and pearl. It was old rose where the snow lay on fields that had been mowed the summer before, and lavender on fields where grasses and weed-stems outtopped the snow. It was mauve on the wooded slopes of the mountains, and pearl, flickering and flushing, on certain stretches of sky.

I had been reading Thomas the night before I woke to this morning of wonder. It was strange, indeed, with impressions from his grey record of Old England uppermost in mind, to look out on a New England so full of color. It was the contrast that struck me at the time, the contrast of an out-of-doors sober and subdued, bedewed and misty, under evening light or rain or the blur of distance, with this snowy landscape so warm-hued and dazzling. I was home again when the news came of his death. I was so absorbed then with the daily routine that I could not realize that my every reading of Thomas after this would be colored by my memories of reading him in circumstances so novel to me. But so it has been.

It is, then, easy for me to overestimate the verse of Thomas because of this association. It is easy for me to overestimate it because its maker cared so much for the English countryside and the presenters of that countryside from old time until to-day. *Country Gentlemen's Contentments,* Walton and Browne, Willoughby and Gilbert White, Cobbett and Borrow, Jefferies and Hudson have long held a first place in my interest, as have our own out-of-door essayists, Thoreau and Wilson Flagg, Burroughs and Muir. Thomas is of this company by his prose. There are passages in his verse, too, that ally him to them. Such a one is "Sedge-Warblers":

REALISTS OF THE COUNTRYSIDE

      sedge-warblers, clinging so light
To willow twigs, sang louder than the lark,
Quick, shrill, or grating, a song to match the heat
Of the strong sun, nor less the water's cool,
Gushing through narrows, swirling in the pool.
Their song that locks all words, all melody,
All sweetness almost, was dearer then to me
Than sweetest voice that sings in tune sweet words.
This was the best of May—the small brown birds
Wisely reiterating endlessly
What no man learnt yet, in or out of school.

  I have had only six weeks in which to observe British birds, and those were weeks of August and September when song is low, so I cannot vouch for the accuracy of this description of the song of the sedge-warbler, but when I compare it to the description in Hudson's *British Birds* I find it in harmony with that.

  It is easy for me to overestimate the verse of Thomas because of my sympathy with his concern for poetry. Next to his family and his countryside came his joy in the reading of poetry. His very regard for poetry made him almost savage at times in his reviewing of what passed for poetry. He put all to the test of comparison with the greatest poetry of the past, and when it fell short of the best he said so. For almost twenty years, from the time he was an undergraduate at Oxford, he was a reviewer of poetry. Thomas was quick to recognize originality. W. H. Davies owed a large part of his acceptance to the early appreciation of Thomas, and Thomas was a stout champion of De La Mare and John Freeman.

  His discovery of himself as poet must have come to Thomas as a great surprise and delight. It was Frost who did most to help him to that discovery. It was a happy meeting, that of these two men, the one English and the other American, both of them so "well-versed in country things." Frost not only encouraged Thomas in his verse-writing, but he was, in a sense, his master. "The Sign-Post," "The Manor Farm," "The Path," "Up in the

Wind," "Wind and Mist," "After Rain," and "The New Year" show in one way and another the influence of Frost. It is now in a fall of words you note it, now in a way of presentation, now in the tone, now in the atmosphere. Each is distinctively of his own countryside, the one of New England, the other of Old England. Thomas had Welsh blood in his veins, but I can find little "Celtic" in his writing. He had tramped over Wales, but he knew it less well than Southern England, and its landscape does not color his verse as does that of Hampshire and Wiltshire. There is testimony from all who knew him that no other writing man of his time had walked so much about the countries south of the Thames, hill-paths, sheep-tracks, old Roman roads, byways as well as highways.

A large part of his verse is a record of these wanderings, his moods brought up by people he met, vistas that opened before him, places that he happened on, chalk-pits, copses, ploughlands. There are not many narratives among these verses, almost all being meditative lyrics, but one of the best of them is partly narrative. I mean "Up in the Wind." There is here a presentation of a wild and unfrequented place, an old public-house and blacksmith's forge back from the roads. In old years its neighborhood was a district of charcoal-burners, but now there are "eleven houseless miles" on one road that runs near it. A girl who is lonely here, but wedded to the place, tells its story to the poet. "Up in the Wind" is a poem of a sort that had he lived he had doubtless done more of. It is the tendency of middle years to be interested in other forms of poetry than the purely lyric. This place of "Up in the Wind" and the girl its narrator stand as samples of many such out-of-the-way corners and people he had stumbled on in his wanderings.

"Lob" is another poem partly narrative. It is concerned with that figure of folklore that appears under so many disguises, as Robin Goodfellow and Puck more often perhaps than as Lob. Thomas is interested in him because he is so definitely a symbol of the time when "This England, Old already, was called Merry."

It is their fidelity to what the poet has seen and felt, their discovery of beauty of landscape and feeling, that is best in these verses of Thomas. There are no "purple patches," and few lines good to quote. I like his picture of

>   . . . The wagtail running up and down
> The warm tiles of the roof slope, twittering
> Happily and sweetly as if the sun itself
> Extracted the song
> As the hand makes sparks from the fur of a cat.

My *Collected Poems* (1920) opens to *"Words."* This poem is a tribute to our English words, so good for all the purposes of beauty and utility:

> older far
> Than oldest yew,—
> As our hills are, old—
> Worn new
> Again and again:
> Young as our streams
> After rain.

Certain lines in Thomas you mark, so that you may return to them and savor them. Such a one is that describing a farmhouse as "So velvet hushed and cool under the warm tiles." Another gives you the very quality of a particular farm by telling you, "The flint is the one crop that never failed." A third is, "When Gods were young This wind was old." And a fourth, perhaps the most haunting he has written, is, "The past is the only dead thing that smells sweet." I am not sure, however, that this other saying of his does not recur to me oftener:

> How dreary-swift, with naught to travel to,
> Is Time.

For all his greyness of landscape and for all his many variations on the greyness of life Thomas has moments of exaltation.

These moments are expressed so restrainedly, so reticently, so quietly, that sometimes you miss the feeling that underlies the expression. Even his Englishman's front of indifference cannot, however, repress the joy in beauty that cries out in:

> Forget, men, everything
> On this earth newborn,
> Except that it is lovelier
> Than any mysteries.

Thomas had never left the England that was his share of the earth that was "lovelier Than any mysteries" until he went to the War in France. England would undoubtedly have been dearer than ever to him had he survived to come back to it in peace. One miracle having happened in the late flowering of poetry in the hardened prose-writer that Thomas was, it could hardly be hoped that the further miracle of the deepening and broadening of his poetic power would have followed. And yet we cannot tell. It happened in Hardy. The verses of his youth count for little. He was old when he mastered the new medium. From Thomas we had only two volumes; *Poems* (1917) and *Last Poems* (1918). Their rhythms are often the rhythms of prose, though their material is always the material of poetry. Only now and then, in "Two Pewits," "Swedes," "If I Should ever by Chance," "Melancholy," "Adlestrop," and "Cock-Crow" are material and rhythm completely at one.

Other sets of verses, many of them, despite strained rhymes and awkwardnesses of expression of one kind and another, are so poetical in feeling that they make their intended effects. The force and directness and utter sincerity of the man, his gift of caring greatly for all things English great or small, compensate in a measure for the shortcomings of his art of poetry.

CHAPTER XV

The Last Romantics

THE child is father of the man even more fully in Walter De La Mare (b. 1873) than in most poets. It is not only that he writes child-verse in the spirit of the child, but that nearly all his other verse is informed by otherworldliness, a suggestion of that no-man's-land beloved by children, and by that make-believe that is part and parcel of their lives. In "Alulvan," a strange country of his imagining, a ghost walks at noonday and a banshee calls all night. In "The Isle of Lone" there are dwarfs of mellifluous names, Alliolyle, Lallerie, and Muziomone, who come to their deaths in the sea, and parrots and apes of ways as peculiar as those of the dwarfs. In "Melmillo" a counting game turns into the description of a witch's dance in a malevolent wood.

There is magic in these verses, and unaccountable things that children love. There are other child-verses about things wholly accountable, such as Nicholas Nye the donkey, "knobble-kneed, lonely and grey." "Summer Evening" is a sleepy song as sure to bring the sandman as that "sheep jumped over the fence" of happy memory. "Five Eyes" is a delectable thing about cats and rats and night in an old mill.

All this, of course, is only child-verse. That is all that *Mother Goose* is, too, but no rhyming has stood more indestructible against the years. De La Mare is not content, however, to be judged by this part of his work. Not a bit of child-verse, not even "Silver," appears in his *Selected Poems* (1927). "Silver" is a study of the familiar dooryard things under soft moonlight. All are lacquered with silver, the fruit on the trees, the paws of the sleeping dog, the breasts of the doves at the doors of their cote, and claws and eye of a scampering mouse.

> And moveless fish in the water gleam,
> By silver reeds in a silver stream.

Nor does De La Mare include here "Shadow," from his verse of general appeal, the poem that stands first in his *Collected Poems: 1901-1918* (1920). It is in this poem that he says the most memorable thing he says anywhere, "The loveliest thing earth hath, a shadow hath." There is a great deal of the man himself in this line. There is his code of beauty, his preoccupation with shadow, the archaism of the "haths." In the very next line he is concerned with death, as he is again and again in his poetry. This concern does not, however, bring to his readers any depression of spirit. Where all is so shadowy, the final passing beyond the veil is not so great a change.

You find among the sixty-eight poems of the *Selected Poems* that he would be judged by most of his best poems. There are here: "The Willow," a poem about a tree that is a fellow to the "birch with silver bark And boughs so pendulous and fair" of Coleridge; "Three Cherry Trees," with his characteristic eeriness; "Nod," that has its only rival in kind in "The Homecoming of the Sheep" of Ledwidge; "England," that is worthy of its subject; "Sotto Voce," that remarkable poem about Edward Thomas, and a nightingale which sang at high noon; "Music," that you must go back to Campion to match; "Winter," with its robin and rose-light and Orion; "Old Susan" and "Miss Loo," character poems of as much body as Overbury's prose; "All That's Past," with its reach back to Eden; and "Arabia," whose beauty is shadowed with dream.

I had intended to make this a list of the ten best poems of De La Mare, but the best of him will not reduce to ten. Every one of the eleven I have listed from *Selected Poems* calls out to be named. Then there are "Silver" and "Shadow." That makes

THE LAST ROMANTICS

thirteen lyrics of De La Mare that it would be difficult to keep out of any anthology of twentieth-century verse.

The subjects of these thirteen poems would seem to indicate a considerable range of dream and life in De La Mare, and it is true that he is interested in many things. His habit of playing at make-believe, however, and his uniformity of tone, his grey-shadowiness, serve to bring most of his poems close together in effects. He fails to include in *Selected Poems* any of his verses on the characters of Shakespeare. He excludes them, I suppose, because they are derivative. They are not criticisms, but revisionings of Falstaff, Mercutio, Iago, Imogen, Ophelia, and the rest.

There is good poetry to be found in *Poems* (1906) and *The Listeners* (1912). The verses of the *Veil* (1921) are not of equal richness. In *The Fleeting and Other Poems* (1933), De La Mare has turned grave. It is death and life that concern him now, not dreams, shadows, and little creatures. He is troubled now, uncertain, his determination to escape from realities shaken. His art, too, is less sure. He seems to be experimenting in at least half of the poems. Only now and then, as in "The Snail" and "Jenny Wren," is he his old sure self. Child-verse was what he began with, in *Songs of Childhood* (1901). *A Child's Day* (1912), *Peacock Pie* (1913) *Down-a-Derry* (1922), and *Ding Dong Bell* (1924) have followed, often with repetitions from one volume to another. There is a considerable bulk of story-telling in prose. It has been highly praised, but it is none of it, either short stories or long, of qualities at all comparable to the fine qualities of his verse.

Among all the verse of De La Mare there has been more to-do about "The Listeners" than about any other poem. It is very interesting technically, with its change of movement from odd to even lines. The rhythm of lines one and three and five is very like the rhythm of prose; the rhythm of lines two and four and six and all their even fellows is unmistakably the rhythm of verse. In "The Listeners" a knight on horseback keeps a tryst, not so perilous as that of him who found the "round squat turret" and put the slug-horn to his lips and blew "Childe Roland to the Dark Tower Came," but one that takes him who keeps that tryst outside "the world of men" and puts him at the mercy of untoward powers. A good many of the effects of "The Listeners" are hardly more than trappings. The moonlight, the phantom listeners, the beating on the door, the bird in the turret that you are told of but that you cannot sense; and the hoof-beats of the horse, are old and tried properties of the romantic poem. Other poems of his have like properties: "an ominous bird," "a tower of Ivory," "a lonely wanderer," "a witch," "sweet Mistress Fell," "False Faerie," the cry of a wolf, a lamplighter like Leerie, a charcoal-burner, and a changeling. De La Mare has moments when he realizes this weakness of his. He then admits:

> My inmost mind is like a book
> The reader dulls with lassitude,
> Wherein the same old lovely words
> Sound poor and rude.

"The Glimpse," the poem from which come these lines, is as near to a credo as he has come. "Life's Ecstacy," he owns, he would see and catch if he could, but "fading dreams" are in his eyes.

There is not much of the natural man in the verse of De La Mare. It is little concerned with the world, the flesh, and the devil. There need be no quarrel with such omissions. It is a relief, indeed, to come on poetry in which sex is held in abeyance. We have in his writing, to delight us, a delicate art busied with various sorts of loveliness, and now and then with a comforting reality. It is not a poetry that plumbs the depths, that makes discoveries about life, that has vision. It has felicities of sound and imagery, but even when its material does not demand it, it is obscured, in a half-light, greyed by the shadow of his mind. It is by design a thing apart from the "workaday" self of the poet. There is no echo in it of his long years with the Anglo-American Oil Company. There is little echo of his days in the hills about Oxford. In his own words it is a poetry written when "Life is no longer a riddle but a dream."

THE LAST ROMANTICS

RALPH HODGSON

Ralph Hodgson (b. 1872) has given us two slim volumes of verse. They appeared ten years apart, *The Last Blackbird* in 1907, *Poems* in 1917. The first is all compact of the stuff out of which poetry is made; the second is all compact of poetry. There is, indeed, no other volume of so few poems, twenty-five in all, that would contribute so many poems to an anthology of the best poems of our day, as this second collection. Such an anthology must have "The Gipsy Girl," "Time, You Old Gipsy Man," "Eve," "The Mystery," "The Bull," and the three fragments about Reason and Babylon and The Idle Rainbow; and it could ill spare "The Song of Honour," long as it is. These seven poems make in number of lines more than half of the volume. Without "The Song of Honour" they make more than a third of it. One and all these poems have magic; one and all they quiver with strange glows; one and all they move to a new music; one and all they surprise and thrill with a leap of imagination that spans the world and time.

Hodgson has tried to suppress *The Last Blackbird*. A fellow-poet and close friend of his had never seen it until I showed him my copy. Said he, after a sitting with it, "Hodgson is right about *The Last Blackbird*. There are only two good poems in it." He meant poems that were really "done," fully realized, of a caliber equal to those of the *Poems* of 1917. What were the two poems that his friend liked I did not ask, but I know that one was the lyric of eight lines that stands first in the volume. It makes "pitted toad" and "meanest slug" possessors of beauty. It is of the lineage of

> He prayeth best who loveth best,
> All things both great and small;
> For the dear God who loveth us,
> He made and loveth all.

Hodgson, of course, knows the detail of out-of-doors better than Coleridge. He is of the house of Bewick, and he shares with that ornithologist a deep love of birds. He writes just as warm-heartedly about beasts, too, in his verses to Dulcina his bulldog; and in the long poem, "The Bull," he composes it all from a woodcut of the great man of his family. He has separate sets of verses about "The Sedge-Warbler," "The Missel Thrush," "The Last Blackbird," and "The Linnet" in his first book; but it is in *Poems* that you find his most memorable poem about birds. "Stupidity Street" visions what will happen to the world if it allows its birds to be killed off. Hodgson sees:

> The worm in the wheat,
> And in the shops nothing
> For people to eat;
> Nothing for sale
> In Stupidity Street.

This poem may savor too much of the propaganda of the Audubon Societies to please some of us, but there is no doubt of the intensity of feeling of the man who made it. He published a poem of four hundred and thirty-six lines in *The London Saturday Review* for September 3, 1910, that is also propaganda raised into rhapsody. It is entitled "To Deck a Woman," and it recounts what will happen to the world if beast and bird are hunted down that lovely woman may stoop to the folly of fur and feathers. Wisely, he did not include these verses in *Poems*. There is not, indeed, more than half of what he published between 1907 and 1917 in *Poems;* and what is included is generally most severely revised from the form in which it first appeared. It must have cost him something to have left out:

> One melody, one lustre lost;
> One loveliness of Earth at end—
> Not Heaven deflowered of all its host
> Were deeper wound or worse to mend.

Yet the poem is too reiterative as well as too long and too definitely propagandist.

It was between 1907 and 1917 that Hodgson came into his own with the little sheaves of verse gathered into *The Flying Fame Chapbooks*, a venture in which he was associated with Lovat Fraser and Holbrook Jackson. *Eve and Other Poems* was the first of these. There followed in the same year, 1913, *The Mystery and Other Poems*, *The Bull*, and *The Song of Honour*. For the last of these Hodgson received the Polignac prize from the Royal Society of Literature.

There is considerable range of subject in the seven poems listed as his best. "The Gipsy Girl," a dramatic lyric, has that in it which makes it a fellow of "The Tiger." It has quick movement; and splashes of color, gold and yellow and purple; and as vivid an image at the end as that at the opening of Blake's famous poem.

> But oh, the den of wild things in
> The darkness of her eyes

loses nothing of its picturesqueness put over against

> Tiger! Tiger! burning bright
> In the forests of the night.

In "Time, You Old Gipsy Man" is music and color and arresting image on arresting image, and such a leap of the imagination as almost stuns you:

> Last week in Babylon,
> Last night in Rome,
> Morning, and in the crush
> Under Paul's dome.

is a record even for Time in annihilation of the ages. Seven millenniums are jumped in as many days.

"Eve" breaks your heart. Eve is such an ingenuous child that even Satan and the snake might have hesitated to take advantage of her. "The Song of Honour" is a garnering of the beauty of the world, and the singing of a pæan of praise to the heaping hills of treasure so gathered. It is a piling of image on image, of loveliness of phrase on loveliness of phrase. We see, with the poet, the whole world kneeling at prayer in the evening light, as we have so often seen it, but without the wit to find so true a phrase to describe it. We pass from reality that is good to dream that is better, and back to reality again. We pass through a catalogue of good things and beautiful that rivals the catalogue of great things in the table of contents of Bacon's essays. We hear, with the poet:

>The song of each and all who gaze
>On Beauty in her naked blaze.

We hear it:

>all, each, every note
>Of every lung and tongue and throat.

The meaning of this long poem is not to be come by quickly, but only after many readings, and much analysis, and with the help of imagination. "The Song of Honour" in the end will come to be to you, as it is to its maker, an apotheosis of "the whole harmonious hymn of being."

"The Mystery" reiterates the truth that the beauty of things is so transcendent that we need no explanation of their meaning. We do not feel in all our moods that this is a truth, but this poem persuades us as we read it that, for the nonce at any rate, the meaning of things does not matter, their beauty being so great.

"The Bull" tells the story of the whole life of the master of the herd, from the picture of him, old and deserted and dying, that was cut on wood by Thomas Bewick. Hodgson outlines the picture in his poem, even to the vultures already on the watch for the beast's fall, but he goes far beyond this. We see the bull a calf with his mother. We see him, a little older, playing with the youngsters of his year, at "butting trees and boulder-stones and tortoises." We follow him on, step by step, and always with sympathy and understanding, until the herd own him "masterhorn" and he is conqueror of leopard and lion as well as of all of his own kind. All this past of his the dying beast lives over in dream, and during all his dreaming and his gradually growing weakness the vultures continue to flock around him "Waiting for the flesh that dies." You can no more forget the story of the bull, once you have read it, than you can forget the woodcut its original, once you have seen it. And there is, of course, always before you that of which the bull is the symbol, the way of all flesh down to death.

There is a trick in:

> God loves an idle rainbow,
> No less than labouring seas.

Those "labouring seas" opposed to the "idle rainbow" are somewhat of the category of the pun as a decorative figure of speech that you find in Milton. It costs the seas no more effort to be "labouring" than it costs the rainbow to be "idle." The end that the poet has in view, however, is most effectively accomplished by the juxtaposition of the two words. He is making out the case, that Emerson made out before him, in "Beauty is its own excuse for being." He puts the case for Beauty as succinctly as it has ever been put.

These seven poems are, I think, the best of Hodgson, but nearly every poem of *Poems* has in it something to delight you. "A Wood Song" reminds you of Emily Dickinson. "After" gives you a stanza in which are six images in four lines, beauties crowded close but never jostling each other. In "The Bride" the girl in her bloom brings back all her generations of grannies who were beauties, too, in their times, a reach into the past that W. H. Hudson must have loved. "The Swallow" records a fear for her child that strikes to a mother's heart. "The Late Last Rook" is a fragment from a longer poem of inequalities. Hodgson could not resist culling out and reprinting these two stanzas of pure gold. "February" reveals a love of

> Swarth yew and ivy kinds
> And iron breeds germane

that is like Herrick's. "The Bells of Heaven" is a little poem quick with pity for beasts man-worried. In "Ghoul Care," without intending it, Hodgson strays into a revelation of himself. He is indeed the man of all men of whom it may be said:

> In the greenwood of his soul
> There was a goldfinch singing.

Light-hearted he is, as are all who know the joys of climbing and of lungs filled with the air of the heights. Merry-hearted, too, for all his awareness of the forces that threaten the beauty of life and the beauty of the loved landscapes of England. With eyes so eager for beauty, Hodgson can always find enough of beauty everywhere and anywhere to furnish forth a world of his own imagining. And when that fails to content him he can always find Arcady round the corner.

JAMES ELROY FLECKER

The bulk of the poetry of James Elroy Flecker (1884-1915) loses substance and significance with each rereading. It is all of it nearly always impeccable verse, the work of an artist in words, but most of it is no more than that, save for an image here and there. Only "The Golden Journey to Samarkand" and "The Old Ships" have the right hardness of material and execution to weather the years. These two poems are finely graven things of that Parnassian fashion that he thought it well his fellow-poets should follow, too. All his critics point to his obligations to Gautier, Leconte de Lisle and Heredia, but there are obligations, too, to English poets, to men as different as Fitzgerald and A. E. Housman.

Of the two poems of Flecker that any anthology of twentieth-century verse would have to include, the one is of the desert and the other of the sea. "The Old Ships" begins with a slow music that we have too little of in English poetry:

> I have seen old ships sail like swans asleep
> Beyond the village which men still call Tyre.

THE LAST ROMANTICS 373

A part of the effect of these lines is due to a succession of syllables that must be accented to bring out the meaning, and that drag the verse as you do so accent them. Another part of the effect is due to the alliteration. The lines are of like sort with "The lone and level sands stretch far away" of the Shelley Flecker so admired. "The Old Ships" is one of his poems that is what Flecker's theory declared all poems should be, a succession of clear and beautiful images from A to Z. The ships with which it is concerned at its outset are so old that they may have been attacked by Genoese galleys. From them we pass to "a drowsy ship of some yet older day," perhaps that very one on which Ulysses sailed from Troy.

"The Golden Journey to Samarkand" has appeared in a good many forms since it was first published in 1913, in a volume to which it gave title. As we have it now it is the end of Act V of his play *Hassan* (1922), and an assuagement, in its great beauty, of the Oriental cruelty of the earlier part of that act. This is, I think, the best version. It has thirteen stanzas of four lines each, a few of them broken up into dialogue, but most of them printed as quatrains. There is about the poem the lure of the desert, one of the most romantic of all the lures there are in the infinite variety of beautiful phases of the world. This lure is one of the elemental lures, like the lure of mountains, or of the sea; of jungle, or of tundra; of pine forests, or of prairie; of upland pastures, or of lakes; of little rivers, or of heaths; of salt marsh, or sand-dunes above the beach. This lure of the desert has found voice in English literature before it found voice in Flecker, in Kingsley's *Hypatia* (1853); in Burton's *Pilgrimage to El Medinah and Mecca* (1855); and in Doughty's *Arabia Deserta* (1888). It has found expression, with very great beauty, since Flecker, in Dunsany's *Tents of the Arabs* (1914).

It is "blazing" moonlight, at a city gate of Bagdad, when we meet "The Golden Journey to Samarkand" at the close of *Hassan*. All manner of people are waiting to make up the caravan when the watchman shall open the gate. The merchants raise the chant first:

374 THE TIME OF YEATS

Away, for we are ready to a man!
Our camels sniff the evening and are glad.

One and another of the crowd join in, the chief draper, the chief grocer, the principal Jews, the master of the caravan, Ishak the minstrel, a woman and an old man who would have all stay in the city, Hassan himself, and the watchman. It is to Hassan that the great moment of the poem belongs. He is given the lines that sum up the magic of the desert:

> Sweet to ride forth at evening from the wells,
> When shadows pass gigantic on the sand,
> And softly through the silence beat the bells
> Along the Golden Road to Samarkand.

Those lines and the opening lines of "The Old Ships" are Flecker at his best, a best that might have risen to even better things had not tuberculosis first debilitated him and then cut him off at thirty.

There are other poems of some power to Flecker's credit. There is "The Ballad of the Student in the South." This chronicles a chance romance of travel of a kind usual in Symons, in a manner that is developed from a study of the narratives of Housman. It has in it one of the few readings of life in Flecker:

> Why should we think,
> We who are young and strong?

There are those, no doubt, who would dismiss this as a declaration facile and cheap, but it is the inevitable outcome of the preachment of Meredith that thought is the beginning of sorrow. "The Ballad of Camden Town" is a fellow to "The Ballad of the Student in the South." There is a naïveté, a simplicity, an everyday sort of air about both that are very winning, but they alike fall short of the poignancy that you feel they should have. "The Ballad of Camden Town" comes the closer of the two to this poignancy. It all but reaches it in the lines that recall the days with Maisie:

THE LAST ROMANTICS

I have so little to forgive,
So much I can't forget.

It is not because this poem is akin to *vers de société* that it misses poignancy, but because, somehow or other, you just don't believe the story. It seems to be gotten-up stuff, invention of the wrong sort, and not a record of a memory.

Two other poems of Flecker, both lyrics, are all but up to his best work. They are "Stillness" and "November Eves." Both are indoor poems and both studies of fear. "Stillness" recurs to the image that ends "Tenebris Interlucentem." There it was a ghost in Hell that "stole forth a hand To draw a brother to his side," and here in "Stillness" it is the poet himself who knows that he should drown "if you laid not your hand on me." The consumptive has often a warning of death long before it comes. It was more than four years, in Flecker's case, from the time of his first attack to his death, and for the last eighteen months he must have known that he was fighting a losing struggle. In those years he felt as a child feels in the dark, that it cannot stand the fear unless there is a strong hand to hold to. "No Coward's Song" puts one phase of the matter, but there is better poetry in the memories of childish fears recorded in "November Eves." Flecker wrote on to almost the very end, knowing the excitement of the early days of the World War in his last months.

The picturesqueness of the man's life; the many bloods in him, English and Viennese German and Jewish and Huguenot French; his passing for a wit at Oxford and Cambridge; his journeyings, in the consular service, about the Near East; and his long and losing fight against disease—all these combined to make him more of a figure than he would have been by his poetry alone. There has been a great deal written about him, too, two books, innumerable articles, and a long introduction to *The Collected Poems* (1916) by J. C. Squire. Douglas Goldring's book on him is called *James Elroy Flecker, An Appreciation* (1922), and Geraldine Hodgson's, *The Life of James Elroy Flecker* (1925). Flecker's books, from *The Bridge of Fire* (1907) to the posthumously published *Hassan* (1922) are all treasures to the bibliophiles and his name is constantly on the book-lists and in the auction catalogues. The old irony of the poet who had difficulty in selling his stuff in his life-time selling at high figures for others' profit after his death is repeated in Flecker's case.

It is difficult, considering the circumstances, to write about his accomplishment with that detachment that criticism demands. Flecker has a place in English poetry, a place as sure as that of his friend Rupert Brooke, but he is, I am afraid, like Brooke, an overrated man to-day. To paraphrase his own phrase, his "golden sentences," despite their artistry, often leave you cold. Flecker is not a poet of many poems, but "The Old Ships" and "The Golden Journey to Samarkand" ought to keep him known to men through their place in the anthologies.

RUPERT BROOKE

Had there been reflected in the verse of Rupert Brooke (1887-1915) any large part of the brilliancy and charm of his young manhood he had been a poet indeed. There was a something shining about the man, a glow of light, almost a splendor. Fellow on fellow of his pays testimony to this quality, a Gibson, a Drinkwater, a De La Mare, a Masefield. There are only glints and flashes of what he was in blood and brain and spirit in his poetry. Read all the little he had time to write before the World War cut him off at twenty-eight. It is sterling work all of it, but it is not the work of a master. It is very interesting as the reaction of a sensitive youth to the changing conditions of his time. Brooke was so concerned with his fears for the loss of youth that he could not see the glory there was in just being what he was, a man in the fullness of youth. The pseudo-psychology of his times drove him into a self-consciousness that was bad for his poetry. Apparently he forgot this self-consciousness among his friends; human fellowship cast out fear. By himself, and writing, he was haunted by the thought of growing old, of love dwindling into habit, of all the keen sweetnesses of youth losing their edge and freshness, of second-bests succeeding first-bests.

As a matter of fact, though, there is no sign in any of the writing of Brooke of a love lifted to the heights of great passion. Love of the usual sort there is in plenty, of the young man awakened to the wonder of mating, of love that lends the poet new eyes with which to see the beauty of the world, of affection and kindliness and tenderness for the girl loved. There is jealousy, too, that revenges itself in the thought that neither the girl who has preferred another, or that other, can save love from the ravages of the years. All this pother about love, however, impresses you as curing its own ills by the expression of them. If there was a grand passion in the life of Brooke it has left no marks in his poetry. It is a boy's love that he sings, a love that the man in after years would think of with a shrug of shoulders, or write down to experience, or cherish as a sentimental memory, as his mood might be, or as life had made him to be day in and day out.

Young people just out of their teens exult in "Kindliness" and "Menelaus and Helen" and "Jealousy" because these poems record what they are experiencing, or dreaming, or fearing. All three poems are natural and frank and clean. All three are understandable to the last word on a first reading. All three are poetry, but they are not high poetry. There is no ire in "Kindliness," but just a sigh that "love has changed to kindliness."

There is an increase of feeling against the wicked truth that love must wither in "Menelaus and Helen." In "Jealousy" the anger against the way things are in love is warped into satire, and yet, somehow, the satire does not precipitate the poetry, as is so often the case when the two are mixed.

There are many verses of Brooke that concern themselves with the life beyond the grave. "Dust" is, indeed, among his earlier verses, being found in *Poems* of 1911, the little volume that made him known as a poet. There is here a wistfulness and a music and a quiet delight in the thoughts of lovers who will:

ride the air, and shine, and flit,
Around the places where we died.

There is in these poems about the hereafter none of that fierce curiosity that marks the verses of like content of Stephen Phillips. Death and what follows it has no threat to Brooke comparable to the threat of what the long years of life may bring. And yet in the third sonnet of "1914" he appreciates:

> the years to be
> Of work and joy, and that unhoped serene,
> That men call age.

It is yet too soon for us to be able to estimate the value of the poems inspired by the World War. We feel it all too much to have that detachment of judgment necessary to criticism. The war has been written of from every angle. It is easy to appreciate the savage satire of Sassoon, the nonchalances of Graves, the homesickness of Sorley, the ceremonial effectiveness of Winifred Letts, but just what will be the value of these several sorts of war poems in after years is another matter. There is so much more of the English countryside than of war in "August, 1914" that we can trust it to wear well.

Just now it seems that the five sonnets of Brooke's "1914" are very fine indeed. Nine people out of ten would pick them out as the best verses of *The Collected Poems* (1915). It may be that there are rhetorical effects in them, but we do not feel it so now. The sonnets seem to be the proper and exact expression of patriotism. All five are eloquent; they speak themselves. All five are free from portentousness and rancor. All five are dignified and high-hearted. It is hard to think of them forgotten as long as there are men to care for England. "The Soldier" sums them all. It is already as well known as any poem of our day. Its deep feeling and slow music are likely to make it, like "Crossing the Bar," almost a part of certain services for the dead.

We can be more certain, however, of other poems of Brooke,

THE LAST ROMANTICS

"The Great Lover" for one, and "Grantchester" for another. These are in a vein in which no other poet has written. They are boyish, witty, tender, true. They are in a sense "catalogue poems," enumerations of the things he loves best, though he does not, for once, praise "the warm strange smell of clover." They are not all things that a boy loves that he lists, or a boy's pleasures, but many of them are. Brooke had, until the end, all the child's joy in touch sensations. He liked the feel of "flowers and furs and cheeks":

> White plates and cups, clean-gleaming,
> Ringed with blue lines; and feathery, faery dust;
> Wet roofs, beneath the lamp-light; the strong crust
> Of friendly bread; and many-tasting food;
> Rainbows; and the blue bitter smoke of wood.

These are collected very much as a boy collects the treasures that are dear to his heart, in some cabinet or closet or bunk that is his to mess up as he will, the treasures that are so often only junk to his parents and sisters, but are the most loved things in the world, next to his pets, to him. It is strange, by the bye, that in so boyish a poet as Brooke we should have no mention of a dog. Fish he writes of more than once, curving round in their bowl and thinking of "Paradisal grubs" they shall find in the future life, but there is never a pat on the head for a dog in all his verse.

Brooke is more confidential in "Grantchester" than in "The Great Lover." It is a poem written in Berlin, in homesickness for England. In Berlin, where everything is "verboten," he thinks of the old vicarage near Cambridge where he had lived, and bathed in Byron's pool, and written verses. There,

> Unkempt about those hedges blows
> An unofficial English rose.

There, at Grantchester, are associations with Chaucer and Tennyson. There,

> spectral dance, before the dawn,
> A hundred Vicars down the lawn.

Brooke has you by the elbow, piloting you about the place he loves, chatting to you about whatever comes into his head, and making it of moment by the way he says it. It is, indeed, a new sort of social verse that he has created, bright and engaging as his own sunny self, and breaking out into little ecstasies about a succession of little things.

England, and all who love England, remember Brooke best for the beauty, brave and cool, of:

> If I should die, think only this of me:
> That there's some corner of a foreign field
> That is for ever England.

That is as it must be now, but I cannot help wondering if the time will not come when we value him most for the trifling confidences, "pitiful with mortality," of these familiar poems.

There is another note in Brooke, a note almost Elizabethan. It rings out now and then, like a chorus in a song. You have it in "Doubts":

> And if the spirit be not there,
> Why is fragrance in the hair?

You have it again in the "Even Love goes past" of "The Chilterns." You have it still a third time in "The Way That Lovers Use." You feel the music of this catch as you feel the music of:

> Kiss me love! for who knoweth
> What thing cometh after death?

Like Morris, too, Brooke had early learned the old secret that, "There's little comfort in the wise."

The spectacle that was Rupert Brooke still overshadows the poetry of Rupert Brooke. We read the grace and buoyancy and brightness of him into his writing, that sunniness that the score of his friends among writing men have paid tribute to. We read his death and his premonition of death into all his lines. When all that speaks for him is those lines themselves, a just verdict on the poet will be possible. To-day it does not seem that such a time could ever come. Can the world forget the death of Brooke at Scyros any more than it can forget the death of Byron at Missolonghi? And yet we are coming to a judgment of the poetry of Byron independent of the story of Byron. When there comes such a judgment of the poetry of Brooke, "the hurried happy lines" of "The Great Lover" and "Grantchester" may mean more than a young man's reaction to life. They may mean more even than the clear-eyed patriotism of a man glad to die for his country.

JOHN FREEMAN

There is a clear revelation of the taste in poetry of John Freeman (1880-1929) in the introduction to *An Anthology of Pure Poetry* (1925). It is in the discussion between Freeman and De La Mare and George Moore, as the last-named records it, that we find the revelation. Poe is the topic. Freeman agrees with De La Mare and Moore that "To Helen," "Dreamland," "The City in the Sea," "The Haunted Palace," and "Ulalume" must be included in the anthology, though he is not whole-heartedly for "Ulalume." "Eulalie" he rules out, and "The Bells," which he calls a trick. He only half agrees with Moore that the highest poetry is a "something that the poet creates outside of his own personality," but his practice in his own verses, as well as his acquiescence with Moore's objections to "ideas, thoughts, reflections" as inhibitory to poetry, show in which camp he belongs. Freeman takes his stand with the lovers of beauty.

The shortcomings of the man are not the result of any wrong theories of verse, or of insufficient artistry; they are shortcomings of power. He labors to make every set of verses he writes beautiful. He fails to make them more than thinly beautiful even at his best. At his second best they are no more than good verse. He wrote too much, for one thing, but even when he seems to have long pondered his material, and to have something definite to say, he lacks emotion and imagination. He chooses fit subjects. There is hardly a theme in the nearly two hundred sets of verses in

Poems New and Old (1920) that might not have kindled into poetry in the hands of a better man. Freeman has temperament. His point of view is always that of the artist, but he cannot fuse his material into a perfect thing of beauty. There is fresh imagery always in his verses, the unexpected phrase that is at one with what it describes or interprets. Yet poem after poem fails to build up into a finished whole.

You see a tree as one thing, trunk, and branches with their leaves, in that unity which is the tree. You see a poem of Freeman not as you see a tree, but as a thing of a trunk, and of separate branches and of bunches of leaves. "That Loveliness Is Yours" is a case in point. Image by image and verse by verse it is beautiful, but all the elements do not blend together into a unified lyric. Clear seeing, solid construction, sound writing are here, but not the genius that shapes all into one effect. There is inconsequence about this poem, as about a hundred poems of Freeman. He has seldom a sure intention, and when he has, he is baffled nine times out of ten in following it out.

Things deeply loved there are in plenty, beechwoods and birds and poplars, the thin strong hands of a woman, silver light and the shimmer of the sea in the distance, the sea off his "green lonely land" at Anerly in Kent, his cherished corner of England. He has tried often and often to make some place of this neighborhood, long delighted in by him, a place to remember because of what has happened there, but in nearly every attempt the description of the countryside swamps the human drama. Even when he has plenty of action in a narrative poem, or pastoral, a certain quality of detachment dulls its poignancy. "The Harp" and "Three" should be moving, but somehow they are not.

What beauty the verses of Freeman have is a wan beauty, a beauty of November skies with "faint purple flushes of the unvanquished sun." Time and again he tries for the human touch, but he nearly always misses it. Nor has he any discoveries about life to tell us. He goes over the old roll-call of subjects essayed by all the poets, love and death and joy in nature. He chronicles many things, but no new thing. Like his master, Bridges, Freeman gives what pleasure is in him to give by his well-put record of the English countryside.

> How many English hills enlarge their pride
> Of shape and solitude
> By beechwoods darkening the steepest side!

is a typical three lines. This reference, or half-picture, call it which you will, brings back, no doubt, loved places to certain readers, but there is no glow in their return. If those three lines seem poetry to the reader, it must be because of his experience of some such place as that referred to, and by his memory of some golden moment he knew there. The reader, in other words, must do the transmuting into poetry of the subject material. He who has written the lines has not done it.

JOHN DRINKWATER

John Drinkwater (b. 1882) has a defter hand at short verses than at longish plays. He writes longish poems, too, "The Fires of God," "Travel Talk," "The Carver in Stone," "David and Jonathan," and "Persephone," but they are not many in relation to his scores on scores of "characters," lyrics, occasional poems, and verse epistles to his friends. These shorter poems are very English, as English in their lesser way as Wordsworth or Kipling. Drinkwater has at intervals clarities that remind you of Cotton. He has read all the poets, great and small, and it is inevitable that there should be echoes of them now and then in his verses. He is Teutonic in his slowness of development. His early verses, as he owns in his autobiography, show meager accomplishment and little promise. He makes a like confession in "Enrichment":

> I hear notes divinely pitched,
> As never my youth enriched.

That couplet is illustrative not only of his progress, but of his technique. He has not worked awkwardness out of his rhymes.

Drinkwater would like to be judged, I suppose, by his three volumes of collected verse, *Poems 1908-1919* (1919), *Collected Poems* (1923), and *Summer Harvest: Poems 1924-1933*. These volumes are of very like quality, though there is a freshness about the earlier verses that one misses in the later. The lyrics of Drinkwater I have most enjoyed are in his earliest collection: "Birthright," with "little Ariadne" crying; "The Feckenham Men," who loved "a sinewy tale"; "For Corin Today," in which we meet an old shepherd with "a loaded wallet of content"; and that "Derbyshire Song" of the girl who had a "grace in any gown." The trouble is we cannot remember these songs, as we can say Housman's, or Hardy's. What we can recall are certain of his "characters," "The Life of John Heritage" from the earliest collections, and "Who Were Before Me" from the second. These two are more pondered, written out of more knowledge of subject and with more feeling than the "come easy, go easy" verses that are his characteristic output. The "American Vignettes" we of the States can forgive, as we can hardly forgive those charades with words masquerading as a play that he calls *Abraham Lincoln* (1918).

COLONEL SIR RONALD ROSS

Colonel Sir Ronald Ross (1857-1932) was concerned with verse all his life. The authority of his race on malaria, with a long government service in India and at home, he was rhyming off and on from youth until old age. In his *Poems* (1928) are verses dated as early as 1878 and as late as 1927. His first volume, *Philosophies,* published in 1910, received a good press, and there were references to him thereafter as something more than the recognized scientist playing with poetry in his off hours. There is a certain freshness about all he writes, a seeing of things for himself and a beating-out a manner of his own. Lascelles Abercrombie declares " 'In Exile' will surely stand as one of the acknowledged masterpieces of modern poetry." He does not, however, make out his case by quotation from this sequence of lyrics. Ross is never, as a matter of fact, thoroughly master of his medium, and he has done no perfectly finished poem. He has pondered on life, he is keenly aware of the transitoriness of all things. It irks him that a man has to pass on when his years have given him the experience and powers that make him an asset to humanity. It irks him that "when true Achievement comes," it is written down by the world as "A trifling doctor's matter—no consequence at all!"

It is not his rendition of Indian scenery that counts, but his observations on life in his gnomic verses, gnomic verses that all too seldom lift to lyric. He has found out:

> We have no rights at all,
> But only duty here.

There is a tonic stoicism in much that he writes, and a contempt for the moderns who do not subscribe to the old code of the gentleman, for "Mean books by, for, and of mean people writ." He is keenly aware of the stars that are for too long hours of the twenty-four blotted out by the blaze of more vulgar light. It is his proud boast:

> I live to buy in every mart;
> To try the hand at every art;
> In every science take a part;
> With every passion prove the heart.

Though he is trite now and obvious again, he never forgets Himalayan winds, snow peaks in the offing, "full-blooded rivers" loose in "vales of vivid verdure." The appeal of his verse is in its intimations rather than in its accomplishment. As you read you regret a man of noble nature can but stutter out the truth.

CHAPTER XVI

The Latest Phases of English Poetry

IT HAD been better for the fame of Gerard Manley Hopkins (1844-1898) had his admirers taken their cue from what Robert Bridges wrote of him in the notes to the Hopkins *Poems* first published in 1918. Bridges calls no poem a completely accomplished creation. He finds "very forcible and original effects of beauty" in several poems, and he laments that Hopkins "died when, to judge by his latest work, he was beginning to concentrate the force of all his luxuriant experiments in rhythm and diction, and castigate his art into a more reserved style." It had been better, too, if the considerable number of verse-writers who seized upon Hopkins's new methods as the way out from what they considered an exhausted mode of poetry had not had such utter faith in him as guide. "Sprung rhythm" and breathless elliptical expression, exclamation and coined adjectives are well enough in their way, but they are a small part of poetry. Hopkins bulks bigger to-day as an influence over younger poets than as a poet, but his value as an originator of new effects has been overemphasized, as well as the intrinsic worth of his poetry.

There are in Hopkins a good few poems of arresting onset, but there is no single one of great and sustained power from first line to last. "In the Valley of the Elwy" is the most completely realized, but it is not the best. If "God's Grandeur" were from beginning to end of the power and beauty of its first line, it would be a great poem. "The world is charged with the grandeur of God" is that first line, but the poem goes to pieces in the very next line, and it regains its initial dignity only once before its close. Your excitement is at a high pitch over the opening of "The Starlight Night" with its:

> Look at the stars! look, look up at the skies!
> O look at all the fire-folk sitting in the air!

but you are let down by the obscurity quickly following. There is loveliness in:

> Wind-beat whitebeam! airy abeles set on a flare!
> Flake-doves sent floating forth at a farmyard scare!

but the errors of taste and decorum that Bridges points out mar it seriously.

"The Lantern Out of Doors" catches your interest by its first figure, but the poem is lost in religiosity as it develops. "Pied Beauty" keeps to a high level of imagination for more than half of its length.

> Glory be to God for dappled things—
> For skies of couple-color as a brinded cow;
> For rose-moles all in stipple upon trout that swim;
> Fresh-firecoal chestnut-falls; finches' wings.

There is beauty in the opening of "Duns Scotus's Oxford," but it quickly goes the way of most of his verses into turgidity and confusion.

His conversion to Catholicism made a breach between Hopkins and his family, and his removal to Ireland after he became a Jesuit priest widened that separation. His self-centeredness and preoccupation with questions of poetical technique that he could share only with Canon Dixon and Robert Bridges, for the most part only by letter, set him still further apart from his fellows. He felt this isolation and loneliness as did Francis Thompson, another poet who owned his speech alien from that of other men. Hopkins wrote:

> To seem the stranger lies my lot, my life
> Among strangers—Father and mother dear,
> Brothers and sisters are in Christ not near.

His verse, too, was not wholly a comfort to him, it fell so far short of what he would have it. He owns that his lines are without "the roll, the rise, the carol, the creation," and that his is a "winter world." At times, indeed, it would seem he was wilful in denying himself certain of these effects. In "Inversnaid," for instance, he clogs up his lines with words that must be stressed on the off beat as on the beat, perhaps to give the effect of the Highland torrent he is celebrating. Then, as if to show what he could do with Wordsworthian directness and simplicity, he writes:

> What would the world be, once bereft
> Of wet and of wildness.

As we have it, "The Woodlark" is only a fragment, but it, too, has a coherence and a clarity almost Wordsworthian. Even as it is, it is one of the memorable bird poems of our tongue, comparable to the master's "Cuckoo" and the rest of that noble lineage that reaches back to the nightingale riddle in the manner of Cynewulf. Whatever he might have amounted to had he lived to attain complete mastery of his art, Hopkins cannot be judged a great poet on what we have of him, but only a poet with moments of greatness here and there in his poems.

RICHARD MIDDLETON

Richard Middleton (1882-1911) is one of the not few writers we are apt to rate higher than they deserve because of the pitifulness or picturesqueness of their lives. His volubility, too, is winning, and a way he has of taking us into his confidence as a child would. There is ease in his rhyming, and color, and a happy sort of surprise, unexpectedness of phrase and turn of thought. It takes you exceedingly on a first reading, a very great deal of this verse of Middleton, and it is only after many readings you come to feel there are only stanzas here and there you would stand up for in argument as good poetry. "Lament for Lillian" is a poem his perfervid admirers laud to the skies. It has a fine onset, a little rhetorical perhaps, but captivating. It ends with youthful cynicism on the cry, "Dear God, what means a poet more or less?" That thought is the climax of a mood in which the poet sees that a girl in her bloom is beyond a poet's praise, a something lovelier than any work of art. More universal, because touching the experience of every man, is his cry at the end of "To Althea, Who Loves Me Not":

> Damn you, in some queer way I love you still!

Middleton is of narrow range, only love and children and his art concerning him much. Had he lived, of course, he must have broadened, but one wonders would he ever have done more of power than he did. His friend, Henry Savage, has collected for us what verses of Middleton he rates as mature work in *Poems and Songs* (1912) and *Poems and Songs: Second Series* (1912). These two volumes and *The Ghost Ship and Other Stories* (1912) are what we have to give Middleton place. The essays are not seasoned writing. I cannot see that the prose is on the whole any better than the verse. Of greater accomplishment than "The Marvelous Boy," Middleton seemed destined to find place beside Chatterton in English poetry as one who never realized his high intentions.

HAROLD MONRO

Harold Monro (1879-1932) is a drab poet. He is drab in his celebration of domestic things in "Solitude" and "Every Thing" and the like. A thoroughly domesticated person myself, I like his references to "large and gentle furniture," and "Crockery and Cutlery," and dogs; but there is no color in him, no vividness, no surprise. He is drab, and dull, too, when he takes to metaphysics. The "real property" he deals with in *Real Property* (1922) is not dreams at all, as he would like to think, or imagination, or a discovery of beauty. It is stony ground, and the seed of thought that falls upon it is soon scorched and withered, for there is no "deepness of earth."

Monro forgets his stifling metaphysic in Part II of *Real Property*. In "Dog" he becomes a fellowy and sympathetic human being, and, reseeking the old way of English poetry, awakens and holds your interest. Like so many of his contemporaries, however, he does not take the trouble to work his poems out into inevitability of phrase and into cadences that keep them in memory. Even when he is considering his dog he cannot forget his speculating self:

> Now, sending a little look to us behind,
> Who follow slowly the track of your lovely play,
> You fetch our bodies forward away from mind
> Into the light and fun of your useless day.

Not only does Monro by chance escape his metaphysic now and then, but he is conscious of a definite hope of escaping it. He writes:

> Oh, that a man might choose
> To live unconsciously like beast or bird,
> And our clear thought not lose
> Its beauty when we turn it into word.

That is a fair sample of Part I of *Real Property,* and of a good deal of his verse in other volumes from 1906, when he began to publish, until 1928, when he published *The Earth for Sale.* His writing has always been bald, with no romantic connotation, little affinity to song, and little deep emotional quality. It is a hard mentality that is his most constant characteristic. He deliberately tries to be cryptic, and you, reading, are driven to wonder if his meaning is worth making out. If you do struggle to make it out, because of the puzzle interest so deep-seated in all of us, you wonder in the end was it worth while. It would seem that Monro, driven back on mind from the ugliness of the London about him, knows, at moments, what is the matter with himself and his verse. He admits that he is "city-soiled." He has lived in the city so long it has tainted all he is and does. He is a stranger in a strange land in beautiful country places. Had he been able ever to put himself out to pasture he might have become more of a poet.

There are thousands of potential W. J. Turners the English-speaking world over. There are thousands of youths who dream of Samarkands and Yucatans, cities and lands of romance in the here and now, but far away from the prosaic places in which those youths live the daily round of hard work and scant play. Of those who so dream few find their way to perpetuating their dreams in patterns of any sort. W. J. Turner (b. 1889) has so perpetuated them for a season, if with little notability of any kind. He began publishing his verses during the World War, *The Hunter* coming in 1916. He has not fallen below the standard set in that volume, and he has not risen to any higher standard. "True," we say, of this stanza, and "romantic" of that. "Here," we say, "is a corner of England rendered that others have passed by," and "there," we say, "is a boy's ecstasy rather freshly phrased." The trouble is you remember none of these sets of verses, save "Romance," and that only because you, too, as a child were fascinated by Chimborazo, Cotopaxi, and Popocatepetl. That set of verses you remember, and this, the first line and a half of *Pursuit of Psyche* (1931) about woman:

> She had no mirror when the world was new
> Therefore she was not.

His youth in the Antipodes and his researches in music color his verses less than you might expect. Though he takes a vagary now and then his main concern is with the old and tried themes.

If you care at all for the verses of J. C. Squire (b. 1884) it is for their material you care. His is not the imagination to light up life with strange fires, his lines fail to fall into cadences that win the ear, and his comment on men and things reveals little to you that has not been revealed before. Reading him in this magazine and that and in *Poems: First Series* (1918) and *Poems: Second Series* (1921) I found no set of verses for that anthology of favorites one assembles consciously or unconsciously but never gets further with than a list of titles.

It was not until there appeared *American Poems and Others* (1922) that lines of his stayed with me, as lines will if they mean anything to you. I carry a good deal of verse in memory, but it has gained its place there without will on my part. If verse appeals to me, I return to it, reread and reread it, and before I realize it passages and whole poems come to my lips without effort.

What Squire finds to write about in America is the coast-line outside New York, the outskirts of Washington, Niagara, the stock-yards and abattoirs at Chicago, and the Western prairies, but none of these subjects are sufficiently known and pondered by him to be productive of beauty. It is just another English tourist giving in obvious fashion his impressions of America. That is the way it is for the most part with Squire: his verses are his casual impressions of things.

D. H. LAWRENCE

The ironies had their will of D. H. Lawrence (1885-1930). Dowered by nature with all the gifts that go to the making of a great writer, he never became a great writer. There were intimations of greatness in the verse of *Love Poems and Others* (1913) and in the prose of *Sons and Lovers* of the same year. In both books there was a way with words, a concern with beauty, an individuality of style, a fullness of characterization and the beginnings of an architectonic power that would have carried him as far as any man of his time had he not been obsessed with fleshliness. The generation he disappointed had no quarrel with the natural instincts of man lived out in life or recorded in letters. It had gone to George Meredith as prophet as well as poet, and it accepted "blood," as it accepted "brain and spirit," as necessary to natural life, and the record of it needful in the literature that reflected that life. Poor Lawrence could not content himself with the three joined "for true felicity." He over-accented "blood," he was blinded by sex to such a degree that he could not read the sign-posts that warned "This way madness lies."

What Lawrence had to give to beauty to English poetry is most of it in *Love Poems and Others*. "Whether or Not," a narrative scene by scene of a love that failed, though not in sonnet form, has its place in the sonnet sequences of our language. There are clouds, though, even over the verse of his youth. Cruelty and unnaturalness cast their shadows over "Cherry Robbers" and "Cruelty and Love" and "Lightning." There are verses in *Look! We Have Come Through!* (1917) that promise beauty, but they fail of its perfection. Even "River Roses" has canker at the heart. The countryside, instead of affording him an escape from man and his mortality, bears for him the attributes of men.

> And now I see the valley
>   Fleshed, all like me,
> With feelings that change and quiver:
> And all things seem to tally
>   With something in me,
> Something of which she's the giver.

Poor, tortured man, there was no escape for him anywhere from the toils of the flesh! Bavarian Alps, Sicilian shores, and painted deserts in New Mexico, wherever he turned, there was that same fleshliness he saw in the valleys of his native Nottingham. Pomegranate, peach, fig, medlar, sorb-apple, and grapes all turned from fruit to flesh under his touch, and even so innocent flowers as anemones and cyclamens put on corruption.

There is a certain grotesque humor that mitigates the effects of the muddied vision with which he sees most animals, but only in "Mountain Lion," of the animal verses in *Birds, Beasts and Flowers* (1923), is there anything to lift the heart. In *Pansies* (1929) Lawrence seems to forget his concern is with poetry. He is satisfied there to offer us disjointed notes and observations on this and that his sick body and tortured mind left him no art to develop toward poetry.

There is little poetry in his so-called philosophical verse, verse that made him for some people the leader of a new evangel. There is far higher poetry in the "lyrical interbreathings" of his prose in *Sons and Lovers* and *The Rainbow* (1915) and *Women in Love* (1921). There might, indeed, be made out a case for Lawrence being a better poet in prose than in rhyme or in the free and Whitmanic measures he so often resorts to. There is not much poetry, either, in his satiric verse. He had no Synge's gift of fusing into one poetry and satire. The Whitman that was a preoccupation with Lawrence off and on for years is patent in "The Evening Land," and in "Spirits Summoned West," and in "The American Eagle." So, too, is Whitman the master of landscape patent in Lawrence's "Autumn at Taos," one of the few poems of his that has in it any savour of peace.

And then to look back to the rounded sides of the squatting Rockies,
Tigress-brindled with aspen,
Jaguar-splashed, puma-yellow, leopard-vivid slopes of America.

That description of our landscape is truer, let us hope, than his questioning of our country in "The Evening Land":

> Oh, America,
> The sun sets in you.
> Are you the grave of our day?

F. S. FLINT

There is the sting of defeat about the verse of F. S. Flint. He is baffled by life and he is baffled by the art of poetry. He seeks therefore, to content him, to make an otherworld which shall be the reflection of what is best in the world about us. He feels he cannot do himself justice in the time-honored forms of English poetry, so he tries unrhymed cadences, upholding his practice by reference to Cynewulf and Chaucer. There is so much sound sense and right feeling in the preface to *Otherworld* (1920), in which he defends his attempts, that you cannot but deplore his attacks on rhyme and meter. He is one of the many who feel that to cry up free verse you must cry down rhyme. "The history of English poetry in verse," he writes, "is the story of the exhaustion of the effects to be obtained from rhyme and metre," a statement manifestly out of keeping with the facts. The exact contrary is, indeed, the truth. Substitute "triumph" for exhaustion, and the statement will closely approach the facts of the case. The history of English poetry is the story of the triumph of the effects to be obtained from rhyme and meter.

It is all Whitman's attack on rhyme brought up to date and justified by a sounder scholarship than was Whitman's. Such preaching should not affect our judgment of a man's writing, and it has not, I think, in my case, affected it any more with Flint than with Whitman. It does not matter to me what he predicates about poetry who wrote "When lilacs last in the dooryard bloomed." Unfortunately we have not a Whitman to consider in F. S. Flint. Great poetry can be written in the contemporary fashion of unrhymed cadences, of course, but Flint has not written it. We have in him a man sensitive to many kinds of beauty, and whole-heartedly of the belief that all great writing is, necessarily, poetry. "There is only one art of writing, and that is the art of poetry; and wherever you feel the warmth of human experience and imagination in any writing, there is poetry, whether it is in the form we call prose, or in rhyme and metre, or in the unrhymed cadence in which the greater part of this book is written." This passage, from the preface to *Otherworld*, is the law and the gospel.

So far as I have read Flint, in *In the Net of Stars* (1909) and *Otherworld*, the poem that gives title to *Otherworld* is his *magnum opus*. In this long poem he attempts to sum up his estimates of the values of things, to prove himself philosopher as well as poet, to snatch many kinds of beauty out of the incoherence of things as they are. There are successes in the poem and there are fallings short of success, which is to say that the poem is not a whole. Its shortcomings are more of detail than of structure. It wanders, it fails to drive home its main purpose, which is to find and express the best self there is in all "the myriad men who bear my nature," to attain to that otherworld that is a reflection of the best there is in this world we know. There are moments of beauty in the poem, moments of human comradeship, moments of delight in out-of-doors, moments of appreciation of domesticities. There is never, however, the power to put such in a telling line. I had wished to quote some such moments, but all are too diffuse in the recording. There are as many moments in "Otherworld" that he has failed to sublimate to beauty as there are of beauty achieved. There are no discoveries at all about life, no sounding of the depths of things. It is his belief that his poems:

> open the mind and the heart
> To a new sunshine and new perfumes.

That is true only fitfully of his poems. Their cataloguing of the things that have brought him pain and joy is at times as dull as that of his master Whitman. Much of such inconsequential writing would have been spared him had he oftener practised the recognized verse forms of English poetry. Their hardness and rigidity would have stripped his verse of the unessential, the puttering, the wordy, that we find so often in evidence there.

Flint is more concerned with himself than with his subject. If he retort that himself is his subject I say that unless the poet is a very great poet there must be concrete objective things in his poetry as well as his moods and emotions. A rich experience of life will hold your attention longer, in a minor poet, than any other of the poet's attributes. Admit, of course, that he must have rhythm, cadence, fall of words, call it which you will. Admit he must have imagination, vision, art. If with all these, but without a rich experience of life, he will quickly bore you, poet in his way though he be. Only the possession of supreme power in some other attribute of poetry, a possession that makes its owner a major poet, can compensate you for lack of experience. His individual accent so compensates you in Poe, his rhythm in Swinburne, his imagination in Francis Thompson. If a minor poet is to be appealing in many rereadings he must have a rich experience of life.

His verse is the proof that Flint has had a hard row to hoe. Yet others with rows as hard have found much more beauty and happiness in the daily grind and in the escape from the daily grind. Even for those of us most fortunately situated and most happily dowered by temperament, life is a half-and-half proposition. If the average man gets only a little less than half of what is due him he is lucky. How many of us can honestly say we have been given our half of the road by half of the people we have met in cars, courtesy from half of the people with whom we deal, consideration from half of our acquaintances, justice from half of the powers that be? It is Flint's insistence on the half you normally do not get that reveals his inferiority complex.

> You spoke of your art and life,
> Of men you had known who betrayed you,
> Men who fell short of friendship
> And women who fell short of love.

Those lines are from "Dusk." This next line is from "Gloom":

> Thinking of men's treasons and bad faith.

Sometimes Flint gets an angry satisfaction out of making a thing of ugliness, as in "Eau-Forte," but more generally his disillusion and sore-headedness bring him no more than the mild pleasure of lamentation:

> I have many things to hurt me,—
> Youth gone and life and friends uncertain.

Things would have been very different with Flint, one cannot help thinking, had he had even a pittance, as had Davies, from "a dead man . . . who couldn't change his mind."

Richard Aldington (b. 1892) writes verse that appeals to you, each time you return to it, as well written, shipshape, newly felt, and neatly phrased. Yet you find it difficult to remember, even if some of its pictures seemed outlined sharply enough as they took form and color to you reading. His things seen and dreamed and remembered range all the way from Greek girls of Sappho's time to London busses and cinemas of to-day. There are war poems, too, in which beauty is found even among the mud and carnage. There are divertissements of the sort old D'Urfey loved to collect. Each fragment of his earlier verse is made vivid for the nonce by a clearly defined image, but that image, unaccompanied by a reading of life or a haunting fall of line, is not of itself enough to keep any such fragment in memory. As you read him now in *The Collected Poems of Richard Aldington* (1933), twenty years after you read him first in the Imagist Anthologies, you wonder how he has found his way to such a George Moorish novel in verse as *A Dream in the Luxembourg* (1930).

Herbert Read (b. 1893) is a critic of a certain independence of attitude. As a poet he is a victim of that attempt to intellectualize poetry that T. S. Eliot has directed so militantly and that Cecil Day Lewis quintessentializes in his plea for a "tetragonal Pure symmetry of brain." There is Gerard Manley Hopkins, too, in Read's intellectual ancestry, but the innate hardness of his writing is such no influence can soften it to lyricism. You cannot but applaud the much good writing there is in *Poems: 1914-1934* (1935), and a clarity unusual among the followers of Eliot, but there are no discoveries about life, no new quality even to his war verse, no natural falterings or victorious bursts. On looking into his collected verse again I find I have ticked on previous readings only two sets of verses as worth remembering, "Harvest Home" and "Day's Affirmation." Reading these two over they shrink in proportions. "Plans, prognostications and strategies" have given him little leisure for the experiences and brooding out of which poetry comes.

ROBERT GRAVES

The gallant gentleman that the war proved Robert Graves (b. 1895) to be forgot his childhood only during those dread years. And even among the battle pieces of *Fairies and Fusileers* (1917) are to be found verses that savor of the nursery. It is his conviction that "The child alone a poet is."

Though Graves is the son of the Irish verse man Alfred Perceval Graves (1846-1931), it is a district of Wales that is the country of his heart. Writing to Siegfried Sassoon from Mametz Wood he sees Snowden and Hebog. It is a poem somewhat in the spirit of Brooke's "Grantchester," but grimmer, as you might well expect. In "Rocky Acres" Graves describes this countryside more particularly. "An English Wood" tells us of another lonely place he loves. It is not generally in such poems as these, however, or in those war poems in which he takes lightly danger and severe wounds that you have what is most characteristic of the man. Read all the verses in *Collected Poems 1914-26* (1929) and *Poems 1926-1930* (1931) and you will find no successful experimentation with any other kind of verse than child-verse. What Graves can do is variations on *Mother Goose* and other old songs. His writing in this vein is as distinct from poetry as is *vers de société*, but very different, in its unsophistication, from the worldliness of *vers de société*. I cannot persuade myself that this forte of his leads to an important kind of verse. There is no such poetry in all Graves as you find in Owen, or even in Sassoon and Nichols.

Charles Hamilton Sorley (1895-1915) was killed in the World War before he had gone beyond promise in his verse. What he had written is preserved in *Marlborough and Other Poems* (1916). He is at his best in those lines in "Return," in which he seems to write with prescience of his end:

> I might have known the things I love,
>   The winds, the flocking birds' full cry,
> The trees that toss, the downs that move,
>   Were longer things than I.

He loved, too, rooks and Richard Jefferies, stony fields and Ibsen, rain and the *Odyssey*. What he had developed into had he survived the war no one can guess. He saw clearly that what he had done was merely tentative. So clear-visioned a critic of his own work might well have come through to things of significance.

ROBERT NICHOLS

It is *Wings over Europe* (1929), his play written in collaboration with Maurice Brown, that has made Robert Nichols (b. 1893) best known. It was as a poet, however, that he made his appeal in the early days of the War. *Invocation* (1915) was his first book of verse, but it was *Ardours and Endurances* (1917) that found him a responsive public. There was realistic reading of war here, if none of the propaganda and the intentionally revolting detail of Sassoon. What was dominant over all else, though, was high heart, and the officer's regard for his men, and the "cool madness" that comes to soldiers in action. It is as a record of a gallant soul under stress, as a cross-section of war, that his verses take their place. There has been a deepening of power with the years, but there is nothing in the later volumes, even in *Aurelia* (1920), that points toward discoveries or a new beauty. The story and the play are engrossing him now, perhaps happily, since he does not seem likely to make a place for himself as a poet.

WILFRED OWEN

His fellow poets who wish to end war by their recital of its horrors consider Wilfred Owen (1893-1918) the first of England's poets of the Great War. Downright and outspoken as he is, he has somehow escaped the hysteria of Sassoon. He is merciless in his pictures of suffering, filth, exhaustion, and bestiality, but he has a continence that enables him always to retain his dignity. His verse is not so effective as propaganda, perhaps, as the sharper-edged invective of Sassoon, but it is, on the whole, closer to poetry. In the preface they found among his papers, after his death at the Sambre Canal, he does and does not claim his verses are poetry:

> Above all, this book is not concerned with Poetry.
> The subject of it is War, and the pity of War.
> The Poetry is in the pity.

It is exactly thus I feel about them. Now I think they are poetry, because of the high indignation against war that is burning in them. Now I think they are not poetry, because they discover no beauty. The protest of "Dulce et Decorum Est" and "Parable of the Old Men" bites sharply, but if they both escape rhetoric, it may be they are still something else than poetry. It seems to me that despite the revelation of a noble personality that *Poems* (1920) makes, its chief value is tractual rather than artistic.

SIEGFRIED SASSOON

The function of the war verse of Siegfried Sassoon (b. 1886) is the function of satire and of propaganda. *Counter Attack* (1918) is written to stop war, if possible, by recounting its horrors. The lacing that its verses give the old death-and-glory boys is merciless and unremittent. It puts, as never had been put before, the attitude of the men who did the fighting to the incompetent commanders behind the lines and to the bureaucrats at home. Its charges made *Counter Attack* popular in the trenches. It raises again and again the despairing cry, "O Jesu, make it stop!"

It is not in such verse that you can expect beauty, and you do not find beauty in the battle-field verse. Once in a while, in the interludes he must write or go mad, you do find beauty, in verses concerned with memories of a hawthorn in bloom or of fox-hunters drawing "The Big Wood."

Sassoon tells us in the *Memoirs of an Infantry Officer* (1930) that when he was on leave in England he tried to have himself court-martialed so that he would bring the wickedness of war officially before the country. It may be that he was half shell-shocked when he made this resolve, happily frustrated by his friends, but there is no doubt that all of the man, the resolute sane self of him, is dedicated to a determination that war shall never again be.

The poem that gives title to *The Old Huntsman* (1917) has in it only echoes of war, but even its preoccupation with fox-hunting affords only a momentary relief to the burden of anti-war verses that give the volume its chief weight, as you read it, and its place in memory. It is Masefield-like, but Sassoon is his propagandist self soon again. Of necessity these outcries against war cannot be of high beauty. It is true they are passionate, with a passion that lifts the verse to eloquence, but it is the eloquence of rhetoric, not the lyric ecstasy that is poetry. Here are such verses at their best, in "Aftermath," from *Picture Show* (1919):

> Do you remember that hour of din before the attack—
> And the anger, the blind compassion that seized and shook you then
> As you peered at the doomed and haggard faces of your men?

It takes time to realize the beauty of quietness there is in the verses of Sassoon's *Vigil* (1936), the beauty of evening light greying away to darkness. "Vigil in Spring" and "December Stillness" are poems to reckon with, poems that go through you with a thrill. Each reading of them reveals more and more in them, grave rewards of his pondering, in country aloofness, over the spectacle of the world and over the years burdening mazed man. The soreness that was once so characteristic of Sassoon has gone out of him, his middle years have brought him peace. Wistfulness and wonder have returned to the familiar ways about him and have made his Wiltshire gracious and kindly again.

A. E. COPPARD

A. E. Coppard (b. 1878) is a genius in little, but he is a genius. His gift of verse is clearly more than a talent. It is all his own, a fine thing of a definitely minor sort. There is nothing of first power about his poetry save its artistry. There is music in much of it, in all of it that is not free verse. It is a gentle music, unobtrusive and of long-established falls, that steals upon you winningly, but it is not a haunting music. There are fresh figures in all his verses, but they are few of them arresting figures. There are observations upon life in his verses, but they are not revelations, and every other one is a variation on an observation made by his forebears.

In his introduction to *Collected Poems* (1928) Coppard protests against a reviewer who finds influence in him of a writer the poet says he is unable to read. "I have never felt a desire to copy anyone, or the need of such assistance." May be so, but Coppard like his betters has echoes of the poets before him. "Betty Perrin" suggests Hardy, "Geography on a Jew's Harp" Edward Thomas, and "The Return" A. E. Housman. There are locutions and material in "The Streams" and "The Tinker" that prove he has read the poets of the Irish Renaissance. Such parallels are inevitable in any poet of our day. They in no way lessen his originality. He has won his way to a manner and tone of his own unique among contemporary poets. And this despite a predilection for paraphrases of nursery rhymes, popular sayings, and often quoted passages from the poets. There is quaintness and truth in:

> One mind has a thousand eyes,
> The tail of the peacock sees nothing.

There is, in fact, nothing more memorable among his observations on life, but he has used the familiar line of Bourdillon as the springboard from which to leap.

What is best in Coppard is his imagery.

> The old thatched house is like a hassock—
> Time itself has kneeled upon it—
> But the cot of doves in the yard
> And the two white hives
> In moonlight make it beautiful.

Fantastic and akin to a conceit though you call that, it has beauty.

There is more than once a seventeenth-century air about this or that set of verses.

> But if truth offend my sweet
> Then I will have none of it

is in the vein of Herrick, and again and again his record of country things recalls Cotton.

There is no one poem of Coppard that is his credo, though "Narcissus" may be close to a credo. There is a waywardness, an antic pose, a faunlike quality about him, though he is lacking in the energy and bounce of the faun. There is nothing of what Yeats calls "the ancient sorrow of man" in his verses. His sorrows do not trouble us deeply. Now and then his experience has been our experience, but in such instances he has not been hurt as we have been, and so we do not much sympathize with him. Nor has his pain, if such you can call it, the power to move us as has the pain of dumb beasts, the beasts he seems to have so little care for in his verses on lost dog and dying horse. For all the beauty of his art, and for all the music of his verses, the sense they give of irresponsibility and of mockery and of playing at life blunts their poignancy.

FRANCIS BRETT YOUNG

It is in certain passages of his prose that Francis Brett Young (b. 1884) comes closest to poetry. There are lyrics of Shropshire in *The Crescent Moon* (1918) that recall Housman, and a love scene in *The Redlakes* (1930), on Burrows Hill, between the hero and Lady Cynthia that parallels "By Wilming Weir" and "Ferdinand and Miranda" of Meredith. *Marching on Tanga* (1918) is a prose epic. Beside the masterly writing of these passages the good writing of his verses in *Poems 1916-1918*, and elsewhere, shows up but indifferently. There are lines here and there in the verse and passages of description that matter, but no one poem of sustained intensity of feeling and sustained felicity of phrase. In the passages of lyric prose and epic prose of his novels and travel book Young has found his way to beauty of a new sort. In his verses he does well in the old modes and he even wins to beauty, but not to beauty that was not before he made it.

Pick up what book you will of J. Redwood Anderson (b. 1883) and you will find a faithful record, in undistinguished verse, of English countryside and English folk. There is better writing in the later volumes, *Walls and Hedges* (1919), *The Vortex* (1928), and *Transvaluations* (1932) than in the earlier *Eros and Psyche* (1908) and *The Mask* (1912), but hardly writing more akin to poetry. His verses have none of those falls of words that are to poetry what melody is to music. There is no strong individuality in the verse, it is wordy and long drawn out, with all the old images used over and over. He celebrates city scenes as well as country scenes, an oil mill, a warehouse, a traction engine pulling a caravan, and chimneys, as well as lanes, evening light over river meadows, a fair, and night by the sea. He is fond of a very loose form of ode, which leads him into detailed description, a weight that English poetry has had all too much of since Wordsworth's day.

SYLVIA TOWNSEND WARNER

For all its show of realism there is no instancy to life in the verse of Sylvia Townsend Warner (b. 1893). Everything she writes is at least one remove from reality. There was high praise for "Nelly Trim" in her first volume, *The Espalier* (1925), but even that stark and ballad-like yarn is only half believable. The epitaphs, too, so satisfying to our natural instinct for irony, never bite with a sense of authenticity. It is not life that the poet gives us, but a playing with life in a way of a sophisticated *littérateur*. There are poems of genuine feeling here and there, but most of the verses are only pawns in a game she is playing and for which she makes her own rules. We do not feel any real horror in "In the Cotswolds." She has a love for the macabre something like that of Theodore Francis Powys, but like him she deadens her effects by over-emphasis.

Time Importuned (1928) has a little more music in its lines than has *Espalier*, but it shows no other development of her art and it lacks such effective lines as

> Autumn is an unkindly thing
> In a town,

and

> You're easy pleased if what you like
> Best be a green field and a stone dyke.

She is hopelessly the city person in her writing of country things. Only the literary townsman could write of the "ewe's reply" in

Between the lamb's bleat and the ewe's reply
A star has come into the sky.

The first time I read *Opus 7* I thought it a travesty of Masefield. Now my guess is that it is intended as another study in the macabre. It is little more, at any rate, than robustiousness for its own sake. In *Whether a Dove or a Sea Gull* (1933) she and Valentine Ackland do not reveal which wrote this poem or that. Her latest verse has not justified the promise of her early verse. She cannot slough off a mannered literariness. Tried craftsmanship in writing has not brought to her verse such felicities as you find in the prose of *Lolly Willowes* (1926) and *Mr. Fortune's Maggot* (1927).

VICTORIA SACKVILLE-WEST

There is little intimation in *Poems of West and East* (1918) of Victoria Mary Sackville-West (the Honorable Mrs. Harold Nicolson) that she would ever be the poet of *King's Daughter* (1929). The earlier volume is no more than sound 'prentice-work, the later poetry of a fresh and arresting tang and savor. It is a new world we have here, a world dreamed from those glimpses of the East her husband's diplomatic missions have revealed to her, but made all her own by an intensity of imagination few poets of her time can equal. There is in her verse strange imagery, and magical phrase and a music unheard before. That there is preciousness a little is not to be wondered at, but it troubles you hardly at all in the scents and sounds of Araby she conjures up. There is simplicity of wording side by side with the preciousness, and clear depths of feeling. Who that knows "lions, tigers, leopards and their kind" but will delight in:

> The greater cats with golden eyes
> Stare out between the bars.
> Deserts are there, and different skies,
> And night with different stars.

I think of "The Gazelles" of Sturge Moore and Blake's "Tiger" as I read, but the accent and atmosphere are an atmosphere and an accent uncaught by her elders. There emerges from these verses a clear realization of two important functions of a poet:

> A poet's but a drudge, that must compress
> Life's great allowance to a strip of lines,
> Love's complication to a word's caress.

In "common words and mean" the poet must make a microcosm of the world in " a strip of lines," and he must so endow an epithet with significance that it suggest a love story. Read "The greater cats," and "If I might meet her in the lane," and "Envoi," and know the frontiers of the old world of poetry left behind and a new world of beauty and brave adventure stretching before you.

No one has more love of the English countryside than Mrs. Nicolson. *The Land* (1926) is a record of that love. She follows the pageant of out-of-doors through the seasons, she knows farm and manor; village and heath; farm beasts and the beasts of the chase; cornfields and woodland: all from the inside, sympathetically, and down to the least detail. The country habit has her by the heart. She knows, too, all the country avocations and trades, the peddler and the reddleman, the tinker and shepherd, the farrier and the farm laborer. They are one and all part of the English scene that is the half of life to her.

ALDOUS HUXLEY

There is next to no emotion in *The Cicadas and Other Poems* (1931) by Aldous Huxley (b. 1894). There is a detached interest in objects of art and stars in the skies. That interest quickens to a mood short of detachment but still of little fervor when decadence nears. "Picture by Goya" is characteristic, and "Caligula," and "Nero and Sporus." The titles connote the subjects and the esthetic treatment. Some of the loosely cast sonnets catch pictures, often pictures of Italian landscape, rather prettily, and now and then with atmosphere, spirit of place. He is most human in the verses that open the slight volume "Theatre of Varieties." Here he is concerned with the eagerness of the "flower faces" of the audience at a variety show. It is this picture-making that is most persistent in his art. It has been present from his first volume, *The Burning Wheel* (1916), with that faint and disillusioned interest that makes him describe everything in nature as if it had already been made over by the concern of men into a painting or piece of sculpture. Now and then he is Puckish as in the "Fifth Philosopher's Song," but his recurrent note is that of Epicurean estheticism. The book-collectors make much of him, asking high prices for all his "firsts." It is as "firsts" they are valuable, for the art he shows in *The Cicadas* was slow in developing. *The Defeat of Youth* (1918) has no such color as his Gautier-like later poems display.

So far as I know, Julian Huxley (b. 1887) has published only the one volume of verse, *The Captive Shrew and Other Poems of a Biologist* (1932). Most of the book is frankly amateur stuff, but it is so much more varied in material and in mood than the verse of Aldous Huxley that you suffer it more gladly than the tired maunderings of the more skilled writer. The scientist is better company than the esthete, and it may be, despite his amateurishness, the better poet. There is one set of verses of his, that which gave title to his collection, that I should include in an anthology of verse of these times of ours. It may be that it is the out-of-door man in me, the lover of small deer in me, that leads to my estimate of these lines. Few men know the shrews that "in hundreds pass" through woods familiar to us, we think, as our dooryards. Shrews figure much in folklore and in everyday speech, but they have, for the most part, gone unhonored and unsung. There is imagination in the verses, things seen from the mite's point of view. The "Timid atom, furry shrew" looks up on a "striding world of booted men," and is afraid. The creature is let go, for to this scientist, as to the best of his fellows, what is under the microscope is more than Exhibit A or Exhibit B.

Gerald Gould (b. 1885) is one of a hundred writers of careful and lucent verse. All that he does is pleasant to the ear and easy to understand, even arresting in a way, but it does not stay with one, it does not bite in upon the memory. I have been reading at him now a quarter of a century, but I could not give you off-hand the material of a single poem of his, or quote you a line of his. I own only the one slight volume, *Beauty the Pilgrim* (1929), but even in the rereadings possession of this little book makes possible I have not got to care for one set of verses enough to want to read it to any one else.

HUMBERT WOLFE

Humbert Wolfe (b. 1885) gets as close to poetry in his verse as the man of cleverness only can ever get. His best verses, outside his satires, are epigrams, and epigrams have always, from the day of Martial on, fallen short of poetry. Even verses that Wolfe intends as lyrics have turned in their writing to epigrams, as surely as does Lyly's "Cupid and my Campaspe played." That, Henley points out unerringly, in his preface to *English Lyrics* (1897), is an epigram. To epigrams, too, turn charming versicles like "Tulip" in *Kensington Gardens* (1924), and "The Grey Squirrel," for which Frost had so warm a spot in his heart.

From *Shylock Reasons with Mr. Chesterton* (1920) down through *The Uncelestial City* (1930) I have come upon no poem of Wolfe that I should include in an anthology of the best English lyrics, and upon no line or couplet I should include in a book of the thousand and one "discoveries" to be culled from English poetry. It is only in epigram and satire that he is himself. Elsewhere, at his best, he is only clever, like the Chesterton he hates, the Shaw he venerates, the Belloc he damns with faint dislike. And when his cleverness fails him he is reminiscent.

Wolfe has written soundly about the art of verse in many places, two very definite declarations of his position being in his "Iliad," and in "The Builder" sections of *Requiem* (1927). It is only too true that

> The word, and nought else,
> In time endures.

. . . . .

In "The Builder" he cries:

> Theories of Art! Believe me, they're no theories!
> To know yourself, to clutch what's now and here
> and set it down for yourself—that's all there is
> in all that chatter about mysteries.

The essence of Wolfe, his satire, ranges all the way from parodies, light but barbed, of Housman, Yeats, and Davies, through the headstone verses, bitter, sardonic, or merry, as may be, on Chesterton, Wells, and Dean Inge, to the grappling with big problems of *News of the Devil* (1926). Wolfe hates cheap journalism, and the kind of business man that battens upon it. Paul Arthur, his protagonist, is a type we have all met. The iron has entered Wolfe's soul, and he eases the hurt it does him by frontal attack and veiled innuendo alike on the system responsible for the wound. He makes us think, in his attack on his loathed kind of business man, of Thackeray's denunciation of "the man of the world, the worst enemy of the world." Wolfe has not, however, the simplicity or directness or naked power to take rank with the great satirists. He can hope, at best, only for a seat at the foot of the table at whose higher end presides Dean Swift.

CHARLOTTE MEW

There is no set of verses of Charlotte Mew (1870-1928) but has in it some touch of poetry, some augustness of feeling, some capture of the beauty of the world. There are only a half-dozen of them that are finished things, "The Farmer's Bride," "Arracombe Wood," "I have been through the Gates," "The Road to Kerity," "In the Fields," and "To a Child in Death." "The Farmer's Bride" is her poem of poems. It tells, from the standpoint of the husband, of the shrinking away from him of the fay-like child he has wed. It is a poem of defeated tenderness, of understanding, of sympathy. It is instinct with pity, the larger share of it for the girl, just a bit of it for the husband on whose lips the words are put, a very natural man deprived of the love and of the children he had expected.

"Saturday Market" is a more typical poem, a dramatic lyric the meaning of which is none too clear but which has moments of tense life. The old man that is dead of "Arracombe Wood" haunts me. There is a sharply incised picture of old folks in "The Road to Kerity," and rain, and young lovers.

All the work of Charlotte Mew, save a few posthumous poems, is comprised in *Saturday Market*, published in America in 1921. Of those posthumous poems "In the Fields" is a perfect accomplishment. Only Frost's "Nothing Gold Can Stay" holds more of the beauty of the world in so short compass as "In the Fields." "The gold stillness of the August sun on the August sheaves" gives as much of late summer as has ever been given in a line. It is only one of a score of fellows that will become part of the equipment of all who would use nobly our English speech. "The music of the world" is another, "one short grey day Of sudden sin" still another. Mates worthy of the two are "You do not miss a rose," "The pebbles pushing in the silver streams," and "If things are so it does not matter why." Her "broken forgotten things" makes me think of "All things uncomely and broken, all things worn out and old" of Yeats. Not that her quality is at all like his, but that the thoughts of the two poets run parallel for the moment. There is hardly ever a suggestion of any other poet in Charlotte Mew. She is tensely individual. What she writes she has discovered for herself, has wrung from life at the top of being, exultantly, and with a thrill that has in it a share of pain.

> . . . when I was half a child I could not sit
> Watching black shadows on green lawns and red carnations burning
>   in the sun,
>   Without paying so heavily for it
> That joy and pain, like any mother and her unborn child
>   were almost one.

There is in none of her contemporaries a more stabbing sweetness. Aging woman that she was, she knew all the tumult and wild joy of youth and of the spring. One of her dreams that takes my breath away is that of the girl in the circus tent:

She stood on a white horse—and suddenly you saw the bend
Of a far-off road at dawn, with knights riding by,
A field of spears—and then the gallant day
Go out in storm, with ragged clouds low down, sullen and grey
Against red heavens: wild and awful, such a sky
As witnesses against you at the end
Of a great battle; bugles blowing, blood and dust—
The old *Morte d'Arthur*, fight you must—
It died in anger. But it was not death
That had you by the throat, stopping your breath.
She looked like Victory. She rode my way.

Charlotte Mew had the gift of poetic imagination. She knew "The Enchanted Thing." They are all so compact of experience, these poems, and of thought, brooding thought, imagination, vision, that you cannot come to a full feeling or a full understanding of them quickly. You must live with them, rereading, learning them by heart, before you will know all that in them is. Then, maybe, they will come to be to you, as they were to Thomas Hardy, the best poems of a woman of her generation; poems to be put, in his estimation, with Edmund Blunden's, and to be turned to again and again.

We have John Buchan's word for it that Mrs. Violet Jacob writes good Scots. We have the many editions of the *Songs of Angus* (1915) to prove their continued appeal to Scots at home and abroad. It is another Scots than that of Ayr that Burns has more or less familiarized the world with, a Scots with a glossary necessary to its understanding. The World War and places in the homeland long lived in and loved are the recurrent themes in the verse. There is humor of a familiar kind. The verse in English in *More Songs of Angus* (1918) is of a kind with the verse in Scots, careful, conventional, without surprises or sudden felicities.

Marion Angus is another Scot writing pleasant verse. She contributes regularly to *The Modern Scot*, "the organ of the

Scottish Renaissance." What she will develop into remains to be seen; there is promise in her writing as there is in that of William Soutar and Hugh M'Diarmid.

ANNA WICKHAM

There is no question about the originality of Anna Wickham (b. 1884), who is, socially, Mrs. Patrick Hepburn. Her verse is all her own, her harvest of beauty and truth from the chaotic experiences of life. Unfortunately, she has not been able thoroughly to assimilate what she has discovered, to transmute it, through rhythm, into the high art of poetry. It is her humorous lament that she is too busy, as wife and mother, to give all the time she would to her art. Yet there is no real regret over the insistence of family affairs in her daily life. She is triumphantly glad of her man and her boys.

The title poem of *The Little Old House* (1921), for instance, is a bit of life, but it has not been brooded over and relived and fashioned so as to take on finality. The five stanzas of the poem are full of good things, but the poem is not a unit; it does not build up, stanza by stanza; it fails to sum its burden and drive home the meaning of that burden in unforgettable phrase. In the very end the poem weakens almost to bathos.

There was freshness in her writing from the beginning, *The Contemplative Quarry* (1915) and *The Man with a Hammer* (1916) being marked by that individuality of outlook and by that vividness of phrase that distinguish her later work. It is hardly true, as she says, that she builds "songs like iron ships," but it is true that her song is "sometimes swift and strong." It is her belief that

> We are outwearied with Persephone;
> Rather than her, we'll sing Reality.

There is a certain vigor in Mrs. Hepburn's work that springs, perhaps, from her colonial origin, her young years in Australia. It is a vigor comparable, in a way, to that of her younger fellow-poet, Roy Campbell, the South African, though the materials of their poetry are far different. England seemed home to her when she came there to live, and it is incidents in England and emotions of a life lived in England that inform most constantly her writing. There is little in *The Little Old House* that betrays her colonial beginnings. There is much there which reveals her as wife and mother and housewife, as a shrewd person devoted to her art, but never afraid to laugh at it, as at all else in life.

MARY WEBB

An enthusiast could make out a plausible case for the priority of Mary Webb (1881-1927) among the women who have written verse in English. Beside the one-poem women, like Lady Caroline Nairn, of whom there are perhaps a score, the women poets are surprisingly few. There are Elizabeth Barrett Browning, Emily Brontë, Christina Rossetti, Emily Dickinson, Alice Meynell—but hardly a sixth that one could, in real seriousness, call major. There have been women whose verse bulked big to a day or generation, like Joanna Baillie, Mrs. Norton, Mrs. Hemans, "L.E.L," Eliza Cooke, Lucy Larcom, and "Laurence Hope," but they have all shrunk away, or they are fast shrinking away, into mere historical importance. Gathered together as they are in a volume of Miles's *Poets and Poetry of the Century* they emphasize the littleness of accomplishment, in the aggregate, of women in verse as compared to the largeness of their accomplishment in prose. Even the best of the women poets are of a lesser stature entirely than Jane Austen and Charlotte Brontë and George Eliot. The verse of George Eliot was taken for more than its worth because of her rating as a prophet and because of her power as a story-teller. Emily Brontë, overpraised as a poet, has a romance almost great, *Wuthering Heights*, to give her rank in the novel. Of all the women who have essayed verse and the prose story, Mary Webb alone might be claimed to have an unchallenged place in both fields.

Full of verbal felicities, fresh in imagery, rich in imagination as is the verse of Mary Webb, it shows in nearly every set of verses the absence of a revising hand. *Poems* was published posthumously in 1929, with a preface by Walter De La Mare, who first had revealed her to the world as a poet by the inclusion of "Green Rain," "The Water Ouzel," and "Market Day" in *Come Hither*, his anthology of 1923. Had she herself gathered her verses together for a volume, she would have noted certain repetitions, the weak insistence on "elphin" things, on intangible presences, on a something discerned in nature beyond the good thing seen by the eyes. There is hardly a set of verses in the eighty-three of *Poems* without the stuff of poetry in them, but the effects of a good many are too closely allied. Had she had a chance to select from her store of them, or to work them over when they came to too like conclusions, there would have been fewer included that progressed after the fashion of a formula.

Mary Webb is, therefore, better to recall than to reread. She is good to reread, for there is always new phrasing and the catching of some beauty of out-of-doors uncaught before she caught it that had slipped your memory. Rereading though, you come on thinness of matter, the result of an impatience on her part to imprison aspects of landscape and personal moods before they had swum into her ken often enough or returned to her enough times to body themselves into the proportions of a poem. There are poems, of course, which are visitations, but most poems are records of recurrences of sights or emotions or moods that grow with each recurrence until they finally almost say themselves aloud and compel the poet to write them down.

So it is dangerous to send friends who care for poetry, but who have missed this particular poet, to the verse of Mary Webb. She is a poet to read first by accident, with no expectation of a find. If you so come upon her you may escape the sense that there is not enough root in her poetry to bear so much blossom. Beauty of a new kind she has unquestionably, a new ecstasy over out-of-doors and over the wonder of life, but not the perfection in poem after poem that comes with disciplined and mature art. You feel similar imperfections in her prose, particularly in the studies of nature, beautiful here, overwritten there. Even the novels, in whose art she was more practised than in the art of the nature essay or of verse, have a like way of falling below the great and thrilling moments they attain to and lead you to expect they will consistently maintain. *Precious Bane* (1924) is the most uniformly of high level of all the stories. *Gone to Earth* (1917) hardly makes credible its strange story, and *Seven for a Secret* (1922) is an in-and-out sort of book. If it all were of the caliber of that early chapter in which Gillian Lovekin, unawakened, comes with her conies, strung on a wire, through the twilight to Robert, what a book it would be!

In both verse and prose, though, Mary Webb has extended the limits of the art in which she worked; in both she did things that had not been done before; in both she created a new romance. She is sure of a hearing as long as there shall be lovers of beauty in the world.

There are several notes dominant in her verse, none more dominant than that old lament of poetry for the transitoriness of all good things. Perhaps she was aware when she wrote certain of her verses that her days were numbered. Perhaps she wrote in pain. Yet there is no faltering of the spirit or any disloyalty to life.

> June droops to winter, and the sun droops west.
> Flight is our life. We build our crumbling nest
> Beneath the dark eaves of the infinite.

That is her most notable declaration of the sort. Aphoristic, and somewhat in the vein of Omar, is this other:

> All things so early fade—swiftly pass over,
> As autumn bees desert the withering clover.
> Now, with the bee, I sing immortal June;
> How soon both song and bee are gone—how soon!

Next oftenest, perhaps, sounds in her verse the intimation of something beyond the thing seen:

> There is a presence on the lonely hill,
> Lovely and chill:
> There is an emanation in the wood,
> Half understood.

In "Viroconium," a poem inspired by the ruin of a Roman city in Shropshire, the place is haunted by:

> One that lives while empires die,
> A shrineless god whose songs abide
> Forever in the countryside.

If there is not this something beyond the thing seen, that thing, good though it is in itself, lacks perfection. In "To the World" she cries out against the world that it has taken away her "small ecstasies." Yet Mary Webb can delight greatly in the tangible sweet things of earth. She and her husband were market-gardeners for a while, taking the stuff they raised themselves to Shrewsbury and selling it from a stall in the market there. "Market Day" is an idyll in little, charming all the way from onset to finale. It parts from you with a conclusion overheard in Arcady:

> If all folk lived with labour sweet
> Of their own busy hands and feet,
> Such marketing, it seems to me,
> Would make an end of poverty.

One wonders how many of these country poems, with the hunger for Shropshire in them, were written after their author went, in 1921, to live in London. It was in London that that other poet from the Welsh Marches wrote his *Shropshire Lad* (1896), and it may well be that Mary Webb remembered the blush rose, and the "red fruits of the orchard," and all the hundred and one other country things that so throng all her verse, after they were gone from the sight of her eyes. "The Happy Life" and "You Are Very Brown" are two of the friendliest of these poems.

There is picture after picture clear in the seeing and equally clear in the rendering in her poetry. Sometimes she flashes one before you in a line, as in "A lone green valley, good for sheep." More often it takes a four-liner to limn it.

There are human dramas in little, too, one of them "Going for the Milk." In this poem of seventeen lines are recounted four chapters of the life story of an old woman in a workhouse who recalls going for the milk as a toddling child, as a girl of seventeen, as a young mother with her first baby sleeping on her arm. Now in her age she is drinking "the pauper's skim." Companion pieces to this are "An Old Woman," and "The Neighbour's Children," studies in pathos both.

There are poems of otherworldliness, too, "The Land Within," "The Ancient Gods," and "Colomen," the last the best of the three. In "Colomen" we are with the Pre-Raphaelites again. There are affinities between the work of Mary Webb and that of many poets her elders and betters, Coleridge, Rossetti, Christina Rossetti, William Morris, Emily Brontë, Emily Dickinson, Yeats, and Housman, but she is here nearest to the Pre-Raphaelites. There is something of the color of "The Goblin Market" in "Colomen," if less of magic. There is more of Miss Rossetti's brother here, though, than of Miss Rossetti, and of the Coleridge who was his master. "Colomen" is a tale of a sorrow and of a death so remote and so long ago it affects you no more personally than do the old airs haunted with Celtic melancholy. It is pleasantly sad, gently sad, sad in a far-off fashion. It is these poems of a No Man's Land that De La Mare picks out for especial praise. Fresher, though, more wholly her own, discovered for herself, are the Shropshire poems, poems all compound of long hours out-of-doors in the southern part of the county. Shropshire has been fortunate indeed in its most recent poets, and it is only just to say that the last of them, Mary Webb, measures up well in comparison with A. E. Housman and John Masefield.

THE SITWELLS

Not all the irritant poets of to-day are Americans, either stay-at-homes or expatriates living in England or France or Italy. The

Sitwells, English of the English, boasting Norman blood and aristocracy, have followed in the footsteps of Ezra Pound and are confounding the conservatives of to-day, even as he confounded the conservatives of yesterday. They owe something of their methods to T. S. Eliot, who, too, owes not a little to Pound. Our own Amy Lowell and Gertrude Stein have been taken seriously, too, by the Sitwells. They have wandered willingly after many strange gods. They owe some of the much publicity they have attained to developments of the antics originated by Wilde, and developed to so much better purpose by Shaw.

And yet in their own queer way the Sitwells seem to be servants of beauty. Edith Sitwell (b. 1887) is the best poet of the three. There are passages in *The Sleeping Beauty* (1924) that are not only poetry but poetry of new quality. There are not many such passages, and their poetry is not of high order, but it is indubitably poetry. She, like her brothers, has written so much strident nonsense that most readers have not taken the trouble to read them through. It is a hard sledding, but it can be accomplished, even if the treasure come upon hardly pays for the effort. There is a certain childish freshness in

> In the great gardens, after bright spring rain,
> We find sweet innocence come once again,
> White periwinkles, little pensionnaires
> With muslin gowns and shy and candid airs.

This childishness of vision and many memories of nursery days and days of wandering in old gardens attest the innate simplicity of Miss Sitwell under all the outward sophistication. The lines that follow, also from *The Sleeping Beauty*, are a discovery in their little way:

> The palace housekeeper, cross Mrs. Troy,
> Who kept all the whimpering sad ghosts locked
> In a cupboard, was grieved and faintly shocked
> If the Princess Jehanne, long since dead,
> Whose hair was of costly long gold thread,
> Would slip her flat body, like a gleaming

> Quivering fish in a clear pool dreaming,
> Through the deep mesh of conversation,
> Making some ghostly imputation.

That is amateur poetry in all save its technique, but it has a quaintness as of child's talk about it as well as the intended grotesquerie.

A better passage is that beginning "Then all the beauty of the world lay deep," but it borrows half its beauty from Yeats. It is not characteristic. What has come to be considered Sitwellian is a kind of hodgepodge of color and sound that shrills out like simian laughter at a cakewalk. If our American mirth is acrid and Asiatic, hers is acrid and African. Such may be natural enough in an age that has made so much of negro dances and rhythms, black bottoms and blues and spirituals, but Miss Sitwell has not been able to extract much poetry from it all. Joseph Conrad and Vachel Lindsay have done much better with such material, in very differing ways. There are times, of course, in which another sort of mirth manifests itself, a sort of child's humor, arch, semi-plaintive, grotesque. And at other times again, the humor is a clown's humor, conventional, weatherworn, forced.

Miss Sitwell writes too much; there is hardly one of her poems, even the semi-epigrammatic short ones, intended as non-sense verses, that would not be the better for compression. She repeats herself again and again. Her tinniness and brassiness of sound may be intentional, but they are tiring, deadly tiring. The colors of her verse, too, are raucous, reminding you irresistibly of the red and yellow flags from the smaller tents that always attend on a three-ring circus. The Sitwells are sideshow performers, of the old proven sort.

In her preface to *Collected Poems* (1930) Miss Sitwell writes: "With the exception of Christina Rossetti's *Goblin Market* there has been no technically sufficient poem written by a woman." That is truer than most of her critical declarations. Read her book on Pope if you wish to see her playing pitch-and-toss with values,

LATEST PHASES OF ENGLISH POETRY 421

and doing her principal no honor by her vagaries. Miss Sitwell obviously intends certain of her own poems to be "technically sufficient," but they are that only in detail. None save the little poems are clearly patterned. The longer ones jibe and run as the wind wills. They leave you with a sense of jumbled assemblies of sharp and screaming images.

Osbert Sitwell (b. 1892) began with *Argonaut and Juggernaut*, a little volume of amateur verse. His writing has tightened up since then, but he has put most of his later effort into prose forms. Sacheverell Sitwell (b. 1897) is less Sitwellian than either his brother or his sister. He has yet to develop a distinctive vein of his own. *The Cyder Feast* (1927) is almost traditional. He has written a good deal of tushery about Baroque art. *The Gothick North* (1929) gives itself away in its first sentence: "I cannot be writing poetry the whole time, and must look about for a subject for prose." It was not until I came upon this statement I was sure of the poverty of the Sitwells. The basic trouble with all of them is that they have not much to write about.

MISS WADDELL'S TRANSLATIONS

A book such as this cannot include translations unless like Fitzgerald's *Omar Khayyam* they have become part of English poetry. There are, however, certain books which must at least be mentioned. *Wine, Women and Song: Medieval Latin Student Songs* translated into English verse by John Addington Symonds (1884) had a certain vogue for almost two generations. Only recently there have been a number of very successful translations, among them those snatches from the songs of the *Wandering Scholars* (1929) by Helen Waddell and her fuller translations in *Medieval Latin Lyrics* (1933). Miss Waddell has read all English poetry, and her recreations of the originals of her medieval poets are as perfectly done as translations ever can be done. She never loses a sense of humor and she never loses lightness of touch. One must also mention the translations of the sonnets of Ronsard by Humbert Wolfe.

EDMUND BLUNDEN

Edmund Blunden (b. 1896) is the poet whom Hardy liked best to read in his last days. That fact tells a good deal of what Blunden is. It means that he is a writer about country things in that southern England Hardy was born to and loved to its least minutiae. It is the counties just east of Wessex that Blunden writes about, Sussex and Kent, but the detail of farm life and ways, the beasts and the birds, the downs and valleys, the cottages and churches, are like enough to those of Hardy's countryside for him to feel thoroughly at home with Blunden.

Blunden is, indeed, a very companionable poet, a just-folks sort of poet we say in the States. All his life is in his poems, his childhood's play, his boyhood's fishing and prying about, his youth's rambles, his manhood's understanding of character and the tears of things. There is in his poetry, too, his experience in the World War, in which he served with the 11th Battalion, Royal Sussex Regiment. Festubert and Ypres come into his verse, but not obtrusively. There is far more mention of place-names in Kent and Sussex than in Belgium and France. Chanctonbury and Cheveney, Beult and Benover, Hardham and Quincey, Yalding and Hunton are mentioned, places few of them famous, but all of them old familiars of his. They are all associated with things he loves greatly, bells at evening, plum-blossom, fish, high downs and dew-ponds, poplars against the sky, owls, leisure, ripe apples, and the coming of autumn.

There is nothing more than promise of what was to come in *Pastorals* (1916). What counts begins with *The Waggoner* (1920). *The Shepherd* (1922) won the Hawthornden prize, and it was worthy to win it. It marks a decided advance in power over even *The Waggoner*. *English Poems* (1925) holds the position he made for himself by *The Shepherd*. In *Half Way House* (1932) he strikes a new vein in "A Tale Not in Chaucer," a dog poem to remember. Blunden has edited *John Clare: Poems Chiefly from Manuscript* (1920) and *A Song to David* (1924) by Christopher Smart, and he has written an understanding essay *On the Poems of Henry Vaughan* (1927). He made a record of a voyage to South America in *The Bonaventure* (1922), and he went out to Japan in 1924 to occupy Lafcadio Hearn's old chair in English at the University of Tokyo. He held the chair until 1927. In 1930 he was "collected."

All poetry is to a large degree autobiographical, and the poetry of Blunden is so wholly memories of his days that a biography of him could almost be built up out of it. "Old Homes" tells us more of his youth, perhaps, than any other poem, but it is only one of many of its kind, the descriptive poem which gives the color and genius of place. This poem takes us to where "beside that thunderous weir, Our lot was cast." Streams deep enough for boating, mill-buildings by them, and the fish in them are a large concern of Blunden. Walton would have delighted in the frequent chronicling of the ways of fish, rudd and dace, ruff and chub, carp and bream, pike and eel, perch and roach. He would have eagerly discussed "The Pike." He might have thought "Perch Fishing" overly sentimental, but he would have appreciated the knowledge it displays of the life history of "The ogling hunch-back perch with needled fin." "A comradeship of twenty summers" was ended when one of the pair was caught, its mate following its hooked fellow to the top of the water when it was drawn out.

I have dwelt on this poem because it illustrates the fidelity to observed fact in Blunden. Such a fidelity runs through all his writing. Gilbert White would have approved his knowledge of birds. Hardy did approve his knowledge of farm ways. Hardy himself was never more faithful in detailing a similar scene than Blunden in "Country Sale." The poem is just as true, as sure in description, as in revelation of human nature, of an auction in New England as of this country sale in Old England.

"Storm at Hoptime" is another rendering of an institution of southeastern England, hop-picking. All through his writing there is due homage to this plebeian vine, its culture, its harvesting, and its effect on the landscape, but nowhere else than in this poem is its importance fully solemnized. And yet, after all, the rendering of the thunderstorm is as impressive as the pageantry of hop-picking.

These pastorals on rural institutions are as well done as the character poems. "The Veteran" lifts to a rich close. "Mole-catcher" is as mellow as the centuried oak of the church whose chimes the old man rings. "Shepherd" is a picture of England to put beside Gray's "Elegy" and Masefield's "August, 1914." Into "Leisure," a pastoral of autumn akin to these character poems, comes an old hedger.

> Now the old hedger with his half-moon-hook,
> Plashing the spiked thorn, musing of bygone men,
> Shakes the crab apples plopping in the brook
> Till jangling wildgeese flush from the drowned fen.
> Nodding he plods in his grey revery,
> Self-sorry robins humouring his thought's cast;
> While scarce perceived, by red walls warm with peaches,
>   By bosque and signal tree,
> The otters'-lodges on the river-reaches,
> The feather-footed moments tiptoe past.

Though he uses blank verse seldom, it is the grave and slow-moving measures that Blunden does best. At times he writes a song, "The May Day Garland," "The South-west Wind," or "The Brook," but, good though they are, they are not of his best. That best is his celebration, in the long line and in detail, of "all the tiny circumstance of peace," seen for himself and clearly, and told in words fresh and unworn and seldom reminiscent of the older poets he knows so well. It would seem that he has gone to the language of the countryside in which his youth was spent, that, like Wordsworth, he bases his diction on peasant speech. It is a true poetry that he builds up from his intimate knowledge of the life and landscape of Sussex and Kent. It is of a singular evenness of texture, "honest English song for England sung."

ROY CAMPBELL

To Roy Campbell (b. 1902) poetry is a thing of all moments and all moods. It is not a thing apart, a sanctified thing, an idol before which man must prostrate himself, but a matter of everyday concern. He rhymes about everything from details of South African politics to the remaking of civilization. He will ride an enemy in a limerick, and he will hitch Noah's ark to a gigantic turtle and send the creature wallowing through the seas of the world, the patriarch and all created things in tow. The greatest questions in the world are to be tackled as offhandedly as inconsequential things that tickle one's fancy in a moment of idleness. Always, though, the poet must be the artist. Always he is tested by whether or not he "can use words with imaginative, emotional, or sensuous effect."

Campbell whoops it up sometimes in true Vachel Lindsay fashion, but he carries his grotesquerie and sumptuous imagery to a height our American poet only rarely attains, and he sustains that level there, often, for a considerable period. There is something of the spaciousness and splash of colors of his own South African veldt in his writing. He has a sense, too, of the freedom of the sea, of its unending reaches, of its openness to sun and stars, of what easy prey it is to drawing moon and roaming wind.

There is largeness to *The Flaming Terrapin* (1922) and primitiveness and bouncing energy; there is imagination and a sense of splendor; there is hurry and brag. There is little in the long poem of the surliness and sore-headedness that are so often in evidence in certain of his verses, and little of the gaucherie and cocksureness that mar the usually sound pronunciamentos of his critical writing. *The Flaming Terrapin* is far ahead of everything he has done. Under all its pretentiousness and stridency and yawpiness it is passionately conceived and artistically executed. It has moments almost Miltonic, that of the appearance of Leviathan, for one. The poet's Terrapin is a symbol of that force in man that drives him onward and upward, that shall make this world over in the image of a regenerated and freed world that is as yet only a dream in the mind of man. But let the poet explain his symbol in his own words:

> This sudden strength that catches up men's souls
> And rears them up like giants in the sky,
> Giving them fins where the dark ocean rolls,
> And wings of eagles when the whirlwinds fly,
> Stands visible to me in its true self
> (No spiritual essence or wing'd elf
> Like Ariel on the empty winds to spin).
> I see him as a mighty Terrapin . . .
> . . . . a great machine,
> Thoughtless and fearless, governing the clean
> System of active things.

"The Albatross" and "Tristan da Cunha" are the other poems than "The Flaming Terrapin" that bulk big in retrospect. Though the one deals with the great gull and the other with the great rock in Antarctic seas, both poems are symbols of the poet, angry cries wrung from him because of his loneliness and because of his inability to find beauty everywhere, and because of the very impatience of youth. The bird, so powerful of wing, is battered down, broken and dying, by a ship's spars. Campbell is as Scottish as Davidson. He has Davidson's belief in the superman, Davidson's insistence on the truth though the heavens fall, Davidson's soreness at the way things are in the world. There is deep in Campbell the Scot's rebelliousness and love of flyting, the Celtic bitterness of speech and sting of satire. If there is one motive predominant over another of five or six that recur and recur in his verse it is the motive of the hatefulness of truth. In "To a Pet Cobra" he says:

> Hate was the surly tutor of our youth:
> I too can hiss the hair of men erect
> Because my lips are venomous with truth.

In "To a Young Man with Pink Eyes" the same image appears. This time it is phrased, "The hissing cobras of the truth." In

"Poets in Africa" he substitutes a spider for the snake, but the figure is very like. And again, in this same poem, we have "We shall grow venomous with truth."

Campbell is as indignant as were Labouchère and Olive Schreiner over the campaigning of Cecil Rhodes in South Africa. Of the very quality of the novelist's *Trooper Peter Halkett of Mashonaland*, and of the journalist's parody of Kipling's "English Flag," is the close of his "Solo and Chorus." All three maintain that subjugation and "beer and Bibles and rum" follow the Flag of England. "Mass at Dawn" almost alone of his poems is without bitterness. A touch of bitterness taints the opening of "The Sisters," which else had been a thing of loveliness.

It is not only that Campbell has a quarrel with the world. That is a common condition of poets in youth. There is the further trouble that the anger in him has blinded him to beauty. The poet may protest that "Beauty has still one faithful heart who watches," but for all that watching he often can only see red. Anger parches imagination and insight. Anger burns out the heart, and leaves the poet only that specter of himself, the satirist and cynic. And after all, despite the knowledge that the years bring that this is not the best of all possible worlds, they bring also the knowledge that things might be considerably worse than they are.

It is unfortunate that Campbell can take pride in little else than his clarity of vision and in his art of verse. He has no pride in life, no loyalty to life. The man can write, there is no doubt of that. He is master of the verse forms he attempts. The danger is that when his anger passes, as pass it must with the years, the glow will go out of his writing, and only sound and fury and cold rhetoric will remain. There is more promise in him than in any man of his years writing in England. It will be a pity if there will not come to him before he is old that tranquillity in which emotion must be remembered before it can be transmuted in a perfect art of words.

PETER QUENNELL

There is a feeling as of rare air about the verse of Peter Quennell (b. 1905). You have a sense of height, too, height in cold sunlight. There is little warmth in these thin numbers, little substance, little association with known and loved things. What he writes in the second stanza of "Ate" describes the very texture of his verse:
>   I come to waste spaces aerial
>   Lo, blossom breaks and clear leaf,
>   Below me, below me.

He is a Grecian, of course, but with a very different treatment of Greek themes, and a very different manner, from all the many who from Milton's days to ours have owned themselves Hellenists. He has not Sturge Moore's power to make the legendary life of Attica instant to us. Quennell makes it even more remote than it was in our school days. He refines it, he removes it out of any world we can believe in, he makes it as tenuous as a dream to one wide awake. He never romanticizes it; he leaves it a far-off, leached-out existence, as distant from experience as the lost Atlantis his Leviathan destroyed. Consonantal rhyme he avoids, but the faint vowel rhymes he uses have a charm unlike anything I have met in English verse. I know only his *Poems* (1926), which are, I hope, intimations of a richer poetry to come. All you can say of his verse as yet is that it is, despite definite images, unsubstantial, vacuous, evasive.

CHAPTER XVII

Of Poetry and Propaganda

IF THERE is poetry in a man it will out. It does not matter much what form of verse he uses, the poetry is the thing. It is easier for the poetry to manifest itself if the poet have a clear utterance, but manifest itself it will, if it be in him. Incoherence will hinder him presenting it in a form that can be understood by all who chance on it, but incoherence will not prevent those who care greatly for poetry from listening to it. A poet's poetry will find its way to an audience more quickly if it is of the traditional sort, but it is no surer of long acceptance because it is traditional. People like patterns that they know, but they are more critical of work done in familiar patterns. They have more parallels with which to compare it, by which to measure it.

If there is poetry in a man it will out no matter what his politics. The poet may more quickly attract an audience if he disagree violently with the accepted system of things in his time, but he will not longer hold his audience because of that difference or that violence. It may be that Shelley's undergraduate rebellion focused attention upon him that would have not been so focused had he been a conformist, but that rebellion has nothing to do with the high place he holds to-day. There may have been more early concern over Coleridge because of his communist propaganda than had he accepted what was placidly, but what we treasure in Coleridge to-day has no relation to that propaganda.

Our young communist poets, W. H. Auden, Stephen Spender, and Cecil Day Lewis, insist loudly that poetry is the better for being inspired by the forward-looking thought of our time, but their own verse does not bear out their contention. Auden, essentially a satirist, may get what power his satire has from current conditions, but he cannot lift his satire to the level of poetry. He is the least of the trio for no other reason than that he has the least poetry in him. Spender, a man who has his moments, clutters up his utterance with deliberate incoherence. When the poetry does break out in his verses it is despite his methods. His temperament, in those moments, gets the better of his vagaries. Lewis is of wider scope than either of his fellows, and he can write so as to be understood. He has not, however, Spender's intensity of poetic speech. Lewis is the publicist of the group. *A Hope for Poetry* (1934) does far more to middleman them than *The Destructive Element* (1935) of Spender, which fathers their "newnesses" on Henry James.

Since the concern of this book is with poetry I do not have to consider all of Wystan Hugh Auden (b. 1907). However important as social propaganda "Paid on Both Sides" may be, and *The Orators* (1932) and *The Dance of Death* (1933) they are not for the most part poetry, not even the poetic satire they have been claimed to be. What of the writings is cast in verse has other purposes than those of the art of poetry and never assumes the purposes of poetry even inadvertently. What entitles Auden to consideration as a poet is the six odes assembled as Book III of *The Orators* but only remotely connected with it, and the thirty sets of verses that are the first part of his *Poems* (1934).

The final test of any poem is: "Would you give it a place among the best poems of our language?" There is but one answer to be made when you ask this question of the thirty-six sets of verses of Auden before mentioned. One answer, that is, if you judge poetry by those standards of criticism by which down the centuries the ballads and Shakespeare have been judged, and Donne and Herrick, Wordsworth and Emerson, Housman and Frost. There is no such set of verses among the thirty-six sets of verses. Number XXIV is nearest poetry. There is some suggestion of that exaltation there that is essential to poetry, it has to do with

OF POETRY AND PROPAGANDA

a high mood even if it does not wholly catch it. There are no lines to remember here, though, or in any other verses of Auden, save in certain satiric or propagandist ones, no lines that are revelations, readings of life, images of power, lovelinesses of language that are part of you from the moment you were first aware of them. There are interesting experiments, perhaps after Hopkins, in the measures of Old English poetry, like, for instance, "Doom is dark and deeper than any sea-dingle." There are images arresting for a trice such as

> lonely on fell as chat,
> By pot-holed becks
> A bird stone-haunting, an unquiet bird.

Most of the parallels between lines of Auden and lines of his predecessors are intentional, as when he ridicules Tennyson or Kipling. Once in a while, however, a parallel slips in unawares, as when he re-echoes a famous passage in Frost's "Death of the Hired Man" in

> Happy only to find home, a place
> Where no tax is levied for being there.

The schoolmaster in Auden breaks out now and then in little pedantries and in passages of sesquipedalian words. He delights in "With underground proliferation of mould" and "For goodness wasted at peripheral fault." He is content to accept a playing with the cryptic, in a sort of gnomic language of special and definite meaning to those "in the know," but that is a hard and only half-intelligible symbolism to the uninitiated reader. The dedication, to Christopher Isherwood, at the very forefront of *Poems*, has an obvious interpretation, but there may be other implications in it:

> Let us honor if we can
> The vertical man
> Though we value none
> But the horizontal one.

And who but the initiate shall be sure they have the full meaning of:

> . . . a hawk's vertical stooping from the sky;
> These tears, salt for a disobedient dream,
> The lunatic agitation of the sea.

To Auden England is the very reverse of the "Merrie England" of old time. The oldsters have handed on a tired and worn world to the youngsters:

> When we asked the way to Heaven, these directed us ahead
> To the padded room, the clinic and the hangman's little shed.

Things are so bad with life as it is lived that he declares:

> If we really want to live, we'd better start at once to try;
> If we don't, it doesn't matter, but we'd better start to die.

There are those who find humor in Auden, citing as proof of it:

> Engine-drivers with their oil-cans, factory girls in overalls
> Blowing sky-high monster stores, destroying intellectuals.

The Dog beneath the Skin (1935), a play in which Auden collaborates with Christopher Isherwood, tries to leaven propaganda with various sorts of humor, but it is poor fooling and ineffective satire.

There is a sort of satire akin to poetry. Donne had it, Swift had it, Synge had it. Auden falls short of it, in nine efforts out of ten to attain it. Satire must be clear to tell. The satirist may, of course, speak in symbols, but they must be symbols capable of interpretation as the satire is read. Satire by secret signs, satire of esoteric meanings unknown to those with whom the satire is concerned, misses fire, scores not at all, recoils upon itself.

The verse of Auden is for the most part raised to an nth power of aloofness from life, from the common human, from what appeals to all sort and conditions of men. It is strange that such an aloofness should be studied, far sought for, in a man theoretically devoted to the brotherhood of man, to the development of a society in which there shall be no chosen or privileged classes. The communists of *The New Masses* had the instinct to condemn Auden and his confrères as no true communists but only bourgeois in disguise. That they unquestionably are, and yet, ironically, sacrificers of what poetry is in them through the burdening of it by propaganda and the wilful avoidance of beauty.

Stephen Harold Spender (b. 1909) has gotten poetry out of his love for his fellow-man, if not specifically out of his communistic creed. You find such poetry in "31" of his *Poems* (1934). The close of that poem has exaltation, high hope for the future, a great wonder. The ultimate lines have surprise, shock even, and, what is so rare in the writing of this group, that sort of beauty, new and old, that has for so many centuries been the distinction of English poetry:

> Watch the admiring dawn explode like a shell
> Around us, dazing us with its light like snow.

Spender has stripped his verses bare of the old trappings of rhetoric, of the used phrases, the obvious rhymes. In "6," which he wantonly refuses to call "Ferry to Wilm," he wisely pursues, however, that search for beauty that is the concern of all art. He retains worn symbolism, perhaps of set purpose to further the ends of that cryptic riddling so dear to his group. He can make play with old counters, such as "hawk" and "paw of dark" and "ape," and such journalese as "health-resort," and school-boy nastinesses, but these weaknesses are forgotten or forgiven as you turn the page and come on "Beethoven's Death Mask" and "I think continually of those who were truly great." The onset of this last poem, "30," is Spender at his best:

> I think continually of those who were truly great.
> Who, from the womb, remembered the soul's history
> Through corridors of light where the hours are suns
> Endless and singing.

Spender tries hard for a poetry concerned with pylons, aërodromes, and great machines, but they resist even his hot lyricism. He can seldom bend them, or exalt them, or twist or turn them to the service of poetry. "The Express" is only a half-success. There are few of his sets of verses, however, without a line here or there that rouses wonder. In "41" he achieves:

> Time solitary will emerge
> Like a rocket bursting from mist.

Such images do not always score. They are too studied in this instance, too theatrical in that. Nor can he always find poetry in that city world that is too much with him:

> The city builds its horror in my brain,
> This writing is my only wings away.

There is, of course, always possible physical escape from the city. "The simple green . . . can heal all sadness." Yet so intense is he from the strain of city life that country things, too, can be too much for him. He owns:

> Town-bred, I feel the roots of each earth-cry
> Tear me apart.

It is such work of his as this I have been quoting that really matters. The propagandist writing and that which cries down tyranny, however highly intentioned and however deeply felt, just does not "come off." *Vienna* (1935) is little more than a tract. It is fortunate for his position in letters that he has not cast aside all those oldnesses that theoretically are but detritus to him. He just cannot restrict himself to being the poet with the social purpose that he would be. Even in "Not palaces," "42" among his collected verses, which is his code, the beauty he derides breaks through. He, because of the poet's nature in him, must be concerned with more than "Time's change."

OF POETRY AND PROPAGANDA 435

It is strange that a man who is so good a critic of English poetry as Cecil Day Lewis should write in Audenese. He did not always so write. In *Transitional Poem* (1929) we find eccentricities but little incoherence, and a poet an Emersonian if there ever was one. In *A Time to Dance* (1935) we find Lewis incoherent, unable to master the detail of the great flight of two airmen from England to Australia in a "shot" plane, arid, journalistic, unfinished. The verse is clogged and bumpy, and the material shoveled in anyway without sifting. In his desire to avoid the old counters of poetry he falls into the very faults he is clear-visioned enough as a critic to see cardinal ones of post-war poetry. In *A Hope for Poetry* (1934) he writes of the post-war poets: "The texture of their verse . . . is apt to be too rigid and uncompromising, a hard concrete surface that gives no resilience, no echo, no sense of depths below." Nor has what stir these post-war poets have caused gone to his head. In *A Hope for Poetry* he writes: "We have also suggested that a great deal of the comparative popularity of the post-war writers with whom I have been dealing is due to an interest in other ingredients of their verse—its political significance, for example, or its contemporary coloring—rather than to a perception of whatever 'pure' poetry there may be in it."

The very title of *A Hope for Poetry* implies adverse criticism of the poetry of his day, though he owns that "there are young writers producing good work outside the particular field with which I am dealing." The title needs, for exactness' sake, a subtitle "as seen in the work of Auden, Spender and Day Lewis." Of the previous generation Day Lewis applauds Yeats, Hardy, Housman, and De La Mare. He even has a good word, in passing, for a line of Roy Campbell. Of older English poets he approves Tennyson, Wordsworth, Blake, Herrick, Donne, and Shakespeare, an orthodox attitude indeed in a young communist.

Day Lewis writes down as the ancestors of the communist poets T. S. Eliot, Wilfred Owen, and Gerard Manley Hopkins. Other influences he cites are those of Wyndham Lewis, James Joyce, and D. H. Lawrence. Such influences are on both the material and form of the young communist verse. Like his fellows Auden and Spender, Day Lewis can get little poetry out of his political and economic and social creeds. He can see little good in the present system in England. He is clearer than Spender and Auden in stating what changes he would bring about in his country, what are the ends he is seeking:

> What do we ask for, then?
> Not for pity's pence nor pursy affluence,
> Only to set up house again:
> Neither a coward's heaven, cessation of pain,
> Nor a new world of sense,
> But that we may be given the chance to be men.

He feels he is a spokesman for the oppressed and for all of those with the rapture of the forward view. He can be guilty of such flatnesses as "Some aimed at a small objective" and "Yes, why do we all, seeing a Red, feel small?" He can write, in music-hall patter:

> Revolution, revolution
> Is the one correct solution—
> We've found it and we know it's bound to win.
> Whatever's biting you, here's a something will put life in you:
> This evening we're inviting you
> To share what's on the air and tune in.

Impute what motive you will for such writing, call it tongue-in-cheek stuff, irony, a trap for the unwary, it is not imbued with enough passion to lift "the common words and mean" to any large significance. The pity of it is there is real poetry in the man. He can say:

> For he must travel light who takes
> An eagle's route,

and

> Mine is the heron's flight
> Which makes a solitude of any sky,

and

> An autumn evening certain of its peace.

This last line has been seized upon by a reviewer of his own point of view as a mere rhetorical counter of the old sort. The restfulness of it is irritating to those who would make a new world through the break-up of the world we know. Day Lewis is himself less leftish, a conservative communist who would "seek a new world through old workings." He is himself in temperament a traditionalist, who finds himself in the red group by violence to his own nature. It irks him to have to say:

> Comrades, my tongue can speak
> No comfortable words.

There are parallels between passages of his and passages of Emerson and Browning, Whitman and Thoreau, Emily Dickinson and Francis Thompson. He is bound by all sorts of ties to yesterday. He is not so much the internationalist as Auden and Spender. After his fashion Day Lewis loves his England, its out-of-doors, its poetry, its undemonstrative people. Like his confrères he bears the tags of a city man, though he knows more of the countryside than they. All of them know the stonechat and the kestrel, though they stereotype the little hawk into a cold symbol. They are fond of upland places from High Stoy to the mountains above Easedale. All of them seem to have summered in the Alps. Trees and flowers and country avocations they know less of than of pylons and aërodromes and office buildings. No one can quarrel with them if they can find poetry in what is most mechanical in the machine age. What one can quarrel with is their failure to transmute industrialism into poetry. No one can quarrel with their attempts at new themes. What one can quarrel with is their failure to infuse the new themes with poetry. Day Lewis can prelude such a theme. The pity is, after such a prelude the theme does not arrive. What does arrive is as inconsequential as the line announcing the new theme; the eighth line below:

> You that love England, who have an ear for her music,
> The slow movement of clouds in benediction,
> Clear arias of light thrilling over her uplands,

> Over the chords of summer sustained peacefully;
> Ceaseless the leaves' counterpoint in a west wind lively,
> Blossom and river rippling loveliest allegro,
> And the storms of wood strings brass at year's finale:
> Listen. Can you not hear the entrance of a new theme?

We cannot hear it. The "visiting angel" that is heralded fails to appear, "the strange new healer." There is no doubt of the need of such an explanation as we have in *A Hope for Poetry* of the origins and aims of the Auden-Spender-Day Lewis group. There had been such explanations by poets before, the much middle-manning of the writers of the Irish Renaissance by Yeats, the articles in *The Germ* by the Pre-Raphaelites, the famous preface to the *Lyrical Ballads* of Wordsworth and Coleridge. We would, indeed, have had Day Lewis go further than he did, and give us detailed explanations of a poem of each one of the trio of the sort Yeats made in the notes to *The Wind Among the Reeds*. Then, perhaps, we would have a key to what "ancestor" means, and "kestrel," and "vertical man" and "horizontal man." Then we might understand what Day Lewis would have us make of:

> It is certain we shall attain
> No life till we stamp on all
> Life the tetragonal
> Pure symmetry of brain.

A reader to whom poetry is the first of the fine arts, and one of the main concerns of life, must approach all attempts at poetry sympathetically. Such a one is always eager for new notes to be struck, fresh revelations of the world to be made, felicities and falls of words unmet before to surprise and delight him. Such a one can but feel there is more fuss and fuming, more propaganda, more log-rolling about this movement of the young communists in poetry than the actual accomplishment of the members of the group warrants. Only Spender belongs in the anthologies. After the much to-do about the young men it is disappointing to find so little poetry in them. The hillock labors and brings forth a shrew.

ANDREW YOUNG

IF ANDREW YOUNG were as much master of the art of poetry as he is of the art of observation of things out-of-doors, he would be a figure of larger stature in contemporary literature. As it is he is paid lesser heed than his accomplishment warrants, but it is not difficult to understand why. Man, outside of Young himself, is not of first moment to him. Birds and trees and farm animals interest him deeply, and even certain phases of farm work, but he is too self-centered to realize that the proper study of mankind is man. His countryside as it is revealed in *Winter Harvest* (1933) has few human figures. In the twelfth set of verses you see a lady in a carved canopy in Romsey Abbey, but it is the twenty-fourth before you meet a girl in the flesh. When human figures do people his landscape, he resents their intrusion. In "The Men" their presence and that of their dog

>   meant small good
> To some of us who owned that wood,
> Badger, stoat, rabbit, rook and jay

and drove him "off like any stealthy beast."

The White Blackbird (1935), a worthy companion of *Winter Harvest*, breaks no new ground. There is again in this volume the catching of the moods of a close observer of nature; photographic accuracy in the description of winter oats and cuckoo, wild pear and swan; and excursions into "the higher pantheism."

In a day when so much fleshliness is unclean you come with a delighted surprise on the clean fleshliness of Lawrence Whistler (b. 1912). That clean fleshliness is the cardinal quality of *Four Walls* (1935), the book of verses to which a committee numbering Binyon, Masefield, and De La Mare among its members awarded the King's Medal. It is a pity he is so insistent on the one topic. It is after all an old subject, and he must be a good man who can say something about it that has not been said by earlier poets in the long line from "The Song of Solomon" through Ovid to Symons. Whistler does contribute a few hitherto unpublished items, some of them skilfully presented and others so unskilfully that even the godly will burst into ribald laughter. The new technique the blurb on the cover of the book refers to cannot sustain the old, old burden. It bogs down under it as would the more usual technique of English poetry.

There is fresh feeling and fresh phrasing and lusciousness in Whistler's writing, and, too often, a confusion of words with no clear thought or imagery emerging. You are constantly aware, as you read his verses, of emotion, lyric mood, tenseness. There are many good lines, chiefly of description. "A valley full at evening of faint bells" is one. "Her hair that blows two shades of gold" is another. "The fascination of still things" a third. Of a different sort is "time That glittered with many millions of eyes." He holds that

> these eyes in my bold
> Quick glancing, rejoicing, are the world
> (Ah the sweet world) so frailly, intensely
> Real is this ecstasy of sense!

There is the feel of poetry in about every second line of Whistler, the feel of poetry, not the fall of lovely words. These verses give you a sense of investment by poetry. You feel the touch of poetry as you feel the touch of south wind in summer. Again the touch of his lines is less agreeable, like the touch of a purring cat that rubs its jowls on you and slavers a bit. One passage will reveal a sense of humor and another the absence of a sense of humor.

It is in "The Burial," suggested perhaps by the ceremonials over Lenin, that Whistler girds up his loins for triumphant achievement. There is true spaciousness in the poem and Miltonic pageantry, a splendid sonorousness that echoes hollowly. The poem has all the trappings of epic, but hardly the substance of epic. Its weakness is in material, not in art. Let us hope that life gives Whistler other topics to write about than love and politics. He has the mien and manner of the poet. There awaits him the experience that will discover to him the realities and vision.

Blanaid Salkeld had a good time in writing *The Fox's Covert* (1935). Her jiu-jutsu with words and thoughts is arresting, amusing, irritating. She happens on poetry now and then, when she can forget masters, a Browning or a Gerard Manley Hopkins. It would seem her eccentricities were deliberate, premeditated, defiant, for she can write simply when she will. She is full of fun, a merry poet despite constant evidence in her writing of tired hours and worn energy. The pity is she has not always the power to fire the fun to poetry. One likes her small-girl sort of play with words and things, "muddy breast bones" and "super-soarer," the old cock pheasant skulking and the "typewriter merry clicks." There are better bits than these I quote, though a Puck's face is always peering through the lines. An image to remember is:

> In my heart's bare branches assemble suddenly,
> Sworn to a spree,
> A clan of small soft birds huddled in jollity.

The Fox's Covert is, of course, a symbolic title, of the secrets she hides in her heart, and flashes on us cryptically or too quickly for apprehension. There are few slight books with more of the material of poetry in them than this sheaf, but poem after poem fails to be perfected. A number in which the verse runs clear proves her power would she take the trouble the poet owes to the art of poetry. Such are numbers XX, LII, LVII, and CXXXV. There is the making of a poet that counts in Blanaid Salkeld.

There are those in Dublin who expect a future for Patrick Kavanagh (b. 1913). He writes with absolute simplicity of the little things of his life. He chronicles country sights, a coltsfoot with yellow blossom for one. He celebrates the attic room which is his home when in town and the faith which is in his heart. He laments "the dark people" who make unlovely in Ireland what things were lovely in Eden.

The freshness of wind over lake water is in the verse of Lilian Bowes Lyon. She writes of country things and of people affected by the sights and sounds and experiences of country life. A curlew's feather falling from the sky brings estrangement to lovers in "The Feather." Fields bare of laborers gone to town for an outing inspire "Saturday Afternoon" in which "golden Time is lengthening to Eternity." "The White Hare" is concerned with the brief life history of this lithe and lively creature "With a creamed belly soft as ermine," a beast "Beautiful . . . among vermin."

These quotations are in *The White Hare* (1934) verses of 1929-1934. Along with this collection she includes "Earlier Poems." Among these are two sets of verses to treasure, "Jenny" and "Resurrection Bill," bits out of bucolic life of a looney and a girl gone wrong. Of her the poem's narrator says:

> An' serve 'em right, that's soft enough
> To follow men for love.

Miss Ruth Pitter has gotten a good press for mocking and satiric verse. Its merriness, too, has been approved. That is as it should be. Fun has not had its due in poetry, and real humor, as distinguished from wit and banter and playfulness, is seldom to be found along with lyric cry, and readings of life and vision. This rarity of humor in poetry is in part because of the feeling that humor, like satire, has a tendency to precipitate in almost a chemical fashion the poetry with which it is mixed. In a first reading of *A Mad Lady's Garland* (1935) you think that here at last is poetry with humor in it. In the end, though, after you have lived with this most companionable little book, and read it many times, you have to come to the conclusion that, in most instances, those verses that are humorous remain verse, and that those verses that are poetry are pretty much without humor.

There are moments, notably in "The Earwig's Complaint," in which there is a fusion of poetry and humor, but even in this poem the laughter is oftenest at the mock heroic, the lady who was "so great, so fair" that she seemed to the mite of an insect "whole continents of beauty." That moment of scorn the earwig enjoys as he spreads his wings and flies is lyric surely: "And she —what knows she of such heavenly things?" His heart is hot with the conviction that, after all, that beauty is but lumpish that is without wings.

A large share of the appeal of Miss Pitter lies in her recapturings of the airs and graces of Elizabethan and seventeenth-century poetry. So it is in "Maternal Love Triumphant," the song of the spider who eats her mate and honeymooning flies; and in "The Kitten's Eclogue," the song of "the sooty whelp" that was spared when her "stripy brethren plumbed the pail." There are reminiscences of Flecker in "The Matron-Cat's Song," of "A Ballad of Camden Town," and "Digdog" wades unmercifully into T. S. Eliot and Company Unlimited. She lays under tribute all poetry from Mother Goose to Homer, paying especially heed to Wyatt and Sidney and Spenser. All her echoes, though, take on new tones.

In "The Pious Lady Trout" humor and lyricism are again at one. In the series "Fowls Celestial and Terrestrial or The Angels of the Mind" the humor has faded out to a wistful playfulness. In this book Miss Pitter hardly dares be wholly serious. There is beauty, and beauty of a kind new to English poetry, in these lyrics of swan and nightingale, bird of paradise and phœnix. Here mythology plays hob with science, as it has a right to do, and surprises that quicken and refresh the reader are come upon line after line. The swan "like an angel" goes "down a most silent stream"; the nightingale utters "peerless notes of sorrowful delight"; the bird of paradise was as "One of the awful burning cherubim"; and the phœnix blooms in the fire where lately she "did fade."

CHAPTER XVIII

The Hope for the Future

THERE are those who think, because the period since the World War has as yet produced no poet recognized as great, that we have fallen on a slack time for English poetry. Maybe we have. There have been other periods, many of them, in the long history of English poetry, in which those to whom it was a large share of life had to wait even longer than the three decades of a generation for an authentic voice of fresh and large utterance. In the old age of Swinburne we were told that there was no one to take his place; a lament heard, too, in the old age of Tennyson not so many years earlier; and, prior to that, in the middle of the nineteenth century, before Tennyson and Browning, Arnold and Rossetti, Morris and Swinburne had come into their own. Sir William Watson, in *Wordsworth's Grave* (1890), published forty years after that great poet's death, could dismiss Swinburne and Browning in this cavalier fashion:

> Lo, one with empty music floods the ear,
> And one, the heart refreshing, tires the brain.

Yeats was then on the threshold of the great poetry of his early period. Housman, a clerk in London homesick for his western hills, was writing the verses of *A Shropshire Lad*. Masefield was doing school-boy rhymes with no presage of the lyrics and sonnets that were to be. Kipling was already to the fore, but of verse too far at variance with the pencraft admired by Watson to be appreciated at his full worth by that traditionalist. Those who look at our day as Sir William looked on forty-five years ago may easily fall into a like error.

There is no need to despair of the future. We may question there is likelihood of major poetry from any of the rising generation of British poets at home or in the colonies. Some of us will be content to say Yeats is with us still, or Masefield, or Hodgson. Others of us will wonder will Spender slough off propaganda, and rise to Shelleyan heights, as certain of his more fervent admirers declare possible. Or will Roy Campbell develop from one who was a marvel in his youth to mastery in his middle years? Or will Victoria Sackville-West concentrate all those great resources in evidence in *The Land* into a poem of sustained power stripped bare of unessential detail and all compact with insight and beauty of imagination and deep knowledge of England? Fortunately I do not have to answer. Criticism is not prophecy, criticism is concerned with what is.

Those who believe that great poetry is born of great movements are optimistic over a civilization in upheaval and look to our shaken times to inspire new voices that will be heard around the world. It has always seemed to me, however, that the men in literature who were most subject to the social influences of their time have passed with it, that the Chaucers have outlasted the Langlands, that the great poets were what they were because they were great individuals, and that they were no more than colored by their times. The great poets have all been quick with wonder at the world, aware that life is the greatest of adventures, men who have by some miracle been invested with "Singing robes" that have, as Francis Thompson says, a "paradisal air." Shakespeare, Donne, Herrick, Blake, Wordsworth, Emerson, Poe, Tennyson, Housman, De La Mare, and Frost had all been voices men must listen to no matter in what age they had been born. Many, too, who wear the colors of their times and are acknowledged as poets of groups or movements, as Milton of Puritanism, or Kipling of Imperialism, are greater for their work that lies outside of their religious or social or governmental preoccupations than for their work that is so circumscribed. There must be a great deal of poetry in a man to get the better of his obsession with ideas, of their dominance over him. Politics and "isms" have never had place on Olympus.

One can say with no attempt at prophecy, but in accordance with the doctrine of probabilities, that an art that has been first in power of all the fine arts in England for century on century is likely to continue its primacy. The great audience that Walt Whitman postulated as necessary for great poetry is here. There are great poets still with us carrying on the great traditions of English poetry. All poets do not come into their highest power in their young years. Certain of the men in their thirties may ripen into true majority. If they do not, the genius of the race for poetry may be trusted to give us others of full stature. England will cease to be England when it fails to breed great poets.

INDEX

A Book of Verses, 34
A Child's Day, 365
A Child's Garden of Verses, 43, 45, 46, 310
A Country Muse, 53
A Dish of Apples, 127
A Doorway into Fairyland, 155
A Dream in the Luxembourg, 398
A Farm in Fairyland, 153
A Full Moon in March, 191
A Harvest of Chaff, 127
A Hope for Poetry, 430, 435, 438
A Hundred and Seventy Chinese Poems, 27
A Hundred Sonnets, 127
A Lay of Ossian, 210
A Lover's Breast Knot, 198
A Mad Lady's Garland, 442
A Merry-Go-Round of Song, 54
A Poetry Recital, 218, 221, 222, 223, 224, 225
A Poet's Alphabet, 349
A Rosary, 61
A Shropshire Lad, 47, 153, 242, 252, 255, 256, 257, 259, 264, 417, 444
A Sicilian Idyll, 296, 297
A Song of Speed, 38
A Time to Dance, 42
A Vision of Giorgione, 304
A Wiltshire Village, 356
Abercrombie, Lascelles, 10, 20, 22, 106, 288, 303, 339, 343, 351-355
Abraham Lincoln, 384
Absalom, 296
Achilles in Scyros, 72
Ackland, Valentine, 406
Adam Cast Forth, 287, 289
Admirals All, 142, 143
"A. E.," 7, 28, 29, 131, 169, 172, 191-194, 211, 219, 238, 250
Aeschylos, 51
Aldington, Richard, 6, 397-398

Aldrich, Thomas Bailey, 313
Alice in Wonderland, 133, 310
Alice's Adventures in Wonderland, 45
Allingham, William, 208
Altdorfer, 300
Ambition, 349
American Poems, 391
Amoris Victima, 157, 307
An Anthology of Pure Poetry, 381.
An Englishwoman's Love Letters, 153
An Offering of Swans, 239
Andersen, Hans Christian, 311
Anderson, J. Redwood, 404
Aphrodite against Artemis, 295, 296
Aquamarines, 204
Arabia Deserta, 23, 284, 285, 286, 293, 373
Arable Holdings, 251
Ardours and Endurances, 400
Argonaut and Juggernaut, 421
Arnold, Matthew, 3, 4, 9, 28, 93, 95, 113, 156, 195, 260, 279, 352, 444
Ainsworth, Harrison, 310
Arnold, Sir Edwin, 127
Artemision, 125
Arthur, 106, 114
As the Wind Blows, 127
Asquith, Herbert, 78
Asquith, Mrs. Herbert, 89
Asquith, Violet, 89
Astrophel and Stella, 72
At the Hawk's Well, 171
Attila, 106
Aucassin and Nicolette, 123
Auden, W. H., 14, 429-433, 435, 436, 438
Aurelia, 400
Austen, Jane, 77, 97, 414
Austin, Sir Alfred, 82, 127
Autobiographies (Yeats), 160, 168, 177
Aylwin, 9
Ayuli, 114

447

448 INDEX

Bacon, Francis, 195
Bailey, Philip James, 285
Baillie, Joanna, 414
Balder Dead, 98
Ballads, 43
Ballads and Barrack Room Ballads, 134
Ballads and Poems, 316, 318, 319, 320, 321
Ballads and Songs, 54, 65
Ballads in Prose, 202, 204
Balzac, Honoré de, 165
Baring, Maurice, 130
Barnes, William, 232, 279
Barrie, Sir James M., 34, 36, 166
Battle and Other Poems, 342
Baudelaire, Charles, 9
Beauty the Pilgrim, 409
Becket, 101
Beethoven, Ludwig von, 36
Belloc, Hilaire, 129-130, 133, 409
Bennett, Arnold, 130
Benson, A. C., 28, 86, 96-98, 110
Bewick, Thomas, 368, 370
Bible, King James, 4, 95, 142, 194, 267, 299
Binyon, Laurence, 28, 67, 71, 106-120, 128, 129, 143, 439
Birds, Beasts and Flowers, 393
Blair, Robert, 93
Blake, William, 4, 158, 218, 226, 287, 295, 323, 369, 435, 445
Blind Thamyris, 297
Bloomfield, Richard, 18
Blue Moon, 153
Blunden, Edmund, 18, 20, 23, 27, 129, 412, 422-424
Blunt, Wilfred Scawen, 48, 286
Bombastes in the Shades, 114
Books of Nonsense, 133
Borrow, George, 345, 358
Bottomley, Gordon, 124, 302-305
Bourdillon, Francis, 121, 122-123, 232, 403
Brett-Young, Francis, 128, 404
Bridges, Robert, 28, 67-77, 108, 120, 143, 286, 287, 353, 383, 386, 387
British Birds, 359
Brittain's Daughter, 307
Bronté, Charlotte, 414
Bronté, Emily, 414, 418

Brooke, Rupert, 14, 17, 64, 237, 315, 343, 376-381, 398
Brother Beast, 126
Brown, Maurice, 399
Brown, T. E., 34
Browne, Sir Thomas, 358
Browning, E. B., 166, 414
Browning, Robert, 11, 20, 93, 127, 154, 218, 276, 344, 351, 437, 441, 444
Browning, Introduction to the Study of, 154
Buchan, John, 42
Buchanan, Robert, 4, 55, 111
Bunyan, John, 142
Burns, Robert, 5, 8, 18, 20, 21, 33, 42, 57, 93, 94, 95, 102, 234, 309, 323, 330, 412
Burroughs, John, 13, 234, 332, 358
Burton, Richard Francis, 373
Byron, 20, 25, 34, 51, 64, 93, 102, 323, 360, 379, 381

Cæsar, Julius, 71
Campbell, Joseph, 8, 212-214, 250
Campbell, Mrs. Patrick, 57
Campbell, Roy, 21, 128, 414, 425-427, 435, 445
Campbell-Bannerman, Sir Henry, 78, 89
Campion, Thomas, 223, 264
Cannan, Gilbert, 132
Canton, William, 225
"Carberry, Ethna," 201-202
Carew, Thomas, 239
Carlyle, Thomas, 3, 56, 57
Carroll, Lewis, 45, 133, 310
Cathay, 27
Cathleen-ni-Houlihan, 183
Catholic Rhapsodists, The, 144-153
Cattledrive in Connaught, 247, 249
Catullus, 117
Chamber Music, 245
Chambers of Imagery, 303
Chatterton, Thomas, 389
Chaucer, 18, 20, 51, 278, 284, 291, 294, 329, 330, 334, 351, 356, 379, 394, 445
Cherry Stones, 127
Chesson, Nora Hopper, 202-205
Chesterton, G. K., 130, 409, 410
Child Lovers, 348
Chinese and Japanese Influence, 26-27

INDEX 449

Christ in Hades, 98, 102, 103, 104
Clare, John, 18, 260, 356
Clarke, Austin, 29, 212, 247-249
Claudel, Paul, 78
Clodd, Edward, 86
Cobbett, Richard, 328, 358
Coleridge, S. T., 47, 93, 97, 279, 323, 367, 418, 438
Collins, William, 93, 97, 125, 257, 260
Colum, Padraic, 242-243
Colvin, Sidney, 41
Come Hither, 347, 415
Complete Poems of Francis Ledwidge, 231
Comus, 71
Congreve, William, 46
Conrad, Joseph, 36, 420
Constantine the Great, 124
Cooke, Eliza, 166, 414
Cope, Edward Drinker, 12
Coppard, A. E., 402-404
Coppée, F., 57
Cor Cordium, 356
Corkery, Daniel, 219
Corot, J. B. C., 36
Cotton, Charles, 260, 303, 403
Counter Attack, 401
Country Gentlemen's Contentments, 358
Coutts, Francis, 28, 121
Cowl, Jane, 100
Cowper, William, 97
Crabbe, George, 110, 264, 336
Craigie, Pearl Maria Theresa (John Oliver Hobbes), 10
Crashaw, Richard, 195
Creatures, 243
Cricket Songs, 53
Cripps, Arthur S., 128
Crockett, S. R., 44
Cromwell, 57
Cuckoo Songs, 198
Custance, Olive, 52
Cymbeline, 31
Cynewulf, 330, 380, 394

Daily Bread, 339, 340
Danaë, 296
Daniell, William, 112
D'Annunzio, Gabriele, 168
Dante, 51, 186, 351
Darwin, Charles, 11, 12, 78

Dauber, 14, 316, 324
David Balfour, 39
Davidson, John, 24, 25, 54-66, 111, 127, 166, 218, 426
Davies, W. H., 15, 23, 255, 330, 344-351, 356, 397, 410
Days and Nights, 154
Deborah, 354
Debussy, Claude A., 163
Decadents, The, 154-166
Deirdre, 168, 170, 171, 176, 177, 183, 221.
Deirdre of the Sorrows, 170
Deirdre Wedded, 214
De La Mare, Walter, 8, 9, 24, 125, 153, 225, 226, 303, 347, 359, 363-366, 376, 381, 415, 418, 435, 439, 445
Demeter, 72
Departmental Ditties, 25, 134
DeQuincey, Thomas, 146
DeVere, Aubrey, 208
Dickens, Charles, 90
Dickinson, Emily, 9, 211, 263, 371, 414, 418, 437
Ding Dong Bell, 365
Dixon, Richard, 387
Dobell, Sidney, 15, 16, 17
Dolmetsch, Arnold, 175
Donne, John, 11, 122, 173, 260, 264, 351, 430, 435, 445
Doughty, Charles M., 23, 284-294, 311, 351, 373
Douglas, Lord Alfred, 51-52, 133
Douglas, Norman, 23
Dowden, Edward, 8, 86, 94
Down-a-Derry, 365
Dowson, Ernest, 53, 157, 159-164, 160
Drake, 311, 312
Drake: An English Epic, 306
Dramatic Legends, 243
Drinkwater, John, 305, 376, 383-384
Dryden, John, 80, 95
Dublin Days, 244, 245
Dunsany, Lord, 9, 27, 28, 29, 186, 227-229, 230, 234, 236, 237, 240, 297, 373
D'Urfey, Thomas, 397
Duse, Eleonora, 111, 155

Einstein, Albert, 267
Eliot, George, 18, 414

INDEX

Eliot, T. S., 6, 11, 13, 21, 29, 390, 419, 435-443
Ellis, Havelock, 131
Emerson, Ralph Waldo, 3, 6, 7, 9, 10, 24, 142, 152, 192, 223, 347, 371, 430, 437, 445
Emperor and Galilean, 61
English Country, 23
English Lyrics, 30
English Poems, 164, 422
English Poetry in Its Relation to Painting and the Other Arts, 107
English Traits, 9
Epigrams, 92
Eremus, 101
Eros and Psyche, 72, 404
Euripides, 51
Eve and Other Poems, 369
Evelyn Innes, 29
Excursions in Criticism, 92

Fairies and Fusileers, 398
Falstaff, 307
Familiar Studies of Men and Books, 4
Farewell to Poetry, 348
Faust, 100, 101
Fennellosa, Ernest, 27
Festus, 285
Field, Eugene, 311
Fielding, Henry, 34, 328
Fifty Poems, 227, 228
Firdausi, 122
Fires, 338, 340
Fitzgerald, Edward, 97, 372, 421
Flagg, Wilson, 358
Flecker, James Elroy, 47, 255, 372-376
Fleet Street, 59
Fleet Street Eclogues, 56, 65
Fletcher, John, 356
Flint, F. S., 394-397
Foliage, 348
Forbes-Robertson, Sir Johnston, 57
For Daws to Peck At, 246
For England, 86
For England's Sake, 37
For Lancelot Andrewes, 11
Forty New Poems, 349
Forty Singing Seamen, 300
Foster, Stephen Collins, 269
Four Plays for Dancers, 171
Four Short Plays, 354

Four Walls, 439
Fraser, Lovat, 369
Freeman, John, 359, 381-383
Freud, The Influence of, 27
From a College Window, 97
Frost, Robert, 10, 235, 341, 343, 346, 359, 409, 411, 430, 431, 445
Fuel, 343

Gale, Norman, 52-54, 91
Galsworthy, John, 330
Gandhi, M. K., 6
Garnett, Edward, 285, 292, 345
Gautier, Judith, 26
Gautier, Théophile, 154, 165, 372
Gay, John, 18
Ghose, Mammohan, 128, 129
Ghosts, 23, 62
Gibbon, Edward, 273
Gibbon, Monk, 245-246
Gibson, Wilfred Wilson, 22, 24, 254, 336-344, 348, 354, 376
Gilbert, Sir William Schwenk, 26, 132, 310, 315
Gissing, George, 308
Gladstone, W. E., 82
Gluck, C. W. R., 37
Goblin Market, 420
Godfrida, 56, 57, 58
Gods and Fighting Men, 232
Goethe, J. W. von, 3, 276, 351
Gogarty, Oliver, 28, 86, 227, 238-242
Goldring, Douglas, 375
Goldsmith, Oliver, 93, 217
Gone to Earth, 416
Good Friday, 333
Gore-Booth, Eva, 208, 209, 309
Gosse, Edmund, 45, 122, 302, 303
Gottfried von Strassburg, 113
Gould, Gerald, 408
Graham, E. B. Cunninghame, 23
Grania, 200
Graves, Alfred Percival, 398
Graves, Robert, 17, 315, 378, 398-399
Gray, Thomas, 28, 93, 95, 97, 152, 257, 260, 323, 330, 331, 424
Greek Myth, 28
Green Arras, 153
Green Branches, 222
Gregory, Lady Augusta, 7, 174, 186, 200, 232

INDEX 451

Grimm, W. K. and J. L. K., 311
Guilbert, Yvette, 157
Guy Mannering, 58
Gwynn, Stephen, 210

Hail and Farewell, 29
Half Way House, 422
Hallowe'en, 207
Hardy, E. L. G., 281
Hardy, Thomas, 9, 18, 19, 20, 21, 22, 23, 77, 126, 127, 167, 171, 218, 232, 233, 261-286, 285, 290, 305, 326, 329, 330, 334, 344, 351, 362, 384, 403, 412, 422, 423, 435
Hardy, The Art of Thomas, 195
Harold, 100
Harte, Bret, 10
Harvey, Sir Martin, 114
Hassan, 373, 376
Hawthorn and Lavender, 32
Hawthorne, Nathaniel, 9
Hearn, Lafcadio, 423
Heldenleben, 155
Helen Redeemed, 125
Hemans, Mrs. Felicia D., 166, 414
Henley, Anthony Warton, 38
Henley, E. J., 31
Henley, W. E., 3, 4, 5, 30-39, 111, 116, 230, 307, 309, 310, 319, 409
Hepburn, Mrs. Patrick, 413
Her Majesty's Rebels, 217
Heredia, José de, 372
Herford, C. H., 303
Herod, 98, 100, 112
Heroes and Hero Worship, 56
Herrick, Robert, 8, 20, 32, 33, 53, 141, 254, 257, 259, 260, 264, 322, 345, 350, 403, 430, 435, 445
Hewlett, Maurice, 23, 124-126, 309
Hicks-Beach, Sir Michael, 82
Higgins, Frederick Robert, 29, 212, 249-251
Hinkson, H. A., 198
Hinkson, Katherine Tynan, 197-200, 203, 236
Historia Monachorum, 112
Hobbes, John Oliver (Pearl Maria Theresa Craigie), 10
Hodgson, Geraldine, 375
Hodgson, Ralph, 27, 235, 257, 330, 367-372, 445

Hogarth, William, 285, 292
Holiday, 65
Homer, 32, 51, 443
Homeward, 193
Hope," "Laurence, 157, 164-166, 414
Hopkins, Gerald Manley, 386-388, 398, 431, 435, 441
Hopper, Nora, 202-205
Horace, 356
Horizons and Landmarks, 216
Household Book of Poetry, 46
Housman, A. E., 19, 47, 70, 91, 153, 211, 242, 252-260, 264, 318, 332, 335, 372, 384, 403, 404, 410, 417, 418, 430, 435, 444, 445
Housman, Laurence, 153, 254
Howard, Newman, 123-124
Howells, William Dean, 272
Hudson, W. H., 9, 23, 254, 293, 350, 358, 359, 371
Hull, Eleanor, 176
Human Shows, 260
Hutton, Richard Holt, 86
Huxley, Aldous, 407-408
Huxley, Julian, 408
Huxley, Thomas H., 12
Hyde, Douglas, 174, 249
Hypatia, 373

I Heard a Sailor, 342
Ibsen, Henrik, 23, 24, 46, 57, 61, 62, 399
Ibsen, The Poetic Suggestion of, 23-24
Idea of Great Poetry, 352
Ideals in Ireland, 7
If, 226
Il Trovatore, 307
Imagism, 27
Immanence, 131
Imperialism, 15-18
In a Music Hall, 59
In Russet and Silver, 122
In the Land of Youth, 221, 222
In the Net of Stars, 395
In the Seven Woods, 186, 188
In Vinculis, 49
Inge, W. R., 410
Insurrections, 218, 219, 222, 223
Interludes and Poems, 353
Internationalism, 13-15
Invocation, 400
Ireland and Other Poems, 196

INDEX

Irish Eclogues, 217
Irishry, 212, 250
Irving, H. B., 99, 100
Irving, Sir Henry, 10, 101
Isherwood, Christopher, 431
Island Blood, 250, 251
Islands, 343

Jackson, Holbrook, 369
Jacob, Violet, 412
Jago, Richard, 232
James Elroy Flecker, An Appreciation, 375
James, Henry, 10, 11, 430
Jefferies, Richard, 9, 19, 309, 356, 358, 399
John, Augustus, 15
John Clare: Poems Chiefly from Manuscript, 422
John Gabriel Borkman, 23
Johnson, Lionel, 9, 180, 195-197
Johnson, Samuel, 30, 86, 87, 238, 351
Jonson, Ben, 80
Josephus, 112
Journeys End in Lovers Meeting, 10
Joyce, James, 245, 435
Judas, 296, 299
Jude the Obscure, 17, 262, 274
Judgment, 213
Judith, 296

Kavanagh, Patrick, 441
Kaye-Smith, Sheila, 129
Keats, John, 51, 64, 94, 95, 97, 98, 106, 109, 112, 230, 236, 279, 294, 295, 313, 323
Kelly, Lawrence, 207
Kensington Gardens, 409
Kerrigan, J. M., 173
Kestrel Edge, 340
Khayyam, Omar, 410
Kiartan the Icelander, 123, 124
King Cole, 324, 325
King Lear's Wife, 302, 303
King's Daughter, 406
Kingsley, Charles, 373
Kipling, Rudyard, 5, 10, 14, 15, 17, 20, 24, 25, 35, 36, 91, 117, 127, 128, 129, 130, 134-142, 166, 192, 309, 312, 318, 319, 335, 344, 383, 427, 431, 444, 445
La Traviata, 307

Labouchère, Henry, 427
Lachrymae Musarum, 92, 93
Lamb, Charles, 164, 195
Landon, L. E., 414
Landor, Walter Savage, 30, 94, 173, 260
Lang, Andrew, 143
Langland, William, 445
Laodice and Danaë, 303
Larcom, Lucy, 414
Last Poems, 165, 252, 255, 256, 257, 362
Last Songs, 231, 237
Late Lyrics, 260, 264
Later Days, 349
Lawless, The Hon. Emily, 200-201, 208
Lawrence, D. H., 27, 392-394, 435
Lear, Edward, 132, 133
Leaves of Grass, 4
Leconte de Lisle, Charles Marie René, 372
Ledwidge, Francis, 212, 229-238
LeGallienne, Richard, 53, 128, 164
Leidy, Joseph, 12
Lenin, Nikolai V. U., 440
Lesbia, 158
Letts, Winifred M., 207, 378
Lewis, Cecil Day, 14, 398, 429, 435-438
Lewis, Wyndham, 435
Lincoln, Abraham, 90
Lindsay, Vachel, 25, 308, 340, 420, 425
Little Eyolf, 23
Lloyd-George, D.
Lolly Willowes, 406
London, 36
London Nights, 157
London Types, 35
London Voluntaries, 35
Longfellow, Henry Wadsworth, 4, 25, 33, 94
Look! We Have Come Through, 393
Loti, Pierre, 165
Louise de la Vallière, 197
Love Is Enough, 86
Love Poems, 27, 349
Love Poems and Others, 392
Lover's Leap, 339
Lowell, Amy, 6, 419
Lyon, Lilian Bowes, 442
Lyric Love, 92
Lyrical Ballads, 93, 438
Lysaght, Edward E., 215-217
Lysaght, Sidney Royse, 215-217

INDEX

Macaulay, 25
M'Diarmid, Hugh, 413
MacDonald, James Ramsay, 14
Macleod," "Fiona, 203
MacManus, Anna Johnston ("Ethna Carberry"), 201-202
MacManus, Seumas, 202
Macpherson, James, 4, 286
Maeterlinck, M., 7, 9, 24, 46, 277
Mallarmé, Stéphane, 9
Malory, Sir Thomas, 113
Mammon and His Message, 59
Mangan, James Clarence, 7
Mansoul, 287, 289, 291, 292
Marching on Tanga, 128, 404
Mariamne, 296, 299
Marlborough and Other Poems, 399
Marlowe, Christopher, 57, 64, 98
Marmion, 323
Marriott-Watson, H. M., 36
Marvell, Andrew, 127, 260
Masefield, John, 5, 8, 14, 20, 21, 22, 24, 25, 27, 29, 91, 136, 172, 215, 254, 264, 303, 315-336, 344, 346, 353, 376, 401, 406, 418, 424, 439, 444, 445
Masters, E. L., 341
Mather, Margaret, 31
Maugham, W. Somerset, 132, 160
Mary and the Bramble, 353
Mazzini, G., 51
Mearing Stones, 213, 214
Medieval Latin Lyrics, 421
Mellish, Fuller, 99
Memoirs of an Infantry Officer, 401
Mendicant Rhymes, 153
Meredith, George, 5, 10, 13, 20, 116, 117, 132, 157, 206, 215, 216, 219, 220, 228, 279, 280, 313, 327, 351, 374, 392, 404
Merry England, 146
Mew, Charlotte, 410-412
Meynell, Alice, 145, 331, 414
Meynell, Wilfred, 145
Middleton, Richard, 388-389
Midsummer Eve, 193, 303, 305
Midsummer Night, 333
Mikado, 310
Miles, A. H., 414
Miles Dixon, 132
Milne, A. A., 45

Milton, John, 20, 28, 29, 33, 37, 51, 57, 71, 72, 74, 80, 84, 93, 95, 98, 109, 150, 167, 177, 185, 211, 226, 259, 279, 284, 287, 297, 351, 356, 371, 425, 428, 440, 445
Milton, Miss Maud, 99
Modern Love, 157, 280
Modern Painting, 36
Moments of Vision, 266
Monro, Harold, 389, 390
Moore, George, 10, 28, 39, 36, 70, 180, 186, 381, 398
Moore, T. Sturge, 38, 172, 191, 287, 294-302, 428
Moore, Tom, 166, 219
More Beasts for Worse Children, 129
More Songs from the Glens of Antrim, 209
More Songs of Angus, 412
Morris, Sir Lewis, 16, 17, 127, 128
Morris, William, 13, 28, 47, 51, 88, 174, 343, 380, 418, 444
Morrison, Arthur, 36
Mother Goose, 133
Mozart, W. A., 239
Mr. Fortune's Maggot, 406
Muir, John, 358
Music Hall Rhythms, 24-26
Mysticism, 131

Nan, 327, 328, 333
Napoleon, 267, 274, 275
Nature and Other Poems, 356
Nature Poems, 349
Neighbors, 338, 341
Nero, 100, 101, 105, 158
Nero Part I, 72
Nero Part II, 72
New Ballads, 56, 65
New Hampshire, 10, 11
New Numbers, 339
New Poems (Thompson), 146
Newbolt, Sir Henry, 17, 67, 71, 127, 134, 142-143, 211
Newman, John Henry, 3
News of the Devil, 410
Nichols, Robert, 17, 315, 399-400
Nicolson, The Hon. Mrs. Harold, 406-407
Nicolson, Violet, 164-166
Nicolson, William, 25

454
INDEX

Nietzsche, F. W., 24, 56, 57
Noel, 132
Noh Plays, 27
North of Boston, 10
Northern Light, 244
Norton, Mrs. Caroline, 166, 414
Noyes, Alfred, 21, 25, 306-314, 344, 346

O'Bruadair, 219
Odes (Binyon), 113
O'Donavan, Fred, 173
Odyssey, 104, 399
Of Human Bondage, 132, 160
O'Flaherty, Liam, 201
Omar Khayyam, 421
On Baile's Strand, 103, 176, 177
On the Poems of Henry Vaughan, 423
On the Threshold, 354
On Viol and Flute, 122
O'Neill," "Moira (Nesta Higginson Skrine), 203, 209-210
Opus, 7, 406
O'Rahilly, 219
Orchard Songs, 53
Ossian, 4, 286
O'Sullivan, Seumas (James Starkey), 211-212
Othello, 307
Otherworld, 394, 395
Our Lord's Coming and Childhood, 198
Our Old Home, 9
Ovid, 356, 357, 440
Owen, Wilfred, 17, 315, 399, 400-401, 435

Pan's Prophecy, 296
Pansies, 393
Paolo and Francesca, 99, 100, 101
Paradise Lost, 37, 71
Parker, Gilbert, 36
Parnell, Charles S., 217
Pastorals, 422
Pater, Walter, 9, 28, 97
Patience, 315
Patmore, Coventry, 24, 32, 144, 153, 195, 294
Peacock Pie, 365
Pelléas and Mélisande, 24
Pencraft, 83
Pepacton, 13
Per Amica Silentiae Lunae, 180, 186

Percival, Right Rev. John, 82
Perry, Commodore M. C., 26
Philip the King, 333
Phillips, Stephen, 28, 67, 72, 98-106, 115, 128, 129, 158, 297, 309, 378
Phillpotts, Eden, 22, 126-127, 329
Philosophies, 384
Picture Show, 402
Pietro of Siena, 100
Pilgrimage, 247
Pilgrimage of Grace, 129
Pilgrimage to El Medinah and Mecca, 373
Pinafore, 132
Pindar, 356
Pitter, Ruth, 442-443
Plarr, Victor, 160
Plato, 76
Plotinus, 208
Plunkett, Sir Horace, 192
Poe, Edgar Allan, 7, 9, 24, 64, 92, 95, 110, 162, 163, 211, 223, 381, 396, 445
Poems 1908-1919, 384
Poems: 1919-1934, 384
Poems 1916-1918 (F. Brett Young), 404
Poems 1926-1930, 399
Poems and Songs (Middleton), 389
Poems at White Nights, 303
Poems in Wiltshire, 356
Poems: New and Old, 143
Poems of the Love and Pride of England, 15
Poems of the Past and Present, 21, 263, 265
Poems of the Unknown Way, 215
Poems of Thirty Years, 302, 304
Poems of West and East, 406
Poems Old and New, 382
Poetry and Science, 11
Poets and Dreamers, 17
Poets and Poetry of the Century, 414
Pomes Penyeach, 245
Pomfret, John, 156, 347
Pompey the Great, 333
Pope, Alexander, 37, 80, 95, 102, 351
Porphyrion, 109, 111, 118, 119
Porphyry, 208
Pound, Ezra, 6, 10, 11, 21, 27, 419
Power, Tyrone, 99
Powys, T. F., 355, 405

INDEX

Precious Bane, 416
Pre-Raphaelites, 9, 197
Pre-Raphaelitism, 28, 46, 254
Primavera, 106, 108, 128, 129
Prior, Matthew, 238
Prometheus the Fire Giver, 72, 75
Propertius, 254, 259
Prose Fancies, 164
Proverbial Philosophy, 24
Pursuit of Psyche, 391

Quennell, Peter, 428

Racine, J. B., 351
Raftery, 185, 219
Read, Herbert, 398
Real Property, 389, 390
Requiem, 409
Responsibilities, 184, 189
Retrospective Reviews, 164
Reynard the Fox, 21, 318, 324, 327, 328, 329, 330, 331, 332
Rhodes, Cecil, 7
Richard III, 57
Ricketts, Charles, 304
Right Royal, 324, 325, 327, 331, 332
Riley, James Whitcomb, 225, 311
Rodd, Rennell, 48
Rolleston, T. W., 4
Ronsard, Pierre de, 421
Roosevelt, Theodore, 34, 83, 136
Rose Leaf and Apple Leaf, 48
Rosebery, A. P. P., 78, 82
Rosmersholm, 24
Ross, Ronald, 384-385
Rossetti, Christina, 121, 414, 418, 420
Rossetti, D. G., 4, 47, 51, 97, 154, 197, 218, 304, 418, 444
Rothenstein, Will, 54
Rowley, Richard, 246-247
Rudyard Kipling's Verse, 140
Rue, 153
Rufinus, 112
Rupert Brooke and the Intellectual Imagination, 226
Ruskin, John, 49
Russell, George W., 7, 28, 29, 191-194, 195

Sackville-West, Victoria May, 406, 445
Sakuntala, 114

Salkeld, Blanaid, 441
Salt Water Ballads, 25, 114, 215, 315, 316, 317, 319, 335
Sappho, 397
Sardou, V., 46
Sargent, John S., 191
Sassoon, Siegfried, 14, 17, 315, 378, 398, 400, 401-402
Satires of Circumstance, 265, 281
Saturday Market, 411
Savage, Henry, 389
Savonarola, 124
Schopenhauer, Arthur, 267
Schreiner, Olive, 427
Scott, Sir Walter, 18, 25, 43, 129, 322, 323, 330
Seaman, Sir Owen, 127
Secrets, 349
Selected Poems (Barry), 131
Self's the Man, 57, 58
Seven for a Secret, 416
Shakespeare, William, 18, 20, 25, 29, 31, 51, 57, 61, 93, 95, 232, 261, 267, 283, 284, 305, 309, 311, 327, 330, 351, 356, 365, 430, 435, 445
Shannon, Charles, 191, 304
Sharp, William, 4, 24, 203
Shaw, George Bernard, 13, 14, 180, 187, 345, 409, 419
Shelley, P. B., 51, 94, 107, 146, 147, 151, 185, 279, 373, 445
Shenstone, William, 232
Sherrard, Robert H., 161
Shorter, Dora Sigerson, 205-206
Shorter Poems, 68
Shylock Reasons with Mr. Chesterton, 409
Sidney, Sir Philip, 84, 326, 356, 443
Silhouettes, 157
Sister Songs, 146, 148
Sitwell, Edith, 419
Sitwell, Osbert, 14, 421
Sitwell, Sacheverell, 421
Skrine, Nesta Higginson ("Moira O'Neill"), 209-210
Smart, Christopher, 423
Smith: A Tragic Farce, 56
Smollett, Tobias George, 34
Socrates, 76
Soldiers Three, 20
Some Experiences of an Irish R. M., 329

456 INDEX

Somerville, E. Œ. and Martin Ross, 329
Song of Roland, 284
Songs and Meditations, 125
Songs from Leinster, 207
Songs from the Clay, 222
Songs from the Glens of Antrim, 209
Songs in Wiltshire, 350
Songs of Angus, 412
Songs of Childhood, 365
Songs of Joy, 348
Songs of Peace, 231, 237
Songs of the Fields, 231, 233, 237
Songs of the Morning, 203, 204
Songs of Travel, 43
Sonnets (Masefield), 316, 320
Sonnets with Folksongs, 132
Sons and Lovers, 27, 392, 393
Sophocles, 51
Sorley, Charles Hamilton, 7, 315, 349, 378
Soutar, William, 413
Spencer, Herbert, 78
Spender, Stephen, 10, 14, 429, 430, 433-434, 435, 436, 437, 438, 445
Spenser, Edmund, 28, 32, 80, 144, 183, 217, 236, 284, 291, 294, 356, 443
Spiritual Adventures, 157
Sprung Rhythm, 386
Squire, J. C., 375, 391-392
Starkey, James (Seumas O'Sullivan), 211-212
Stars of the Desert, 165
Stein, Gertrude, 419
Stephen, Leslie, 35
Stephens, James, 172, 217-226
Sterne, Laurence, 127
Stevens, G. W., 36
Stevenson, R. A. M., 36
Stevenson, Robert Louis, 4, 8, 31, 35, 36, 39-46, 122, 147, 177, 211, 215, 225, 232, 260, 310, 311
Stonefolds, 339
Strauss, Richard, 155
Street, G. S., 36
Strindberg, August, 167
Strong, L. A. G., 29, 212, 243-245
Summer Harvest, 384
Swift, Jonathan, 30, 97, 176
Swinburne, Algernon Charles, 8, 17, 28, 47, 51, 113, 127, 157, 166, 204, 206, 279, 308, 313, 338, 344, 396, 444

Symonds, John Addington, 4
Symons, Arthur, 11, 28, 47, 53, 105, 154-159, 166, 307, 440
Synge, James Millington, 8, 29, 132, 169, 173, 186, 201, 321, 322, 323, 334, 345, 394

Tabb, John B., 151
Tain bo Cuailgne, 176
Tales of the Mermaid Tavern, 310
Tamburlaine, 57
Tennant, Margot, 89
Tennyson, Alfred, 15, 18, 28, 33, 47, 80, 93, 95, 97, 101, 109, 113, 142, 154, 230, 252, 267, 313, 322, 323, 344, 356, 379, 431, 435, 444, 445
Tents of the Arabs, 373
Terence, 76
Terry, Dame Ellen, 10
Tess, 262, 305
Thackeray, W. M., 410
The Adder, 354
The Admirable Crichton, 34, 160
The American Invasion, 3-11
The Angel in the House, 24
The Autobiography of a Super-Tramp, 345, 349
The Ballad of the White Horse, 130
The Battle of the Bays, 127
The Bird of Paradise, 348
The Birth of Song, 346
The Blithedale Romance, 9
The Bonaventure, 423
The Book of Earth, 310, 313
The Book of Jade, 26
The Bounty of Sweden, 167
The Bride of Lammermoor, 24
The Bridge of Fire, 376
The Bull, 369
The Burning Wheel, 408
The Campden Wonder, 327
The Canterbury Tales, 329
The Captive Shrew, 408
The Cause, 115
The Celtic Renaissance, 28-29
The Celtic Twilight, 187
The Centaur's Booty, 296, 297
The Charwoman's Daughter, 221
The Cicadas and Other Poems, 407, 408
The Cliffs, 285, 290
The Clouds, 285, 288, 289, 290, 293

INDEX 457

The Collected Poems of Lord Alfred Douglas, 51
The Collected Poems of Richard Aldington, 398
The Contemplative Quarry, 413
The Countess Cathleen, 102, 167, 168, 177, 178, 188
The Crescent Moon, 404
The Crier by Night, 303, 305
The Crock of Gold, 220, 221
The Cuchullin Saga, 176
The Cyder Forest, 421
The Daffodil Fields, 14, 316, 323, 324, 327, 328
The Dance of Death, 430
The Dark Breed, 251
The Dawn in Britain, 285, 286, 289, 293
The Death of Adam, 114, 118
The Death of Tristram, 118
The Defeat of Youth, 408
The Demi-Gods, 220, 221
The Deserter, 354
The Destructive Element, 430
The Divine Vision, 94
The Dog Beneath the Skin, 432
The Dynasts, 274, 275, 276, 285
The Early Life of Thomas Hardy, 262
The Earth Breath, 194
The Earth for Sale, 390
The Elfin Artist, 311
The End of the World, 354, 355
The Espalier, 405
The Everlasting Mercy, 14, 316, 317, 321, 323, 325, 326, 327, 328
The Faithful, 27, 333
The Farmer's Wife, 22
The Fleeting and Other Poems, 365
The Fires of Baal, 247, 248
The Five Nations, 137
The Flaming Terrapin, 21, 425
The Flower of Old Japan, 306, 310
The Forest of Wild Thyme, 306, 310, 311, 312
The Four Winds of Erinn, 201
The Fox's Covert, 441
The Gamekeeper at Home, 17
The Garden of Kama, 165
The Gate of Smaragdus, 303
The Gazelles, 300
The Germ, 28, 438

The Ghost Ship, 389
The Gods of the Mountain, 227
The Golden Helm, 339
The Golden Room, 343
The Gothic North, 421
The Green Helmet, 171, 176, 184, 189
The Growth of Love, 72, 73, 74
The Heart of Darkness, 128
The Heart of Peace, 153
The Higher Provincialism, 18-23
The Hill of Trouble, 97
The Hill of Vision, 218, 220, 221
The Hodgiad, 124
The Hour of Magic, 345
The House at Pooh Corner, 45
The Hunter, 391
The Idols, 116
The Inalienable Heritage, 200
The Inn of Dreams, 52
The King of Elfland's Daughter, 227
The King of the Great Clock Tower, 190, 191
The King's Threshold, 187
The Knave of Hearts, 158
The Knight of the Maypole, 57, 58
The Lady of the Lake, 323
The Land, 407, 445
The Land of Heart's Desire, 182
The Last Blackbird, 367
The Last Voyage, 310
The Life of Charles M. Doughty, 285
The Life of James Elroy Flecker, 375
The Listeners, 365
The Little Old House, 413, 414
The Little School, 296
The London Academy, 146
The London Athenaeum, 146
The Loom of Years, 306
The Love Songs of Connacht, 249
The Lowery Road, 244
The Magazine of Art, 36
The Man Who Saw, 83
The Man with a Hammer, 413
The Marble Faun, 9
The Mask, 404
The Masque of Dead Florentines, 125
The Master Builder, 24
The Mickle Drede, 303
The Mikado, 26
The Modern Scot, 412
The Muse in Exile, 91

INDEX

The Mystery and Other Poems, 369
The National Observer, 36
The Nets of Love, 339
The New Criterion, 11
The New Inferno, 101
The New Masses, 433
The New Review, 36
The Nigger of the Narcissus, 36
The Night Has a Thousand Eyes, 122
The Old Huntsman, 401
The One and the Many, 208
The Only Jealousy of Emer, 176
The Orators, 430
The Origin of Species, 11
The Path to Rome, 129
The Phoenix, 354
The Pierrot of the Minute, 163
The Playboy of the Western World, 173
The Poems of A. C. Benson, 96
The Poor Man and the Lady, 281
The Praise of Life, 109, 119
The Prince's Quest, 81, 88
The Queen of Cornwall, 171, 260
The Queen's Vigil, 339
The Queen's Chronicler, 210
The Rainbow, 393
The Return of the Native, 9, 276
The Return of Ulysses, 72
The Riding to Lithend, 302, 303, 305
The Ring and the Book, 276
The Rocky Road to Dublin, 222, 225
The Romantic Movement in English Poetry, 155
The Rout of the Amazons, 296, 297
The Scarlet Letter, 9
The Scot's Observer, 36
The Sea Is Kind, 296, 298
The Seven Seas, 17, 135
The Shadowy Waters, 159, 168, 169, 170
The Shepherd, 422
The Shorter Poems of Robert Bridges, 76
The Sale of St. Thomas, 352, 353
The Sin of David, 99, 101
The Sleeping Beauty, 419
The Song of Empire, 134-143
The Song of Honour, 369
The Song of Life, 349
The Song of the Plow, 124, 125

The Song of the Sword, 35
The Soul's Destroyer, 345
The Spires of Oxford, 207
The Staircase, 354
The Story of My Heart, 19
The Superhuman Antagonists, 78
The Sword of the West, 248
The Tablet, 146
The Testament of a Man Forbid, 60, 62
The Testament of a Prime Minister, 60
The Testament of a Vivisector, 60
The Testament of an Empire Builder, 60, 61
The Testament of Beauty, 28
The Testament of John Davidson, 55, 60
The Theatrocrat, 57, 59
The Three Sorrows of Story Telling, 170
The Titans, 289
The Torchbearers, 314
The Tower, 25, 184, 186, 189, 190, 294
The Tragedy of Nan, 321
The Trembling of the Veil, 59
The Trial of Jesus, 333
The Triumph of Mammon, 59
The Utmost Isle, 285
The Veil, 365
The Vengeance of Fionn, 247, 248
The Village Wife's Lament, 125
The Vinedresser, 294, 295, 296
The Vortex, 404
The Waggoner, 422
The Wanderings of Oisin, 174, 175, 178. 188
The Watchers of the Sky, 310, 313
The White Blackbird, 439
The White Hare, 442
The Widow in the Bye Street, 14, 316, 317, 323, 324, 325
The Wild Swans at Coole, 184, 185, 189, 294
The Wind among the Reeds, 171, 182, 191, 438
The Wind in the Trees, 197
The Winding Stair, 184, 190
The Woodlanders, 276
The Year of Shame, 82, 86
The Yellow Book, 54, 128
Theocritus, 32, 218
Theseus, 296

INDEX

Thomas, Edward, 8, 10, 13, 17, 23, 288, 302, 303, 315, 343, 345, 353, 358-362, 364, 403
Thomas, Helen, 343
Thompson, Francis, 9, 24, 144-153, 195, 206, 240, 294, 310, 312, 396, 437, 445
Thomson, James, II, 4, 55, 146
Thoreau, Henry David, 6, 7, 8, 9, 358, 437
Through the Looking Glass, 45
Thus Spake Zarathustra, 155
Time and the Gods, 227
Time Importuned, 405
Time's Laughing Stocks, 21, 263, 265
To Leda, 296
Todt und Verklarung, 155
Tolstoi, Leo, 14, 15
Towards Democracy, 4
Tragedies, 158
Transitional Poem, 435
Transvaluations, 404
Treasure Island, 35, 39
Tree, Sir Herbert Beerbohm, 59, 100
Trench, Herbert, 214-215
Tristan and Iseult, 156
Tristan and Isolt, 333
Trooper Peter Halkett, 427
Tupper, Martin Farquhar, 24
Turgenieff, I. S., 9
Turner, J. M. W., 54
Turner, W. J., 390
Tynan, Katherine, 180, 197-200, 206

Ulysses, 99, 100, 101
Under Quicken Boughs, 203, 204
Under the Greenwood Tree, 19, 269
Underhill, Evelyn, 131
Underwoods, 41, 42
Urlyn the Harper, 338

Vaughan, Henry, 423
Verdi, Giuseppe, 307, 308
Verlaine, P., 154, 157
Verschoyle, Mrs. (W. M. Letts), 207-208
Verses, 200
Victoria, Queen, 15
Victorianism, 3
Vienna, 434
Views and Reviews: Art, 33
Vigil, 402

Villon, François, 8, 322
Voices of the Stones, 194
Volsunga Saga, 284
Voltaire, F. M. A. de, 267

Waddell, Helen, 421
Wagner, Richard, 64
Waley, Arthur, 27
Walker, Stuart, 305
Wallace, Alfred Russell, 12
Walls and Hedges, 404
Walton, Izaak, 18, 32, 33, 358, 423
Warner, Sylvia Townsend, 405
Washington, George, 90
Watson, E. L. Grant, 23
Watson, Sir William, 17, 28, 55, 77-96, 127, 309, 444
Watts, G. F., 82
Watts-Dunton, Theodore, 8, 9, 17
Webb, Mary, 289, 414-418
Webster, John, 92
Weir of Hermiston, 39, 43
Wells, Herbert George, 13, 14, 130, 410
Wetmore, Frederic, 15
Wessex Poems, 21, 263, 271, 277
Western Flanders, 113
When We Were Very Young, 45
Whether a Dove or a Sea Gull, 406
Whibley, Charles, 36
Whistler, Laurence, 439-441
White, Gilbert, 53, 358, 423
Whitman, Walt, 3, 4, 5, 6, 13, 127, 172, 215, 276, 307, 345, 351, 393, 394, 395, 396, 437
Whittier, J. G., 46
Wickham, Anna, 413, 414
Wilcox, Ella Wheeler, 166
Wild Apples, 241
Wild Earth, 242, 243
Wilde, Oscar, 28, 46-51, 158, 180, 315, 419
Williams, Alfred, 356-357
Wine, Women and Song, 421
Wings over Europe, 399
Winner, Septimus, 269
Winter Harvest, 439
Winter Words, 265, 266, 272
With the Living Voice, 321
With the Wild Geese, 200
Wolfe, Charles, 121, 122
Wolfe, Humbert, 409-410, 421

INDEX

Women in Love, 393
Womenkind, 339, 341
Woods, Margaret L., 123
Wordsworth, William, 15, 18, 19, 21, 28, 29, 33, 36, 50, 51, 80, 84, 86, 93, 94, 95, 109, 127, 144, 155, 197, 255, 261, 267, 279, 294, 302, 330, 339, 356, 383, 388, 405, 424, 430, 435, 438, 445
Wordsworth's Grave, 55, 91, 92, 444
World War, The, 17, 24, 45, 83, 114, 125, 229, 246, 292, 312, 370, 378, 398, 399, 400, 401, 402

Wuthering Heights, 414
Wyatt, Thomas, 443

Yeats, Jack B., Jr., 173
Yeats, J. B., Sr., 8, 172, 191
Yeats, William Butler, 11, 15, 24, 25, 28, 29, 59, 64, 67, 71, 106, 113, 154, 158, 159, 160, 167-191, 192, 195, 200, 211, 219, 231, 237, 239, 242, 250, 280, 294, 318, 335, 344, 346, 404, 410, 418, 420, 435, 438, 444
Young, Andrew, 439
Young, Edward, 351

[1]